KU-446-782

To bathe or not to
bathe... 216

17 Sex and Genitals 217

Embarrassing bits 218
Sex and libido 220
Men's health 221
Women's health 222
Menstruation 227

**18 Animals – Small
and Large 229**

Skin invaders 230
Small biters 233
Small bad beasts 238
Snakes and nasty
  reptiles 243
Dangerous large
  mammals 247
Dangerous domestic
  mammals 249
Small wild mammals 252

19 Ailments 253

Medical evacuation and
  treatments 254
Risks of medical
  treatment 255
Exotic diseases 255
Coughs and chest
  pains 260
Abdominal symptoms 263
Head, nose and
  throat 266
Eye problems 269
Glasses and contact
  lenses 271
Dental problems 272

20 Accidents 273

Collapse 274
Immediate responses and
  safety 274
Unconsciousness and
  fits 275

Maps

Yellow fever 45
Japanese encephalitis 46
Epidemic meningococcal
  disease 47
'European' tick-borne
  encephalitis (TBE) 48
Rabies 50
Malaria 133
Dengue fever 151
Leishmania 153
Schistosomiasis
  (bilharzia) 179
River blindness
  (onchocerciasis) 181
'European' tick-borne
  encephalitis in Europe
  inside back cover

Tables

Regional health risks:
 – Europe 53–4
 – Central America
   and the Caribbean 55
 – Africa 56–7
 – Asia 58–9
 – Pacific 60
 – South America 61
Commonly used
  preparations to
  counteract motion
  sickness 88
Sizes of microbes
  responsible for
  travellers' intestinal
  infections 108
Microbes commonly
  detected from stool-
  gazing after a trip to the
  tropics 118
Commonly used anti-
  malarial prophylactic
  tablets 136–7
Geographical distribution
  of vector-borne
  diseases 144
Diseases transmitted by
  small biters 148–9
Animal hazards and
  where they occur 232–3

Strains, sprains, bruises and
  wrenches 278
Cuts, wounds and bites
  280
Fractures and
  dislocations 282
Something stuck... 283
Swallowing things
  accidentally 285
Exposure to CS gas 286

21 Expatriates 287

Health and hygiene 288
Special concerns for
  expatriates 289
Psychological welfare 291
Babies and children 294

When You Get Home

22 Return 297

A post-trip check-up? 298
Psychological welfare 300

Reference

Useful Addresses **301**

Bibliography **306**

Index **308**

5th edition published 2009

Cadogan Guides is an imprint of
New Holland Publishers (UK) Ltd
London • Cape Town • Sydney • Auckland

New Holland Publishers (UK) Ltd	80 McKenzie Street	Unit 1, 66 Gibbes Street	218 Lake Road
Garfield House	Cape Town 8001	Chatswood, NSW 2067	Northcote
86–88 Edgware Road	South Africa	Australia	Auckland
London W2 2EA			New Zealand

cadogan@nhpub.co.uk
t 44 (0)20 7724 7773

Distributed in the United States by Interlink Publishing Group
46 Crosby Street, Northampton, Massachusetts 01060
www.interlinkbooks.com
www.cadoganguidesusa.com

Copyright © Jane Wilson-Howarth 1995, 1999, 2002, 2006, 2009
© 2009 New Holland Publishers (UK) Ltd

First published in 1995 under the title *Bugs, Bites and Bowels: The Essential Guide to Travel Health*

Cover photographs: front cover © Image Source/Corbis; back cover © iStockphoto.com/Nieves Mares
Pagán, iStockphoto.com/John Bell, iStockphoto.com
Illustrations © Betty Levene
Map design (disease risk areas): Tracey Ridgewell, adapted by Stephen Dew, Pete Gwyer and Angie Watts
Cover design: Jason Hopper
Senior Editor: Louise Coe
Proofreading: Susannah Wight
Indexing: Isobel McLean

Printed and bound in Finland by WS Bookwell Ltd
A catalogue record for this book is available from the British Library

ISBN: 978-1-86011-424-3

Acknowledgements

Jane Wilson-Howarth

Laura Fleminger first convinced me I could write this book but it would never have been completed without help from my busy, generous friends and relations, notably Drs Mary Styles, Mark Howarth and Jill Sutcliffe, Hilary Bradt, Lorna and John Howell, Andy Robinson, Dr Jim Waddell, Dr David Wilks, Shane Winser, Professor David Bradley, Dr Anne Denning, Dr Andy Pollard and Dr Paul Stewart. Suggestions also came from Kate Cooper (La Paz), Dr Matthew Ellis (Bristol), Ramsay Hovell MRCVS, Dr Catherine Howarth (Aberystwyth), Dr Helen Hutchinson (Cambridge), Mary Kedward RGN (Cambridge), Dr Gil Lea (London), Dr David Shlim (Jackson Hole), Dr Vaughan Southgate (London), Claire Verlander (Ipswich) and Joseph Wilson (my ever-encouraging Dad). Despite all the expert advice I have received, though, I am to blame for any errors or omissions (but let me know about them please). At Cadogan's office in London I owe thanks to Rachel Fielding for taking the risk in first publishing this book, and for the hard work and support given by my editors, especially Louise Coe. I am grateful to my many patients and fellow travellers who continue to educate me.

Without the quiet but unstinting support of my best friend, mentor, chief editorial advisor and husband, Simon Howarth, who has read various versions of the text *ad nauseam* and distracted our children at critical points, the book would not have appeared in five editions.

Cadogan Guides

We thank St John Ambulance for permission to reproduce the image of the recovery position shown in the Accidents chapter on p.278. Copyright 2009 St John Ambulance. Recovery position illustration correct at time of going to press.

About the author

Jane Wilson-Howarth BSc, MSc, BM, DCH, DCCH, DFSRH, FRSTM&H, FFTM RCPS trained first in zoology and then medicine. Her 11 years' residence in Asia honed a particular loathing of parasites. She's worked on various health promotion and child-survival programmes overseas as well as acting as GP to expatriate neighbours. She organized expeditions to the Himalayas, Peru and Madagascar (twice) and has enjoyed a dozen treks in Nepal with children from the age of three months. Her travel memoirs *Lemurs of the Lost World* and *A Glimpse of Eternal Snows* describe some of these experiences. She has written a regular medical feature for *Wanderlust* magazine since it was first launched in 1993 and contributes on occasion to the *Independent* newspaper. She is currently a general practitioner and also medical director of the Travel Clinic, Cambridge. Further information about Jane and photos are at *www.wilson-howarth.com*.

To three compassionate and inspiring physicians: Dr Hugh Dawson, Dr Julie Draper and Dr Jim Waddell.

Introduction

01

Picture this: you've awoken in your hotel bed having just flown in to a town you don't know, in a country where you don't speak the language. You don't feel good. Your belly aches and you have a horrible watery sensation in your mouth. You get up and the room spins. You are ill, but how ill? Is this simply a stomach upset or do you need a doctor's prescription? What do you do? Where will you find reliable medical advice? Or is it safe to self-treat this most frequent affliction of travellers?

The answers to these questions are all in the pages of this accessible and comprehensive guide. You'll also find information about all other health concerns you might have, many you haven't thought of, as well as advice on when and how to find a local doctor. All the exotic horrors people love to talk about are included too – not because you're likely to encounter them, but just because you might like to know and this knowledge should help stop you worrying.

As you leaf through these pages, you will see that hazards from tropical diseases and noxious animals are often over-stated. The candiru fish, for example, is just not worth worrying about (see pp. 181) and bites by venomous creatures are rare. The diseases that afflict travellers are mostly trivial, like colds, sore throats and diarrhoea. Even so, this book will help you avoid disease. The advice will work as well in Miami or Malawi as it does in Morocco or Mumbai.

Treatment suggestions are given, but only where there is good scientific evidence that they are effective. Those alternative remedies that work are mentioned, but untested remedies are not listed. This is not, though, a do-it-yourself doctor kit and it isn't intended to replace a consultation with a doctor (if you can find one). The first-aid guidance given is of the kind needed in situations where secondary aid might be poor or absent. It is intended to supplement proper first-aid training; if you are going somewhere remote you should ensure that you or a travelling companion are trained at least in some first-aid basics.

Styles of medical practice vary even between English-speaking countries. Most of us are used to doctors offering a diagnosis and explaining the purpose and possible side effects of prescribed treatment. Many doctors around the globe may be unused to patients who know enough about their bodies to discuss medical conditions and treatments. Tactfully ask what you wish to know, and be aware that linguistic and cultural difficulties may make him (or you) seem rude. You can then use this book to discuss alternatives and to check that the doctor's prescription makes sense.

I've offered advice on what to do, rather than provide lists of medical names. It's been tough condensing my 27 years of medical experience on four continents into a portable reference book, so if you find deficiencies or omissions, do write to tell me.

Stay cool; have fun. Take care, *bon voyage*, *salamat jalan* and *pheri betau la*!

J. M. W.-H., Cambridge, winter 2008/9

Naming medicines

Generally medicines are given two names: the trade or brand name, which tends to vary a great deal from country to country, and the longer **generic** name, which should be similar everywhere. This generic name is what you should look for when buying medicines overseas. It is usually written in small print somewhere on the packaging. Throughout this book the generic names of all medicines I suggest are written in *italics*.

Before You Go:
Features

Is it safe...is it legal? 10
  Unexpected delays 10
  Different countries, different laws 11
  The downsides of drinking 12
  Don't skimp 12
An end to malaria? 13
  Other new vaccines 13
  Even better protection 14
Flying and DVT 15
Outbreaks and plagues: when should
  we panic? 18
  Avoiding epidemic hysteria 19
Travelling responsibly 20
  Patching up the locals 20
  Skin infections 22
  Responsibilities 22

02

Is it safe...is it legal?

Would-be travellers who consider the risks to their health abroad tend to think of infectious disease. However, many health problems overseas are either due to non-infectious health problems like heart attacks or 'non-natural' causes such as accidents. Tens of thousands of people die and perhaps two million are injured on European roads every year. The countries with most fatalities within the European Union are Germany, Poland, Italy, France, then Spain, with Britain coming in sixth. The first five countries each have more than 5,000 deaths on the roads a year. A third of all American fatalities abroad are due to road accidents. The latest US non-natural mortality statistics make a sobering addition to that statistic.

Astonishing numbers of tourists, travellers and expatriates get into trouble with the law while away from home. It is foolish to assume that foreign laws are similar to our own. Surprisingly, for example, possession of beef is forbidden in Nepal, and pork (including bacon) is illegal in many Muslim states. Some prescription medicines may not be imported into some countries, even for your own use. The Foreign and Commonwealth Office, State Department or specific embassy websites should forewarn you. It is important to check.

Unexpected delays

Over a million Britons visit the United Arab Emirates (UAE) annually. Many flights to South and Southeast Asia transit through the oil states and travellers might find themselves with an unscheduled stop-over or might even be sent back to the Middle East if there are visa problems at their destination. It is therefore worth knowing how strict laws are in most Middle Eastern countries. More than 230 Britons were arrested in the UAE in 2007 and some were imprisoned for more than a year.

Two Britons who were accused of having drunken sex on a Dubai beach were sentenced to three months in prison, and, although their appeal was successful, they still spent time behind bars. Was it bad luck that they fell foul of local laws or should they have known that in Dubai you can be arrested for kissing, having sex outside

Non-natural deaths in US citizens overseas: 1 July 2005 – 30 June 2008
Information from *http://travel.state.gov/*

Cause of death	Number of deaths	Percentage
Vehicle accident	721	33
Homicide	321	15
Suicide	281	13
Drowning	266	12
Air accident	128	6
'Terrorist' action	83	4
Drug related	66	3
Maritime	24	1
Execution	7	0.3

Total deaths 1,897 (out of an unknown number of people)

marriage, for obscene gestures, for being gay and for drinking alcohol in public? Since ignorance is no plea in the eyes of the law – even an exotic law – other travellers should heed the example made of Michelle Palmer and Vince Acors; they weren't the first European visitors to be imprisoned in Dubai, nor will they be the last.

Different countries, different laws

Drugs in the bloodstream count as possession according to Dubai's courts and what is illegal in Dubai may be permissible elsewhere. *Codeine* can be bought over the counter in the UK as a component of pain-relieving remedies including Solpadol, but a British visitor was held in prison for seven weeks because a urine test showed she had *codeine* and *temazepam* in her system; the prosecution said that she should have been carrying a prescription justifying her need to take the drugs but she managed to avoid a prison sentence which could have been four years. In February 2008 an unfortunate German citizen was arrested on arrival in Dubai and – surprisingly – jailed for four years for possessing the jet lag cure melatonin. In a different incident a Swiss man was held after poppy seeds (from a roll) were found on his clothes.

Expatriates often have a brush with the law. Many drive their own vehicles and so they are at high risk of a road accident, and some are accused of infringing local regulations. Very strict Muslim states – like Saudi Arabia – even have religious police who may club people who show too much skin – or even hair. World travellers must respect local sensibilities. In February 2008 a 37-year-old American businesswoman was arrested, strip-searched, thrown in jail, threatened and forced to sign a false confession by the 'Mutaween', Saudi Arabia's religious police. Her crime was sitting with a male colleague at a Starbucks coffee shop in Riyadh. Fortunately the woman's husband was able to use his influence to find her, then get her released, but she was bruised and crying when she was set free. In Saudi, people die in prison; there are lashings and on average more than two executions a week; most victims are foreign nationals, albeit mostly from neighbouring Middle Eastern countries.

Imprisonment isn't great for your mental health, or your career. Some regimes encourage 'trusties' (inmates who are used to control other inmates). This happens in Nepal and Thailand (where there are stories of unexpected deaths among prisoners). Prisoners in places including Columbia and Venezuela suffer violence. It

TIPS
→ Check the rules both for your destination and at any stop-overs.
→ Carry a doctor's letter if you have packed prescription medicines or hypodermics; an NHS GP will probably charge you for such a letter.
→ Never carry items for others.
→ Be wary of carrying white powders.
→ Think carefully about what you carry across borders.
→ Do your homework; visitors can be targeted for political reasons.
→ Travellers who look tidy and 'respectable' usually get less hassle at immigration and customs.
→ Think about the location and company you are keeping if celebrating with intoxicants.
→ It is no longer illegal to be left-handed in Albania.

is sobering to realize that 59 countries still impose the death penalty, including China, Nigeria (which has the highest number on death row: 763 in October 2008), Thailand (especially for drug trafficking), the USA, Indonesia, Iran (one of five countries that executes children) and Japan. Thailand, Mexico and Guatemala are the three countries where US citizens have been executed recently.

When I was last in Amritsar I was approached by missionaries to take food to Western travellers who had been incarcerated for trying to take drugs across the Indo–Pakistan border. The prisoners were miserable and at risk of becoming ill because relatives were unable to supplement the basic food provided by the prison. Misery is one outcome but the death penalty is certainly a possibility for anyone entering Thailand with illegal drugs. Carrying hypodermics and syringes can get you misjudged as a drug addict unless they are obviously part of a first-aid kit or for diabetes-certified medication with a doctor's letter.

The downsides of drinking

The Westerners most recently jailed in Dubai committed their 'crime' while drunk, and alcohol is certainly responsible for a lot of grief – if not deaths – in travellers. Enjoyable as intoxication may be, it reduces the defences and encourages risky behaviour. If you are in an unfamiliar environment this can lead to rape, robbery, a road accident or drowning. And immunizations don't protect travellers' lives from those hazards. Of Westerners who die abroad:

→ approximately half succumb to problems like heart attacks and similar 'at home' problems which the victim would get wherever. These are time bombs waiting to go off, although it seems that, in those who are susceptible, medium- and long-haul flights increase the chance of having a heart attack by about three times.

→ Of the other half of deaths abroad, most are due to accidents and violence in various forms. Getting drunk or intoxicated in other ways and/or getting arrested certainly increases the chance of undesirable outcomes.

Britain has unusually lax drinking laws, and behaviour that is permissible in the UK may be illegal overseas; drink-driving limits are generally much stricter even in Europe and Australia than in the UK. In Britain drivers will get into trouble with the law if their blood alcohol is more than 0.08%. In many other European countries as well as Canada, Australia and South Africa the legal limit is nearly half at 0.05%; in Japan and Russia it is 0.03% and in Estonia and Brazil it is a mere 0.02%. In the Czech Republic, Hungary, Slovakia, Romania, UAE and Saudi Arabia it is zero. Be aware that travellers are more likely to fail breath tests even the morning after a night of heavy drinking.

Don't skimp

Dressing sensitively and behaving soberly allows a merging into the background so that violent crime, sexual attack and arrest will be less likely. Contravening informal local dress codes can attract trouble. Travellers experience serious sexual assault and sometimes this can be precipitated by wearing skimpy or inappropriate clothes. It pays to understand your risks and know how much of a target you might be in certain regions. Check *www.fco.gov.uk* or *http://travel.state.gov/travel* for security information and entry regulations.

An end to malaria?

When the World Health Organization (WHO) was set up in the 1940s, malaria, venereal diseases and tuberculosis were seen as the most devastating health problems globally and the Malaria Eradication Division of WHO was formed to combat one of the biggest killers. By the mid-1970s, though, it had become clear that 'eradication' was impossible and the word was removed from the divisional name. Research continued; indeed in the early 1980s I worked towards understanding how malaria damages blood vessels and thus causes the dreaded cerebral malaria. I looked at how parasite-loaded red blood cells clump against arterial walls – especially in the brain – and cause leakage. We didn't get very far in our researches but contributed a little towards understanding of the disease process.

Then at the end of 2008 scientists in Melbourne headed by Prof Alan Cowman announced how they had identified the substance responsible for the stickiness of infected red blood cells, which promotes survival of malaria parasites. It stops them circulating and so they avoid being filtered out by the body's normal defences. This breakthrough opens possibilities of developing a medicine or even perhaps a vaccine that will make malaria less of a killer.

The first glimmer of hope for a vaccine came in the late 1980s when an unknown Colombian scientist claimed he could immunize against New World malaria. Trials in Asia and Africa though found it protected only about 30% of the population. The scientific community remained pessimistic – so much so that in the last edition of this book I quoted experts who felt that 'malaria vaccines are always at least five years off.'

Since this, though, GlaxoSmithKline (GSK) has been running field trials on a vaccine that protects 71% of immunized adults, and in Mozambican under-fives, where children expect to be hit by a bout of malaria perhaps five times a year, the vaccine cut the risk of developing severe and life-threatening malaria by 58%. This then is a useful vaccine in a resource-poor setting where malaria is a big killer of children, but it is not yet good enough to have us ordinary travellers abandoning our antimalarial pills. Research continues and there is hope for developing a more effective version which might absolutely protect within a few years. Recent decades will be remembered by tropical physicians as the time when radical new treatments and even perhaps eradication of malaria looked achievable again. Even so, the prospect of absolute protection is still a long way off. Meanwhile, sadly, we'll all just have to go on taking the tablets.

Other new vaccines

The first modern travel vaccine – a whole-cell typhoid inoculation – was developed during the Boer War. Interestingly, despite the fact that the burden of disease is often much greater among citizens of the tropics, advances in tropical medicine have so far mostly been driven by war. Medical developments have rarely emerged to benefit the needy of the developing world, but aim to protect relatively wealthy citizens or soldiers. Despite causing quite unpleasant side effects, the original typhoid vaccine was only superseded in the early 1990s. Typhoid vaccine capsules became available again in March 2006. The few new vaccines developed in the 20th century were all aimed at mass protection from common diseases of industrialized nations. Vaccines to protect minorities or to avoid exotic diseases have been seldom commercially viable.

Things are changing fast though. With easier, cheaper air travel, the world is shrinking. UK residents alone make around 100 million overseas visits annually. This means that markets for travel vaccines are expanding, so there is new investment in research. Field trials on one dengue fever vaccine in Thailand have proved very encouraging and there are plans to test another new vaccine in Brazil. At least five other dengue vaccines are being researched, but clinical trials need to be slow and meticulous; Sanofi hope to submit for regulatory approval in 2012; GSK are working on competing product. Currently the WHO is pushing for a low-cost dengue vaccine aimed at protecting locals. It is most encouraging that resources are finally being channelled towards producing more vaccines for the world's poor – who need them the most.

Even better protection

GSK's vaccine against hepatitis E is also looking promising; a six-month trial in men showed it was 96% protective but research continues on how long the protection lasts and on safety. Meanwhile there are encouraging results from scientists who mutated the common cold virus to produce an anti-H5N1 bird-flu vaccine. A better vaccine against tuberculosis (developed in Oxford) has passed the first stage of clinical trials, a meningitis B vaccine (developed in Oxford with Novartis) gives 96% protection and two American biotech companies are racing to produce a new anthrax vaccine. Other scientists strive to develop a West Nile vaccine, and a new safer Japanese encephalitis vaccine is expected in the next one to three years.

A new injection has been launched by GSK against rotavirus, aka winter vomiting virus. It is a two-dose course given only to babies between the ages of six and 28 weeks. Rotavirus is common throughout the world so, while all babies would probably benefit from this vaccine, it should be of particular interest to families living in regions of high population density.

The cholera vaccine, Dukoral, a course of two fizzy drinks, is available on prescription in the UK, some European countries, Canada, Latin America, New Zealand and now in Australia, but not in the USA. Unlike the sore-arm-inducing predecessor, this gives effective cover against cholera for a full two years. It was hoped that this vaccine might give protection against the commonest cause of travellers' diarrhoea because the vehicle for the active ingredients is sanitized ETEC (see p.51). A study in Mexico suggested that the level of protection is disappointingly low at 52%, but the vaccine gives better cover against the serious heat-labile variant of ETEC and against mixed infections, as are common in the Indian sub-continent. There is more information at *www.medsafe.govt.nz/consumers/cmi/d/dukoral* and *www.travellersdiarrhea.com*.

New, 'purer' vaccines are being launched all the time. These 'cleaner' antigens are good news for those who are allergic to components of current products, although egg-allergic people still await a yellow fever or 'flu vaccine that they can tolerate.

There are now not only more vaccines against more infections, but a greater choice of products and means of administration. Vaccine combinations reduce the number of jabs taken before any trip, although when the different components have different booster intervals (as with hepatitis A and B, and also the new hepatitis A and typhoid) immunization schedules become complicated. So be patient with your clinic nurse and allow her plenty of time to work it all out.

Flying and DVT

Way back in 1946, a doctor flying the 14 hours between Boston and Venezuela suffered a **deep vein thrombosis (DVT)**. He was convinced that the cause was the flight. During the Second World War Blitz, too, doctors noted that Londoners who slept all night in the Underground in deck chairs had a high rate of blood clots. Their special risk factors included immobility in the sitting position and inhibition of blood circulation in the legs due to the chair frame pressing against the calves and/or thighs. Doctors, then, have long recognized that being immobile is a risk factor for DVT. It makes clinical sense. While the heart pumps blood out under pressure in arteries, blood returning within the veins has to be massaged back by movement and muscle contractions, facilitated by non-return valves in the legs. Immobility slows circulation and allows pooling of fluids at the low points of the body. A stint in a hospital bed after a fracture or operation encourages stagnation of the blood and is well known to cause clots in a significant minority.

The term 'Economy Class Syndrome' was coined in 1977 but is was not really rediscovered until October 2000 when there was much journalistic interest in the tragic death of 28-year-old Emma Christofferson minutes after completing a 20-hour flight from Sydney. Subsequently, because of ever-increasing numbers of journeys, it was noticed that significant numbers of people are being affected by DVT. There are around 900 million international plane arrivals each year, yet the size of the DVT problem is difficult to estimate, not least because even a competent specialist doctor cannot diagnose the condition without an ultrasound scan.

Clots are fairly common in the general population: on average 1 in 2,000 people are diagnosed with a DVT annually. Estimates early in the millennium suggested there were perhaps 1,000 cases of flight-associated DVTs in Britain each year among around 50 million arrivals in the UK, although those in the business of selling 'flight socks' felt there were as many as 30,000. A believable, unbiased estimate is between one and four cases of DVT per 10,000 long-haul travellers. The risk of dying from a blood clot after a transatlantic flight though is less than one in a million.

DVTs that are big enough to cause symptoms are treated in hospital. A few are fatal but more than 98% of sufferers survive. The symptoms are: swelling of a leg (although most often swelling is due to the pooling of normal tissue fluids that is common on long flights), a painful calf or thigh and/or a reddening or darkening of the leg making it feel hot. This classically comes on 10 days after a period of immobility but can (rarely) start on the flight itself, or weeks later. The danger is that a big clot in the leg can break off and travel to lodge in the lungs. A clot in the

Why DVT is known as 'Economy Class Syndrome'

→ **Cramped seating** discourages movement, while movement that mimics walking promotes normal circulation.

→ **Lack of leg room** can create pressure on the calves, impeding normal blood flow in leg veins.

→ **Dehydration**, which effectively thickens the blood, is caused by low humidity and air pressure in the aircraft and by drinking too much alcohol or strong coffee.

→ **Reduced oxygen** in flight slightly increases the clotability of blood.

lung will usually cause a sudden onset of breathlessness, and often chest or shoulder pain. This is a medical emergency. Whether the sufferer survives this or not largely depends on the size of the clot.

The reason DVT is called 'Economy Class Syndrome' is that although DVT occurs in first class passengers and on any journey where people sit for more than five hours, conditions in the economy section of long-haul flights contribute to the problem. **Cramped seating** and a **lack of leg room** discourage movement and inhibit normal circulation of the blood (so listen to the flight attendants and put your bags in the overhead locker). On top of this, the **reduced oxygen** during the flight and the fact that passengers are often **dehydrated** means that the blood has a greater tendency to clot (*see* also **Flight**, pp.85–92).

Certain people are at increased risk of DVT (*see* box, opposite). People who have had a previous clot may be prescribed *warfarin*, which will protect them from a further clot. Otherwise, a shot of *heparin* may be suggested just for the flight.

There is good evidence that a meal of oily fish eaten in the 24 hours prior to a flight has protective properties. It has fewer side effects than *aspirin*. Statins probably afford some protection but shouldn't be started for this reason alone. Immunization against influenza also seems to be somewhat protective, especially in people under 50 years of age and especially women taking the combined pill. The risk of clotting is lowest in people with the O blood group.

Moving around the cabin, simulating walking movements and avoiding dehydration are definitely protective. So long as they are not already taking *warfarin*, are not asthmatic and are not upset by *aspirin*, higher-risk travellers might consider taking 300mg *aspirin* for three days before flying (although experts are still arguing about how protective *aspirin* is against DVT).

The best (proven) protective 'gizmos' are properly measured and fitted, graduated **support stockings** or **flight socks** (*see* 'Contact information: DVT', opposite). These should be put on before getting out of bed on the day of travel – not when in the sitting position. While flight socks are protective, those passengers with significant varicose veins, especially if they are in the upper calf, may experience inflammation of the skin of the upper calf where the socks slightly inhibit superficial circulation of blood. This may lead to uncomfortable phlebitis, although this is not dangerous. Wearing long support stockings will avoid this complication.

Small, foldable, inflatable devices, such as the **Airogym** or a **Pocket Gym**, can be taken on board and used to stimulate the circulation. For these devices to be effective, the calf muscles need to be tensed and relaxed as they would be during walking. Don't cheat by moving thighs up and down rather than using the calf

People especially prone to deep vein thrombosis (DVT)

→ Those who have had a DVT or pulmonary (lung) embolus (PE) previously.

→ Anyone who has had major surgery, a serious leg injury, a leg fracture or hip or knee replacement or varicose vein stripping in the previous three months.

→ Cancer sufferers or those treated for cancer in the previous six months.

→ Those who have ever had a stroke.

→ People with heart disease.

→ Those with close blood relatives who have had a clot – they may have an inherited tendency to clot because they carry the Leiden V gene.

People with a slightly increased risk (compared to others with no risk factors)

→ Smokers.

→ The very obese.

→ Pregnant women or those who have had a baby in the previous six weeks.

→ Women who are taking the combined oral contraceptive pill or HRT (*see* also pp.224–8). Consider stopping four weeks before a long flight.

→ People over 40 years of age.

→ Very tall people (over 6ft) or short people (under 5ft tall).

→ People with very severe varicose veins. (Thread veins do not increase risk.)

muscles. Appropriate use of these gadgets does promote blood flow, but so does getting up out of your seat every hour or so.

Contact information: DVT

Further information is available at *www.nathnac.org/travel/factsheets/dvt.htm* or visit the Aviation Health Institute website *www.aviation-health.org*. Also *www.thrombosis-charity.org.uk* provides factsheets and information on diagnosis.

The following companies sell anti-DVT products:

Activa Healthcare Ltd, Units 26–7 Imex Business Park, Shobnall Road, Burton on Trent, Staffordshire DE14 2AU, UK **t** (01283) 540 957, **f** (01283) 845 361, *www.legshealth.com*. Produces flight socks; note that flight socks need to be fitted by a pharmacist.

Airogym, 10 Crystal Business Centre, Ramsgate Rd, Sandwich, Kent CT13 9QX, UK **t** (01304) 614 650, *info@airogym.com*, *www.airogym.com*. Cost £11 including postage and packing.

Mediven Travel Ltd, Fields Yard, Plough Lane, Hereford HR4 0EL, UK **t** 01432 373 500, *www.mediuk.co.uk/travelsocks.html*. Flight socks.

Pocket Gym Ltd, Corbin Way, Gore Cross Business Park, Bradpole, Bridport, Dorset DT6 3UX, UK **t** (01308) 421 150 or **t** (order hotline) 0800 072 0898, *salespocketgym@btinternet.com*. Cost £17.95.

Scholl, Freepost, Scholl, UK **t** 0800 074 2040, *www.schollfootcare.co.uk*. Produces support stockings and flight socks.

Support Hose Store, 2300 S. Bell, Suite 2, Amarillo, Texas 79106, US **t** 1 800 515 4271, *www.supporthosestore.com/mediven.html*. Flight socks.

Zinopin is sold in pharmacies, or buy from *www.jscurr.com*.

Protective actions for all travellers

→ Consider eating some oily fish in the 24 hours before your flight.

→ Take exercise (a run, brisk walk or a swim) before and after the flight.

→ Get up and move around the aircraft every 1–2 hours.

→ An aisle seat allows more mobility.

→ Do calf-tensing exercises every hour. The in-flight magazine may detail special exercises.

→ Pressing the balls of the feet down hard against the floor or footrest improves blood circulation in the legs.

→ Breathing deeply several times an hour stimulates circulation and oxygen supply to the brain and body.

→ Avoid excessive tea and coffee; drink plenty of juices or still water.

→ Avoid taking sleeping tablets, excessive quantities of alcohol or any other form of sedation.

→ Consider breaking long journeys into shorter stages; flights of more than 12 hours are the most dangerous.

→ Consider the advantages of upgrading to business class if space is going to be a problem.

→ Avoid carrying aboard large, bulky items of hand baggage that will cramp you in your seat.

→ Sitting with your calves pressed against the seat or against a footrest inhibits blood flow; don't do it.

→ Avoid sitting with crossed legs.

→ Avoid tight ankle socks on long flights. Wear loose clothing.

→ Consider having a flu jab: it seems to reduce the risk of a clot by 23%.

→ Don properly measured and fitted flight socks.

Natural ways to reduce the risk of DVT

→ **Eat tropical fruit**: papain (found in papayas) and bromelain (in pineapples) may help to prevent thrombosis.

→ **Garlic** (a clove a day) and also **ginger** are traditionally used to thin the blood.

→ **Ginkgo biloba** and **cat's claw** may help to reduce the stickiness of red blood cells.

→ The **flavinoids** in grape seed extract and skins, as well as tea, red wine and berries may help to reduce the risk of clots.

→ Tea made from **holy basil** or **tulsi**, *Ocimum sanctum*, is said to have mild antithrombotic activity (*see* box on p.84).

→ **Essential fatty acids** (in oily fish, cod liver oil and cold-pressed vegetable oils) reduce blood cell stickiness by modifying levels of prostaglandins.

→ French maritime pine bark extract (*Pycnogenol*) with ginger, sold in capsule form as **Zinopin**, may reduce the risk and helps control ankle swelling on long flights.

Outbreaks and plagues: when should we panic?

'DON'T PANIC – there's enough tetracycline', said the headline in the *Kathmandu Post*. Plague was expected to arrive in the city but residents weren't reassured; the newspaper coverage precipitated panic buying of the antibiotic that cures the infection. It was a tense time. Expatriates fled; tourists cancelled; thousands of deaths were predicted but the disease remained far away in India, and the final death toll was 52. Any deaths are unacceptable but this number pales into insignificance against the Indian death toll on the roads, which runs to hundreds a day. Risk can be presented in ways that make it seem scarier than it need be. Something that doubles your risk of an early death sounds worth taking seriously, but what if your risk of untimely death is infinitesimally small? Doubling a minuscule risk still leaves you with only a negligible risk.

During the **Severe Acute Respiratory Syndrome (SARS)** 'epidemic' there was also fear and bewilderment. Only slowly did it emerge that survival rates in people infected with SARS were over 90%. The problem is that in any new outbreak the first cases will be severe – that's how the problem is noticed. Severe disease, fatalities and mystery illnesses make good eye-catching headlines and it is easy to assume a new microbe will kill most of the people it meets. Fortunately this is rarely the case. Outbreaks tend not to harm those who keep fit, don't smoke and are in reasonably good health.

When bird flu first crossed into humans, newspapers again carried predictions of global disaster and there was widespread concern. Again fortunately – thus far – outbreaks remain almost exclusively confined to birds. Only on rare occasions do infections cross to people and then this almost exclusively occurs in people living in poor conditions in intimate contact with their fowl.

It does seem as if health scares are part of life, and yet scares where experts suggest an outbreak might lead to deaths across the world on a huge scale – as happened with the 1919 influenza pandemic – will understandably lead to concern. The biggest barrier to staying calm is difficulty in discovering the real story. Early in any outbreak the scientists may not know how things will evolve but withholding information can be equally alarming. The scandal in China in 2008 when milk was contaminated with melamine caused widespread panic and people stopped buying milk completely. The problem with any outbreak or scare is that there is often suspicion that the local administration has suppressed information. Many regimes fail to inform and – sadly – it isn't only foreign governments that withhold the facts from the public.

Avoiding epidemic hysteria

Epidemics continue to rage in various corners of the globe, in addition to those reported from war-torn regions like Sudan or drought-stricken Somalia. Few can be unaware of the AIDS pandemic and we now appreciate the precautions we can take to avoid it. Knowledge surely is the best vaccine against epidemic hysteria. Travellers may be aware of the resurgence of cholera in southern Africa, but cholera is not a risk to ordinary travellers who are in good health. It hits the poor and debilitated. Routine precautions, which most travellers take to avoid diarrhoea, will protect them. Meanwhile epidemics of kala-azar fever continue unabated in northeastern India and southern Sudan, but since outsiders are unlikely to contract this treatable disease it is unnewsworthy. Nor do newspapers choose to focus on the five million or so children who die each year from diarrhoea.

How strange it seems that the media can fire our imaginations and play on our own ignorance, thus causing us to worry so much about diseases that harm mainly the desperately poor who are compromised by being perpetually half-starved.

Further outbreak information
Centers for Disease Control and Prevention (CDC), *www.cdc.gov*.

Health Protection Agency, *www.hpa.org.uk*.

World Health Organization (WHO), *www.who.int*.

Tips for people travelling into an epidemic area

If you wish to travel during an epidemic, check your facts from a reliable source before you go:

→ **Where is the outbreak now?** If it is restricted, say, to the industrial area of Surat (which few travellers visit anyway) in the Gujarat state of India, it is likely that other parts of this huge country will be unaffected – except by panic.

→ **How is it caught?** Consider whether it comes from contaminated, unhygienically prepared food (which you can avoid) or from flea bites in slum dwellings (which you are never likely to enter). Transmission routes for most diseases are covered later in the book (*refer to* Index, p.307–12).

→ **Does my lifestyle** mean I am more likely to catch the disease than other travellers?

→ **Do I have a medical problem** that makes me more at risk than most?

→ **Is it particularly dangerous** if I catch it?

→ **What precautions can I take** to avoid it?

→ **Is there a vaccine?**

→ **If I catch the disease how will I recognize it?**

→ **What treatment is there?** Should I carry a suitable treatment course?

→ **Do I now feel I have sufficient information** to be armed against mass panic all around?

Travelling responsibly

Some of my most rewarding encounters with delightful people have been when travelling by local public transport. Getting on a plane or being chauffeur-driven keeps you aloof, whereas getting out and mixing is not only the green option, it also allows you to experience more and enjoy more. Admittedly, though, employing a local as a guide or driver can really draw you into the community.

Travelling may mean meeting less privileged people. It can be inspiring to see that a materialist way of life isn't the only way, but thoughtful travellers will also realize that living with limited access to resources and health care is challenging. The realities of poor or non-existent medical care in the developing world can shock and appal, too. It can be hard for visitors to cope with facing such injustices.

In the West – even with our health services' problems – most of us can access any treatment we need. However, even the simplest surgery, and effective courses of cheap antibiotics, are denied to most poor citizens of emerging nations. Proper medical care with the right medicines is not affordable.

We're also unused to being confronted with disability, handicap and chronic disease; such unpleasantness is sanitized in the West, but images of struggling people are so common and obvious in resource-poor parts of the world that it can be a shock. It makes many of us want to help. Others respond by criticizing.

Tourists often try to treat simple medical complaints but locals really don't need Westerners dabbling just to salve their own consciences. It is important to offer only what you are competent to help with. Never be tempted to promise what you can't deliver and never just throw money at a problem.

Patching up the locals

If you want to 'patch up the locals' while travelling, think carefully about what you are doing and why. There is little harm in offering a couple of *paracetamol*, but do a little research if you want to do more. Try to avoid supplying a quick fix. Few diseases respond to a single dose of a drug, and unless you stay to supervise treatment you can never be sure that medicine has been taken properly. If your treatment does seem to work, the recipient may lose any confidence he had in the few facilities that are available locally. Furthermore, if your patient doesn't take your exotic tablets properly and so your treatment fails, he will lose confidence in allopathic treatments and you may wreck opportunities for health workers who follow. Also there may be a lost opportunity for the patient to learn how to avoid future health problems.

You may be tempted to hand out antibiotics. This can lead to harmful antibiotic resistance in the community. Even educated Europeans and Americans have a bad record of taking medicines as prescribed, and villagers who have had little exposure to Western treatment are unlikely to take a full course as required. In most places where I have worked, local practitioners, Western and traditional, prescribe selections of medicines. One so-called Ayurvedic practitioner in Sri Lanka prescribed for a woman with fever: *amoxicillin* (antibiotic), *valium* (tranquillizer), *paracetamol* (to reduce the fever), *propranolol* (heart medicine) and a vitamin capsule – one of each. Even qualified doctors sometimes prescribe part-courses of antibiotics. So, when villagers acquire a course they may take one or two and save the rest for when they are ill again. This promotes resistance to antibiotics, so that when serious infection strikes antibiotics may be ineffective. Giving out antibiotics is harmful in the long term unless you are prepared to stay for a week and supervise taking of the medicine; this is the kind of commitment you should be ready to make if you feel treatment is so necessary. Treating people properly is probably best done by a local medic.

The big killer in the developing world is diarrhoea; people die of dehydration because they do not realize how much fluid is lost or how to replace it. A traveller interested in helping people he meets may save lives by teaching villagers how to make and use sugar and salt solution (*see* p.111). It is easier perhaps to hand out packets of oral rehydration solution, but this on its own will not do much to make villagers self-sufficient in the next diarrhoea outbreak.

If you want to help, give it serious thought before plunging in, and allow lots of time (days perhaps) to teach people about what you are giving them. If you are desperate to hand out pills, note there are some that you can give away with relative impunity, and even do some good. Many women of child-bearing age in developing countries are anaemic, due to a combination of poor diet, constant pregnancies and hookworm infestation. Consequently they suffer chronic fatigue, are less efficient workers and breadwinners, and are more likely to die in childbirth

Play it safe

→ Don't be tempted to treat diseases you know nothing about.
→ Consider your motives: will giving treatment be conscience-salving, but harm your patients?
→ Try to offer locally bought medicines. *Paracetamol* or *aspirin*, packets of rehydration salts, iron tablets and antiseptic does a lot of good.
→ At the end of your trip donate your medical kit to a clinic, not to a non-medical local friend.
→ Resist practising on local people.
→ If you want to contribute money channel it through a charity with local links.

or deliver small, weaker babies. Dishing out iron tablets (*ferrous sulphate*) to women and older girls is useful (but note that an overdose of iron is dangerous, especially to young children). Locally made tablets are usually very cheap.

Also relatively harmless is *paracetamol* (Tylenol), which reduces fever and pain. Explain carefully to any recipient what the tablets can and cannot do. Again, you will do your patients a service if you give them recognizably local pills. They will be able to buy the next supply, and avoid being exploited by an unscrupulous practitioner or pharmacist. The poor spend too much of their tiny incomes on tonics and medicines, yet many are useless and some are actually dangerous.

Skin infections

Travellers are often asked to treat skin infections. This is one problem that is fairly safe to treat, and you can demonstrate how to deal with the next episode so that the sufferers learn to help themselves. Superficial impetigo (*see* p.212) is easy to treat, but festering sores need a week of supervised six-hourly *flucloxacillin* capsules.

In India and Nepal little packets of *potassium permanganate* crystals (sufficient to treat 100 people) cost a few rupees, and it's easy to carry a handful of them. Demonstrate dissolving a few crystals in water (*see* p.206), then rub the solution into the infected area with cotton wool or a scrap of clean cloth, and leave the packet with the family. Try to explain that grazes and wounds should be treated like this three times a day for a few days and that future infections can be avoided by cleaning even the smallest wounds with *potassium permanganate*. Even this level of explanation takes time, and ideally you should devote some hours at least to keeping an eye on your patient to see they are following your advice. Remember that local paramedics will be experts in treating skin infections, so if there is an accessible clinic it may be best simply to encourage your 'patient' to go there, and perhaps donate unwanted medical supplies to the local clinician.

Responsibilities

When venturing into difficult conditions we cannot assume that any locals who help us or travel with us are immune to health problems. Indeed it is likely that locals will have less ready access to good clinical facilities because they will probably have no insurance, may have limited finances and may be a long way from home. People do find casual employment by working for tourists but we should also keep a look out for obvious exploitation or negligence. The charity Tourism Concern (*www.tourismconcern.org.uk*) publicizes and champions victims of abuse. And why not check out *www.stuffyourrucksack.com*, where you can find out what you can take to help the region you are visiting or make suggestions on your return.

Before You Go:
Getting Ready

Planning 24
  Is your destination safe? 24
  What might kill you? 25
Insurance 25
Homework 27
  A first-aid kit 27
Clothes 28
Fit enough? 29

03

Summary

→ There's more to ensuring a healthy, enjoyable trip than immunizations and malaria tablets.

→ Arrange adequate health insurance when booking your trip so that you are covered for accidents or illness even before departure.

→ Travel agents won't want to scare you, so seek reliable, independent information about health and security risks. Certain internet sites under-emphasize health hazards. Equally, some expert sites might scare the pants off you. Face-to-face consultations are usually most reassuring.

→ Travel clinics usually offer the best personalized information, and will give you time.

→ Arrange a dental check to reduce your chances of needing treatment overseas (and thus reducing risk of HIV and hepatitis B infection).

→ Sort any niggling health concerns; an exacerbation could ruin your trip.

→ Pack a note of the dose and generic name of any medicines you take or may need to take.

→ Travel with a copy of your spectacles prescription in case you need a replacement.

→ Become safety conscious when travelling; of those few travellers who die overseas about half succumb to accidents.

→ For security information, check *www.fco.gov.uk/knowbeforeyougo*, the UK Government's travel advice website or the US State department's *http://travel.state.gov/travel/cis_pa_tw/tw/tw_1764.html*.

Planning

Is your destination safe?

News travels fast, yet a surprising number of travellers get caught up in riots and civil unrest; some are held by armed robbers or even terrorists. It can be difficult to sort out whether your particular destination is dangerous but your first pre-trip chore should be to check as best you can. Some travel clinic printouts include security warnings. The **UK Foreign and Commonwealth Office** or **US State Department** websites carry useful advice; diplomats are sometimes over-cautious, but that is because they bale out innumerable foolhardy adventurers. Good sources of information are recently returned expatriates, expeditionaries, missionaries and travellers, as well as newspaper websites, consulates and embassies. Advice can also be obtained through the Royal Geographical Society's **Expedition Advisory Centre**, organizations like the **South American Explorers** and smaller bodies like the London-based Anglo-Malagasy, Anglo-Peruvian, Anglo-Indonesian or Britain-Nepal Societies. Restrictions, such as whether an HIV test is required before entry, will be detailed with visa application paperwork.

Contact information: planning resources

Expedition Advisory Centre, Royal Geographical Society, 1 Kensington Gore, London SW7 2AR, UK t (020) 7591 3030, f (020) 7591 3031, *www.rgs.org, eac@rgs.org*.
South American Explorers, 126 Indian Creek Road, Ithaca, NY 14850, US t (607) 277 0488.
UK Foreign and Commonwealth Office, UK t (020) 7008 0232/3, *www.fco.gov.uk*.
US State Department, US t (202) 647 4000, *www.state.gov*.

If 100,000 people visit a resource-poor region for a month:
→ Half will develop some kind of illness.
→ 8,000 will visit a doctor.
→ 5,000 will be confined to bed.
→ 500 will require repatriation by air.
→ 300 will be admitted to hospital during their trip or on return.
→ One will die.

Source: Prof Robert Steffen, International Society of Travel Medicine

What might kill you?

Of those who die on their travels more than half succumb to diseases that would have taken them wherever they were, while most of the other deaths are from accidents. Less than 4% of those who die succumb to communicable disease. Road accidents are common: at least 300 people are killed on the world's roads every day. In the developing world vehicles are often poorly maintained because spares are both expensive and difficult to obtain, safety has a low priority, legal controls may be lax and some people drive crazily or while tired or intoxicated. Inside buildings, electrical equipment may be dangerous, so burns and electrocution are not uncommon. Drowning takes many travellers' lives. Poisoning from stoves in tents or badly maintained gas/kerosene fires is another hazard. Hotels may not have adequate fire alarms or escapes. Even if you're not usually safety conscious, take care when travelling. Hazards will not be signposted in the way you are used to at home.

Accident prevention, then, is especially important abroad. Jet lag, culture shock, not understanding local signs and signals, interesting distractions, wandering animals, unfamiliar vehicles and vehicles on the 'wrong' side of the road all contribute to the risk of mishap. In the less developed world accidents can be a double disaster because rescue services may not exist and emergency medical facilities may be poor or distant. Do not attempt a dangerous sport for the first time in a place where they do not seem geared up for beginners. If, for example, you wish to learn to scuba-dive, check that the instructors are properly qualified. Travel with safety equipment as appropriate, such as life jackets if you will be trying any watersports, helmets if you plan to hire motor bikes or cycle, or a car-seat for the baby.

Insurance

Arrange insurance to cover medical care and accidents, including air repatriation. Evacuation by 'air ambulance' costs the equivalent of at least three full-price seats,

Case history: Pakistan
Some keen Japanese venturers set out to canoe the Indus. They were kidnapped by dacoits (armed robbers). Had they enquired, they would have been told that this was a lawless area where foreigners are seen as rich and vulnerable. They were released once a ransom was paid. In Pakistan kidnapping is common.

plus nursing care. You need to be quite well and clinically stable to be medically evacuated, so if, say, you have a bad car smash, you may stay in intensive care locally for a while before you are fit enough to be evacuated. Your insurance must cover all these expenses. Be aware that medical care in the USA is the most expensive in the world, so if you are travelling in North America, or might be evacuated there, make sure the worst case is covered: £2–4 million worth of cover is a sensible target for travel in the New World. Health care in Asia, Africa and parts of Europe can be cheaper than private care at home (see 'Medical Tourism' box, p.74). Note that if you choose to travel to a destination against Foreign Office or State Department advice, this might invalidate insurance. Check, too, that the policy that you buy gives you what you need for your trip, such as a helicopter rescue from Everest Base Camp. Altitude is often a limiting factor in travel insurance; many companies put an upper limit of 2,000m (6,500ft), which is easily reached even in the Atlas Mountains. Insurance for mountain rescue is not usually included in standard policies, even if they do cover hill walking. The UK is unusual in having free mountain rescue from volunteer teams or RAF helicopters. Some insurance policies include emergency administration of screened blood (see 'Contact information: travel advice and insurance', below).

In addition to adequate insurance, try to have another back-up (such as a credit card), in case of unforeseen events, such as an earthquake or terrorist attack. Travel insurance is available through insurance companies, banks, travel agents and tour operators. Many household insurance policies can be extended to cover trips abroad, but domestic and standard travel policies often exclude extended or remote trips and adventurous activities (such as skiing or diving), in which case you should call a specialist firm. Conventional insurers often refuse even short-term cover if you have any long-standing medical problems or are pregnant. Travellers with specific health requirements are covered in **Special Travellers** (see pp.63–84). The RGS Expedition Advisory Centre can suggest on companies that insure expeditions (see p.24).

Within the **European Union**, emergency treatment is provided free or at reduced cost to EU residents with an **EHIC form**. This does not cover long-standing complaints. The free UK Department of Health booklet *Health Advice for Travellers* explains how to get medical treatment inside and outside the EU (see below). It is still wise to have medical insurance too. Reciprocal arrangements (where certain countries share free or subsidized treatment) are unusual elsewhere. Countries without reciprocal agreements with the UK include Switzerland, Turkey, Cyprus, Canada, the USA, Mexico and all South American nations, most Caribbean islands, all Middle Eastern countries, all African countries, all of Asia, and the whole Pacific region except Australia and New Zealand. Note that many governments, including the UK, don't want to make it easy to discover who is entitled to free health care. Know how to arrange treatment at your destination before you go.

Contact information: travel advice and insurance

To obtain the free UK Department of Health booklet *Health Advice for Travellers*, call UK t 0845 606 2030, or collect a copy at a post office or doctor's surgery. Look at *www.bloodcare.org.uk* for how to obtain properly screened blood.

Age Concern Insurance Services, UK t 0845 600 3348, *www.ageconcern.org.uk*. Covers most medically stable passengers and has no age limits.

Case History: travel insurance for the USA

Joe, aged 81, keeps active and cycles to the pool twice a week for a strenuous, fast-lane, quarter-mile swim. About six years previously he'd suffered 'funny turns' due to night epilepsy. He was put on treatment and had no further problems. He had not needed even to see his own GP except for repeat prescriptions. He decided to visit his son in Washington DC and do a bus tour to enjoy the fall colours of New England. Since his home was insured with Saga, he phoned for a travel insurance quote. Saga, which specializes in cover for the over-50s, say they have no upper age limit, yet they refused cover: with his epilepsy America was too risky for them. Joe phoned around and found that most insurers would not cover someone over 80, although several said that cover might be possible if he obtained a medical certificate confirming fitness to travel. Surprisingly, Joe's GP didn't feel he could provide such a certificate because of Joe's 'heart block' that had been fully investigated seven years before and was causing no symptoms. The GP suggested a provate referral to a consultant cardiologist and for an echocardiogram. Reluctant to pay the fees for this, Joe tried Age Concern; once he could confirm that he had not been in hospital during the previous year, they offered cover for himself and his 75-year-old wife for £309; the policy was valid for up to 31 days' travel any time during the following 12 months. What insurance companies need to know is whether travellers are stable. The fact that Joe hadn't been in hospital for six years demonstrated that his epilepsy and heart problems were stable; he was not a high-risk traveller. People with other medical conditions would be well advised to shop around for insurance or consult a patient support group for advice or special deals.

Columbus Direct, UK t 0870 033 9988, *www.columbusdirect.com*.
Saga Services, UK t 0800 015 8055, *www.saga.co.uk*.
Tourism For All, UK t 0845 124 9971, f 01539 735 567, *wwwtourismforall.org.uk*, *info@tourismforall.org.uk*. Offers information for travellers with health problems and a list of sympathetic insurance companies.
Worldwide, UK t (01892) 833 338, *www.worldwideinsure.com*.

See also **Special Travellers**, pp.63–84, for firms offering travel advice and insurance to those with particular health conditions and over-65s.

Homework

A first-aid kit

If you are planning a remote or long trip, try to attend a first-aid course before you go; in Britain, possible choices are **Red Cross**, **St John's**, **Wilderness Medical Training** or **Life Support** (*see* 'Contact information: first-aid courses and supplies', overleaf). It might also be worth investing time in gaining other skills that will be helpful if you are heading for remote places; reflexology, for example, relieves pain without medicines, and I have seen it used as a self-treatment to great effect in the mountains. Mobile phones are a useful item of safety equipment: as long as children or travelling companions carry a note of the number, they allow people to find each other or call for help. You can call for help (if you know the local emergency number) if, say, you are left in a ski lift for the night.

If you ask your doctor to prescribe medicines to take abroad, British NHS rules say that a private prescription fee should be charged, even if you are prescription-charge exempt. A specialist service like **Nomad** might be cheaper. Sterile medical packs containing needles, etc. may be purchased from Nomad or other travel clinics, Homeway

Medical, BCB (*see* 'Contact information: first-aid courses and supplies', below) and many others. Guidelines on medicines and first-aid kit to take are given on pp.32–4.

If you are going somewhere hot, pack one or two large (one-litre) water bottles. Thermos flasks are also useful, even in the tropics (*see* p.105).

Contact information: first-aid courses and supplies

BCB International, Clydesmuir Road, Cardiff, CF24 2QS, UK, *www.bcbin.com*.

Life Support, UK **t** (01229) 772 708.

St John Ambulance, UK **t** 08700 104 950, *www.sja.org.uk*.

Wilderness Medical Training, UK **t** (01539) 823 183, *www.wildernessmedicaltraining.co.uk*.

See also **Useful Addresses**, pp.301–4.

Clothes

What will you wear? If travelling to a hot region, I suggest you pack at least one long-sleeved, 100% cotton shirt and long, loose trousers; these will help protect you from biting beasts, barbed vegetation and the sun. Dark clothes attract insects (blue in particular attracts tsetse flies) and absorb sunlight, so light colours keep you coolest. Clothes may be cheaper at some destinations than at home, and in much of South and Southeast Asia you can get garments made to measure very quickly. Jeans are unsuitable travel wear: they're heavy, dry slowly, are hot and clingy in hot weather and yet not warm enough in cold climates. T-shirts are not particularly comfortable tropical wear, either; they are hotter than ordinary cotton shirts and do not protect the back of the neck from sunburn. They are, however, very useful as additional layers if the weather is unexpectedly cold or you ascend to cooler conditions from a hot, low area. Layers are warmer than one thick garment, and more adaptable if travelling through several climatic zones. Try to discover how hot it will be at your destination and decide which is the kindest season climatically.

Even in tourist destinations, dressing modestly seems to be appreciated and those who do so are treated with more respect. Ask people who have travelled to your intended destination about local dressing customs. Even men can offend by stripping off, and if women dress as they would at home they may encourage problems and even sexual assault. In many cultures it is unacceptable to be scantily clad, while figure-hugging clothes and leggings may not be appreciated (or, on women, may be appreciated too much). In some Muslim countries and many Asian cities it would be considered almost obscene for men to go out in public bare-chested or wearing shorts. Men and women wear loose-fitting garments that cover all but the head, hands and feet. In many places where outsiders are a rarity, stripping down to a bathing costume is never done and, if women bathe at all, they bathe fully clothed. Until recently, women in Malawi were not allowed to wear trousers at all.

In warm climates my favourite outfits include long wide skirts. These are especially good when on long bus rides since – by spreading the skirt wide and squatting – it is possible to take a discreet pee. The long tails of the sub-continental *shalwar-kameez* are also good for this purpose. Loose skirts allow healthy circulation of air, reducing the problems of thrush commonly experienced by women travelling in hot, humid climates. A tube of cloth sold as a sarong in the Far East or lungi in South Asia is also great for bathing in public, and a drawstring skirt can be pulled up under the armpits for a complete bath at the village tap.

It is common for the girth to shrink dramatically on tropical trips: women's waists seem particularly variable. Heat tends to reduce the appetite, there may be fewer tempting snacks, there may be a bout or two of diarrhoea and there is often more exercise. Pack a belt.

Fit enough?

It is easy to be swept up by the excitement of travel while overlooking the fact your body has to cope with what is to be thrown at it during the experience. A routine **medical check-up** is rarely necessary in people who feel healthy. However, when planning any journey, consider whether you are fit enough for what you plan to do: a surprising number of ill-exercised people book trekking holidays in high mountains, which makes for a miserable as well as risky trip. Of the million Britons who head for the ski slopes annually, 1% will have their trip curtailed by injury; sprains are commonest in the unfit.

Inexperienced travellers and **smokers** are more likely to become ill abroad. Smokers are the group most likely to contract legionnaires' disease or another significant chest infection, and there are many countries where smoking in public places is illegal. **Overweight people** (with a body mass index, BMI, over 30) are at higher risk of heat exhaustion and blood clots. Severely underweight people (BMI less than 18) may not weather a bout of travellers' diarrhoea well. Women whose periods have stopped because they are underweight should take medical advice before undertaking extended trips to resource-poor regions. **Backpackers** and **independent travellers** also have a high share of problems. A survey by the UK Foreign Office found that one-third of British independent travellers experienced a 'major problem' for which they sought help from an embassy: of these, 20% were ill, but had no travel health insurance.

Try to sort out any recurrent medical problems, as an exotic trip can make them a lot worse. And be aware that previous injuries leave a joint susceptible to a new sprain. Pack sports supports if you have a vulnerable knee or ankle.

Teeth

Have a pre-trip dental check-up. Dentists may not charge much abroad but the standard of treatment is variable, and if equipment sterilization is deficient there is a risk of contracting hepatitis B or HIV. Stones in rice and lentils often cause dental trouble, so consider taking temporary fillings or a dental 'first-aid kit'; travel clinics often sell them. Meat in the developing world is often very stringy, so pack dental floss, too; you should floss daily wherever you are in any case.

Ear and sinus problems

Those with active middle ear or sinus congestion or infection, or severe hay fever, may suffer from a great deal of pain if they fly. Anyone suffering from a middle ear infection (*otitis media*) should delay flying until they have taken at least 36 hours (several doses) of a course of an appropriate antibiotic. Anyone who has had an operation on the inner ear should avoid flying for two months. Wait 10–14 days before flying after a tonsillectomy or any operation on the middle ear.

Eyes

Conjunctivitis is common on tropical trips, and **contact-lens** wearers should travel with a pair of glasses so that they can manage without lenses in case of infection. Those with a **cataract** should pack a peaked cap to cut down glare. During surgery for a retinal detachment, a gas bubble is often injected into the eye and it is necessary to wait for this to be reabsorbed before flying; the wait is two weeks if sulphahexafluoride or six weeks if perfluoropropane gas was used. Surgery for cataracts or corneal laser surgery is not influenced by air travel but wait a week after any penetrating injury to the eye. Check with your eye doctor. Travel with a spare pair of glasses and your spectacles prescription.

Recent surgery, serious illness and fractures

If you have just had an operation, ask your surgeon when it is all right for you to travel. Most doctors would say you should wait at least a week before flying. If you fly soon after **laparoscopy** you may feel very uncomfortable, as gas left in the abdomen expands by about 30% in low cabin pressures; this expansion can also stretch a surgical scar if you fly within 10 days of an **abdominal operation**. After an **operation in the chest**, wait at least three weeks before flying. Air travel should also be delayed for three weeks after significant bleeding from a **stomach** or **duodenal ulcer**, since pressure changes can stimulate another bleed, which could be life threatening. People with **colostomies** may find that they produce more waste during a flight so should use a large bag and travel with extra in the carry-on luggage. Anyone with their **jaw wired** after a fracture should either be accompanied by an escort with wire cutters, or with some self-activating quick release in case of vomiting. After a **leg fracture**, flying is not advised for 48 hours due to risk of swelling within the cast; back-slabs and casts that are split in two should avoid harmful swelling. If there is a full-length or above-knee plaster, or if the leg needs to be kept raised, it may be necessary to travel first class or to buy two seats. Fractures or other significant injuries or operations on the leg, including to varicose veins, carry an increased risk of blood clots. For the kinds of **surgery** which increase risk of a clot *see* 'Flying and DVT', pp.15–18; *see also* 'Fit to fly?' box, p.65.

The disabled

Whether the disability is temporary or permanent, the biggest challenge, especially during flight, is likely to be the toilet; airline facilities can be very difficult and travellers usually need to be able to manage alone (*see also* 'Tips for wheelchair travellers' box, p.73).

Contact information: disabled access

www.justmobility.co.uk: good for links to other helpful sites.
www.dmoz.org/Society/Disabled/Travel: good for US travellers.
The Society for Accessible Travel & Hospitality, US **t** (212) 447 7284, *www.sath.org*. Useful resources.

Before You Go:
Medicines

What to take 32
  Dressings and bandages 32
  Carrying hypodermic syringes 34
  Thermometers 34
Taking medicinces abroad 35
  Beware of injections and drips 36
Useful medicines 36
Reasons for not taking medicines 38
'AIDS kits' and blood transfusions 39

04

Summary

→ Medicines are widely available the world over. Pharmacies in big cities are likely to be better stocked than in small towns.

→ Some medicines that are available over the counter in Europe need a doctor's prescription in North America and vice versa.

→ Most remedies and many antibiotics are available over the counter in southern Europe, Asia, Africa and South America.

→ Medicines that have been banned in the West are sometimes sold in developing countries.

→ Counterfeit medicines are on offer in some developing countries. Be especially careful in Asia and sub-Saharan Africa. Buy properly packaged tablets made by drug companies whose names you recognize and reject packets with spelling mistakes.

→ Take medical advice from a doctor where you can.

→ Know which medicines upset you and find out the generic names of these and their chemical cousins. Trade names vary – even between Australia and the UK.

→ Only self-medicate if you understand what you are taking and are aware of potential side effects and disadvantages of the preparation.

→ Check what you are taking. In many regions, combinations of medicines are the norm, and you may get more than you bargained for.

→ New formulations and some contraceptive pills may be hard to find in some destinations.

→ Palatable preparations for children can be difficult to find. Pack Calpol (*paracetamol* suspension) or soluble Tylenol.

What to take

People the world over have health needs so generally medicaments or a reasonable substitute can be found overseas. I carry less and less on my trips therefore, although good dressings always come in handy. A list of what I consider a fairly comprehensive kit can be found opposite, although of course some destinations will have better products on offer than at home.

If you wish to take a comprehensive medical kit because you are going on a major expedition, get professional advice. **The Royal Geographical Society** (RGS; *see* 'Contact information: what to take', p.34) runs seminars in London on expedition planning, medicine and independent travel. You can also buy custom-made medical kits from travel stores. Many organized tours and treks carry a comprehensive medical kit, which means you need to carry less medical clutter of your own.

Sharp objects in your hand luggage may be confiscated at the airport (*see also* 'Packing sharp objects', p.91). Such objects include tweezers, scissors, nail files, razor blades and needles, which may form part of your first-aid kit.

Dressings and bandages

If you plan to do anything remotely athletic, adventurous or dangerous, shop around for good dressings and bandages. In particular, those with recurrent tendencies to injure a particular body part need to pack supports for their weak joint; these are available in pharmacies. Knee/ankle supports take up very little room.

Contents of a first-aid kit

→ *Antimalarial tablets* – Paludrine is never available abroad.

→ *Insect repellent*, DEET-based; sticks or roll-ons are least messy.

→ *Sunscreen* and **lip screen**.

→ Soluble *aspirin* or *paracetamol* (*acetaminophen*, Tylenol).[1]

→ A strongish **painkiller** containing *codeine*[2] but check about local laws on importing such medicines, *see* pp.11–12.

→ Sore-throat **pastilles**.

→ Heavy **moisturizer** (e.g. white soft paraffin, petroleum jelly or Vaseline).

→ **Oral rehydration sachets** or a *measuring spoon to make sugar and salt rehydration solution.

→ **Anusol** or **Sudocrem** – especially if prone to piles.

→ Drying **antiseptic** of your choice (*see* p.204–6).

→ An **antifungal cream** such as Daktarin (*miconazole*) or Canesten (*clotrimazole*) cream.

→ *Calamine lotion* or **After Bite**.

→ **Crêpe bandage** and **safety pins**.

→ *Plasters/Band-Aids* (which stick and stay stuck when you sweat).

→ *Non-stick dressings* (e.g. Melolin).

→ *Micropore tape* to stick on dressings or to tape sore eyes closed.

→ *Steri-strips* or **butterfly closures**.

→ **Injection swabs**.

→ **Cotton buds** for removing grit from the eye (10 is plenty; *see* pp.269–71).

→ *Dental first-aid kit*/temporary fillings.

→ **Antihistamine tablets** such as *cetirizine* (e.g. Zirtek) or *diphenhydramine* (e.g. Benadryl).

→ **Fine-pointed tweezers** for removing splinters and coral.[3]

→ **Scissors**.[3]

→ **Artery forceps**.[4]

→ **Paperclip** for releasing blood under a nail (*see* p.282).

→ *Condoms* and **contraceptive pills**.

→ A **torch/flashlight**.

Notes

* Asterisked items are those that are scarce or difficult to come by abroad, or may be of poor quality. Some destinations will, of course, have better products on offer than at home.

1. Soluble tablets allow gargling when the throat is sore.

2. Painkillers like DF118, Distalgesic or *codeine phosphate* also calm abdominal cramps in severe diarrhoea. Mixes of *paracetamol* (Tylenol/*acetaminophen*) and *codeine* are also good. All cause constipation. Some countries demand a doctor's letter to import codeine even for your own use.

3. Sharp objects (e.g. tweezers/scissors) must be packed in hold luggage; they may not be carried on board flights as hand luggage.

4. Useful for pulling out thorns, clamping off spurting arteries, repairing tents and removing fish hooks from people – and fish.

Extra first-aid items for some particular conditions

→ **Thermometer**: if travelling with medicines for self-treatment of malaria.

→ **Mouth ulcer gel** (*Bonjela or Teejel): for travellers taking Paludrine or Malarone, in case of mouth ulcers.

→ Low-reading **thermometer** and **space blanket**: if going to cold places.

→ **Steroid ointment** (e.g. 1% *hydrocortisone* or Eumovate) if you have eczema or react to stings.

→ **Aciclovir* (*acyclovir*, Zovirax) **cream**: if a cold-sore sufferer.

→ **Adrenaline** (*epinephrine*) **injection** (0.5% or 0.1% or 1:1,000): if allergic to stings, nuts, etc. (*see* pp.69–70).

→ Two different courses of **antibiotics**: if going somewhere remote.

→ *Paracetamol/acetaminophen* (Calpol, Panadol, Tylenol) or *ibuprofen* syrup: for children.

→ Perhaps an **anti-motion sickness preparation** (*see* pp.88–90).

→ A fine-toothed **louse comb**: especially if travelling with children.

For most wrenches and sprains a simple crêpe, ace or rayon/elastic bandage is excellent and is also perfect for first aid after a snake bite (*see* 'Venomous land snakes', pp.243–6). Hydrocolloid dressings are great for healing blisters; they stay on until the blister falls off. A condom filled with ice makes a good soothing emergency cool-pack to be placed on swollen, painful joints or even piles.

Carrying hypodermic syringes

If you take an 'AIDS kit' and/or your own needles (*see* '"AIDS kits" and blood transfusions', pp.39–40), remember that some countries, notably Malaysia, will assume you are a drug addict unless the syringes are obviously part of a medical kit and/or you have a medical certificate. Diabetics and other legitimate syringe- and needle-users should carry an official-looking doctor's letter, ideally in English and the relevant local language(s), with lots of rubber stamps if travelling to a country where bureaucracy is complex.

Thermometers

Mercury-filled thermometers haven't been allowed on aeroplanes for some years and European regulations now forbid their use on the ground, too. Alternatives are the inaccurate and unreliable forehead strips or various electronic devices. The in-the-ear versions are accurate if somewhat bulky. Another alternative is a single-use clinical thermometer; it can be used several times or for several people if cleaned adequately, but they are so cheap, small and light that each person could carry his or her own (they are made by Zeal and sold by TALC, *see* below, for 15 pence). They read from 35.5°C to 40.5°C in 60 seconds when placed under the tongue or in three minutes when under the arm.

Contact information: what to take

Expedition Advisory Centre, Royal Geographical Society, 1 Kensington Gore, London SW7 2AR, UK **t** (020) 7591 3030, **f** (020) 7591 3031, *eac@rgs.org*, *www.rgs.org*.

TALC (Teaching-aids at Low Cost), PO Box 49, St Albans, Herts AL1 5TX, UK **t** (01727) 853 869, **f** (01727) 846 852, *talc@talcuk.org*, *www.talcuk.org*.

Taking medicines abroad

Some resource-poor countries lack adequate policies to control the use of medicines. This means it is sometimes possible to buy unsuitable, poor quality or even dangerous preparations over the counter. Buying medicines abroad is also confusing, as many trade names are very different from those you will be used to at home. Try to know the **generic** names (in *italics* throughout this book). Most drugs have at least two names: the trade name, snappy and memorable but often different in different countries, and the generic name, usually in much smaller print on the packet, which should be similar everywhere.

The next challenge is finding out what is available. Pharmacists may say that a drug does not exist, when what they mean is that they simply don't have it and would rather sell you something they do have. On the other hand, some medicines, even common and very useful ones, are just not available in some countries. Pills containing combinations of drugs are best avoided, unless you have already been prescribed it by a doctor you trust. When buying meds, check that the generic name is correct and that the expiry date hasn't been and gone. Also make sure that you will take the correct dose at the correct frequency by checking the packet insert.

Very few out-of-date tablets are dangerous (an exception is *tetracycline*, which degrades into toxic products), but even out-of-date *aspirin* is likely to be ineffective. Syrups and liquids have a shorter shelf life than dry medicines, especially in hot climates, so opt for tablets if you can. When taking antibiotics, complete the course.

Most medicines you buy in the European Union, North America and Australasia are of acceptable quality, but some medicines beyond these shores are made to very poor standards. Manufacturing standards are known to be poor in Nigeria and

Buying medicines abroad: checklist

Before you buy, check that:

→ The **generic** name is correct.

→ The preparation contains only **one medicine**.

→ The **expiry date** is still in the future.

→ There are **no misspellings** on the packet.

What to avoid

→ Do not take steroids or corticosteroids unless prescribed by a doctor you trust.

→ Try to avoid injections. If in a resource-poor region and an injection is needed, provide or buy your own syringe.

→ Do not buy or use medicines that are more than a year out of date.

→ Never take *chloramphenicol* (called Chloromycetin, Catilan, Enteromycetin) except as eye or ear drops. It should only be used during hospital treatment.

→ Enterovioform was banned as a dangerous cure for diarrhoea. Avoid it.

→ 'Mexican aspirin' or *dipyrone*, which is sold as a 'stronger' variety of *aspirin*, is dangerous; avoid it.

→ Women trying to conceive should be wary of taking medicines. Some drugs are dangerous in pregnancy, especially in the first three months; take advice.

Thailand, for example. Try to buy pills made by local branches of international drug companies, or, in Nepal, by the national drug company, Royal Drugs. Spelling mistakes on packets sometimes betray counterfeit tablets.

Beware of injections and drips

In all Asian countries in which I have worked, locals like the powerful placebo effect of a hypodermic. I have seen Afghan and Nepali medics giving intravenous saline infusions to treat weakness, but in such small quantities (20ml or so) that even if the patient was dehydrated it would not have had any effect. This treatment is considered very 'strong', earning paramedics high prestige. It can be dangerous to have unnecessary injections though. Serious allergic reactions are more likely, and there is a risk of an abscess or infection from dirty needles. In addition, serious reactions are more likely if the remedy is suspect: there have been deaths in 2008 in China, for example, after *ciwujia* (Siberian ginseng) injections, which are claimed to treat thrombosis, weak liver and kidneys, coronary heart disease and menstrual problems. Before accepting any proffered injection, ask if the medicine is available in tablet form. Dirty needles, including those for acupuncture, unsterilized body-piercing and tattooing needles can give you hepatitis B or HIV. Beware.

Useful medicines

Painkillers

Aspirin (*acetylsalicylic acid*) is an underrated and underused medicine. It is a good painkiller, reduces inflammation and swelling and is a good, cheap drug for lowering fevers. It can cause wheezing in some asthmatics. Those with stomach ulcers or a lot of indigestion should probably not take it. Nor should *aspirin* be given to children under 16.

The alternatives are *paracetamol* (*acetaminophen* or Tylenol in the USA) or *ibuprofen*. The **non-steroidal anti-inflammatory medicines** (**NSAIs**) are excellent for treating aches and pains, sprains, strains, wrenches and breaks, though they may make some people with asthma wheeze. Start with *ibuprofen* (e.g. Nurofen in the UK; Motrin, Nuprin, Advil in the USA); if it is not strong enough move on to *naproxen* (e.g. Naprosyn in the UK and USA; Anaprox in the USA) or *diclofenac* (e.g. Voltarol). If you get indigestion or nausea while taking these, stop and use a combination of *paracetamol* and *codeine* instead. The prime side effect of *paracetamol*, *codeine*, DF118, Distalgesic and other painkillers is constipation.

Avoid 'Mexican aspirin', *dipyrone*. It is sold as a 'stronger' variety of *aspirin*, but can cause agranulocytosis: a fatal AIDS-like condition. Pain lasting more than a day is best controlled by regular painkillers. Letting pain return before taking another painkiller makes pain control harder. You can take painkillers and antibiotics at the same time.

Antibiotics

Antibiotics have no effect on viral infections (including common colds). *Penicillin* in its various forms is probably the most useful antibiotic for travellers. However, allergy to it is common, and allergic people should not take *penicillin*,

Emergency treatment for HIV exposure

The risk of being infected with HIV may be reduced by 80% by giving emergency treatment with AZT. A one-month course is normally undertaken only with expert assessment and counselling, but this is often hard to find in developing countries. Travellers heading for environments with a high risk of occupational or sexual exposure to HIV should check to see what help is available in the event of accidents. If anti-HIV drugs are unlikely to be available, ask a knowledgeable specialist (such as a GU consultant, see below) to give you a private prescription for an emergency starter pack before departure. The **treatment** recommended by the UK Department of Health is one month of triple therapy with AZT 250mg twice daily, *lamivudine* (3TC) 150mg twice daily and a protease inhibitor such as *nelfinavir* 1250mg twice daily. Common **side effects** are nausea, vomiting and diarrhoea. Current information suggests AZT is mostly safe in pregnancy but there is less information about other drugs. The cost of a five-day starter pack is approximately £50 for AZT, £40 for 3TC and £80 for *nelfinavir*. The added benefit of three drugs over AZT alone is unknown, but three drugs might be important if the source has developed drug resistance. Treatment is best started within two hours, following first aid (allowing any wound to bleed freely, then thoroughly washing or irrigating the area). You should seek expert advice about the next step as soon as possible.

If you have special occupational risk of HIV, you may be able to negotiate a special package which includes repatriation in case of a needle stick accident. **Club Direct** or the **British Medical Association** may be able to help.

Dr John Richens, University College Medical School, London

Sources of information: exposure to HIV

www.doh.gov.uk/eaga/pepgu2ofin.pdf. Advice on HIV post-exposure prophylaxis from the UK Expert Advisory Group on AIDS.

BMA, BMA House, Tavistock Square, London WC1H 9JP, UK **t** (020) 7387 4499, **f** (020) 7383 6400, *info.web@bma.org.uk*.

Club Direct, UK **t** 0800 018 6638, *www.clubdirect.com*.

UK & Republic of Ireland Directory of Genito-urinary Medicine Clinics, *www.agum.org.uk/directory.htm*. GU clinics should be able to provide advice as to how to obtain a private prescription for a starter pack.

amoxicillin, ampicillin, flucloxacillin, cloxacillin or *co-amoxiclav* (Augmentin). The generic names of most (but not all) penicillins end in *–icillin*. The common alternative for allergic people is *erythromycin*. All these antibiotics are safe to take in pregnancy.

Flucloxacillin (250mg four times a day) is excellent for clearing skin infections, but is not available in much of Asia; **cloxacillin** (500mg four times a day) is the alternative. The **tetracyclines** (including *doxycycline*) are good, broad-spectrum antibiotics for sinus, respiratory (i.e. a green-gunk producing cough) and many other infections; they should not be taken in pregnancy, while breast-feeding nor given to children under 12. *Trimethoprim* is excellent for urinary tract infections but should also be avoided in pregnancy (*see also* 'Travelling while pregnant', pp.75–8). Cautions regarding **ciprofloxacin** (which can be taken by those allergic to penicillins) are given on p.113. **Metronidazole** (e.g. Flagyl) is a good, safe antibiotic for treatment of *giardia* and amoebae as well as some dental and gynaecological problems.

Mixing them

If you drink alcohol while taking *metronidazole* (Flagyl) you will vomit. It is also unwise to drink alcohol when taking medicines with sedative effects, such as *codeine*, and also sedative *antihistamines* (e.g. Phenergan, Atarax or Piriton). Don't combine alcohol, medicines and driving. This is an especially important precaution when driving in unfamiliar conditions, such as on the 'wrong' side of the road. Many antibiotics make contraceptive pills less effective (*see* pp.223–6). There is no problem taking painkillers at the same time as antibiotics.

Reasons for not taking medicines

A wise physician once said, 'Show me a drug without side effects and I will show you a drug that does not work.' There are costs to any treatment, and a doctor's job is to weigh up the costs and benefits of any treatment he/she prescribes. There are some antibiotics (such as *chloramphenicol*) that treat travellers' diarrhoea very effectively, but in a minority of patients they shut down the body's immune system and kill. Be wary of taking drugs that you do not know, particularly steroids.

The side effects of most medicines are trivial and short lived, but they are still better avoided unless genuinely necessary. If prescribing for yourself, consider the length and severity of your illness and compare them to the possible side effects of any drug. Simple travellers' diarrhoea, for example, usually lasts 36 hours, so is a course of antibiotics justified?

Antibiotics tend to deplete the body's protective and useful bacteria; losing them can have a variety of effects, from mild loosening of the bowels to serious diarrhoea needing hospital treatment. Absence of these friendly bacteria can allow troublesome bugs to establish themselves, such as thrush, which causes soreness and white plaques in the tongue, mouth or vagina. Profligate use of antibiotics also promotes resistance to all antibiotics, so that when there is a real need for effective antibiotic therapy it will not work. This is the most powerful argument against taking antibiotics too readily. Antibiotic resistance is much less likely to develop if antibiotic courses are properly completed, so do not change your mind after a few days and certainly do not stop the course part-completed just because you feel better. Most courses run for five to seven days. In general, avoid using medicines as your first resort in dealing with any symptoms.

Some medicines (including *doxycycline* and other antibiotics, anti-inflammatories and many others) can render the skin super-sensitive to the sun, so if you notice that sun-exposed areas become unexpectedly sunburned, and you are taking a

Carrying certain medicines into other countries and across borders can cause difficulties even if these have been prescribed for you. Some painkillers, especially those containing *codeine*, and also medicines for anxiety (including diazepam for flight phobias), can cause problems. Keep them in their original packets and consider carrying an official-looking letter or prescription for them from your doctor. This is particularly recommended if travelling to or transiting through the Middle East, or countries with very strict drug laws such as Thailand.

Herbal remedies

Many essential medicines have been developed from herbs and natural sources: *aspirin* comes from willow bark and *digoxin* from foxgloves, for example. There are undoubtedly many other effective cures among the remedies offered by herbalists and alternative practitioners, but how are we to judge which are effective and which might even be dangerous? Doctors of medicine always try to consider the evidence when prescribing any treatment, balancing the risk of possible side effects against the expected benefits from the treatment. It is harder to do this with herbal remedies, because herbal extracts usually contain several active ingredients and good, controlled studies are rarely done. Although there was a Cochrane Review of the benefits of echinacea in preventing and treating the common cold. Given the number of colds that are apparently acquired on board international aircraft, the conclusions were encouraging.

Echinacea is a popular remedy in Europe and the USA, with millions of people taking it in the belief that it stimulates the immune system. There are over 200 preparations containing extract of echinacea available in Germany alone, and these are made from either the roots or the leaves or the whole plant of one of three species of echinacea. The review looked at 40 clinical trials and concluded, 'Preparations containing extract of echinacea probably can be effective in the prevention and treatment of common colds.' They point out, however, that if any trials that showed little effect were left unpublished, this would result in a bias in favour of the remedy.

The big problem concerning herbal remedies is quality control and variability of effective doses. You may not know what dose you are taking and – worse – unusual components that can have harmful effects may be added. A dramatic if very unusual example of this involved a 58-year-old woman who went into a coma after taking Chinese 'herbal' Xiaoke Wan tablets. These contain *glibenclamide*, which in Britain is a prescription-only medicine used to lower blood sugar in diabetes. This incident illustrates that if you feel unwell after taking any unprescribed remedy – even if it is 'natural' or 'herbal' – it is best to stop taking it and see if you feel better.

Contact information: herbal remedies

Further information on herbal medicines can be found on **www.herbs.org** and **www.herbmed.org**.

www.24DrTravel.com can supply echinacea and other remedies by mail order.

medicine that can be safely d iscontinued, try stopping it; the symptoms should improve within days. Meanwhile, avoid further sun exposure (*see also* 'Hazards of the heat and sun', pp.160–4). A true allergic reaction to any medicine usually means an itchy red rash or, less often, breathing problems, swelling of the face and collapse. Mild diarrhoea or slight stomach ache (common in takers of antibiotics) are not signs of allergy. Many medicines are unsuitable for pregnant women (*see* p.78).

'AIDS kits' and blood transfusions

After a major accident the victim may lose blood and so require a transfusion. The dangers of transfusing unscreened blood and blood products are now well known, but some developing countries do not have the resources to carry out this screening. The situation in Bolivia is not untypical: only 30% of its hospitals screen blood, and a survey found that 54% of blood was contaminated with Chagas parasites (*see* p.154), hepatitis B, syphilis or HIV. The Red Cross has introduced a system of accreditation to monitor hospitals claiming to screen blood, which means that it should be possible to identify clinics or hospitals where screening is reliable. These kinds of projects are currently functioning or starting up in many

Case history: Lombok

A member of our small expatriate community in Indonesia was riding his moped when someone felled a tree on him. The handlebar of the bike penetrated our friend's abdomen and he sustained multiple perforations of his intestine. The expats rallied round and, mindful that this is a region where hepatitis B is prevalent, offered their 'AIDS kit' containing intravenous fluids. They also offered to donate blood. All this help was spurned by the local doctors. The patient survived the trauma without being infected, but nearly died because he was given blood of the wrong group. The best way to escape such risks is to be safety conscious, avoid accidents and realize that riding a motorcycle abroad could be the death of you. The Blood Care Foundation could have sent a paramedic to infuse screened blood of the correct group.

developing countries. Also, screened blood is now available in almost every capital city throughout the world, although there may not always be enough of every group. **The Blood Care Foundation** (*www.bloodcare.org.uk*) sends safe, screened blood with a paramedical courier to members who have suffered an accident; they have blood banked in Europe, Hong Kong, Florida and Lagos, and so far have always delivered within 12 hours. This is covered by some insurance policies.

Because of the dangers of infection with HIV or other diseases from blood or contaminated needles, some people travel with 'AIDS kits'. These kits (sold by travel clinics) comprise needles, syringes and a small amount of intravenous fluid, which could be used in case of an emergency admission to hospital. The largest AIDS kit is bulky, because it includes 500ml of intravenous fluid. However, the volume of these fluids required in a real emergency is large, and it is impractical to carry enough saline or plasma expander to be really useful. I also know of situations where an AIDS kit has been produced but was not used by the local medical staff.

Many doctors regard a comprehensive AIDS kit as a useful precaution and, clearly, if you are travelling with someone with paramedical skills, it could be life-saving. I never carry intravenous fluids, but it is worth considering whether you wish to carry a few needles, syringes and sutures; then you can ask the local doctors to use them if you go to hospital. You should also consider how drug-sensitive your destination is (*see* p.11–12). Pack Steri-Strips.

The risks associated with emergency treatment make it doubly important to avoid accidents in the first place. Many sane people become reckless when away. They do not wear motorcycle helmets or car seat belts, and they drive drunk and travel in unsafe vehicles. It's much better not to take the risk.

Before You Go:
Immunizations

Immunizations 42
  Immunizations for trips abroad 43
  Immunizations required for some areas 45
Special or occupational risks 49
Regional health risks 51
  Europe 52
  The USA and Canada 54
  Central America and the Caribbean 54
  Africa 57
  Asia 57
  Pacific Islands, Australia and New Zealand 59
  South America 60
Non-disease hazards 61
  Mines and explosive remnants of war 61

Summary

→ Make an appointment with the immunization nurse at least a couple of months before departure – longer if you are going on an extended trip.

→ Last-minute immunization is possible but may leave you less well protected, for the same financial outlay.

→ Keep up to date with immunization against tetanus.

→ Travelling children must also receive the usual childhood vaccines.

→ Trips to northern Europe require few extra precautions, but walkers and campers should check whether tick-borne encephalitis (TBE) is a risk (see pp.48–9).

→ It is increasingly important to take competent advice to tailor immunizations to your individual requirements.

→ Find out if your destination is malarious. Are tablets necessary and how will you prevent bites?

→ Identify non-disease health risks too. Mines and unexploded bombs are an issue in many previously war-torn regions including Southeast Asia (especially Laos), the Balkans and southern Africa.

→ Accidents take many travellers' lives; others succumb to malaria and many suffer from dysentery, yet there are no vaccines against these health risks.

→ Think prevention as well as 'what jabs do I need?'.

Immunizations

Start preparations for your trip as soon as you can. Know which vaccines are likely to be offered and why before attending a clinic and make sure you get to a travel clinic at least two months before departure. Immunization schedules are becoming more complex and requirements can vary within regions of countries and by season. Disease outbreaks mean that situations change, so these notes are a guide to the immunizations available and who should have them. Further up-to-date advice can be obtained from the Internet and also from specialist travel clinics who will provide a print out specific to the area of the country that you are visiting with information on any recent outbreaks (see **Useful Addresses**, pp.301–4).

Once you know what injections you need, **British** readers can organize immunization free from their GP against hepatitis A, tetanus and typhoid; others may also be administered but at a charge. Special vaccines such as Japanese encephalitis are not usually available, and BCG is now only available from the NHS at special hospital clinics for at-risk people. New vaccines are constantly under development. Specialist clinics usually hear about them first. Travel clinics can provide everything, but charge the full rate for all that they give. You pay for convenience although if you are less mobile or travelling with more than one small child, some clinics may not offer easy wheelchair or buggy access.

In **North America**, check locally with the public health department for travel clinics in your town. **Australians** can arrange immunizations through local doctors. Many carry or can prescribe vaccines and antimalarial tablets, but some don't, so check that they are available when you make an appointment. Travel clinics will probably prove more convenient because they keep more vaccines, so that you can avoid getting scripts, then going to the chemist and then coming back to the doctor to get the vaccine administered. It may be wise to contact a travel clinic if your destination is off-beat, you are visiting several countries, or if you have medical problems that could complicate your situation. The cost of a consultation with a local doctor and in a travel clinic is comparable and Australians can claim these on Medicare.

Immunizations for trips abroad

Vaccines against **malaria** that have been developed so far are insufficiently protective for use by travellers so antimalarial tablets still need to be taken in a great many regions. Travel clinics will say what is best for which area. For details of tablets and other precautions, *see* **Malaria**, pp.129–40.

Tetanus

You will probably have been immunized against tetanus, polio and diphtheria as a child, but check if you need a booster to protect you from these very serious diseases. Tetanus is acquired from deep, dirty skin wounds, and also from puncture wounds contaminated by soil, cow or horse droppings. It is safe to be immunized against tetanus during pregnancy. It is a **killed vaccine** and needs boosting every 10 years. In the UK this is now given with diphtheria and polio.

Polio

Poliomyelitis is still a danger to travellers; it is a filth-to-mouth disease so may be a risk in countries where standards of environmental hygiene are poor. It continues to circulate in Nigeria, Niger, Egypt, Sudan and East Africa, Pakistan, India and Afghanistan. There are still sporadic outbreaks beyond these countries, so it is wise to keep polio immunity up to date for travel to any resource-poor destination since paralytic polio will ruin your life. Polio immunization used to be a **live vaccine** given as drops in the mouth, but the safer, **killed**, **injectable form** is normally given now. It needs boosting every 10 years.

Diphtheria

Diphtheria is spread by droplets in the air; it is still prevalent in Africa, Asia and Central and South America, and is a risk in Russia and the Ukraine. If you already have immunity from previous diphtheria immunization, it can be unpleasant to have the full-strength jab; a special, low-dose vaccine is given as the booster. There is now also a low-dose diphtheria vaccine combined in a single injection with tetanus toxoid and polio, so all three can be boosted at once. Immunity needs boosting every 10 years; it is a **killed vaccine**.

Tuberculosis and BCG (*Bacille Calmette-Guérin*)

Tuberculosis (TB) is on the increase worldwide. For notes on the disease, *see* p.262. Most British adults will have been immunized against TB with BCG at about the age of 13, but this was stopped in 2005, and now only at-risk babies are routinely immunized. Check whether this was done; it leaves a little scar on the upper arm. It is unlikely to need boosting again. British children under the age of 13 should be given BCG if they are living abroad in high-risk areas. The most convenient time to get this done is in the first few days of life before leaving hospital. People who have reduced immunity (e.g. those with cancer or HIV) or are pregnant should avoid this **live vaccine**. There is a debate about the efficacy of BCG, but European doctors favour it since it protects against two fatal forms of TB (TB meningitis and miliary TB). American physicians do not give BCG because it makes diagnosis of TB more difficult; if you see an American doctor about symptoms that might be due to TB, be sure to mention whether you have had BCG.

Hepatitis A and E

Infective viral hepatitis affects 5% of unimmunized travellers to the developing world. The most common form is hepatitis A. Among British travellers there has been an eightfold fall in imported cases of hepatitis A since 1989 and this is probably due to the availability of a good vaccine with few side effects. Gamma globulin, being derived from human blood, carries some theoretical risk and has been superseded; it gave only partial, rapidly waning protection. There are several effective **killed vaccines** (Havrix and Avaxim) and a version for children (Havrix junior), which can be given from the age of one year. Two injections give at least 10 years' protection. There have been some recent problems with the vaccine, though. Unfortunately, during 2001 Aventis Pasteur announced that people previously immunized with VAQTA or VAQTA paediatric hepatitis A vaccines were not protected and that these people need to be reimmunized with the SmithKline Beecham vaccine (e.g. Havrix). Travel clinics and GPs are aware of this problem and should be able to tell their patients whether reimmunization is necessary before their next trip.

If you have had jaundice due to hepatitis A (this can be checked with a blood test), you will have life-long immunity to A and further immunization against it will be unnecessary. Immunization does not protect against the similar hepatitis E (or the other causes of hepatitis) but a vaccine is being developed.

Typhoid

Typhoid is rare in travellers. Around six international visitors per million journeys catch it. Some experts argue that immunization against it is not strictly necessary for travel to sub-Saharan Africa or Southeast Asia, since the likelihood of contracting the disease is similar to that in southern Europe. The risk is higher among travellers to the Indian subcontinent (around 100 cases per million travellers) and some areas of tropical South America, notably Peru (174 per million). It is also quite common in Central Asia, particularly Tajikistan.

The first typhoid vaccine was given in 1896 and caused a sore arm, but the new typhoid vaccines cause fewer side effects and if you are one of the unfortunate 7% to experience pain, swelling and/or redness at the injection site after one product, you can try the other. Immunity is boosted every three years. Children under the age of 18 months don't develop good immunity from this vaccine. People over 35 who have had four or more typhoid courses do not need further immunization. The vaccine gives only 75% protection to typhoid but none at all to paratyphoid. Travellers in risk areas still need to avoid raw or partly cooked food and dubious water (*see* pp.101–8). The oral typhoid vaccine was re-introduced in the UK in March 2006 after being withdrawn in 2002. This is given to people over the age of six years as capsules on days 1, 3 and 5; they are more expensive than the injection and need boosting yearly.

Immunizations required for some areas

Yellow fever

This is an untreatable, killer disease spread by day-active mosquitoes in much of sub-Saharan Africa, Central America and parts of South America (*see* map, below). The live vaccine protects for 10 years. For public health reasons, many countries require an international vaccination certificate if you are travelling from an endemic area. There are mosquitoes capable of spreading the disease in many warm regions, and no one wants to see it spread into new areas. Anyone with a severe allergy to eggs, infants under nine months, pregnant women or people who are immunosuppressed (such as cancer sufferers) should avoid this **live vaccine**. Anyone taking steroids by mouth at a dose equivalent to 40mg prednisolone or more (in children this is 2mg/kg/day or more) for more than a week must also avoid this vaccine. There is a higher risk of severe and life-threatening side effects from yellow fever immunization in the elderly, so it is important to ensure that immunization is actually needed, especially in the over-60s. Discuss this with your doctor before travelling. You cannot enter a yellow fever area without being vaccinated unless you have a medical exemption certificate. Check *www.fitfortravel.nhs.uk/advice/diseases/yellowfever.htm*.

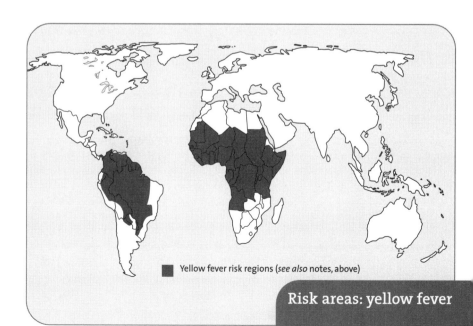

■ Yellow fever risk regions (*see also* notes, above)

Risk areas: yellow fever

Japanese encephalitis

This is another mosquito-borne killer. It occurs in Sri Lanka, India, Nepal and as far north as Pacific Russia; it also occurs sporadically in Southeast and East Asia, particularly where pigs are kept. It generally infects villagers living near pigs and rice fields, but the vector has been known to bite 20km from its breeding grounds. It is said to be rare in Muslim countries, but has been reported in Pakistan, where egrets may be the intermediate hosts. In Indonesia its association with pigs has made it an unacceptable disease and so cases are not reported. Transmission in seasonal climates is mainly April–October (peaking at the onset of the monsoon); closer to the Equator transmission tends to happen throughout the year.

Fortunately it is unusual for travellers to contract Japanese encephalitis. There were only three proven cases among all the Australians travelling in South and Southeast Asia from 1970 to 1991. The risk in tourists and business travellers is estimated to be one case per million travellers, because in more than 99% of people bitten by an infective mosquito there are no symptoms and no illness. However, in those who develop symptoms, the death rate can be as high as 30% and half of the survivors are left with long-term neurological disability. It is a nasty, incurable disease, and those travelling long-term or working in rural Asia may wish to be protected. The vaccine has caused severe allergic reactions, which occurred most commonly (88%) within three days of immunization but happened up to two weeks after the last dose; this was attributed to a bad batch of vaccine. A significant reaction is more likely if you have asthma, eczema or hay fever. Discuss with your doctor whether you are at particular risk; if you decide to be vaccinated have the last dose at least two weeks before departure. Immunization is three doses; a single shot offers no protection whatsoever; two doses a week apart will give no protection in a fifth of those immunized but some short term protection in the rest. Full immunity after the proper three-dose course takes up to a month to

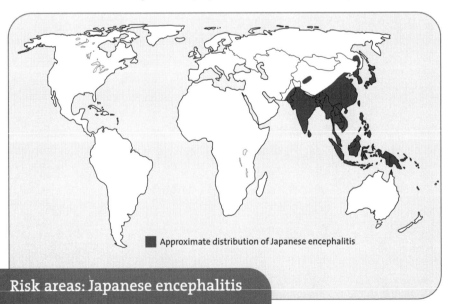

■ Approximate distribution of Japanese encephalitis

Risk areas: Japanese encephalitis

develop. The vaccine protects for at least two years; boosters are required after two or three years depending on the vaccine given. A new safer Japanese encephalitis vaccine is under development and is expected in the next one to three years.

Meningococcus

No vaccine protects against all forms of meningococcal disease, which means devastating meningitis or meningococcal septicaemia. The latter is actually more of a killer than meningitis. There are 13 serotypes of meningococcus and the commonest circulating in Britain are meningococcus B and C. The travel vaccine is different from that given in routine childhood immunizations and protects against four types: A, C, W and Y. This vaccine is needed for travel to India, Nepal and the 'meningitis belt' of Africa (mainly in latitudes 15°N to 5°N, but extending to the Equator in Kenya and Uganda). This includes sub-Saharan Senegal, Mali, Chad and Sudan; all of Gambia, Guinea, Togo and Benin; and southwest Ethiopia, northern Sierra Leone, Liberia, Ivory Coast, Nigeria, Cameroon and the Central African Republic. In the 'belt', epidemics commonly occur at the onset of the dry season (December–February) and usually stop with the first rains (May–June); cases occur from November to April. There have also been outbreaks in Moscow. All pilgrims to Mecca, Saudi Arabia, are required to show proof of immunization with the quadrivalent meningococcus ACWY vaccine, issued not more than three years and not less than 10 days before arrival in the country. Meningococcus is a killed vaccine and can be given to anyone aged over 18 months as a single injection. Boosters are given after three to five years.

Pneumococcus

Pneumococcus immunization is required for those who have lost their spleen or have sickle cell disease. Originally such people were told that they needed immunization once in a lifetime, but experts now recommend that asplenic travellers

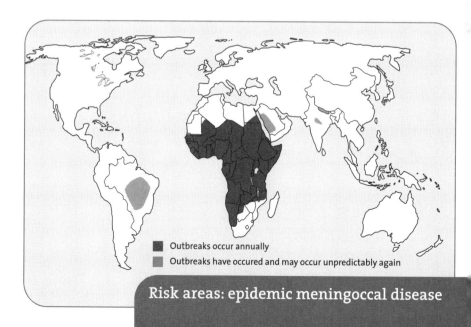

Outbreaks occur annually
Outbreaks have occured and may occur unpredictably again

Risk areas: epidemic meningoccal disease

05 Before You Go | Immunizations

Risk areas: 'European' tick-borne encephalitis (TBE)

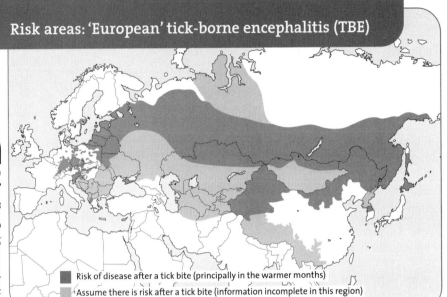

■ Risk of disease after a tick bite (principally in the warmer months)
■ Assume there is risk after a tick bite (information incomplete in this region)

should receive boosters every five years. Pneumococcal immunization is also now recommended in the UK once in a lifetime for people over 65 or with long-standing illnesses, including those with asthma and diabetes. The incidence of pneumococcal infection in travellers is hard to research, but it does seem unusually common in otherwise healthy people. A few doctors advise immunization for all travellers. Your doctor or travel clinic can arrange this. It is a **killed vaccine**.

'European' tick-borne encephalitis (TBE)

TBE is a risk for people walking or camping in forest areas in parts of Scandinavia, former Soviet countries, eastern and central Europe (Czech and Slovak Republics, Hungary, the Balkans, Austria, Germany; *see* map, inside back cover); April to August are high-risk months. The virus can also be acquired from consuming unpasteurized products made from goat, sheep or cow's milk.

The vaccine is not available in the USA, and does not protect against other tick-borne diseases. 'European' TBE occurs in Asia (*see* map, above), where it is

TBE pseudonyms

TBE comes in western and eastern subtypes but the vaccine protects against both. 'European' TBE occurs in Asia and is also variously called:

→ Russian spring-summer encephalitis
→ Central European encephalitis
→ Taiga encephalitis
→ Far East Russian encephalitis
→ Biundulating meningoencephalitis
→ Diphasic milk fever
→ Kumlinge disease
→ Schneider's disease

known under a variety of names, listed opposite under 'TBE pseudonyms'. Most Asian cases (about 10,000 a year) occur east of the Urals in Siberia and Far Eastern Russia. It also occurs in parts of China (including inner Mongolia and northern Tibet), Mongolia, the north of South Korea and the island of Hokkaido in Japan.

Special or occupational risks

Hepatitis B

Immunization against hepatitis B is worthwhile for expatriates and health workers; it is probably not indicated for short-term tropical travel, but its value can be discussed with your doctor or travel clinic. It is a **killed vaccine** with few side effects, gives good immunity and protects from possible hepatitis B infection from blood transfusions or dirty needles during treatment after a road accident (see pp.39–40). Hepatitis B can also be acquired from unsterile tattoo and acupuncture needles and from barbers using unsterile cut-throat razors. The primary course is three doses at zero, one month and six month intervals; immunity can be checked (by blood test) to see if a fourth dose is required. A booster is often offered after about five years. In adults the injection is given in the arm, and in small children in the thigh.

Influenza

'Flu vaccination targets the three most virulent strains in circulation that year, and aims to especially safeguard people at particular risk from influenza: those with diabetes, long-standing heart or respiratory problems (including asthma), those taking steroid tablets and other ongoing illnesses. In Britain it is offered each winter to everyone over 65 years of age and it would be a sensible immunization for many travellers, including the elderly going into the southern hemisphere winter. It is a **killed vaccine**. Egg-allergic people should not have it. One in-house study suggested that 'flu immunization reduces the likelihood of coughs and colds for five years. It also seems to reduce the chance of DVT (see p.15–18).

Rabies

Rabies is a risk in most countries, and confusingly some countries which are officially rabies free can have rabies in the bats. Any bat bite sustained anywhere should be assumed to come with a rabies risk. Bites by other animals in the UK, Ireland, Antarctica, Cyprus, Faeroes and some parts of Scandinavia are considered to carry no rabies risk. In much of southern Europe the risk is low and post-exposure vaccination easy to access so pre-trip immunization is rarely necessary. Australasia is 'rabies-free' but there have been two deaths there following bat bites, after which rabies-like viruses were identified.

There is a debate about who should be immunized and some travellers are not vaccinated because of cost. The advantage of pre-trip immunization is that those who are bitten but who are already immune need only two booster injections to give full cover against developing the disease. Those who haven't been immunized need to find a source of vaccine and also rabies immune globulin. There is currently a world shortage of the latter and there is also a theoretical risk of acquiring a slow virus infection such as Creutzfeldt-Jakob with any such pooled blood product. The other concern is that some remote clinics in developing countries offer the Semple vaccine after a rabies-prone bite (*see* pp.250–2). It is best avoided; the improved vaccine that is given into the arm is available in many capital cities.

Rabies is an innocuous immunization and a sensible precaution for people travelling long-term, going to remote regions or living in the Indian subcontinent (including Pakistan and Sri Lanka), South and East Asia or wherever there are a lot of stray dogs; it is also wise for those intending to enter caves in the Americas. Rabies vaccination is a must for veterinary surgeons or zoologists doing field work. The incubation period (the amount of time you have to get treatment after a bite) depends on the distance of the bite site from the brain and the severity of the bite. Small children often get bitten on the face, so that there is very little time to get medical help. It is important that young children visiting endemic areas are vaccinated.

It is a **killed vaccine**. Two injections are given a month apart, with a reinforcing dose after 6–12 months, then boosters every three years. The cheapest way to be immunized is with a part dose (eight to nine people can be injected intradermally from a 1ml vial) and travel clinics can sometimes arrange this. The vaccine's efficacy is reduced if you are taking *chloroquine* when you receive it, so get immunized well before you start your malaria tablets or, if this is impossible, have an intramuscular (larger) dose of rabies vaccine.

Cholera

Cholera is very rare in travellers, even in epidemic areas; the risk is estimated at perhaps two cases per million travellers. The best way to remain cholera-free is to avoid contaminated food and water (*see* pp.101–5), but people going to work

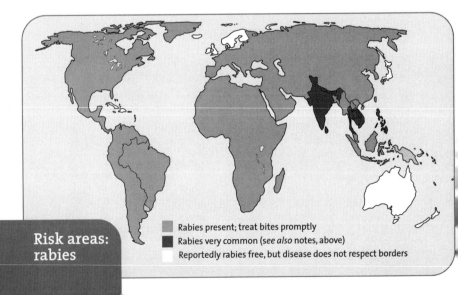

Risk areas: rabies

Rabies present; treat bites promptly
Rabies very common (*see also* notes, above)
Reportedly rabies free, but disease does not respect borders

on aid or relief projects might consider protection, as might travellers going to stay in villages with poor sanitation during epidemics. The **oral vaccine**, Dukoral, is available in Europe, Australia, New Zealand and Canada, but not the USA. It gives two years' protection, and may also offer some protection against travellers' diarrhoea caused by heat-labile toxin of ETEC, but only for three months (*see also* p.14; *www.travellersdiarrhea.com*).

It is now internationally agreed that immunizing travellers does not prevent the introduction of cholera infection into a country and so certificates of immunization are no longer required anywhere. Unofficial demands do occur, however. This is rare and is confined to a few remote land borders. Travel clinics should be able to supply a certificate confirming that the vaccine is 'medically contraindicated'.

Plague
Few travellers need immunization against plague even during an outbreak. Rodent ecologists or medical staff are sometimes immunized if working during an epidemic. It is not a particularly effective vaccine. Side effects are unpleasant, especially after booster doses, which need to be given every six months.

Regional health risks

Travel anywhere involves risks. This section and the immunization tables (*see* pp.53–61) highlight the risks in different geographical regions: the tables mention vaccines that will be required for travellers. These are not comprehensive and are intended to aid a traveller to focus on whether to travel to a particular destination and what preventative strategies might be wise. Things change with new disease outbreaks, so check on a suitable website (e.g. *www.fitfortravel.scot.nhs.uk*) or with a travel clinic.

Everyone should keep up to date with routine immunizations, including MMR (measles, mumps, rubella) and tetanus. People going on long trips to rural regions or to poorer regions should consider immunization against hepatitis B, rabies and perhaps TB (BCG). Those working overseas long term should probably also arrange diphtheria cover. People passing through countries where yellow fever is recorded – even if not visiting a region where the disease is transmitted – may find border crossings easier if they are immunized and are carrying an international vaccination certificate. I know of several instances of forced vaccinations on buses in South America; a vaccination certificate therefore doubly protects travellers.

Leishmania has been listed as a preventable disease in the tables that follow. There is no vaccine and treatment is not straightforward, but it can be avoided by bite prevention.

Key to regional health risk tables on pp.53–61

O	malaria risk patchy or seasonal; prophylaxis may vary across the country; check with an expert source
●	small risk of contracting malaria; no tablets are necessary, but bite prevention is still important
●	malaria risk: recommended prophylaxis is indicated
Mf	*Mefloquine* (Lariam)
Dx	*Doxycycline* (Vibramycin)
Ml	Malarone (*proguanil* with *atovaquone*)
C+P	*Chloroquine* and *proguanil* (Paludrine)
C	*Chloroquine* alone
*C	*Chloroquine* alone in certain parts of the country (as indicated)
✖	immunization recommended
(✖)	disease risk present; immunization requirements depend on length of stay and activities during visit; immunization may be wise for backpackers
*✖	immunization recommended for some parts of the country
*(✖)	disease risk present in some parts of country
M	mandatory immunization
(M)	immunization mandatory unless staying for less than two weeks and arriving from non-endemic country
n	in the northern part of the country
s	in the southern part of the country
!	significant risk if walking in forest in summer
(!)	risk for walkers and campers in parts of country
L	leishmania risk present
m	meningococcal meningitis and septicaemia risk present in some seasons (*see* p.47)
sh	schistosomiasis (bilharzia) risk in freshwater bathers (*see* pp.179–81)
*sh	schistosomiasis risk in some parts of the country
rb	onchocerciasis (river blindness) present in some parts (*see* pp.181–2)
ty	trypanosomiasis (sleeping sickness, Chagas' disease; *see* p.154)

Europe

As with all destinations, there is a risk of gastrointestinal infection, and this risk is greatest in the south and east of the region during the summer and autumn. **Hepatitis A** is fairly common in Eastern European countries. **Legionnaires' disease** occurs amongst hotel holiday-makers but seldom causes symptoms even amongst the people exposed to the bacteria (*see* p.216). Those travellers who enjoy woodland walks or orienteering or who camp may expose themselves to tick-borne infections: both **Lyme disease** and **tick-borne encephalitis** (**TBE**) exist in much of the area and TBE immunization is wise for summer hikers in the countries indicated (*see* table, opposite, for risks). The last indigenous case of **polio** recorded in Europe was in Turkey in 1998, and at the time of writing Europe remains free of the disease.

Health risks: Europe

(*see key*, p.52)

	Malaria	Hepatitis A	Typhoid	Diphtheria	TBE	Rabies	Leishmania
Albania		✖	(✖)	(✖)	!	(✖)	L
Andorra						(✖)	
Armenia	**O** C: Jun–Oct	✖	(✖)	✖	!	(✖)	
Austria					!		
Azores		(✖)				(✖)	
Belarus		✖	(✖)	✖	!	(✖)	
Bosnia		✖	(✖)	(✖)	!	(✖)	L
Bulgaria		✖	(✖)	(✖)	!	(✖)	L
Canary Islands		(✖)				(✖)	
Croatia		✖	(✖)	(✖)	!	(✖)	L
Cyprus		(✖)				(✖)	L
Czech Republic		✖	(✖)		!	(✖)	
Denmark					(!)		
Estonia		(✖)	(✖)	✖	!	(✖)	
Finland				(✖)	(!)		
France					(!)		L
Georgia	**O** Jun–Oct	✖	(✖)	✖	!	(✖)	L
Germany					(!)		
Gibraltar						(✖)	
Greece and Islands		(✖)			(!)	(✖)	L
Greenland		(✖)				(✖)	
Herzegovina		✖	(✖)	(✖)	!	(✖)	L
Hungary					!		
Iceland							
Ireland							
Italy		(✖)			(!)	(✖)	L
Kosovo		✖	(✖)	(✖)	!	(✖)	L
Latvia		✖	(✖)	✖	!	(✖)	
Liechtenstein					!	(✖)	
Lithuania		(✖)	(✖)	✖	!	(✖)	
Luxembourg							
Macedonia		✖	(✖)	(✖)	!	(✖)	L
Madeira		(✖)					
Malta and Gozo							L
Moldova		✖	(✖)	✖	!	(✖)	
Monaco		✖	(✖)	(✖)			
Montenegro		✖	(✖)	(✖)	!	(✖)	L
Netherlands							
Norway					(!)		
Poland		(✖)	(✖)	(✖)	!	(✖)	
Portugal		(✖)				(✖)	L
Romania		✖	(✖)	✖	!	(✖)	
Russia (European)		✖	✖	✖	!	(✖)	L
San Marino							
Serbia		✖	(✖)	(✖)	!	(✖)	L
Slovakia		✖	(✖)	(✖)	!	(✖)	L
Slovenia		✖	(✖)	(✖)	!	(✖)	L

Health risks: Europe (cont.)
(see key, p.52)

	Malaria	Hepatitis A	Typhoid	Diphtheria	TBE	Rabies	Leishmania
Spain		(✖)					L
Sweden					(!)		
Switzerland					(!)		
Turkey (European)	see p.59	✖	(✖)	(✖)		(✖)	L
Ukraine		✖	(✖)	✖	!	(✖)	
ex-Yugoslavia		✖	(✖)	(✖)	!	(✖)	L

Rabies immunization is not necessary for travel in Europe, but treatment must be sought after any mammal bite (see pp.250–1). In southern Europe insect bites can be a nuisance and there is a slight risk of **insect-borne infection,** including leishmania and some other rarities. There has been a rash of reports of holiday-makers returning from the Mediterranean suffering from a nasty fever, muscle aches and severe headache. They had viral sand-fly fever (see p.153 for bite avoidance). All recovered without specific treatment, but these cases highlight the good sense in avoiding insect bites, even in Europe. There is no longer any **malaria** in Europe, although it does occur in Georgia, Armenia and Asian Turkey.

The USA and Canada

The risk of **gastrointestinal disease** is present although small. **Tick-borne infections** are a concern to those enjoying outdoor activities and so bite avoidance is wise (see pp.143–9) and symptoms after a tick bite should be properly treated. Rabies is a risk after any mammal bite.

Although there are no immunizations required for entry into the USA or Canada, children and some university students must show documented evidence of immunization against diphtheria, measles, polio, rubella, and usually also against tetanus, pertussis, mumps and hepatitis B. Chickenpox immunization is also required by some institutions. Health insurance may be expensive for the USA but adequate cover is crucial. **Scorpions** in Arizona and New Mexico are dangerous but antivenom is available; venomous **snakes** rarely cause harm because of the availability of medical services and antivenom.

Central America and the Caribbean

This is a high-risk region for **food-borne gastroenteritis, hepatitis A and E, worms** and **typhoid. Rabies** is a significant risk after any mammal bite. Bats may carry rabies even on 'rabies-free' islands. There are plenty of **insect-** and **tick-borne** infections on offer, so bite precautions are important, especially in mainland forests.

Health Risks: Central America and the Caribbean

(see key, p.52)

	Malaria	Hepatitis A	Typhoid	Diphtheria	Rabies	Yellow Fever	Leishmania	Other
Anguilla		✘	(✘)	✘	✘			
Antigua and Barbuda		✘	(✘)					
Aruba		✘	(✘)					
Bahamas		✘	(✘)					
Barbados		✘	(✘)					
Belize	● C	✘	✘	✘	✘	(✘)	L	
Bermuda		✘						
British Virgin Islands		✘	(✘)					
Cayman Islands		✘	(✘)					
Costa Rica	O C	✘	✘	✘	✘	(✘)	L	ty
Cuba		✘	(✘)	✘	✘			
Dominica		✘	(✘)	✘	✘		L	
Dominican Republic	● C	✘	✘	✘	✘		L	sh
El Salvador	O *C	✘	✘	✘	✘		L	ty
(only Santa Ana province)								
Granada		✘	(✘)	✘	✘			
Grenadines		✘	(✘)					
Guadeloupe		✘	(✘)			(✘)		sh
Guatemala	● C	✘	✘	✘	✘	(✘)	L	rb
Haiti	● C	✘	✘	✘	✘	(✘)		
Honduras	● C	✘	✘	✘	✘	(✘)	L	
Jamaica		✘	(✘)			(✘)		
Martinique		✘	(✘)					sh
Mexico	O C	✘	✘	✘	✘		L	ty
Montserrat		✘	(✘)					
Neth. Antilles		✘	(✘)	✘	(✘)			
Nicaragua	● C	✘	✘	✘	✘		L	ty
Panama	O C+P	✘	✘	✘	✘	✘	L	
Puerto Rico		✘	✘	✘	✘		L	sh
Saint Kitts and Nevis		✘	(✘)					
Saint Lucia		✘	(✘)					sh
Saint Vincent		✘	(✘)					
Trinidad and Tobago		✘	(✘)	✘	✘	*✘		ty
Turks and Caicos Is.		✘	(✘)					
Virgin Islands (US)		✘	(✘)					

Dengue and **dengue haemorrhagic fever** occur, and there are unpredictable outbreaks. **Schistosomiasis (bilharzia)** is present in the Dominican Republic, Guadeloupe, Martinique, Puerto Rico, St Lucia and may be present in other islands (see pp.179–81). **Elephantiasis** has been recorded in Haiti and some other islands. The Americas was declared free from polio but polio immunization requirements are under constant review.

Health risks: Africa

(see key, p.52)

	Malaria	Polio	Hepatitis A	Typhoid	Diphtheria	Rabies	Yellow Fever	Meningitis	Other
Algeria	○	✖	✖	✖	✖	(✖)			L, sh
Angola	● Mf, Dx, Ml	✖	✖	✖	✖	(✖)	M	(✖)	sh, ty
Benin	● Mf, Dx, Ml	✖	✖	✖	(✖)	(✖)	M	(✖)	L, sh
Botswana	○ Mf, Dx, Ml	✖	✖	✖	(✖)	(✖)			sh, ty
Burkina Faso	● Mf, Dx, Ml	✖	✖	✖	✖	(✖)	M	(✖)	L, sh, ty
Burundi	● Mf, Dx, Ml	✖	✖	✖	✖	(✖)	✖	(✖)	sh, ty
Cameroon	● Mf, Dx, Ml	✖	✖	✖	✖	(✖)	M	(✖)	sh, ty
Cape Verde	○	✖	✖	✖	(✖)	(✖)	✖		L
Central African Rep.	● Mf, Dx, Ml	✖	✖	✖	✖	(✖)	M	(✖)	sh, ty
Chad	● Mf, Dx, Ml	✖	✖	✖	✖	(✖)	✖	(✖)	*sh, ty
Comoros	● Mf, Dx, Ml	✖	✖	✖	✖	(✖)		(✖)	L
Congo	● Mf, Dx, Ml	✖	✖	✖	✖	(✖)	M	(✖)	sh, ty
D. R. Congo (Zaire)	● Mf, Dx, Ml	✖	✖	✖	✖	(✖)	M	(✖)	sh, ty
Djibouti	● Mf, Dx, Ml	✖	✖	✖	✖	(✖)	✖	(✖)	L, sh
Egypt	○ *C (El Faiyum)	✖	✖	✖	✖	(✖)			L, sh
Equatorial Guinea	● Mf, Dx, Ml	✖	✖	✖	✖	(✖)	✖	(✖)	sh, ty
Eritrea	○ Mf, Dx, Ml	✖	✖	✖	✖	(✖)	M	(✖)	L, sh
Ethiopia	○ Mf, Dx, Ml	✖	✖	✖	✖	(✖)	✖	(✖)	L, sh
Gabon	● Mf, Dx, Ml	✖	✖	✖	✖	(✖)	M	(✖)	sh
Gambia	● Mf, Dx, Ml	✖	✖	✖	✖	(✖)	✖	(✖)	L, sh, ty
Ghana	● Mf, Dx, Ml	✖	✖	✖	✖	(✖)	M	(✖)	sh, ty
Guinea	● Mf, Dx, Ml	✖	✖	✖	✖	(✖)	✖	(✖)	L, sh, ty
Guinea-Bissau	● Mf, Dx, Ml	✖	✖	✖	✖	(✖)	✖	(✖)	L, sh, ty
Ivory Coast	● Mf, Dx, Ml	✖	✖	✖	✖	(✖)	M	(✖)	ty
Kenya	● Mf, Dx, Ml	✖	✖	✖	✖	(✖)	✖	(✖)	L, sh, ty
Lesotho		✖	✖	✖	✖	(✖)	(✖)		sh
Liberia	● Mf, Dx, Ml	✖	✖	✖	✖	(✖)	M	(✖)	sh, ty
Libya		✖	✖	✖	✖	(✖)			L
Madagascar	● Mf, Dx, Ml	✖	✖	✖	✖	(✖)			sh
Malawi	● Mf, Dx, Ml	✖	✖	✖	✖	(✖)		(✖)	sh, ty
Mali	● Mf, Dx, Ml	✖	✖	✖	✖	(✖)	M	(✖)	L, ty
Mauritania	○ C+P	✖	✖	✖	✖	(✖)	M	(✖)	L, sh
Mauritius	○	✖	✖	✖	(✖)	(✖)			
Mayotte	● Mf, Dx, Ml	✖	✖	✖	(✖)	(✖)			L
Morocco	○	✖	✖	✖	(✖)	(✖)			L
Mozambique	● Mf, Dx, Ml	✖	✖	✖	✖	(✖)	M	(✖)	sh, ty
Namibia	● Mf, Dx, Ml	✖	✖	✖	(✖)	(✖)		(✖)	sh
Niger	● Mf, Dx, Ml	✖	✖	✖	✖	(✖)	M	(✖)	L, sh, ty
Nigeria	● Mf, Dx, Ml	✖	✖	✖	✖	(✖)	✖	(✖)	sh, ty
Reunion		(✖)	✖	✖	✖	(✖)			sh
Rwanda	● Mf, Dx, Ml	✖	✖	✖	✖	(✖)	M	(✖)	sh, ty
Saint Helena and Ascension		(✖)	✖	(✖)	(✖)	(✖)			
Sao Tome and Principe	● Mf, Dx, Ml	✖	✖	✖	✖	(✖)	M	(✖)	L, sh
Senegal	● Mf, Dx, Ml	✖	✖	✖	✖	(✖)	✖	(✖)	sh, ty
Seychelles		✖	✖	✖	(✖)	(✖)			sh, ty
Sierra Leone	● Mf, Dx, Ml	✖	✖	✖	✖	(✖)	✖	(✖)	L, ty
Somalia	● Mf, Dx, Ml	✖	✖	✖	✖	(✖)	✖	(✖)	sh
South Africa	○ Mf, Dx, Ml	✖	✖	✖	✖	(✖)			sh, ty

	Malaria	Polio	Hepatitis A	Typhoid	Diphtheria	Rabies	Yellow Fever	Meningitis	Other
Sudan	● Mf, Dx, Ml	✘	✘	✘	✘	(✘)	✘	(✘)	L, sh
Swaziland	● Mf, Dx, Ml	✘	✘	✘	(✘)	(✘)	✘		sh
Tanzania	● Mf, Dx, Ml	✘	✘	✘	✘	(✘)	✘	(✘)	sh, ty
Togo	● Mf, Dx, Ml	✘	✘	✘	✘	(✘)	M	(✘)	sh, ty
Tunisia		✘	✘	(✘)	(✘)	(✘)			L
Uganda	● Mf, Dx, Ml	✘	✘	✘	✘	(✘)	✘	(✘)	sh, ty
Zambia	● Mf, Dx, Ml	✘	✘	✘	✘	(✘)	✘	(✘)	sh, ty
Zanzibar (Tanzania)	● Mf, Dx, Ml	✘	✘	✘	✘	(✘)	✘	(✘)	sh, ty
Zimbabwe	● Mf, Dx, Ml	✘	✘	✘	✘	(✘)	M	(✘)	sh, ty

Africa

The three big threats to health in much of sub-Saharan Africa are **road accidents** – from bad roads, old cars and erratic driving styles – **violent crime**, and **malaria**. Bite prevention and correct antimalarial tablets are essential. Most of South Africa is malaria-free, but northeastern South Africa, including the Kruger National Park, carries a risk of severe *falciparum* malaria. The region of risk expands after heavy rains. There have been some cases of **sleeping sickness** in visitors to Tanzania's game parks. Dangerous **snakes** exist but rarely attack or cause problems.

The region is fairly risky for **food-borne infections**, and travel to Mediterranean Africa, including Egypt, carries a substantial risk of contracting debilitating **diarrhoea** or **dysentery** and other filth-to-mouth infections. **Meningococcal infection** is a considerable risk to those living and working, and probably to those backpacking, in much of Africa (*see* p.47); the risk is seasonal.

Schistosomiasis is a problem in some of Africa (*see* pp.179–81), particularly in the Rift Valley. Most cases imported into Britain come from Malawi but it occurs in patchy distribution over much of the continent and also in parts of Madagascar.

Asia

Middle East

Food-related **gastrointestinal infections** including tapeworm are quite common throughout the region and there is a significant risk of **hepatitis A, dysentery**, etc. There is some vector-borne disease including **leishmania** and also **rabies** in dogs and wild animals. **Scorpions** are quite dangerous. **Summer temperatures** are fierce and, if driving across desert regions, arrange contingency in case of break-down (water may be hard to find).

There are special requirements for **Hajj pilgrims** including a certificate of **polio** immunization for some visitors and **meningococcus** ACYW certification for all visitors.

Health risks: Asia

(see key, p.52)

	Malaria	Polio	Hepatitis A	Typhoid	Diphtheria	TBE	Rabies	Jap. Encephalitis	Other
Afghanistan	O C+P	✘	✘	✘	✘	(!)	(✘)		L
Andaman Islands	● Mf, Dx, Ml	✘	✘	✘	✘		✘	(✘)	L,m
Armenia	O C: Jun–Oct	(✘)	✘	(✘)	✘	!	(✘)		
Azerbaijan	O C: Jun–Oct	(✘)	✘	✘	✘	!	(✘)		L
Bahrain		(✘)	(✘)	(✘)	(✘)		(✘)		L
Bangladesh	O Mf, Dx, Ml	✘	✘	✘	(✘)		(✘)	(✘)	L
Bhutan	O C+P^S	✘	✘	✘	(✘)		(✘)	(✘)^S	m, L
Brunei Darussalem	O	(✘)	✘	(✘)	(✘)		(✘)	(✘)	
Cambodia	O Mf, Dx, Ml	✘	✘	✘	✘		(✘)	(✘)^S	
China	mostly O C	(✘)	✘	(✘)	(✘)	(!)	(✘)	(✘)^S	sh
Georgia	O Jun–Oct	(✘)	✘	(✘)	✘	!	(✘)		L
Hong Kong	○	(✘)	✘	(✘)	(✘)		(✘)		
India and Islands	● Mf, Dx, Ml	✘	✘	✘	✘		✘	(✘)	L,*sh,m
Indonesia	● Mf, Dx, Ml	✘	✘	✘	✘		(✘)	(✘)	*sh
Iran	O C+P	✘	✘	✘	✘		(✘)		L, sh
Iraq	O C	✘	✘	✘	✘		(✘)		L, sh
Israel		(✘)	✘	(✘)	(✘)		(✘)		L
Japan		(✘)	✘	✘	(✘)	(!)	(✘)	(✘)	*sh
Jordan		✘	✘	✘	✘		(✘)		L,*sh
Kazakhstan		✘	✘	✘	✘	(!)^n	(✘)	(✘)	L
Korea	O	✘	✘	✘	(✘)	(!)	(✘)	(✘)	
Kuwait		✘	✘	(✘)	(✘)		(✘)		
Kyrgyzstan	O C	✘	✘	✘	✘	!	(✘)		L
Laccadive Islands	● Mf, Dx, Ml	✘	✘	✘	✘		✘	(✘)	L,m
Laos	● Mf, Dx, Ml	(✘)	✘	✘	✘		(✘)	(✘)	
Lebanon		✘	✘	(✘)	(✘)		(✘)		L
Macao		(✘)	✘	✘	(✘)		(✘)		
Malaysia	O Mf, Dx, Ml	(✘)	✘	✘	(✘)		(✘)	(✘)	
Maldives		(✘)	✘	✘	(✘)		(✘)		
Mongolia		(✘)	✘	✘	✘	(!)^n	(✘)		m
Myanmar (Burma)	● Dx, Ml	(✘)	✘	✘	(✘)		(✘)	(✘)^S	
Nepal	O *C+P (below 1,500m/5,000ft)	✘	✘	✘	✘		✘	(✘)^S	L, m
Nicobar Islands	● Mf, Dx, Ml	✘	✘	✘	✘		✘	(✘)	L,m
Oman	○ C+P	✘	✘	✘	(✘)		(✘)		L, sh
Pakistan	O C+P	✘	✘	✘	✘		(✘)	(✘)^S	L
Philippines	O C+P	(✘)	✘	✘	✘		(✘)	(✘)	*sh
Qatar		✘	✘	✘	(✘)		(✘)		L
Russia (Asian)		✘	✘	✘	✘	(!)^S	(✘)	(✘)^S	
Sabah	● Mf, Dx, Ml	(✘)	✘	✘	(✘)		(✘)	(✘)	
Saudi Arabia	O C+P	✘	✘	(✘)	(✘)		(✘)		L,m,sh
Singapore			✘	✘	(✘)				
Sri Lanka	O C+P		✘	✘	(✘)		(✘)	(✘)	
Syria	O C May–Oct	✘	✘	✘	✘		(✘)		L, sh
Taiwan		(✘)	✘	✘	(✘)		(✘)	(✘)^S	
Tajikistan	O C Jun–Oct	✘	✘	✘	✘	!	(✘)		L
Thailand	O Dx, Ml	✘	✘	✘	✘		✘	(✘)^S	
Timor-Leste	● Mf, Dx, Ml	✘	✘	✘	✘		(✘)	(✘)	L

	Malaria	Polio	Hepatitis A	Typhoid	Diphtheria	TBE	Rabies	Jap. Encephalitis	Other
Tibet		✗	✗	✗	✗	(!)	(✗)		
Turkey	O C	(✗)	✗	✗	(✗)		(✗)		L
Turkmenistan	O C Jun–Oct	✗	✗	✗	✗	!	(✗)		
United Arab Emirates		✗	✗	(✗)	(✗)		(✗)		L
Uzbekistan	O (SE only)	✗	✗	✗	✗	!	(✗)		L
Vietnam	O Mf, Dx, MI	✗	✗	✗	✗		✗	(✗)[s]	
Yemen	● C+P	✗	✗	✗	✗		(✗)		L, sh

Far and Southeast Asia

The risk of **food-borne diarrhoeal disease** is less than for South Asia but it is still wise to follow the rules of safe eating found on pp.102–8. Insect-bite avoidance protects against **malaria, dengue fever, leishmania, elephantiasis** and **Japanese encephalitis**. There are venomous **snakes**, but it is unusual for travellers to encounter them. Leeches are an inconvenience in wet forest areas. Immunization against **hepatitis A** and **typhoid** is less important for short stays in smart hotels.

India, Pakistan, Nepal, Sri Lanka, Bhutan and Bangladesh

Transmission of **diarrhoea, dysentery, hepatitis A and E, worms, typhoid** and paratyphoid (for which there is no vaccine) via contaminated food is very common in this region and the highest risk season is in the two months before the onset of the monsoon in June. This is also a time of very **high temperatures** and risk of heat stroke in lowland areas. Venomous **snakes** occur but are rarely seen. **Leeches** are a nuisance during the monsoon in rural regions.

Pacific Islands, Australia and New Zealand

Many **sea creatures** of the Pacific region are armed and dangerous, and there have been reports of **shellfish poisoning** (*see* pp.124–5). **Malaria** is a big problem in Papua New Guinea, West Papua, Vanuatu and the Solomons, but other islands are malaria-free. There are frequent but unpredictable outbreaks of **dengue fever** in most of the islands as well as some cases of **elephantiasis** and **Ross River fever** (*see* 'Arboviruses', pp.151–2), so it is important to avoid insect bites. **Rabies** is thought not to be a problem, but there have been two deaths after bat bites in Australia. The Western Pacific region was declared polio-free in 2000, but seek up-to-date advice on any new outbreaks.

In **Australia** and **New Zealand**, the risk of **gastrointestinal disease** exists, although it is low. There are several unpleasant **mosquito-borne infection**s on offer to those bitten in the northeast of Australia; **Japanese encephalitis** immunization is worth considering if going to live in the Torres Strait Islands. The Australian continent boasts a range of venomous **spiders** and **snakes**, so it is best to treat even small wildlife with respect.

Health risks: Pacific

(see key, p.52)

	Malaria	Polio	Hepatitis A	Typhoid	Diphtheria	Jap. Encephalitis	Rabies
American Samoa		✖	✖	(✖)			
Australia					(✖)		
Cook Islands		✖	✖	(✖)			
Easter Island		✖	✖	(✖)			
Fiji		✖	✖	(✖)			
Fr. Polynesia (Tahiti)		✖	✖	(✖)			
Guam		✖	✖	(✖)	(✖)		
Kiribati		✖	✖	(✖)			
Marshall Islands		✖	✖	(✖)			
Micronesia, Fed.		✖	✖	(✖)			
Nauru		✖	✖	(✖)			
New Caledonia		✖	✖	(✖)			
New Zealand							
Niue		✖	✖	(✖)			
Palau		✖	✖	(✖)			
Papua New Guinea	● Mf, Dx, Ml	(✖)	✖	✖	(✖)	(✖)	(✖)
Saipan					(✖)	(✖)	
Samoa		✖	✖	(✖)			
Solomon Islands	● Mf, Dx, Ml	✖	✖	(✖)			
Tokelau		✖	✖	(✖)			
Tonga		✖	✖	(✖)			
Trust Terr. Pacific Is.		✖	✖	(✖)			
Tuvalu		✖	✖	(✖)			
Vanuatu	● Mf, Dx, Ml	✖	✖	(✖)			
Wallis and Futuna Is.		✖	✖	(✖)			
W. Papua (Irian Jaya)	● Mf, Dx, Ml	(✖)	✖	✖	✖	(✖)	(✖)

South America

Food-borne diseases, including **diarrhoea**, **hepatitis A** and **worms**, are common. There is a great range of **insect-** and **tick-borne** disease in the jungle and tropical parts of the region and bite prevention is crucial. Sand-fly-borne **leishmania** is a significant risk in the moist, tropical forests of South America (see pp.153 and 213), while **schistosomiasis** exists in areas in the east (see pp.179–81). **Leeches** also occur. There are dangerous **snakes** but envenoming is rare in travellers.

Immunization against **rabies** would be wise for backpackers, cavers or anyone going far from medical facilities. Sleeping in huts carries a small risk of **Chagas' disease** (American trypanosomiasis, see pp.154).

Health risks: South America

(see key, p.521)

	Malaria	Hepatitis A	Typhoid	Diphtheria	Rabies	Yellow Fever	Leishmania	Other
Argentina	O *C or P (northern border)	(✖)	(✖)	(✖)	(✖)		L	
Bolivia	O Mf, Dx, Ml	✖	✖	(✖)	(✖)	✖	L	
Brazil	O Mf, Dx, Ml	✖	✖	✖	(✖)	✖	L	m, sh, rb, ty
Chile		✖	(✖)	(✖)	(✖)			ty
Colombia	O Mf, Dx, Ml, C+P	✖	✖	✖	(✖)	✖	L,	rb, ty
Ecuador	O Mf, Dx, Ml	✖	✖	✖	(✖)	✖	L,	rb, ty
Falkland Islands		(✖)	(✖)	(✖)	(✖)			
French Guiana	● Mf, Dx, Ml	✖	✖	(✖)	(✖)	M	L,	sh, rb, ty
Galapagos		✖	✖	(✖)	(✖)			
Guyana	● Mf, Dx, Ml	✖	✖	(✖)	(✖)	✖	L,	sh
Marguerita Is.	O Mf, Dx, Ml	✖	✖	(✖)	(✖)	✖		
Paraguay	O C Oct–May	✖	✖	(✖)	(✖)	(✖)	L,	ty
Peru	O Mf, Dx, Ml	✖	✖	(✖)	(✖)	✖	L,	ty
Surinam	O Mf, Dx, Ml	✖	✖	(✖)	(✖)	✖	L,	sh, rb
Uruguay		✖	✖	(✖)	(✖)	(✖)		ty
Venezuela	O Mf, Dx, Ml	✖	✖	(✖)	(✖)	✖	L,	sh, rb, ty

Non-disease hazards

Mines and explosive remnants of war

Few would choose to venture deliberately into a war zone, but once a conflict is over host countries are often keen to attract visitors back. Indeed this can often be a rewarding time to go. It is therefore easy to overlook the hazards of the explosive legacy of war. The problem is that explosive devices take years or decades to find and clear: Southeast Asia is the most heavily affected following wars in Indo-China during the 1950s, '60s and '70s combined with limited resources to fund the very expensive process of clearing mines and unexploded bombs. Currently Laos is the worse affected country. Closer to home, clearance from the Kosovo region of Serbia and Montenegro has been more achievable. Cluster bombs (10% of which never exploded) were strewn over a geographically limited area but, even so, a good level of clearance was achieved at the cost of lives of deminers and peace keepers.

Complete clearance is never achieved though (cluster bombs can penetrate 50cm into the soil), and Second World War bombs are still uncovered from time to time. Conflict-torn regions of southern Africa too have their risky regions, although as time goes on the chances of someone innocently stepping on a mine will become less and less. Locals tilling the soil are at highest risk and mines can be uncovered by flooding.

Avoiding explosive risk

→ Beware of souvenir-hunting metal or plastic objects in regions of conflict; this is an issue that is particularly relevant for parents of curious small children.

→ Efforts are made to protect civilians from unexploded bombs, and often minefields will be marked and fenced until expert deminers can clear the area.

→ It is madness to ignore warnings: the skull-and-cross-bones sign is often used.

→ If in a region where there has been recent conflict, keep to paths and don't venture onto untrodden ground, even if you want privacy for a pee.

→ Take care when visiting areas of previous conflict that have been affected by floods: the water might have uncovered old mines.

ICRC, Geneva, www.icrc.org

Finally, scuba-divers should be aware that it is still possible to stray across live Second World War mines even in British waters. Be careful what you handle anywhere.

Before You Go:
Special Travellers

Special health risks 64
  Pre-existing conditions 64
  Diabetes 65
  Epilepsy 67
  Asthma 68
  Lungs and breathlessness 69
  Allergic reactions and hay fever 69
  Heart conditions and pacemakers 71
  Hypertension 71
  Takers of anticoagulants 72
  Cancer and HIV 72
  People without a spleen 73
  Kidney stones 74
Therapeutic travel 74
  Travelling for treatment 74
  Travel for religious reasons 75

Travelling while pregnant 75
  Flying during pregnancy 76
  Miscarriage 77
  Disease and diet 77
  Medicines and pregnancy 78

Taking the children 78
  The journey 78
  Disease and infection in
  children 80

Senior travellers 81
  Insurance 81
  Health preparations 81

06

Summary

→ Few medical conditions absolutely preclude travel, but some travellers will need to prepare more carefully than others.

→ Recent illness, injury, an operation or an unstable medical condition can preclude travel.

→ Travellers with a long-standing medical condition may be refused insurance by some insurers, but it is crazy to travel without cover; shop around.

→ Resist the temptation to conceal any health problems, past or present, from insurers since this can invalidate your policy.

→ If you have any particular health issues, check with your regular doctor about whether you are fit for your trip.

→ Airlines can advise on fitness to fly; a medical information form is available from airlines and travel agents, part of which is completed by your doctor.

→ Inform the airline ahead of time if you need help getting aboard or with your luggage, if you need to travel with a wheelchair or have special seating or dietary requirements.

→ In-flight oxygen has to be pre-ordered too.

→ Carry a complete list of your medicines, doses and generic names plus a clinical summary written by your regular doctor.

Special health risks

Pre-existing conditions

Anyone with an ongoing medical problem (diabetes, asthma, epilepsy, heart conditions, etc.) must declare these to the insurer. Policies need not cost more than for other people, if your condition is stable, well controlled and you search around. Specialist insurers, as recommended by patients' organizations, can help, but many other insurers are also suitable. Self-help medical groups (which your doctor may know about) have often negotiated special deals. Residents of the European Union who have an EHIC form are entitled to subsidized emergency medical treatment. However, this arrangement does not cover treatment of existing conditions.

It is probably wise to travel with a written doctor's summary; a physician's letter of explanation is especially useful if travelling with syringes and needles. Make careful note of your medicines with their generic (medical) names. Carry plenty to last the trip, allowing for changes of plans or delays, and do not pack them all in one place (in case your luggage gets delayed or lost). NHS rules say that only a three-month supply of medicines may be given to people staying overseas. Private prescriptions are required for larger quantities, even if you are normally exempt from paying for medicines. If possible, avoid making changes to any medication just before travel. If you are unsure whether you're fit to travel, ask your doctor. If you don't like what you're told, get another opinion from a travel clinic. Be well informed and assess your particular risks with the help of your usual doctor.

Fit to fly?

The following conditions usually make air travel too hazardous and medical advice/clearance should be sought before boarding:

→ **Anaemia**: haemoglobin below 7.5g.

→ **Breathlessness** at rest or making traveller unable to walk 50m (50 yards).

→ **Contagious** or **communicable disease** in its infectious period – including chickenpox.

→ **Deep vein thrombosis (DVT)**: recent, unstable and untreated.

→ **Ear infection** or **severe congestion**; it will hurt if you fly.

→ **Epileptic fit** in the previous 24 hours.

→ **Haemorrhage** from stomach or duodenum that has happened recently; you could bleed again.

→ **Heart attack** within the last seven days.

→ **Heart failure**: uncontrolled.

→ **Fracture** of leg and full plaster applied within previous 48 hours.

→ **Jaw wired**: unless you can release or cut it.

→ **Operations** within the last five to 10 days.

→ **Pneumothorax** (collapsed lung) that has not been treated.

→ **Sinusitis**: severe; it will hurt if you fly.

→ **Stroke** within the last three days.

→ **Unstable medical conditions** of any sort.

For further information visit *www.britishairways.com/health*.

Contact information: travellers with special requirements

Age Concern Insurance Services, UK **t** 0845 600 3348, *www.ageconcern.org.uk*. Covers almost anyone with very few exclusions; like many insurers they would not cover those travelling against medical advice. They have no age limits.

Blood Care Foundation, *www.bloodcare.org.uk*.

The MedicAlert Foundation, Freepost, 1 Bridge Warf, 156 Caledonian Road, London N1 9UU, UK **t** 0800 581 420, *www.medicalert.org.uk*; or MedicAlert Foundation International, 2323 Colorado Avenue, Turlock, CA 9538, US **t** 888 633 4298, *www.medicalert.com*. Supplies bracelets alerting medics to medical conditions; allow 28 days for delivery.

The Stroke Association, Stroke House, 240 City Road, London EC1V 2PR, UK **t** (020) 7566 0300, **f** (020) 7490 2686, **t** (helpline) 0845 303 3100, *www.stroke.org.uk*.

Tourism For All, UK **t** 0845 124 9971, **f** (01539) 735 567, *wwwtourismforall.org.uk*, *info@tourismforall.org.uk*. Has information on holidays for those with health problems and a list of sympathetic travel insurers.

Diabetes

People with diabetes may need help or advice from their doctor on rescheduling medicines, and should be aware of special problems they face if they start vomiting or get diarrhoea. It is safe to take oral rehydration solutions containing glucose; pack

Notes for travellers with pre-existing medical conditions

Sufferers of long-standing medical conditions including **diabetes mellitus**, **liver** or **kidney failure**, those **without a spleen**, and those with **immune disorders** (*see* box, p.70) should be aware that:

→ Malaria may be more severe, although the risk of infection is no greater than for any other traveller.

→ Levels of protection given by vaccines may be diminished.

→ Live vaccines (oral polio, oral typhoid, BCG, MMR and yellow fever) may be unsuitable, however immunization against pneumococcus, haemophilus influenzae (Hib) and influenza vaccine are beneficial.

→ Some antimalarials don't mix with some prescribed regular medicines.

→ Travellers' diarrhoea may be more severe.

→ A MedicAlert bracelet is a useful precaution.

Recommended precautions

→ Carry a card and/or written clinical summary, so that an overseas doctor can understand your condition and the medicines you take.

→ Ask your doctor whether it is necessary to travel with an emergency course of antibiotics or other specific medicines.

→ Don't even think about travelling without adequate insurance and always declare your condition to your insurers.

some. Diarrhoea can upset normal diabetic control and tablets or insulin doses may need to be adjusted. It is important to be aware that you can become particularly ill, and may need treatment with an insulin infusion in hospital if you suffer any infection or upset. Discuss risks and warning symptoms with your doctor. Hot climates tend to make low blood sugars (a 'hypo' or hypoglycaemia) more likely, unless your insulin dose is reduced. Careful monitoring is therefore necessary initially, and throughout the journey. Some people with diabetes are hardly aware of the warning signs of a 'hypo'; these travellers should travel with a companion. All travellers with diabetes should carry sweets and probably also injectable glucagon to raise blood sugar. It is worth asking the manufacturer about the insulin(s) you use. Insulin should remain stable at room temperature for up to a month. Generally, clear, fast-acting insulins are more robust and can survive freezing, while cloudy, medium- to long-acting and bimodal insulins are more delicate and are best kept cool. Using a basal bolus regime (*see* box, opposite) has the advantage that, in an emergency, control can be achieved with short-acting insulin alone. Sun-sensitive rashes can occur – albeit rarely – in those taking *chlorpropamide* and *glipizide* tablets to control diabetes (*see* p.163).

Contact information: diabetes

The American Diabetes Association, US **t** 1 800 342 2383, *www.diabetes.org*.

Diabetes UK, Macleod House, 10 Parkway, London NW1 7AA, UK **t** (020) 7424 1000, **f** (020) 7424 1001, *www.diabetes.org.uk*. Issues fact sheets about individual countries, including which insulins are available; they also offer travel insurance, but compare their rates to other deals.

FRÍO, PO Box 10, Haverfordwest SA62 5YG, UK **t** (01437) 741 700, **f** (01437) 741 781, *www.friouk.com*. Sells various wallets that, after immersion in water, keep contents cool for several days.

Managing diabetes on the road

Travellers with diabetes are not more prone to infections, but insulin requirements often increase during even mild illness and in those taking tablets to control blood sugar. Gastroenteritis is therefore best avoided (*see* p.100–8). Medical professionals can advise on precautions, danger signs, adjusting doses and food intake when ill.

For insulin users, a basal bolus regime is very flexible. A long-acting (basal) dose is taken around bedtime, and sometimes each morning, too, and a short-acting (bolus) dose is taken with each meal (usually three). When flying west across time zones, extra meals can easily be managed with extra shots. It helps to have a watch set on both home and local time. Insulin is quite robust (manufacturers are helpful in providing storage information), but should be protected from heat or freezing. Keep it in an unbreakable vacuum flask or in a plastic container which can be stored in a hotel fridge. Plenty of spare injection pens or syringes should be carried. Consider taking a spare blood glucose meter. Kit needs protection from temperature extremes, knocks and water. If travelling to the Americas, carry a blood glucose conversion chart.

Diabetics who know enough of the local language to be able to read menus and labels will enjoy their trip more; vegetarians and fussy eaters may have difficulties. Liking all local carbohydrates helps. Carry emergency food: biscuits, cereal bars and wrapped sweets are good; sometimes fruit, vegetables, meat or dairy products may not be taken across certain state or international borders. Diet soft drinks may not be widely available, yet bottled water gets boring. Low sugar drink powder or citrus juice covers the taste of chemically treated water, or you can add vitamin C after iodine treatment (*see* p.106).

Jean Sinclair RGN MSc, Cambridge

Mountains for Active Diabetics (informal international group) *www.diabetic.friendsinhighplaces.org.*

Epilepsy

Stable epilepsy should not compromise travel, although it may take some searching to find an adequate insurer. Airlines say that someone who has had a *grand mal* seizure in the previous 24 hours should delay their flight. People who have epilepsy are limited in the **antimalarial tablets** that they may take (*see* pp.134–9). Those with epilepsy or a past history of epilepsy should avoid taking *mefloquine* (Larium) and also *chloroquine* as these two medicines can cause seizures in those prone to them. Find out which other prophylactics will protect you for your particular journey and then choose between the other tablets. Malarone and *proguanil* (Paludrine) may be taken safely. If *doxycycline* is suggested and you take *carbamazepine* (Tegretol), *phenytoin* (Epanutin) or *phenobarbital* (phenobarbitone), you need to take 100mg capsules twice daily, which is twice the normal dose. If Maloprim is suggested and you take *phenytoin* or *phenobarbitone*, it should be taken with *folic acid* 5mg daily.

Contact information: epilepsy

Epilepsy Action, UK **t** (0113) 210 8800; **t** (helpline) 0808 800 5050, *www.epilepsy.org.uk.* For 50p, the helpline will issue an 'epilepsy passport', which can be personalized, containing first-aid information about epilepsy (translated into six European languages).

Epilepsy Ontario, Suite 308, 1 Promenade Circle, Thornhill, Ontario, Canada L4J 4P8, Canada **t** (905) 764 5099/(416) 229 2291, *info@epilepsyontario.org*, *www.epilepsyontario.org*

Epilepsy Research Foundation, PO Box 3004, London W4 4XT, UK **t** (020) 8995 4781, **f** 0870 838 1069, *www.epilepsyresearch.org.uk*. Publishes a helpful leaflet entitled 'Epilepsy and Anti-malarial Medication'.

The National Society for Epilepsy, UK **t** (01494) 601 400, *nse.jamkit.com*.

Tysers, UK **t** (020) 3037 8000, *www.tysers.com*. Insurance brokers who are sympathetic to epileptics; they realize that well-controlled epilepsy is not risky and will often offer cover with no extra loading.

Asthma

Anyone who has ever had an inhaler prescribed or who has been told they are asthmatic should be aware that travel might trigger an asthma attack. It is best to be prepared. It can be precipitated by taking *aspirin*, *ibuprofen* and other non-steroidal anti-inflammatories (*see* pp.36–8). Asthma can emerge as a new problem – or a childhood tendency returns – in travellers to congested big cities. Polluted Mexico City, at an altitude of 2,895m (9,500ft), is probably not a good destination for asthmatics or people with respiratory problems. In well-chosen destinations, though, many asthmatics improve, having escaped the pollen of temperate plants and the house dust mites of richly carpeted homes or dingy student garrets. Asthma is unpredictable; it is a serious disease that kills about 1,500 Britons annually. If you have ever been admitted to hospital with asthma you should discuss your travel plans with your doctor who may suggest that you carry a course of steroid tablets. In case of needing to buy more inhalers while abroad, it is important to know exactly what you are taking. Many of the newer inhalers or devices will not be available overseas. Carry plenty, including a *salbutamol* (Ventolin) inhaler in your carry-on bag in case the stuffiness of the aircraft climate makes you breathless. Although *salbutamol* (Ventolin) and *beclomethasone* (Becotide) inhalers are available in many countries, proprietary names differ and doses may vary, so be careful. (*See also* 'Allergic reactions and hay fever', opposite.) If you may need to use a nebulizer on board make sure it is battery operated and you have permission. Use is not usually permitted on take off or landing.

Contact information: asthma

Asthma UK, Summit House, 70 Wilson Street, London EC2A 2DB, UK **t** (020) 7786 4900, **t** (helpline) 0800 121 6244, *www.asthma.org.uk*. Has information on travel insurance for asthmatics.

http://elitesportgroup.com. Provides information on drugs banned for athletes, including some steroids commonly used by asthmatics.

Lungs and breathlessness

Anyone who has had symptoms of breathlessness should get a diagnosis and adequate treatment before flying. Being breathless at rest, or breathlessness that prevents walking 50m (50 yards), will mean you are not fit enough to fly, although oxygen may be provided by the airline if a request is made in advance; there is a charge for this and the traveller needs to make his or her own arrangements during transfers. An untreated **pneumothorax** (partially 'collapsed' lung), for example, might get considerably worse during a flight. Those with **cystic fibrosis** may also have problems due to decreased oxygen and, since they lose lots of salt in sweat, may also have problems acclimatizing to heat if the destination is steamy.

Allergic reactions and hay fever

Allergy is an overreaction of the immune system which causes symptoms of variable severity, from a mild rash or persistent drippy nose, to itching, to tingling of the lips, tongue or roof of the mouth, stomach pain, diarrhoea or sickness through to a more serious reaction (anaphylaxis) which may include facial swelling, difficulty breathing, weakness and/or collapse. Serious reactions tend to come on in minutes but always within six hours of exposure to even a small quantity of allergen to which the victim is sensitive.

Those who have experienced swelling that causes breathing difficulties or collapse (after a sting or eating a certain food) should carry injectable *adrenaline* (*epinephrine*) in the form of an Epipen. Your doctor will prescribe it and explain when and how to use it. If you want to carry this in your hand baggage during a flight you will need to prove it is essential to you. The US site *www.foodallergy.org* offers a sample letter for your doctor to sign. The Medihaler EPI (make by Riker) is an alternative for those who cannot face injecting themselves but it is less effective than the injection and it is not available in the UK; it is like an asthma inhaler. It might also be worth getting a MedicAlert bracelet or pendant (*see* **Useful addresses**, p.301).

The commonest **food allergy** is to peanuts and some true nuts. There are understandable worries about exposure to nut particles in air – on board a plane for example – but this is unlikely to cause a severe reaction, though some soreness of the eyes or a runny nose can occur. You could ring the airline to ask if they serve peanuts on board or contact the Anaphylaxis Campaign (*see* 'Contact information: allergies', overleaf), which has a list of which airlines serve peanuts and which do not.

Consider getting cards to explain your allergy. Those in European languages are available from £6 each or £20 for English, French, German, Italian and Spanish; contact *www.dietarycard.com*. Otherwise look at *www.allergyaction.org*, which offers translations of key phrases into Spanish, Italian, French, German, Greek and Dutch; *www.x-sitez.com/allergy* and *worldlingo.com* also offer translations into more exotic languages including Japanese, Korean and Portuguese.

About one in every 200 people may be allergic to nuts and the number is growing, but 25% of children who are allergic to peanuts grow out of their allergy, while a proportion of children have milder reactions as they get older.

Desensitization treatment can be risky and requires commitment: it involves two to three years of monthly injections at a specialist allergy clinic.

Those who suffer – or have ever suffered, and/or have lots of close family members who suffer – from hay fever and/or eczema and/or asthma are most likely to get an 'out of the blue' allergic reaction to something exotic. These travellers would be well advised to travel with some antihistamine tablets such as *fexofenadine* (Telfast) or *cetirizine* (Zirtek) or *loratadine* (Clarityn). *Chlorpeniramine* (Piriton) or *diphenhydramine* (Benadryl) also help; these last two preparations may cause drowsiness so are useful if symptoms disrupt sleep. All these antihistamine tablets are also useful to relieve itching from **insect bites**. Persistent troublesome hay fever can be treated with an antihistamine tablet and/or a steroid nasal spray (e.g. *beclomethasone*) and/or sodium cromogycate eye drops. True pollen-induced hay fever often gets better overseas, especially at coastal destinations.

Contact information: allergies

Allergy UK, 3 White Oak Square, London Road, Swanley, Kent BR8 7AG, UK **t** (01322) 619 898, **f** (01322) 663 480, *www.allergyuk.org*.

Anaphylaxis Campaign, PO Box 275, Farnborough, Hampshire GU14 6SX, UK **t** (01252) 542 029, *www.anaphylaxis.org.uk*.

British Society for Allergy and Clinical Immunology, Suite 268/269, Queen Anne's Business Centre, St James' Park, 28 Broadway, London SW1H 9JX, UK **t** (020) 7340 9614, **f** (020) 7340 9617.

MedicAlert, 1 Bridge Wharf, 156 Caledonian Road, London N1 9UU, UK **t** 0800 581 420, *www.medicalert.org.uk*.

For more on nuts try: ***www.users.globalnet.co.uk/~aair/nuts.htm***.

Travelling when immunosuppressed

There are some issues for people whose immune system has been suppressed by disease or medical treatment. Immunosuppression commonly occurs in HIV, cancer (*see* p.72), after transplants and in those taking long-term steroid (and certain other) tablets. Your prescribing doctor will be able to tell you, and your usual doctor or a specialist travel clinic will be an important first port of call in the planning stage of your trip. Organizing adequate insurance is crucial; be aware of the information highlighted on pp.25–7 and p.207.

Human Immunodeficiency Virus (HIV)

Infection with HIV should not prevent individuals from travelling. The CD4 count suggests the degree of suppression of the immune system and correlates well with the potential risk of infections. A CD4 count below 400/mmD precludes the administration of live vaccines – especially yellow fever vaccine – and advice should be sought from an experienced travel medicine practitioner. There are potential mismatches between antimalarial tablets and some anti-HIV agents, and consideration must be given to this. *Ciprofloxacin* (often prescribed for travellers' diarrhoea) and *doxycycline* (for malaria prophylaxis) may also interfere with anti-HIV agents and must be given either several hours before or after these other medicines.

Travellers with HIV infection should find out about any current political restrictions prior to travel (*see* 'Contact information: immunosuppression and blood transfusion', p.72).

Other immune disorders

Travellers with immune systems that are suppressed by medicines should seek advice from both their regular hospital consultant and a travel medicine specialist. The administration of vaccines in particular, as well as other medicines, will depend on the dose and duration of immunosuppressive treatment being received. Live vaccines (oral polio, oral typhoid, BCG, MMR and yellow fever) cannot be given, and inactivated vaccines may provide limited protection. Live vaccines may be administered six months after completion of chemotherapy.

Transplant recipients are also immunosuppressed and must not receive live vaccines. These travellers are at increased risk of skin cancer and must avoid exposure to strong sun. Travellers with challenged immune systems must pay particular attention to bite prevention (pp.142–9) and avoidance of travellers' diarrhoea (pp.101–2).

Dr Jane N. Zuckerman, Royal Free Travel Health Centre, London

Heart conditions and pacemakers

Most aircraft are pressurized to the equivalent of about 2,000m (6,600ft); people with long-standing heart disease may suffer from the 10% reduction in oxygen supply and could become unwell during a flight. Many people with heart conditions are at increased risk of **deep vein thrombosis** (DVT) or a blood clot (see pp.15–17). Doctors may advise taking a 75mg *aspirin* before the flight, though most heart patients will already be taking daily *aspirin* or an equivalent such as *clopidogrel* (Plavix).

The 'high altitude' conditions on board the aircraft stress the heart so it is inadvisable to fly within 10 days of a heart attack. After a severe attack wait a month. Postpone flying for at least two weeks after major surgery to the heart or chest. Anyone with breathlessness due to any heart condition should to ask their doctor whether they are fit to fly. Generally, though, if you are able to walk 50m (50 yards) without resting, you are probably fit enough. If in doubt, your doctor can discuss particular medical conditions with the airline's medics. Airlines can often provide supplementary oxygen but it must be arranged well in advance and there is a charge. Oxygen needed in transit must be arranged by the passenger.

Pacemakers can be affected by the metal-detecting loops used in security checks at airports. Ask to be hand searched, and carry a doctor's letter explaining that you have a pacemaker.

Contact information: heart conditions

British Heart Foundation, Greater London House, 180 Hampstead Road, London NW1 7AW, UK **t** (020) 7554 0000, *www.bhf.org.uk*. Has information on insurance for people with heart problems including angina and high blood pressure.

Hypertension (high blood pressure)

As with many conditions, well-controlled blood pressure should impinge little on travel, although it is crucial to travel with enough medication. It may be difficult to find or identify your particular medicines overseas. Running out, and the consequent rebound rise in blood pressure, is dangerous. People who take **diuretics** (e.g. *furosemide/frusemide, bendrofluazide/bendroflumethiazide*) must not stop them for convenience when travelling. Seek medical advice early in case of profuse diarrhoea, since it is easy to develop problems due to an imbalance of body salts, especially lack of potassium.

Takers of anticoagulants

People who take anticoagulants (usually *warfarin*) to 'thin the blood' should avoid intramuscular immunization, because it is likely to cause bleeding into the injected muscle. Many immunizations can be given subcutaneously instead. Those on anticoagulants must also consider their special risks when travelling. Taking an anticoagulant makes disastrous bleeding after any kind of accident more likely, or there could be bleeding into the brain after a fall, and such dangerous complications are a significant risk where emergency services are not of a high standard and supplies of fresh frozen plasma and other treatments are not readily available. People who are taking anticoagulants are also more likely to need **blood transfusions** in emergencies; the risks are described on pp.39–40.

Anticoagulant control is affected by changes in diet, by alcohol consumption and by illness; necessary blood tests may be difficult to organize in less developed countries. It is now possible to carry your own testing kit, but proper training in its use is necessary in hospital outpatients' clinics.

Cancer and HIV

Those who have had treatment for cancer will have lost immunity gained from previous immunizations. Travel and routine childhood vaccinations may therefore need to be repeated after cancer treatment is completed and once the immune system has recovered. **Live vaccines** should be avoided in people who are immunosuppressed, such as those who have active cancer. Those who have contracted human immuno-deficiency virus and who are HIV-positive should avoid BCG and also immunization by mouth with typhoid capsules (although injected typhoid vaccine is safe). Yellow fever immunization is also unsafe. **Killed vaccines** and also the live polio and MMR vaccines are safe.

Patients who have been treated with **radiotherapy** or **chemotherapy** should avoid live vaccines until six months after the end of treatment. Those with cancer who are stable are often fit to travel although the condition must be declared to insurers. Sufferers from certain cancers may have an increased tendency to blood clots, so ask your oncologist whether you should take an *aspirin* before any long flight.

See also 'Travelling when immunosuppressed' box, p.70.

Contact information: immunosuppression and blood transfusion

Aidsnet, *www.aidsnetpa.org*. Lists entry restrictions for individual countries.

Blood Care Foundation, *www.bloodcare.org.uk*.

The Body, *www.thebody.com*. In-depth HIV/AIDS-related information.

Tips for wheelchair travellers

See also p.30.

→ **Preparation**: If possible, book accommodation, equipment hire and assistance in advance. Use travel agents, disability advice centres and Internet forums to find information.

→ **Hospitals**: Have contact details of the nearest medical facilities in case of emergency.

→ **Insurance**: Your insurance company must be aware of your disability; don't forget to insure your wheelchair.

→ **Medicines**: Find out what's available at your destination without prescription, or take enough for your whole trip.

→ **Flying**:

Baggage: Pack enough essential items in your hand luggage for a few days in case your bags get lost.

Legroom: Ask the airline for an upgrade or bulkhead seats for more legroom and to ease transfers.

Wheelchair: Stay in your own wheelchair until you get to the plane. To be sure you get it back in one piece, ask airport staff not to take the wheels off before stowing.

Skin: Use your pressure-relieving cushion on the plane. You can replace their cushion with yours (they're only fixed with Velcro).

→ **Railways**: Check country-specific requirements, but the general rule is to inform stations early of your intended journey.

→ **Punctures**: Use solid (puncture-proof) tyres or carry a repair kit.

→ **Stay cool**: If you can't cope with heat, use a plant spray bottle to chill out.

→ **Washing**: A bin liner over the wheelchair keeps it dry during a shower (not to be done with powerchairs!).

Gordon Rattray, quadriplegic from diving accident in Mali, www.able-travel.com

People without a spleen

Anyone who has had their spleen removed after an accident or suffers from a red blood cell disorder, including **thalassaemia** or **sickle cell disease** (not the trait), is more likely to become severely ill if they develop a pneumococcal or meningococcal infection. The risk of serious infections is highest in the first two years after the loss of the spleen. Previous advice had been to receive pneumococcal immunization once in a lifetime; recently though, it has been realized that asplenic people may not maintain enough protective antibodies to pneumococcus, so five-yearly boosters are recommended. Asplenic people also need regular boosters against meningococcus. All vaccines – including live ones – are safe for them. Asplenic people need to be aware that they have lost one component of their immune system and in case of any sign of infection they should not hesitate to seek medical help. They should travel with a course of *amoxicillin* antibiotics to treat any chest infection. Should such people contract malaria they are likely to become rapidly ill and die. As a result, travel to a high-risk malarious area (including much of lowland sub-Saharan Africa, *see* map, p.133) is probably not worth the risk. There are, however, large areas within the Republic of South Africa that are malaria-free.

Kidney stones

People who have had kidney stones in the past may get them again when in hot climates; they must make a special effort to drink plenty of liquids (*see* p.160). For advice for those with troublesome and recurrent kidney or bladder infections, *see* 'Cystitis', p.223.

Therapeutic travel

Some conditions improve in warmer climates. Aches and pains in joints and muscles, fibrositis and arthritis often get better. Acne and severe eczema (but *see also* 'Allergic reactions and hay fever', pp.69–70) can worsen in strong sunshine, although eczema may also diminish in the heat, especially with plenty of moisturizers. Psoriasis improves with plenty of exposure to sunlight, but can be aggravated by taking *chloroquine* or Malarone.

Travelling for treatment

People sometimes travel abroad specifically for specialist or pioneering treatments, or for quick or cheap operations. This should be done with caution and after seeking as much advice as you can find from medical professionals and patient advisory groups, since – just as at home – the quality of medical care is variable, and the advantage of treatment at home is that your usual doctor should know or can find out how good your treatment will be. There are undoubtedly economies to be had, indeed British patients can travel to the USA for dental implant work and a whole trip and treatment cost that is less than treatment at home. The danger is that if anything goes wrong, follow up and damage limitation can be difficult and expensive. Be cautious if arranging long haul travel for an operation on the leg or to rehabilitate after such an operation since your risk of DVT will be increased.

It is likely that it will become more commonplace for Europeans to be treated in other European countries; however, it is also worth considering the non-medical/technical aspects of opting for this. Travel itself causes stress, and undergoing medical treatment or an operation is also stressful. Language and

Medical tourism

With the inadequacies of the NHS forcing patients to consider care in the private sector, many people now travel abroad for medical and surgical attention, including to Hungary, the Czech Republic and India. Many go, however, without arranging proper insurance and an apparent cost economy can turn into financial ruin. About 150,000 tourists from around the world travelled to India in 2004 for medical treatment in both conventional hospitals and ayurvedic centres. The Indian government now offers medical visas which will enable people to stay in the country for up to a year to undergo heart or eye operations, neurosurgery, transplants and plastic surgery at one of 80 accredited centres.

Dr Iain McIntosh, chair of the British Travel Health Association

communication can be a problem, different assumptions and senses of humour are common and can make for misunderstanding and upset. There are, too, the practicalities of knowing what a hospital in-patient is expected to provide on admission. And travelling for treatment, of course, will probably isolate you from the support of family and friends.

Travel for religious reasons

Involvement in a religious celebration or pilgrimage can take travellers into astonishingly crowded places. Congestion alone makes such a journey physically stressful for pilgrims who are ill, frail, young or pregnant. The biggest religious gathering annually is the Hajj, in the course of which two million pilgrims from 140 countries gather in Mecca. Fully aware of the stress of performing the Hajj, Saudi authorities actually discourage pilgrims if frail and elderly, pregnant or with children. Indeed such people may not be able to manage the large amount of walking involved: the distance between Mecca and Mount Arafat, for example, is around 20km (12.5 miles). Pilgrims are sometimes crushed in stampedes, too.

The season for the Hajj varies, and when it falls in the hottest season many pilgrims suffer from heat exhaustion. It is wise for intending pilgrims to check with their usual doctor about whether the trip is wise, and anyone visiting Saudi Arabia for any reason should read the section on heat illnesses on pp.160–4. Gastroenteritis and bacterial skin infections are common in hajjis and there are often outbreaks of pneumonia, Rift Valley fever, and hepatitis B from head-shaving by barbers. Meningococcus (ACWY) immunization at least 10 days prior to arrival in Saudi is mandatory. Some visitors also need to carry proof of polio immunization too.

Travelling while pregnant

If you feel well during pregnancy, and feel like travelling, do it! The late Alison Hargreaves managed a successful ascent of the north face of the Eiger when six months pregnant. There are, of course, special considerations if your trip is long or the destination is without reasonable medical facilities.

Ideally a travelling woman should arrange as many travel immunizations as she can before conception, since all **live vaccines** and most **killed vaccines** are best avoided, especially during the first three months of pregnancy. If immunization is being considered after the first 12 weeks of pregnancy, an assessment of the actual risk of the disease to the woman and her unborn child must be balanced against the risk to the foetus of the immunization itself. Some women will delay or reschedule travel plans accordingly. Immunization against polio may be required since there is an increased risk of disease and paralysis in the pregnant woman and also of foetal death. Ideally, the pregnant traveller will already be immune from previous immunizations. If immunization is necessary during pregnancy, the injection is safer than the oral live version.

The safest time to travel when pregnant is during the middle three months, from the 12th week of pregnancy (when the risk of miscarriage and ectopic pregnancy has largely passed) until about the 26th week (when the risk of early delivery starts to increase). Organize as many routine antenatal checks as your travel plans will allow; some can be done overseas. Keeping in touch with doctors will make it easier for them to certify that flying is not an undue hazard. Flying when very anaemic (haemoglobin lower than 7.5g) would be dangerous. Pregnancy must be declared to insurers. It is important to make sure that the policy covers any complications of pregnancy and even care of a premature newborn! Some insurers or the airline may ask for a doctor's letter and this is a common request after the 28th week; GPs will charge a fee for this. Even if such a letter is not a requirement, carry a document confirming the estimated date of delivery and the number of foetuses.

It is best to avoid taking medicines during pregnancy as far as possible and this even includes herbal treatments. If remedies are needed, consult a properly qualified doctor. Any health problems that arise overseas for a pregnant woman will need to be dealt with, at least initially, within the local health set-up, and yet facilities may be less favourable than at home: blood for transfusion may be unscreened (*see* pp.39–40.) and it may be difficult to find an English-speaking doctor. These may or may not be issues for the travelling pregnant woman.

Flying during pregnancy

Airlines discourage flying in late pregnancy, not because it is unsafe but because cabin crews do not want women to give birth in the cramped conditions of a plane. Having attended to people who had merely fainted in a jumbo jet, while people climbed over us to get to the toilets, I find it hard to imagine a more unpleasant place to give birth. Airlines vary in their rules and requirements (insurance companies are the most stringent). For most long-haul airlines the deadline for flights is before the 36th week of pregnancy, but it can be as early as 28 weeks, and varies with the length of flight. Multiple pregnancies are usually delivered well before the normal 40th week so airlines do not like carrying women with twin pregnancies beyond the 32nd week. Sometimes a pre-flight medical examination is required a day or two before boarding.

Long-haul flights take passengers to an altitude where there is increased exposure to radiation. Ideally, unborn babies – especially during the first three months of the pregnancy – should have minimal exposure to unnecessary radiation, so frequent fliers may wish to reschedule overseas meetings or use the phone.

Pregnancy increases the clotability of the blood and so increases the risk of **DVT**, especially on long flights. Wearing flight socks would be wise. It is crucial that long-haul travellers exercise during the flight and follow the other advice detailed on pp.15–18.

Miscarriage

Miscarriages are very common: perhaps one-fifth of 'normal' pregnancies miscarry. Having a miscarriage in a remote place could be a horrendous experience. Subsequently some women need a surgical dilatation and curettage under general anaesthetic to remove retained products of conception. There are many developing countries where I would be reluctant to undergo such a procedure. If you are planning a shortish trip (less than four months) you should be able to delay your departure until after the 12th week, when the risk of miscarriage is largely passed.

Disease and diet

Malaria is a very real risk throughout pregnancy. Pregnant women are highly susceptible to the parasite and more likely to die if they contract it. Malaria is also a common cause of miscarriage and premature labour. Most doctors (myself included) therefore counsel against travel to high-risk malarious regions (especially sub-Saharan Africa, certain Pacific Islands and Indo-China) when pregnant unless there are very good reasons for going. Those travelling overseas to live are better able to protect themselves from bites, so they might consider the risks acceptable. Measures to avoid mosquito bites from dusk to dawn are essential.

Antimalarial tablets must be taken rigorously (see **Malaria**, pp.129–40, for a discussion of the antimalarial options). Taking nothing is not the 'safe option' as some people believe. It is best to discuss malaria prophylaxis with an expert (see 'Sources of advice on malaria', p.132). *Chloroquine* can be taken in pregnancy; this is often taken with *proguanil* (Paludrine) and, if this is taken, it must be accompanied by *folic acid* 5mg daily. However, this gives poor protection in high-risk destinations like sub-Saharan Africa. *Mefloquine* (Lariam) is also relatively safe to take in pregnancy but those planning a pregnancy should **avoid conceiving** for three months after stopping *mefloquine*, and also for one month after taking Malarone.

Hepatitis E can make pregnant women desperately ill; it may be wise to avoid the highest risk regions (the Indian subcontinent and tropical Latin America), and stringent precautions must be followed against filth-to-mouth diseases (see pp.115–18).

Chickenpox and **'slapped cheek' disease** (see **Ailments**, p.257) can be dangerous in pregnant women who have not already become immune to these viral infections; blood tests may be necessary, so if there is any doubt medical advice should be sought.

All pregnant women need to observe **dietary precautions**; travellers need to be extra careful. Milk and dairy products should be pasteurized or boiled. Unpasteurized soft cheeses, meat pâté, shark, marlin, swordfish and raw eggs should be avoided. Dried egg is safe.

Medicines and pregnancy

Be very careful about taking any medicines in pregnancy, especially in the first three months and when trying to conceive. *Amoxicillin* and *erythromycin* are safe to take while pregnant or breast-feeding. Avoid *doxycycline* (e.g. Vibramycin) and other *tetracyclines*, and do not take *co-trimoxazole* or *trimethoprim*.

Taking the children

Whether a trip overseas with a child is sensible or reckless depends largely on your knowledge, temperament and experience. Parents planning a trip to a poorly resourced region who were experienced travellers in the years BC – before child – will do best. Children cope with most things and so misfortune tends to strike when parents are at the limits of their ability to cope. Many 'southern' countries are wonderfully child-centred and child-friendly but there are hazards, especially for the under-threes. Wherever you are, remember that safety regulations are different from at home. Unsafe electrics can be accessible to a crawling child even in quite good hotels, so check around whenever you arrive in a new place and before you set the toddler loose.

The journey

Travel with children is relatively easy before they become independently mobile, at around the age of nine months. The easiest and safest age to travel – assuming parental confidence and energy – is when the baby is still at the sleeping and eating stage, from the age of a month and while exclusively breast-fed. As soon as an infant takes anything other than breast-milk, there is a risk of filth-to-mouth infection: diarrhoea is dangerous and difficult to manage in babies. There are also theoretical risks of taking in unsatisfactory formula if it is bought abroad – as illustrated by the scandal in China in 2008 where milk was contaminated with melamine.

With mobility comes the chance of the child wandering away and into danger. Some kids cling; others are natural explorers so when you are queuing to check in they may go to find something more interesting. Label your little ones. At the airport, a note should state destination, airline and flight and mobile phone number. At your destination, collect the card of your hotel, and either put it in a pocket or pin it to their clothes (out of reach and out of sight). Mothers travelling with sons, or fathers with daughters, may have problems when there is a need to go to the toilet. Usually boys are tolerated in the Ladies while they are small – up to the age of about five – although young boys may be reluctant to venture into female facilities. However you solve this problem, be aware that standards vary throughout the world. In many 'southern' countries a child can go alone into the appropriate lavatory as soon as they can manage alone, but a New York City policewoman screamed at a friend for waiting for her 11-year-old son outside

Travelling with children: points to note

→ If crossing international borders – Portugal is currently strict – with children who aren't your own or who don't look like your own, carry documents confirming parental credentials or permission.

→ The most difficult age to travel with children is from the time when they begin to crawl until the age of about three years.

→ Involve the children with planning and reading before departure, and only allow them to take toys and books that they can carry themselves.

→ If using an antihistamine to prevent motion sickness, dose at least three hours before travel (see pp.89–90).

→ Travelling children are at high risk of infectious disease and so must be fully immunized against the usual childhood infections as well as any vaccines recommended for their destination.

→ Check with a travel clinic to see if you are planning to visit a region with a high risk for malaria.

→ Malaria or not, pack a good insect repellent, plus sunscreen and plenty of long, loose, 100% cotton clothes.

→ The best insect repellent is DEET and physicians recommend a 10% solution for children. Even at this dilution, it stings if rubbed into the eyes, so explore other bite-avoidance techniques, see pp.142–9.

→ Travellers to the tropics or the less developed world run at least a 50:50 risk of each member of the family contracting travellers' diarrhoea; children under three have an even higher hit rate, so plan for it. Take extra nappies and bottom cream.

→ Plan how your child will take safe drinks; true mineral water can be very high in salts and so is unsuitable for bottle-fed infants.

→ Accidents are the main killers of travellers in every age group; become safety conscious.

→ Keep emergency entertainment (e.g. playing cards, paper, coloured pens and balloons), snacks and safe drinks to hand at all times. Look out for children's mini books to counteract boredom on journeys.

the men's room rather than taking him into the Ladies, where he would have refused to go.

Diarrhoea risk increases when children start to crawl and put things into their mouths. This is the age when they are easily bored if restrained on long flights; they have little sense of danger, yet they cannot be distracted effectively. Between the age of about nine months and until the age they really start communicating properly, usually around the age of three years, travel can be exhausting. A long flight with an unsympathetic aircrew can be a waking nightmare. Motion sickness can become a trial and is common from the age of two or three; dose early and frequently to stop it before it starts, and see p.89–90 for further advice.

At any unfamiliar destination, small children are at risk of mishaps and of accidentally swallowing something noxious. Medicines may not be in childproof containers; children mistake pills for sweets, or paraffin stored in drinks bottles as Coke (see also **Accidents**, pp.273–86).

Disease and infection in children

Gastrointestinal disease may strike especially on trips to warmer regions including southern Europe. Some doctors say that children under the age of three are too vulnerable to visit high-risk, poorly resourced countries because they are likely to suffer from diarrhoea or dysentery. Toddlers who get bacillary dysentery can get really very ill with high fever and profuse diarrhoea and become dangerously dehydrated surprisingly quickly. It is certainly important for parents/carers to be confident about oral rehydration treatment (*see* **Bowels**, pp.110–12). Find out about safe, locally available drinks that will tempt.

Most destinations offer plenty of **foods** suitable for toddlers, but fussy children might have problems finding foods that they will eat. Quality may not be the same as at home either. In less hygienic destinations, small children should not be allowed to eat ice cream, lettuce or strawberries: these items carry a high risk of gastroenteritis. If bringing disposable nappies/diapers from home, plan for diarrhoea and pack some washable bottom-wear. In Asia and South America disposables are at least double the price they are at home and eco-responsible disposal is just not possible.

Infectious disease is potentially an issue for small children who travel. In the West even unimmunized children are partially protected because their peers are immunized (so-called 'herd immunity'); currently 88% of British children over the age of 13 months are vaccine-protected from measles, mumps and rubella whereas in Nepal coverage is around 40%. The success of Western immunization programmes makes it easy to forget that measles and mumps can kill even well-nourished, previously healthy children. Both infections can also leave children deaf or with long-term problems. It is crucial that travelling children receive the usual childhood vaccines as well as specific travel jabs.

Young children are highly susceptible to **malaria**, and are more likely to die if they contract it. Any travel to highly malarious regions (especially sub-Saharan Africa, *see* map, p.133) with children under the age of five needs to be meticulously researched and parents must think seriously about whether a trip is necessary – until the children are old enough to report any symptoms. Read chapter 11, take expert advice and check the immunizations and risks for your intended destination (pp.42–51).

Sunburn in childhood is associated with a risk of **skin cancer** in later life so take sunscreen and UV protective clothes; repellents protect from insect-borne disease and avoid the misery of itchy hot skin. Pack colourful sticking plasters and a good, drying antiseptic (e.g. Savlon Dry) for the inevitable **grazes**. Small people sustain bumps and scratches and it is very important – especially in warm climates – to clean and cover any wound properly to prevent infection. Pack this book too, so you will know when to panic – or not.

Contact information: stockists of UV-protective clothes

Young Explorers, 1 Brookhampton Lane, Kineton, Warwickshire CV35 0JA, UK **t** 0870 879 3741, *www.youngexplorers.co.uk*.

Senior travellers

Insurance

Providing that older travellers are fit for what they intend to do on their trip, the main challenge is finding insurance. Some companies that offer cover for senior travellers are listed below. Most have upper age limits. It is also worth checking with your household insurers. Travelling through a specialist company like Saga (*see* 'Contact information: senior travellers', p.83) may carry the added bonus of included health insurance, but it is important to check exactly what you are buying. Arrange insurance well ahead of departure so that if you are taken ill you won't feel pressured to travel anyway. Don't be tempted to mislead insurance companies (you may not be covered in case of illness), tour operators or anyone else about any medical condition or your capabilities.

Health preparations

Start fit and return fit. Over the age of about 40 it becomes more important to prepare properly for whatever you plan to do on your trip. Older bodies are less forgiving than younger ones and even a relatively trivial 'failure' – like a filling falling out of a tooth – can cause a lot of distress and inconvenience. Do as much as you can to get any potential problems sorted out well before travel and try to avoid changes in any medication just before departure. People on regular medication often forget their supplies. This could cause considerable problems if, for example, the medication is for heart disorders and/or to control fluid overload in the lungs. Ideally know what treatment you are taking, for what purpose and what the consequences of stopping treatment might be. Travel with a note of the tablets you take, including the generic name and the exact dose in milligrams. Armed with that information, you should be able to procure a new supply of your medicines if you forget them or your luggage is lost or delayed. But pack extra supplies in different pieces of luggage.

Plenty of over-70-year-olds are active and adventurous, but as the years roll on it is important to think through the consequences if things go wrong. If you fall you are more likely to fracture a bone, and a thrombosis is more likely if that fracture immobilizes you. Those who take diuretic or 'water' tablets (to control blood pressure or swelling of the ankles) will suffer sooner from imbalance of the blood electrolytes in the case of diarrhoea and/or vomiting, so it is especially important to know about oral rehydration therapy (*see* **Bowels**, pp.110–12) and replacement of lost potassium. Epidemics of vomiting can strike cruise ships and even touring buses so know how to rehydrate safely.

If you are going on any kind of activity trip, do a little fitness training beforehand. This doesn't need to be a full work-out, but something appropriate to what you will be doing such as, perhaps, a brisk daily walk. This will make the trip itself more enjoyable and less exhausting.

Tips for senior travellers

→ People over the age of 75 may face problems finding travel insurance. Sort out insurance as soon as you book your trip.

→ A recent study suggested that older travellers get fewer side effects and better tolerate taking mefloquine antimalarials than younger people.

→ Take expert advice on the vaccines you need. Tick-borne encephalitis (TBE; a risk to those walking and camping in parts of Eastern Europe) is more serious in older victims. Make sure, though, that you don't receive vaccines that you don't need: the risk of a serious adverse reaction to yellow fever immunization is greater in the over-60s.

→ Consider 'flu immunization; the 'flu season in the southern hemisphere is April to November.

→ Get fit for your trip: older bodies need to train for unfamiliar activities. Intrepid older adventurers invest a lot of time in keeping in condition.

→ Anyone who can walk 50m (50 yards) without becoming breathless should tolerate the reduced oxygen in flight and should be fit to fly.

→ More than 10% of long-haul travellers over the age of 50 have small, silent thromboses, most of which resolve without causing problems.

→ When planning a long intercontinental journey that you expect to be tiring or stressful, consider buying a business-class ticket. The check-in environment is less hostile and you will arrive feeling fresher.

→ If you are less than mobile or need help, notify the airline well before your flight so that assistance or a buggy can be provided.

→ Consider if cramped economy-class will seating suit you. Do stiff hips make it difficult for you to squeeze in?

→ People over the age of 80 have a high risk of dangerous deep vein thrombosis (DVT) especially on flights of more than five hours (see also pp.15–18). Those who are taking statins appear to be at reduced risk.

→ Some car hire firms will not rent to drivers over the age of 75 or the cost may be high. Enquire before you travel; don't assume you can organize it on arrival.

→ Know your medication. What is it for? What if you stop taking it? Carry extra supplies in different suitcases with a note of the generic name and doses. You may not be able to get more at your destination.

→ Those taking tablets for diabetes must realize that if they become even mildly ill – say with an attack of travellers' diarrhoea – they may need treatment with an insulin infusion in hospital.

→ Anyone taking diuretic ('water') or blood pressure tablets who suffers a significant attack of diarrhoea should seek medical help promptly if they start to feel dizzy on rising out of a chair or from bed. This is a sign of dehydration (see **Bowels**, pp.110–12) and may indicate loss of electrolytes as well as essential fluids.

→ People with ongoing medical conditions should ask their doctor about travel precautions. Long car journeys and jarring bus rides will make even bad backs worse.

→ If illness strikes just before departure, consider postponing the trip. Insurance should cover rebooking costs. Travelling while ill is dispiriting and unfamiliar doctors may not be reassuring.

→ Make a hard, rational assessment of your capabilities before any trip and ensure that you are up to it. Be honest about medical conditions and any disability.

Case history: Venezuela

On a boat trip up the River Orinoco we stopped to bird watch, swim in the 90-feet-deep water and drink rum punches. Then we discovered it was two hours before we would be back in our hotel and there was nowhere to 'spend a penny'. Why we didn't think of using the Orinoco we will never know but there was a huge feeling of relief when we got back.

Esther Wagstaff, Eastbourne

Lavatories can be a challenge for less nimble travellers. In many public facilities with pedestal lavatories, there may be no seat. Consequently, one needs to be able to hover over the pan, a trick that may be difficult for older travellers or those with hip disease. Some remote places or budget destinations may only offer squat toilets. If you can't squat to relieve yourself, limber up or re-book; otherwise, North American women might invest in a **Whizzy**, an ingenious foldable, disposable, gutter-like device that allows you to pee standing. The British alternative is the **Shewee**. These are also good for the squeamish who want to keep clear of less-than-salubrious lavatories. Another solution is the disposable **Mini Potti** urinal (*see* below). Never restrict the amount of fluid you take in to reduce the amount you need to pee and do not miss out taking any prescribed 'water tablets' when you are travelling. Both strategies can be harmful.

Contact information: senior travellers

Age Concern Insurance Services, UK **t** 0845 600 3348, *www.ageconcern.org.uk*. Covers most medically stable passengers, unless travelling against medical advice. No age limit.

BCB International, Clydesmuir Road, Cardiff CF24 2QS, UK **t** (02929) 433 700. Produces the Mini Potti urinal, costing £5 for three.

New Angle Products, Box 25641, Chicago, IL 60625, US **t** (773) 478 6779, *www.whizzy4you.com*. Produces the Whizzy, priced $10 for 10.

Saga Services, UK **t** 0800 015 8055, *www.saga.co.uk*. Travel for over-50s, but their insurance isn't age-friendly.

www.shewee.com. Sells the Shewee, priced £6 each.

www.whennaturecalls.com. Sells the Mini Potti urinal online.

Companies offering travel insurance for over-65s:

Club Direct, UK **t** 0800 083 2466, *www.clubdirect.co.uk*. Up to age 74.

Coventry Building Society, UK **t** 0845 766 5522. Up to age 75.

MRL Insurance, UK **t** 0845 676 0691, *www.mrlinsurance.co.uk*. Insures people up to age 89.

Perry Gamble, UK **t** (01404) 830 100, *www.perrygamble.co.uk*. Up to age 79.

Tulsi – possible protection against air travel health problems

Dr Narendra Singh of the International Institute of Herbal Medicine (IIHM), Lucknow, India, and Dr Marilena Gilca, Assistant Professor of Biochemistry, 'Carol Davila' University of Medicine and Pharmaceutics, Bucharest, Romania, recommend using tulsi (*Ocimum sanctum, fam. Labiatae*) or holy basil to combat the multiple symptoms arising after long flights. Tulsi is used in many rituals in India and Nepal, and has been recognized for its health benefits for millennia. It is described in several ancient scriptures including the *Rig Veda, Padma Purana* and *Tulsi Kavacham* written between 5000 BC and AD 1200. Tulsi has many pharmacological activities and appears to be beneficial in a variety of stressful situations and stress-related diseases. Tulsi exhibits more potent adaptogenic/anti-stress activity than Siberian ginseng (*Eleutherococcus senticosus*), Korean/Chinese ginseng (*Panax ginseng*) and 50 other Indian medicinal plants.

Tulsi's multiple biological activities suggest it may be useful in managing various air travel related ailments.

→ Tulsi has mild anti-coagulant/antithrombotic activity.

→ It is claimed to increase endurance and survival time during anoxic stress.

→ It may protect from ill effects of cold/heat induced thermal stress.

→ It may have antipollutant effects.

→ It may help in the detoxification of xenobiotics.

→ It is said to be an immunomodulator with antiviral, antibacterial and antifungal activities.

→ It is also claimed to be a radioprotector.

→ It may posses antioxidant activity.

→ It is calming and helps combat fatigue.

→ It is said to be antiemetic, carminative and has good digestive effects.

→ It is claimed to prevent the stress-induced changes in corticosteroids level and thus may attenuate detrimental effects of different types of in-flight stress.

Tulsi consumption before, during and/or even after air travel as tea (3 cups daily; 1–2g dried leaves per cup) or capsules (1–2 capsules twice daily; each capsule contains 400mg of powdered dried leaves) may help to prevent or reduce the ill effects of air travel on the human body due to its multiple pharmacological effects.

Before You Go:
Flight

Coping with flight 86
Pressure effects and low oxygen 87
Food, drink and exercise on board 87
Motion sickness 89
Sneezes and colds 90
Packing sharp objects 91
Jet lag 91
  Melatonin and friends 92

07

Summary

→ Medicines to deal with motion sickness are very effective (and may help you to sleep on long flights), but some need to be taken 3–4 hours before travel.

→ Loud, chaotic airports and cramped seats are at odds with jet-set and holiday brochure glamour, but lower expectations make for a less stressful trip.

→ Chewing gum helps keep the ears clear and pain free.

→ Go easy on (free) alcohol but take lots of non-fizzy, non-caffeine drinks.

→ Exercises that mimic walking reduce ankle swelling and also the risk of deep vein thrombosis (DVT); blood clots are unlikely after flights of less than five hours.

Coping with flight

You will feel better if you exercise both before and after any long flight. Plan what you will and won't check in so that you aren't overburdened with excessive hand baggage. Avoid having to pack it around your legs. This is uncomfortable, restricts movement and contributes to the risk of a blood clot (*see* 'Flying and DVT', pp.15–18). Don't check in essential regular medication, especially if it is temperature sensitive. Contents of aircraft holds get frozen. Checked baggage gets lost, delayed or stolen.

Most people find at least some aspects of flying unpleasant and it is worth giving some consideration to what especially winds you up. International air travel involves submitting to the control of others. This loss of control can be stressful and in itself adds stress to other stressors: anxiety about being on time, queues, delays, service failures, separations from loved ones, unfinished business, health concerns, a bewildering environment where the senses are assaulted with incomprehensible announcements, etc. You can do a little to insulate yourself from all this: take some light reading, use an iPod to play relaxing music, take something to help you sleep, wear ear plugs or learn to meditate. Pay attention to the safety briefings and to in-flight announcements. Knowing what to do in case of an in-flight emergency improves your chances and helps contribute to feeling more in control. Finally, if the level of service has been poor, use your flying time to write a letter of complaint. Such letters will help diffuse any frustration and anger.

Over three-quarters of people who fly admit to feeling anxious; as many as one in five have felt severely incapacitated by the fear of flying and some people are so scared they cannot fly at all. *Stress-free Flying*, by R. Bor, J. Josse and S. Palmer (Quay Books, Wiltshire), may help. Or there are one-day courses to help people cope with flying phobia, which end in a flight with a specially trained crew. Alternatively you could try treatment by a psychologist (*see* below).

Contact information: flying phobia courses

British Airways/Aviatours, UK **t** (01252) 793 250, *www.aviatours.co.uk*. Courses for £198 + VAT at seven British airports.

Fear of Flying Clinic, 1777 Borel Place, San Mateo, CA 94402, US **t** 650 341 1595, *www.fofc.com*.

Royal Free Travel Health Centre, Pond St, London NW3 2QG, UK **t** (020) 7830 2885, *www.travelclinicroyalfree.com*. Offers treatment by psychologists.

Virgin Atlantic, UK **t** (01423) 714 900, *www.flyingwithoutfear.info*. Regular courses at main British airports cost £199 + VAT.

Pressure effects and low oxygen

Pressure changes (most rapid on take-off and landing) bother some adults and many children. Any trapped gas expands by 30% in flight. Pressure problems are most noticeable if you have a cold or ear or sinus problems, in which case try a single dose of a decongestant such as *pseudoephedrine* (Sudafed, Actifed, Drixoral) a couple of hours before take-off or use an *ephedrine* nasal spray (athletes note: this is a banned drug; see also *elitesportgroup.com*, *www.wada-ama.org*). Sucking a sweet, chewing gum, yawning or swallowing equalizes the pressure either side of the eardrum. Airwaves menthol gum by Wrigley might be worth a try if flying when you are congested. If you experience earache on or after take-off, grasp the nose, close the mouth and suck in to reduce pressure in the ears as it drops in the aircraft; if the pain is on descent, grasp the nose, close the mouth and gently blow to increase pressure in the ears. Giving babies a drink during ascents and especially descents should help stop them suffering earache. If ear pain is a recurrent problem, investigate **reflexology** since stimulating the appropriate point on the sole of the foot can relieve the pressure spectacularly. Tooth pain in flight suggests a loose filling or may be due to expansion of gas remaining after a recent filling or from tooth decay. Don't leave your pre-travel dental check until just before you travel.

Food, drink and exercise on board

The cabin environment is dry and low in oxygen and leads to feelings of irritability and discomfort, which are compounded by sleep deprivation. You will feel better during long flights if you move around every hour or so and do some exercises. Keeping hand baggage to a minimum will allow you more space to move. Loose-fitting clothes, support tights, ankle-flexing and calf-tensing exercises also help avoid ankle-swelling. These measures – especially movement – also protect against the rarer but serious risk of thrombosis (blood clot); any car or plane journey that involves sitting for more than five hours carries a risk of thrombosis.

Dehydration is common on long flights, and adds to the effects of jet lag. Use a skin moisturizer. Abstain from alcohol (one drink on the ground is worth two in the air). Go easy on tea and coffee. Drink plenty of non-fizzy fruit juices or water. The gas bubbles in carbonated drinks expand at reduced pressures on board the aircraft and will contribute to bloating, abdominal cramps and flatus. Take only light food.

Case history: swollen ankles

Sid, a sprightly 81-year-old, turned up at a morning clinic complaining that his legs were swollen and that the left one had become quite sore. He'd travelled from Scotland to the south of England by bus three days before to spend time with his daughter and grandchildren. He was on seven different prescribed tablets, didn't know what they were or what they were for and had forgotten to pack any of them. His legs were indeed very swollen and the left one was hot and red. I was concerned that he had a deep vein thrombosis (DVT) after his 10-hour bus trip. Even without travel, his risk was already high. It is about 1 in 500 annually for over-80-year-olds, compared with about 1 in 3,000 in people under 40. Luckily, the hospital was able to reassure me that he didn't have a clot.

I phoned Sid's GP to find out which tablets he should have been taking. Restarting his diuretics ('water tablets') soon cured the ankle-swelling.

Alcohol and smoking also aggravate jet lag and flight fatigue. If addicted to nicotine, get patches or gum to get you through the flight without air rage, or get help by phoning the **Quitline** (*see* opposite). Prescribed sleeping tablets can be very useful if you are poor at sleeping naturally, although getting heavily sedated will increase your risk of a blood clot on a long-haul flight (*see* 'Flying and DVT', pp.15–18). Sleeping pills take about half an hour to work and are effective for six to eight hours. Some are good mind–body relaxants too, so they are helpful if you are tense about flying. Don't try any new medicine for the first time on a flight in case it doesn't suit you; Phenergan (*promethazine hydrochloride*), an antihistamine that is also often used to sedate children, for example, can make some individuals hyperactive.

Frequent fliers are exposed to greater doses of radiation than those of us who keep our feet on the ground; taking **vitamins C and E** after a long flight is said to help mop up the free radicals produced by irradiation. Another consequence of long flights can be that they stimulate what is effectively a moult: hair loss about three months after the flight. This is an alarming but temporary phenomenon.

Commonly used preparations to counteract motion sickness

Generic name	common names	adult dose
cinnarizine	Stugeron (UK, India); Vertigon (India)	15–30mg
cyclizine	Valoid (UK); Marezine (USA)	50mg
dimenhydrinate	Dramamine	50–100mg
diphenhydramine hydrochloride	Dreemon, Medinex, Nytol (UK); Benadryl (USA)	10–50mg
hyoscine	Joy-rides, Kwells (UK); Scopolamine (USA, Canada)	0.15–0.6mg
hyoscine	Scopoderm (UK); Transdermscop (USA)	1.5mg
hyoscine		0.2mg
meclozine/ meclizine	Sea-legs (UK); Antivert, Dramamine II, Bonine (USA)	12.5mg
promethazine hydrochloride	Phenergan (UK, USA)	10–25mg
promethazine hydrochloride	Phenergan	50mg
promethazine teoclate (theoclate)	Avomine (UK, India); Anergan Prorex (USA)	25mg
ginger		500–2,000mg

Contact information: air travel

For further information on the health effects of flying, check the Aviation Health website, *www.aviation-health.org*, or look at *www.britishairways.com/health*. If you want to know about air quality on board, look at:
www.boeing.com/commercial/cabinair.

Quitline, UK **t** 0800 002 200, *www.quit.org.uk*. Offers help and advice for smokers.

Motion sickness

Motion sickness is the response of a confused brain trying to unscramble conflicting messages coming from the eyes and the balance organs in the inner ear. Your position in any vehicle or vessel affects the amount of motion sickness you experience: choose the place that rolls and pitches least. In a plane this is between the wings; in ships it's in the middle, amidships, and it is best to look at the horizon rather than close to. Alternatively, try lying down with your eyes shut, if possible.

preparation type	onset of effect	duration	notes
tablet	4hrs	8hrs	less sedating; not available in the USA
tablet	2hrs	8–12hrs	less sedating
tablet	2hrs	8hrs	can cause hallucinations in overdose; no longer available in UK
tablet or syrup			very sedating
melt in the mouth or chewable tablets	30mins	4hrs	very sedating; dry mouth; most rapidly effective
patch	6–8hrs	72hrs	fewer side effects than tablets; prescription in UK only
injection	15mins	4hrs	
tablet	2hrs	8hrs	less sedating
tablet or elixir	2hrs	18hrs	usually very sedating
injection	15mins	18hrs	usually very sedating
tablet	2hrs	24hrs	sedating; take at bedtime or 3–4hrs before travel; used in pregnancy
by mouth	30mins	4hrs	

This will work best if you have some distraction – like music playing via an iPod. In a car or bus, sit in the front seat, look forwards (not sideways) and do not read or try to navigate. Back seats on buses 'roll' the most. Travel sickness is aggravated by eating heavy meals and drinking large volumes. It often strikes on unfamiliar forms of transport.

Cures for travel sickness

The table on pp.88–9 lists preparations to ease travel sickness that you can buy while travelling. With the exception of *hyoscine* and ginger, the medicines in the table are all antihistamines and so they are also useful for treating stings, allergies and itchy rashes. Some are sedating, others are less so. Responses vary; if one preparation doesn't work, try another. Many of the antihistamines are best taken three to four hours before travel, or if you are setting out early, take them at bedtime. Further doses are then taken usually every eight hours.

Hyoscine patches need to be applied five to six hours before the journey. Patches can be used in people over the age of nine. *Hyoscine* tablets start working fastest so are great if nausea comes on unexpectedly, but they have the disadvantages that (a) they are only effective for about four hours (antihistamines generally last about eight) and (b) further doses increase the likelihood of troublesome side effects, namely dry mouth, drowsiness, dizziness and even blurred vision. *Hyoscine* is good for journeys of less than four hours because when a single dose is used, side effects are rarely a problem. Tablets and syrups are often useless once motion-induced nausea or vomiting has started. *Metoclopramide* (Maxolon) is not effective against travel-induced nausea, but can be used in gastroenteritis. It is also safe and effective in the **nausea of pregnancy**.

Natural remedies

Elasticated wrist bands called sea bands or travel bands press on acupuncture points and work well for some people in preventing travel sickness, even in children. They have no side effects. Trials by the Royal Air Force, however, concluded that the effect wasn't enough for their own stringent conditions (but if it works for you, who cares?). Ginger is of proven benefit in preventing nausea of any kind, whether it is due to motion sickness, cancer treatment or pregnancy. An effective dose is one gram of ginger extract taken as a tablet; this is equivalent to a handful of fresh root ginger. In two studies this was found to be as effective as *metoclopramide*, a commonly prescribed anti-emetic. It might also be worth a try in the queasiness of travellers' diarrhoea.

Sneezes and colds

The dry cabin atmosphere can cause itching, discomfort and bouts of sneezing. A bland grease like white, soft paraffin (petroleum jelly, Vaseline), anointed inside the nose, should help. Taking any decongestants (e.g. Sudafed *pseudoephedrine* tablets or *ephedrine* nasal spray) just before or during a flight will make a dry nose, mouth and throat worse.

Minor air-borne infections are commonly acquired during a long flight. There is also evidence that TB transmission may occur on flights of longer than eight hours – if someone with the disease is on board – although no cases of active TB have been identified as a result of exposure on a commercial airline. The WHO states that the risk is no greater than to those travelling by train or bus. Smokers are at greatest risk of such droplet-spread infections because tar inhibits particle clearance from the lungs. Airlines are aware of these infection risks (although they would rather this wasn't publicized) and they occur despite the fact that modern planes are now fitted with high efficiency particulate air (HEPA) filters that remove bacteria and viruses. If you are sitting close to someone with a cold or other infection the chances are that you will catch it. I have family members who on two separate occasions caught chickenpox during a flight. Even in the best-filtered planes, infection transmission happens because there isn't a dedicated filter for each passenger and air is usually drawn to the sides of the aircraft. The air circulation and filtration systems in older aircraft used to 'cost' fuel and aircrews were said to reduce the amount of air that was moved around the cabin, particularly at night. In modern aircraft this is no longer the practice. If, though, you are in some ancient airliner and the air seems stale, you might ask the cabin crew to increase flows, or purchase a mask.

Packing sharp objects

Sharp objects are not permitted in hand luggage on board the plane and may be confiscated at the airport. They should be packed in the luggage you are checking in to the hold. Such objects include: scissors, corkscrews, tweezers, pen-knives, Swisscards, nail files, cutlery and hypodermics (check in your first-aid kit). Toy guns, catapults, razorblades, knitting needles and darts are also banned from carry-on baggage. Read any instructions before check-in and follow them to the letter. That way you are more likely to retain your belongings.

Jet lag

Long-haul flights often precipitate a horrible set of symptoms including insomnia, dullness of mind, fatigue, daytime sleepiness, impaired concentration, decreased alertness, trouble with memory, physical clumsiness, weakness, lethargy, light-headedness and a general feeling of awfulness. This is jetlag. There is no 100% effective treatment for it so if you have crossed more than five time zones, don't expect to be at your best for some days. It takes roughly one day to adjust to each hour of time difference; your bowels may need more. Adjusting after flying east takes longer than flying west.

The timing of flights influences jet lag and flight fatigue, and it can be worth paying more to avoid inconvenient times. If there is a choice – this applies especially to inexperienced or lone travellers arriving in an unfamiliar country – avoid arriving in the dark, and beware of who offers you a lift; ask advice from locals and team up with other travellers. On eastward flights an evening departure may mean that you arrive the next afternoon, in time for a meal and relaxation before bed. You will adjust faster if you try to slot into local times immediately; go to bed at the right time at your destination. If you are tired or tense before your flight, expect jet lag to hit harder. Certain routines are said to limit the effects of jet lag, but they are probably no better than rest and pacing yourself.

Try influencing your natural *melatonin* levels; the body normally produces this hormone in the evening and it aids sleep. Its secretion is inhibited by sunlight so getting outside into sunshine helps improve the quality of sleep after a long flight (but don't get burned). Protein-rich meals also help the body produce the hormones needed for a full day, and a light evening meal with plenty of carbohydrate provides those necessary for sleep. Some experts also recommend artificial *tyrosine* and *tryptophan* supplements, which you can buy from herbalists and pharmacies. The homeopathic remedy *arnica* seems to help some people get over their jet lag. **No-Jet-Lag** is another homeopathic alternative.

Melatonin and friends

Melatonin is the hormone that synchronizes the body's internal body clock, and given as a supplement it shifts circadian rhythms and thus improves sleep and should reduce the symptoms of jet lag. *Melatonin* tablets were available from herbalists in Britain until it was realized that this product had important physiological effects: it interferes, for example, with human ovulation. It is still on sale over the counter in the USA, South Africa and Australia as a 'dietary supplement'. It is probably quite safe to take in the short term, but since it hasn't undergone stringent Food and Drug Administration safety testing it is probably unwise to take it long-term (claims are made for it helping combat cancer and Alzheimer's for example). In common with other 'herbal' treatments, doses and tablet components are non-standard, and analysis of 19 commercial melatonin products revealed problems of pharmaceutical quality and consistency. However melatonin has beneficial effects on sleep so if you suffer, it is worth a try – unless planning a pregnancy.

In the UK *melatonin* can be obtained for about £10 for 60 x 3mg tablets by mail order from stockists listed below. Since 2008, *melatonin* has become available on prescription as sustained release Circadin but it is only licensed for people aged over 55 years with sleep disorders (2mg is taken once daily 1–2 hours before bedtime for three weeks). Clinical trials on an artificial *melatonin*, *tasimelteon*, make this look promising.

Contact information: stockists of melatonin
www.agestop.co.uk
PharmWest, 520 Washington Blvd No. 401, Marina Del Rey, CA 90292, US **t** (310) 301 4015, Ireland **t** (46) 943 7317, UK **t** (freephone) 0800 8923 8923, US **f** (310) 577 0296, Ireland **f** (46) 943 7310, *www.pharmwest.com*.
Worldwide Health, Freepost, Alderney GY1 5SS, UK **t** (01481) 824 877, *www.wwhonline.com*.

On the Ground:
Culture Shock

Coping 94
  New arrivals 94
  Phases of adjustment 95
  Loss of control 96
Reverse culture shock 97

Summary

→ Any trip has its ups and downs, highs and lows.

→ Travel is tiring, as well as exciting; be patient with yourself and others.

→ Eat regularly and drink plenty of safe juices and/or water.

→ Don't try to do everything and see everything.

→ Allow time and space to chill.

→ Try to sort out any physical health problems that worry you.

→ Write lots of postcards, emails and letters to keep in touch with home.

→ Make social contacts locally too.

→ Link up with other travellers to share excitements and frustrations.

Coping

Culture shock is commonly experienced by travellers arriving at a new destination, or sometimes when they return home after a long absence. It is a sense of unease and often anxiety. Feelings range from disorientation and mild disquiet through to near panic. They are compounded by factors such as lack of preparation, fatigue and illness, or even concern about loved ones or tasks left undone at home. If you are not feeling very emotionally robust when you leave home, culture shock may hit hard.

New arrivals

Travel experiences are emotionally loaded. Often there is excitement and stimulation. The tingle-factor, though, comes partly from the fact that we're stressed, just a little. On top of the delightful sensations of arriving in a new country, you have to deal with a lot of things – all at once. Yet you are fatigued and jet-lagged, bombarded with sights and sounds, bewildered by unfamiliar signposting, disorientated, bereft of familiar support systems and you may have experienced a painful separation. You may feel hounded by touts and beggars, or people may seem to stand far too close and just won't leave you alone.

Accomplishing simple tasks, such as finding a decent room for the night, buying a bus ticket, extending a visa or finding out about onward flights, can take hours and life becomes exasperating. Yet you are here to enjoy yourself, and you ought to be having a good time. You resent feelings of homesickness, and are reluctant to admit to them. You may start to resent the people around you, especially if they seem to be putting up barriers for no apparent reason. However, if you listen to locals (or maybe even employ a local guide), you will start hearing jokes about how cumbersome systems are: there is talk of especially slow 'Peruvian time', of mañana, insh'Allah, or just, 'that's life'.

It is important to slow down, and to accept that in some cultures, things just move a little more slowly and at a more relaxed pace than you may be used to.

The adjustment process
Not all travellers will progress through all the feelings listed, but many experience most stages during adjustment.
→ Excitement, delight and euphoria.
→ Honeymoon period.
→ Pining for the familiar, family and old friends (homesickness).
→ Anger, shock and numbness, in response to poverty and inequality around you.
→ Guilt at being a rich Westerner.
→ Frustration, depression and apathy (see 'Symptoms that you are struggling to cope', overleaf).
→ Acceptance and greater understanding of your environment.

Phases of adjustment

Understandably, travellers – and especially expatriates – often go through a process of emotional responses. On arriving in an unfamiliar environment, there is frequently a sense of excitement, delight and even euphoria. Next comes a honeymoon period, when you don't see any problems, or problems and disadvantages are minimized. Then there may be some pining – for Marmite/Vegemite, a decent cup of tea or coffee or a friend – and some of the ugliness and inconvenience starts to intrude. You may have periods of feeling angry, shocked or numb, in response to the injustice of poverty, the inequality of healthcare, or even just the levels of waste and inefficiency around you. Then you may feel guilty at having so much in comparison to the people you are travelling among. As the adjustment process continues, you might even become depressed and apathetic, particularly if people's impatience shows every time you try to get a sentence out in a new language; the difficulty of basic communication can be particularly frustrating if you are already feeling isolated.

Alternatively, you may become adjusted and simply accept your surroundings as understanding evolves. However you respond to your destination, though, culture shock can hit unexpectedly and take you by surprise – again and again.

What kind of person are you?
It can be helpful to consider what kind of person you are. What are your attitudes to illness? Do you worry about symptoms or are you confident that nothing serious ever happens to you? When you have had an unexplained symptom in the past, how have you reacted? Have you needed the immediate reassurance of a doctor that you trust? Have you had bad experiences or do you know people who have suffered so that you have a particular dread? Where will you find help and advice if you need it? Have you found out the local phone number to call an ambulance? Is there a local ambulance service? There are plenty of stress tests on the Internet, should you wish to assess your anxiety rating, character and stress level (see 'Contact information: coping', p.97).

Loss of control

At home we exert a great deal of control over our lives; we have established routines and life is safe and predictable. We know how to avoid undue hazards: we know which parts of the city are unsafe after dark; we wear seat-belts in cars, or a helmet when on a motorcycle. Many of us travel to take a break from such predictability, but this means surrendering some loss of control. Again, this adds to the excitement, but when things go a little wrong, such as when there are seemingly avoidable delays or there is illness, travellers will cope better if they become fatalistic.

In comparison to the controlled environment we have been used to, travel often puts us into difficult situations and, during adventurous trips, we may find ourselves in a situation which is truly beyond our control. It is then good to be able to recognize your limits and work within the bounds of what you are able to do. Getting through such challenges is life-enhancing and often makes a person more capable back home, too. Most adventurers set themselves targets, such as circumnavigating Annapurna, reaching a certain altitude or a remote glacier, or seeing every listed site, and such goal-driven trips can lead to disappointments and frustrations. There may be unavoidable delays, or plans can be scuppered by bad weather or a strike, and yet, if the journey, rather than the goal, is the main objective, the trip will still be enjoyable. I have met many trekkers whose opening response on what they'd seen in Nepal was about the failed objective rather than the delights that they had seen. Those who loiter and are not driven by goals see more, meet friends along the way and feel more satisfied.

People sometimes leave home so as to find meaning to life, perhaps after some relationship crisis or other loss. Inner journeys comprise a whole literary genre, in which travel is rather idealized as a healing experience. It can be, but it can be hurtful, too, if travel adds stress to unbearable stress. If you set out on your journey in a fragile state or are too starry-eyed trying to find your idyll you may be disappointed. Set up some safety nets. Consider linking up with other travellers, ensure that you can get to somewhere that feels safe wherever you are, and go properly insured.

Symptoms that you are struggling to cope include:

→ Overreaction to minor problems or inevitable delays.
→ Racism and angry, irrational outbursts.
→ Lack of interest in learning anything about your destination.
→ Withdrawal and negativism.
→ Feeling that everyone is relaxed/beautiful/fulfilled except you.
→ Excessive eating or drinking or loss of appetite.
→ Feelings of uneasiness with strangers.
→ Fear of dirt and disease.
→ Great fatigue.
→ An overwhelming sense of doom.

Panic attacks

If the travel experience becomes a major stressor, it may be tempting to seek solace in alcohol or other recreational drugs. These not only hold dangers in themselves, but they can also lead to accidents and/or unsafe sexual behaviour. Look for other ways to unwind or de-stress, before the situation worsens. A well-recognized symptom of stress is having panic attacks. These are associated with an overwhelming sense of dread, and they cause physical symptoms that include breathlessness, weakness, dizziness, sometimes chest discomfort, often nausea, and cramps or tingling in the hands and feet. If stress levels have reached this pitch find somewhere to chill out and, if a few days of doing nothing in a restful place doesn't help, you may need to find a doctor. Treatment of stress and panic attacks is straightforward, but it is probably best done by someone who speaks your language and has experience of Western lifestyles. The best anti-depressant drugs are taken as a course of at least four months, so they are not necessarily a 'quick fix'.

Treating culture shock: natural approaches

St John's wort is effective in treating many of the symptoms common in culture shock, including low mood, panic or anxiety. It takes about a week to have any noticeable effect. **Ginkgo** improves poor memory. The herbal remedy *kava* has some activity in helping anxiety but it is judged too risky to use. A good alternative to treatments you swallow is behavioural help. It is often possible to develop **meditation** or relaxation techniques through courses on yoga or Buddhism, aimed particularly at foreign travellers. Massage is also beneficial.

Contact information: coping

Internet stress tests can be found on the useful ***www.medicdirect.co.uk*** website, or refer to the excellent ICRC booklet for relief workers, *Coping with Stress*, which can be downloaded from *www.icrc.org* or ordered by post from the **International Committee of the Red Cross**, Distribution Sector, 19 avenue de la Paix, CH 1202 Geneva. The booklet includes a stress and trauma self-evaluation test.

Reverse culture shock

Culture shock and travel-induced stress seldom get this bad, however. Most people adjust and enjoy themselves, and are changed forever by their exotic experiences.

People who have been on a long trip can be surprised by the extent of the reverse culture shock they experience on returning home. Many people feel this is worse than the first culture shock. The length of time it takes to adjust once you get home is partially determined by the length of time you've been away but also depends on whether you have had any life-changing experiences. Those who have been moved deeply by seeing profound poverty or disfiguring disease may find it difficult to talk of this back home. It is possible that friends and relations who have stayed at home may not understand and remain disinterested. This is isolating.

Strategies for dealing with the home-coming blues

→ Get routine back into your life: eat regular meals, take regular exercise and schedule some treats for yourself.

→ Recognize that readjustment takes time. Give yourself space to chill.

→ Discuss symptoms that go on for more than a few weeks with your GP or a counsellor.

→ Deal with any physical health problems that you may have brought back with you. Talk through with your GP any worries you have about health-related souvenirs from your trip. Don't let them play on your mind.

→ The longer you've been away, the longer it will take you to readjust: if you've been away for years, it might take 12 to 18 months to settle.

→ Consider signing up for courses on meditation, yoga or relaxation techniques; those who have been to Asia will love that link back to where they've been.

→ Write lots of emails and letters to keep in touch with the new friends you left behind and are missing so much.

→ Try to link up with other returned travellers and talk things through with them.

→ Understand that those who have stayed at home may feel a touch threatened by your mind-broadening experiences and so may block you out; it's nothing personal.

→ St John's wort is effective in treating many of the symptoms common in culture shock and reverse culture shock including low mood, panic attacks and anxiety; it takes a week to start working.

The process of readjustment after years away may take as long as a year or 18 months. During this time, it is especially important to develop links with others who have had parallel experiences; travel clubs are often good places to find kindred spirits. Long-term travellers often enrol on long or short academic or development courses. If you have been employed overseas long-term, some organizations offer debriefing and/or counselling. If you feel seriously down on your return, however, remember that your family doctor should be able to help.

On the Ground: Bowels

Travellers' diarrhoea 100
  Why get travellers' diarrhoea? 101
  Prevention 101
  Which foods are unsafe? 102

Safe drinks 104

Water treatment 105

Preventing diarrhoea with
  medicines 109

Natural preventatives 109

Treating diarrhoea 110

Replacing lost fluids 110
  Home-made ORS 111
  How much do you need to drink? 111
  The gastro-colic reflex 112
  What to eat when diarrhoea
  strikes 112
  Treatment of children 112
  When to use medicines 113

Filth-to-mouth diseases 115

09

Summary

→ Diarrhoea kills 3.5 million children in resource-poor regions every year, yet treatment is simple and avoidance possible with the information in this chapter.

→ It is common in travellers but mostly it is inconvenient rather than dangerous; symptoms usually settle in 36 hours.

→ Gyppy tummy is side-stepped by eating piping hot, thoroughly cooked food. Avoid salads and other raw foods; do not take ice or ice cream.

→ It is dehydration caused by diarrhoea that makes you feel bad. Drink at least three litres of clear fluids a day if you are off your food.

→ Drink in sips if you are vomiting or nauseated.

→ Headache and dizziness are symptoms of dehydration.

→ Three good-volume urinations of light yellow-coloured wee is normal; less implies dehydration so drink more.

→ A very light, plain diet will usually cure the abdominal cramps of travellers' diarrhoea, and also reduce nausea.

→ Avoid fatty and oily foods and dairy products if your stomach is upset.

→ Taking hot or iced drinks or a hot meal often provokes a reflex bowel action (the gastro-colic reflex), accompanied by abdominal pain.

→ In the absence of medical advice, the safe remedy for childhood diarrhoea is rehydration drinks. Breast-feeding is protective.

→ If you use iodine crystals to sterilize water, pack one 20ml screw-top non-plastic bottle, a 10ml measure (e.g. a syringe) and a 1-litre (1³/₄-pint) water bottle.

Travellers' diarrhoea

About a third of British visitors to southern Europe (including Spain) will suffer from travellers' diarrhoea, with the risk being highest during the warmest months. Approximately half of those visiting a developing country for a month are hit; maybe that's why there are so many names for it. Runny tummy, diarrhoea, gastroenteritis, food poisoning, the squits, Montezuma's revenge, gyppy tummy, Delhi belly, Kathmandu quickstep, Tandoori trots, the Aztec two-step, *turista*, the runs, or whatever you call it, this is the most common medical problem for travellers. The symptoms depend on the microbe. Some gastroenteritis, which has a short incubation period, provokes a prompt puke. Those microbes that travel further down the 8m (25ft) of tubing that is the adult human alimentary canal take longer to cause mischief and cause more diarrhoea than vomiting.

Travel anywhere carries a risk of travellers' diarrhoea, and the chances of it are greater when visiting warmer climates. Hot climates make food preservation more difficult and where unreliable electricity allows refrigerators to get warm, food can incubate troublesome bacteria. Cracked or seldom-cleaned water filters also harbour microbes. The most common cause of travellers' diarrhoea is ETEC (enterotoxigenic *Escherichia coli*), which are nasty forms of normally friendly intestinal bacteria. There are many other causes (*see* 'Diseases avoided by eating safe foods' box, p.103), but do not be put off by the list of diseases. Identical precautions will protect you from them all.

Why get travellers' diarrhoea?

Travellers' diarrhoea comes from getting other people's faeces into your mouth, usually via other people's dirty hands or via food. It is a bad hygiene disease. Yet in a survey of visitors to East Africa, only 2% took adequate protective dietary precautions. Dirty water can be a source, but is much less risky than contaminated food. The risk of developing disease is related to the number of microbes consumed, and bad food contains large numbers. As you travel more, you develop some immunity to some kinds of diarrhoea (notably ETEC). Only the foolish do not continue to take precautions, though, as the transmission route for ETEC diarrhoea is the same as for many other diseases.

Diarrhoea and other filth-to-mouth diseases are a problem anywhere that environmental sanitation is poor. Although more common in warm, humid climates, they are not restricted to tropical countries. Cholera was a problem in Victorian cities in Britain until there were improvements in housing and sanitation. The highest-risk regions are the Indian subcontinent (including Nepal) and tropical Latin America.

Prevention

There is not yet a vaccine against travellers' diarrhoea. Infection is avoided by eating sensibly. Although there are many causes of diarrhoea, the avoidance strategies are the same for each type: eat food that has been prepared and stored hygienically, wash your hands with soap before eating anything, and drink safe water.

Food is the main problem: expatriates who cook for themselves, or employ a reliable cook, are able to ensure that hygiene is maintained. Travellers staying in hotels have less control, so they are at much greater risk. Ordering cooked-to-order hot meals in restaurants is safer than eating ready-made dishes. Be most cautious when you are staying in large centres of population, since the more people there are around you the more faeces there will be. The star ratings of hotels are no guide to hygiene but you can reduce the risks by taking some simple precautions (*see* 'How to reduce the risks' box, p.104).

Do not allow anyone to cook for you if they are ill. It is especially tempting to expect an ailing travelling companion to cook while he or she is recuperating in camp or your holiday flat, but this is the best way to ensure that the whole family or team goes down with the same tummy-bug. Short fingernails are easier to keep clean than long ones.

If you find yourself consuming something that you suspect is unsafe, take as little of it as possible. The less you eat the less likely you are to become ill: the severity of diarrhoea usually depends on the number of microbes that get inside your insides. Never assume that you are immune. The body is never able to build up immunity to *Shigella*, which causes bacillary dysentery, for example, so it is possible to suffer from dysentery several times a year.

Clinical trials suggested that the cholera vaccine Dukoral would also protect travellers from gastroenteritis. Dukoral is protective against cholera but its effectiveness against other infections has been disappointing. It gives only partial protection and works best against mixed infections. In Bangladesh immunized locals had 67% fewer episodes of diarrhoea caused by heat-labile ETEC but protection was only for three months; it was also 86% protective against life-threatening heat-labile ETEC. Among tourists from Finland in Morocco it gave 52% protection against any ETEC diarrhoea, 60% protection against heat-labile ETEC, 71% protection when there was infection with ETEC and another diarrhoea-causing microbe and 82% protection when ETEC and *Salmonella* were present. A study of US students in Mexico found Dukoral was also 50% protective against ETEC diarrhoea. Since Dukoral doesn't give complete protection against diarrhoea, it has not been given a licence as a diarrhoea preventer in the UK or USA.

Which foods are unsafe?

In unhygienic environments, uncooked foods are unsafe. Food can be contaminated with human faeces while it is growing, during transport, preparation, cooking, storage or serving. 'Nightsoil' is a traditional fertilizer in Nepal and China, and in parts of the Andes irrigation water is at such a premium that farmers break into sewage mains to water their crops with untreated effluent. Thorough cooking will sterilize even highly contaminated food, however.

Salads are a likely source of diarrhoea, and lettuce can only be rendered safe by being vigorously boiled. Take tomatoes and smooth-skinned items that can be washed and, preferably, soaked in dilute chlorine ('Milton' or bleach) or iodine (12 drops per litre) for 30 minutes. **Fried rice** is risky: it is often made with 'bits' lying around in the kitchen, and flash frying may not sterilize everything. **Ice** may have travelled from an ice factory on the back of someone's bike and been deposited at the roadside on the way to your drink. It may be handled by unwashed fingers when it is put into your drink. It is safer to pack ice around the outside of the glass or bottle to keep it cool. **Ice cream** is risky, though the acidity of **sorbets** kills many bacteria (including *Salmonella*), so they are fairly safe. **Strawberries** are uncleanable and grow close to unpleasant brown deposits on the ground; they are high risk unless grown in a hygienic environment. The maxim that will protect you is:

'peel it,
boil it,
cook it,
shell it, or
... forget it.'

Eggs

Raw or lightly cooked eggs carry a risk of *Salmonella* food poisoning; pregnant women and anyone frail should eat eggs which are properly cooked. Fresh mayonnaise, tiramisu and mousse are made with raw eggs.

Diseases avoided by eating safe foods

These filth-to-mouth microbes cause diarrhoea in careless travellers and stay-at-homes alike, but the precautions for avoiding all of them are similar and straightforward (see 'How to reduce the risks' box, overleaf).

→ ETEC (enterotoxigenic Escherichia coli).

→ Enteroadherent, enteroaggregative and other strains of Escherichia coli.

→ Campylobacter, which causes a lot of griping pains with diarrhoea.

→ Shigella causes severe bloody diarrhoea (see pp.113–15) and fever.

→ Other bacterial diarrhoea, like Salmonella food poisoning.

→ Giardia (see p.117).

→ Various other parasites (see p.118) and worms (see pp.120–3).

→ Amoebic dysentery (see pp.115–16).

→ Cryptosporidium; causes 14-day diarrhoea with cramps (see p.116).

→ Cyclospora (see p.116–7).

→ Rotaviruses or winter vomiting virus.

→ A catalogue of rarer diarrhoea-causing viruses.

→ Cholera (see p.116).

→ Typhoid (see p.267).

→ Paratyphoid A, B and C (see p.267).

→ Hepatitis A and E (see pp.262–3).

→ Polio.

→ Cystocercosis (worm cysts in the brain; see p.122).

Milk

I have found wood shavings and buffalo hair in 'pasteurized' milk, so in resource-poor regions it is worth boiling milk, even if it claims to be pasteurized. Unboiled milk (and/or the water used to adulterate it) can give you TB, brucellosis, Q-fever, typhoid, paratyphoid and polio, as well as dysentery and diarrhoea. Powdered or tinned milks are as safe as the water used for reconstitution. Yoghurt is usually safe. Goat's milk is not much safer than cow or buffalo milk; it can also carry brucellosis, tick-borne encephalitis and other organisms. Cheese is only as safe as the milk it was made from, while drinks containing yoghurt and ice (e.g. lassi in Nepal) are risky because ingredients are handled during preparation. In the Indian subcontinent milk is usually safe because it has been boiled, but always check. Finally, be aware that milk should probably be avoided when you have diarrhoea or a stomach upset. A temporary (six-week-long) **milk allergy** can be the consequence of continuing to take dairy products during profuse diarrhoea; this will make the diarrhoea go on longer.

Flies

It is unaesthetic to see these six-legged filth-mongers running around uninvited on your food, but it seems that flies do not spread much disease – except trachoma and other eye infections. You can estimate the length of time an expatriate has lived in the tropics by his response to a fly dive-bombing his beer. A recent arrival will discard the beer and pour another. A settled expat will fish out the fly and finish his pint. But a truly acculturated expatriate will drink the beer, eat the fly and extol the virtues of this ready source of protein: 'The chicken is so stringy, you see.'

How to reduce the risks

→ Avoid salads, especially lettuce and watercress.
→ Vegetarian food is usually safer than meat dishes.
→ À la carte is safer than food from a buffet.
→ Any meat that you eat must be thoroughly cooked and steaming hot.
→ Piping hot, freshly cooked foods are safe; sizzling hot street snacks are usually safe.
→ Fried rice may be risky where reliable electricity is lacking (*see* p.102).
→ Avoid ice and ice cream when in less hygienic places.
→ Refuse soft fruits like strawberries that cannot be peeled.
→ Be wary of seafood; make sure it is properly cooked (*see* pp.124–6).
→ Few diseases are transmitted via dirty cups or cutlery (exceptions are typhoid and Bornholm disease) but it is best to avoid obviously soiled spoons, cups and glasses, and plates that have been licked by dogs.
→ Only drink safe water (*see* pp.105–9).

Safe drinks

Village drinking water isn't the microbe soup that some imagine – unless there has been some huge disaster. Many travellers are surprised to discover that true water-borne disease outbreaks are rare. Most gastroenteritis, diarrhoeal disease, dysentery, typhoid, cholera and the so-called faecal–oral (or filth-to-mouth) diseases come via contaminated or unhygienically prepared food. Even so, it is sensible when travelling in less developed destinations to purify your drinking water, because water can also make you ill. The riskiest water is in towns with intermittent piped water supplies; water is often cleaner at source than it is after it has been treated and delivered to the taps, because there is suction into the pipe when water starts flowing along it, and any slight leaks will allow material in the soil to enter the water supply. This is quite a common problem in congested Third World cities. Tap water in North America, the European Union, Australasia and other destinations with good infrastructure should be of drinkable quality. In francophone Europe ordering a *carafe* or *pichet d'eau* will get you tap water and will avoid you getting charged for bottled drinks; empty mineral water bottles have become a litter problem in many areas. Bottled water, which may just be treated (or untreated) tap water, is less safe than boiled water, even if the seal is intact. Studies in India, Nepal and Pakistan have found faecal

Case history: Nepal

We stepped into an eerily deserted restaurant in Kathmandu. I ordered a Mexican dish but said that I did not like lettuce. My food arrived topped with chopped raw tomatoes, and accompanied by a dish of cold sour cream. I had expected the cream to be cooked in a sauce. I awoke in the small hours knowing I was going to pay for ignoring my own rules, and lay awake all night, waiting. I spent the morning emptying my stomach. By lunchtime I had drunk six glasses of cooled hot lemon (with a pinch of salt and plenty of sugar) and a cola (with another pinch of salt). I felt a lot better. That evening I nibbled a few crackers with my hot lemons, and was fine by the next morning, although I kept to a light, plain diet for the rest of the day.

105

09 On the Ground | Bowels

Case history: Indonesia

An expatriate family living in a smart suburb of Jakarta was meticulous about sterilizing food: family members soaked all fruit, tomatoes and cucumbers in soap powder then in dilute bleach, rinsed them in boiled water, dried them and stored them in the refrigerator. They also boiled their water for a full 20 minutes before filtering it. All their food came from a very plush ultra-clean supermarket used almost entirely by expatriates. The family came down with typhoid. Their disease came from locally made ice cream bought at the supermarket.

The family's health precautions were mostly sound, even verging on the obsessional, yet they had not realized that ice cream – even from an apparently hygienic supermarket – is very risky stuff. There are frequent power cuts in Indonesia. Frozen foods may have been allowed to thaw and then been refrozen. Many Jakarta residents say that they avoid buying frozen foods for a week or so after any long power cut; this may reduce the risk – so long as other shoppers are not all doing the same.

bacteria in sealed bottles of 'mineral' water, and bottled water in other developing countries may be contaminated too. That said, this is the source I use when I'm thirsty and unprepared.

As alternatives to water there are other safe drinks: hot lemon, fresh lime soda, tea and coffee; in Indonesia *air putih* (boiled water served warm, but beware of added ice); in Madagascar *ranovola*; in Latin America camomile tea (*manzanilla*). Starting a meal with hot soup also provides tasty and safe liquid.

Water treatment

Boiling

Boiling is the most effective means of sterilizing water; it kills amoebae and other cyst-formers that are resistant to iodine and chlorine. Purists say that to sterilize water it should be brought to a rolling boil and kept there for a full minute, and that at high altitude (e.g. 5,800m/19,000ft, where water boils at 81°C/178°F) water should be boiled for five minutes. Pressure cookers reduce boiling times and save on fuel. However, merely bringing water to the boil makes it safe enough for most purposes. The flat taste of boiled water disappears if it is left standing for several hours in a partly filled, covered container, or if it is shaken vigorously for a minute in a container with an air gap.

Boiled water is safer than water treated with iodine. Iodine is safer than using chlorine- or bleach-based water sterilization tablets. *Cryptosporidium* and amoebae survive in chlorine, and *Cyclospora* is resistant to iodine and chlorine, but all of these microbes are killed by boiling. If you need water to be completely sterile (e.g. for feeding to babies) ask the restaurant or hotel for some boiling water and fill a thermos flask with it; it will soon be sterile even if it was not absolutely boiling.

Clearly, obtaining boiling or boiled water is not always easy and so most travellers will carry tablets to purify water chemically; note, though, that purification takes time, and that this time is longer if the water is cold. It is best to crush tablets into your water bottle to speed up dissolution and in cold conditions allow an hour for the chemical to work – leave it overnight if possible.

Iodine

Iodine comes in liquid or tablet or crystal forms and produces drinkable water in 20–30 minutes. Add four drops of **tincture of iodine** (usually 2% iodine) or use 3% Lugol's iodine to 1 litre of water, shake and leave to stand for at least 20 minutes. If the water is very cloudy or cold, double the iodine concentration or leave the water to stand for longer (a few hours if possible). Nomad sells tincture in a convenient dropper bottle with neutralizing vitamin C for £7. Lugol's iodine is available for $7.95 from *www.altcancer.com*.

Iodine crystals may be better for longer-term travellers. Make a saturated solution of iodine by roughly quarter-filling a 20ml screw-top bottle with crystals (but note that this form of iodine eats through plastic). Top up with any water. Shake for a few seconds (the crystals settle and nothing appears to dissolve) and leave for at least half an hour. Shake again. Pour about 10ml of the solution (not the crystals) into a 1-litre (1³/₄-pint) bottle and dilute with water; shake and leave for at least 20 minutes. Top up the 20ml bottle ready for the next time it's needed. This should make up to 1,000 litres. A 20ml bottle with volume marks on the side makes it easy to estimate the 10ml volume. A neat alternative is to use crystal iodine, available for $9.49 from *www.campingsurvival.com*.

The somewhat unpleasant taste of iodine is improved by adding vitamin C (*ascorbic acid*) after the 20–30 minute period of sterilization. Alternatively, you can add enough drink powder to cover the taste without making the water sweet, or add a squirt of citrus juice. In Latin America, limes are cheap, available in most markets and travel fairly well; they are also easy to find in much of Asia and parts of Africa.

Toxicity of iodine

It is safe to use iodine – including iodine in iodine-resin water filters – for months at a stretch, but be cautious about using it very long term, especially if you have a thyroid problem, are pregnant or are treating water for young children. It is best to take a variety of safe drinks, including hot or bottled drinks, and boiled and cooled water; thus it will not be necessary to swallow much iodine. Travellers' folklore warns that swallowing concentrated iodine or iodine crystals is dangerous. Nothing dramatic will happen to you; seek medical advice if you feel unwell in the following couple of weeks. Doctors looking after Peace Corps Volunteers recently reported reversible thyroid enlargement (goitre) and other mild symptoms, which were attributed to absorbing at least 330 times the recommended daily intake of 0.15mg iodine. These volunteers were working in Niger, where extremely hot desert conditions required them to drink 5–9 litres of water a day, and the volunteers with symptoms treated their water with a two-stage iodine matrix filter. It was felt that use of a three-stage filter, including a carbon-based third stage to remove iodine, would have reduced or avoided the problem. A cheaper option, and one already adopted by most expatriates, would be to use more boiled water, soups and other safe fluids, and rely less on chemically sterilized water, which in any case doesn't taste as good.

Chlorine and silver

If you don't wish to use iodine, chlorine is the next most effective chemical sterilizer and it comes in tablets such as **Aquatabs**. They cost £3.50 for 50 from

Nomad or $11.95 from *www.purewater2go.com*; the chlorine is pervasive and you'll probably need to add cordial to disguise the flavour, but this must be done after the 30-minute sterilization time. Silver-based sterilizing tablets (Micropur) are tasteless and have a long shelf life but are less effective than both iodine and chlorine products.

Filters and water purification units

Portable filters and purification devices are available for travellers. The newer, pump-action models are a huge improvement on the heavy, slow gravity versions, but they are expensive. Many of the bacteriological filters work well, but check that they remove viruses as well as bacteria: in some places viruses cause over half of diarrhoea cases, and filters that do not remove hepatitis viruses do not render water completely safe unless they also include a form of chemical sterilization. There are various ways of delivering iodine and matrixes are the costliest. Many travel shops now stock a range of filters. For very remote and difficult travel conditions, you may like to take the Millbank bag; this is a canvas bag developed by the British Army and designed to remove sediment before boiling or treating with chemicals. It can produce drinkable water from liquid mud.

The neat, light **SteriPEN** range of devices look useful. They are said to produce safe water in 48 seconds but the cheapest in the range costs more than £68 or $89; they also need batteries or a solar charger. Nomad, Cotswold and REI sell them.

Ceramic water filters designed for use in the kitchen are readily available in the Indian subcontinent (but not Indonesia), and they allow expatriates to organize a ready supply of safe water. The Ceramic filter candles might seem crude but they effectively exclude bacteria as well as sediment: Dalton filter candles, for example, have a pore size of 0.22 microns. Do check the filter candles for cracks and clean the filter by scrubbing, then boil the candles for 20 minutes once every couple of weeks; otherwise you may introduce more bugs than were in the original water supply. Ideally, you should filter the tap water first, boil it in a large covered saucepan, and allow it to cool a little, then pour it into bottles for refrigeration.

Interesting research from Dhaka reported dramatic reduction in cholera cases in people who filter their water through clean but worn out saris. Single cloth gives a pore size of 150 microns but folded into eight gives a 20-micron filter. *Cholera vibrio*s survive well in rivers and ponds because of their taste for chitin (the protein common in plankton and crustaceans) so filtration even at a crude level improves water quality and reduces the chances of disease transfer. The message, then, is drink from as clean a source as you can and filter with whatever you can improvise if you are caught out in a survival situation.

What's swimming about in your glass of water

There is a huge range of sizes among the mischievous microbes that may contaminate drinking water. Knowing the pore sizing of your water filtration device will help you judge what it can do. The Aqua Pure Traveller, for example, has a 0.2-micron filter, which means it will exclude all the organisms listed overleaf except hepatitis and other viruses.

Sizes of microbes responsible for travellers' intestinal infections

Microbe (cysts, eggs, etc.)	Approx sizes of cyst/egg in microns (smallest diameter)	Water treatments (boiling also kills all of these)
Hepatitis A virus	0.03	killed by iodine (chlorine is less effective)
Listeria bacterium	0.5 x 1	killed by chemical treatments
Most bacteria (Shigella, ETEC, Campylobacter, Salmonella)	0.5 x 2	filterable; usually killed by iodine and other chemicals
Cholera bacterium	3–6	filterable; killed by iodine and chlorine
Cryptosporidium cyst	4	filterable; chlorine resistant
Giardia cyst	7	filterable; iodine usually kills but chlorine resistant
Cyclospora cyst	8	filterable; iodine and chlorine resistant
Entamoeba (amoebic dysentery) cyst	10	filterable; killed by iodine (chlorine is less effective)
Tapeworm (Taenia) egg	31	readily filtered
Roundworm (Ascaris) egg	35	readily filtered; extremely resistant to chemicals
Hookworm egg	36	readily filtered
Schistosome egg	70+	readily filtered
Fluke (Fasciola)	100	readily filtered
Guinea worm	500–700 long	readily filtered, even through only a cloth

Few filters will take out viruses like hepatitis A and, even if the filter is fine enough to exclude this virus, it will clog up easily and is impractical for travel use. Iodine or chlorine or boiling kills viruses. Boiling kills all the microbes listed. See the table above for a list of microbes and their sizes.

Contact information: stockists of water filters

The following offer a wide choice of water filters:

Camping Survival, US **t** 1 800 537 1339, *www.campingsurvival.com*.

Cotswold, UK **t** (01285) 860 612, **f** (01285) 860 483, *www.cotswoldoutdoor.com*.

Nomad, UK **t** (020) 8889 7014, **f** (020) 889 9529, *www.nomadtravel.co.uk/catalog*. Sells water treatment supplies, bottles and Millbank bags; *see* **Useful Addresses**, pp.301–4, for details of Nomad stores.
REI, US **t** 1 800 426 4840, *www.rei.com*.

Preventing diarrhoea with medicines

Taking medicine to prevent diarrhoea can create more problems than it solves. The US Navy is particularly active in researching ways to avoid travellers' diarrhoea. Interestingly, even they (perhaps less interested in the long-term health of their personnel than civilian doctors) do not recommend prevention with antibiotics, even on short missions. The best precautions are to travel with '*peel it, boil it, cook it, shell it or forget it*' in your mind, knowledge of rehydration procedures, and perhaps a course of *ciprofloxacin*.

Natural preventatives

The idea that it is beneficial to eat certain kinds of fermented foods goes back centuries, and today there is a vogue for eating live yoghurt, 'probiotics' or other products containing 'friendly' bacteria. *Lactobacilli* and their friends don't seem to be much help in preventing travellers' gastroenteritis but they are of benefit after you are struck with the squits. In a bout of travellers' diarrhoea, the bacteria normally inhabiting the bowel take a hammering, and replacing battle-worn friendly bacteria with fresh reinforcements helps you heal. Pharmacies, drug stores and health food shops sell *lactobacilli*-loaded drinks, capsules and powders. These are also useful to replenish friendly bacteria after a course of antibiotics has been completed.

Charcoal also has some modest effect on diarrhoea, and some travellers find it helpful, especially if the upset is associated with a lot of bloating, as charcoal absorbs noxious gases. North American travellers often take *bismuth subsalicylate* for their gastrointestinal symptoms and this probably helps a little.

Stomach acid is the body's first line of defence against any swallowed pathogens so people who take antacids or acid blockers like *ranitidine*, *lansoprazole* and *omeprazole* are probably more prone to diarrhoeal disease and other intestinal infections. Antacids will also increase the risk of acquiring brucellosis, so veterinary surgeons should think twice about taking them. Boiling milk products before consumption will eliminate brucellosis and Q-fever organisms.

In infants, the best protection against diarrhoea is **breast-feeding**, so if you plan to travel with small children try to ensure they are breast-fed rather than formula-fed if possible. Ideally, children should not be weaned off the breast until the age of a year. In many developing countries, it is common for local children to be breast-fed for two or three years (and this is what the World Health Organization, WHO, recommends); this is an excellent and healthy practice, and good for Mum's figure too.

Case history: Nepal

Two Nepalis supported a middle-aged American man on a horse. The American had suffered a sleepless night disturbed by diarrhoea; this, along with trekking the Annapurna circuit, had finished him.

'Dehydration is making you feel awful. You need to drink three litres a day to keep your body's fluids topped up – as well as replace all that you have lost to diarrhoea and breathing hard at altitude,' I said.

'I drank a quart this morning and one of those rehydration salt packets, so I'm not dehydrated.' He ordered a cola and I suggested adding a pinch of salt. 'No, I got all the salts I need from that packet.'

The salt would help him absorb the water in the drink, but he did not want advice and struggled on. He needed to drink a lot more. He also misunderstood the role of rehydration packets. They are not a once-only medicine, but a vehicle for fluid transport into the body. They also give a glucose-fired energy burst, which makes you feel really good and enthusiastic enough for serious (non-alcoholic) drinking.

Treating diarrhoea

Diarrhoea is a good thing. It is the natural process of expelling the poisons that cause disease. Unnatural 'blocking' medicines can prolong the time you feel unwell. A healthy adult is unlikely to come to any great harm from travellers' diarrhoea: a light, bland diet and lots of clear fluids will settle the symptoms quickly. In the very few travellers who become especially ill, it is adequate fluid replacement that saves life, not antibiotics or anti-diarrhoeal medicines. Passing blood and/or mucus and/or having a fever with diarrhoea probably means you have dysentery, which may require treatment in addition to fluid replacement (*see* below). If you have to get on a bus while ill with diarrhoea, beware of the gastro-colic reflex (*see* p.112). Mild diarrhoeal symptoms should respond to a couple of doses of the natural remedy **ispaghula husk**; *see* **Ailments**, p.264.

Replacing lost fluids

A normal adult diet provides about 3 litres (5 pints) of fluid a day, so when you stop eating, you need this PLUS anything that is being lost down the toilet. The usual processes of food and fluid absorption become less efficient when you have diarrhoea, yet simple mixtures of sugar, salt and water continue to be well absorbed by the stomach and upper intestine. In fact, they are taken in more efficiently than plain water. Complex carbohydrates (salty crackers, dry bread, unbuttered toast and jam, pasta, plain rice or boiled potatoes) also aid absorption of the fluids you need to replace those you are losing into the toilet. The fastest road back to health, then, is to take lots of clear fluids. If you are hungry, take a light, bland diet for 24–36 hours; if you do not feel like eating, do not eat. Avoid milk and alcohol.

Good drinks to take are clear soups, young coconut, drinks made from Marmite, Bovril or stock (bouillon) cubes , herbal infusions, Malagasy *ranovola*, hot lemon, lemon tea and fizzy drinks (cola or Fanta); weak black tea and coffee may also be taken. Combinations of sugar and salt are absorbed best, so add a pinch of salt to sweet drinks or a spoonful of sugar to savoury drinks. Alternatively, drink oral rehydration salts (ORS). These are available in most countries: Electrolade, Dioralyte, Rehidrat in the UK, Oralit in Indonesia and Jeevan Jal (literally 'water of life') in Nepal. ORS are best for children, the frail, those with long-standing medical problems and anyone with very profuse (12 times a day) diarrhoea. Most adult travellers, though, will be fine taking clear fluid and/or their own home-made sugar-and-salt solution.

Home-made oral rehydration solution (ORS)

Two heaped teaspoons (or a four-finger scoop) of glucose (or sugar) and a three-finger pinch (less than a quarter of a teaspoon) of salt should be mixed in a large glass of boiled, cooled water, or eight level teaspoons of sugar and a level teaspoonful of salt in 1 litre (1³/₄ pints). Otherwise, use a sugar and salt measuring spoon (which may be bought from travel clinics or TALC, see **Useful Addresses**, pp.303). The solution should taste no more salty than tears.

Most forms of sugar can be used; raw, unrefined sugars or molasses (ghur in Hindi/Urdu) are better than nice white stuff as they are rich in potassium, which the body loses during diarrhoea and vomiting. You can also use palm syrup or honey. Fresh lemon, lime or orange juice improves flavour and adds therapeutic potassium.

How much do you need to drink?

Dehydration is a common complication of diarrhoea, and makes sufferers feel really awful. Most people make the mistake of not drinking enough. To maintain fluid balance, a healthy person of normal build who is not eating needs to drink about three litres a day. Fluid requirements are greater in heat, at altitude, in high winds, travelling in cars with the windows open or on a bike, or when breast-feeding. If you have diarrhoea or fever you need still more. Drink two glassfuls each time you open your bowels, and more if thirsty. Vomiters can absorb fluids if they drink slowly, in sips.

Case history: Peru

A phone call: 'Julian looks awful, feels faint, can hardly get out of bed, bad diarrhoea, dizzy, splitting headache. Could it be cholera? Isn't there a cholera epidemic in the country? Should he fly home?'

I asked a few questions. Most of the symptoms seemed to be due to fluid loss and fear that he was desperately ill: he did, after all, feel deathly. Why else could he hardly stand up? They had rehydration salts (ORS) in the house. 'See if you can drink at least a litre of clear fluids in the next hour; slow the drinking rate if you feel nauseated.'

I called round 90 minutes later to find a pale, stocky man in his twenties looking very sorry for himself. I estimated he had lost 5% of his body fluids: he was badly dehydrated.

'How are you getting on with the drinking?'

'Fresh orange juice gives me stomach ache. I've had half a glassful.'

He needed to replace 4.5 litres, plus two glassfuls every time he opened his bowels. He was surprised at the volume and by the need to take only clear fluids, but was now convinced enough to settle down to some real drinking. He could not stomach ORS. Diluting the juice made it easier on his aching belly, and he made some glucose and salt solution too. Two hours later, the headache and dizziness had gone, and he felt much better.

Dehydration can make you feel dizzy (or even faint) when getting out of bed or a chair. Drink more, move slowly and sit with your legs over the side of the bed before rising. If you are passing only a scant amount of dark-coloured urine, you must drink more.

The gastro-colic reflex

Very hot or very cold drinks and foods tend to provoke a reflex bowel action and abdominal pain. This gastro-colic reflex can be useful if you are constipated; a hot drink first thing in the morning encourages a bowel action. However, beware of what you take just before boarding a bus. If you have diarrhoea with a lot of abdominal crampy pains, take only food and drink that is tepid or at room temperature. Cramps are more likely if you eat indigestible food when your stomach is upset. Then, take only a light, fat-free diet.

Abdominal pains and **irritable-bowel-type symptoms** are common during or just after an attack of diarrhoea. *Hyoscine* (e.g. Buscopan) 20mg when needed (up to four times a day), *mebeverine* (e.g. Colofac) one 135mg tablet three times daily, or *peppermint* (e.g. Colpermin) 1–2 capsules three times daily, can help. If pain persists, get a stool test. Finally, be aware than an over-active bowel can increase the appetite and make you more **hungry**.

What to eat when diarrhoea strikes

Drink plenty, but if you have no appetite, eat nothing. Otherwise, try a little light food. Bananas help stop diarrhoea and also contain plenty of essential potassium. Yoghurt can help settle the stomach by replacing diarrhoea-causing bacteria with friendly ones, but avoid other dairy products. Dry biscuits or bread can also be comforting to an aching, empty stomach. When the appetite returns, start by eating only pure unadulterated starch: plain boiled rice, potatoes, couscous, pasta, butterless toast and jam, etc. Children who have diarrhoea should be encouraged to eat when and what they can. All sufferers should avoid solid, greasy foods, which often cause abdominal pains as the bowel tries to expel them.

Treatment of children

When children have diarrhoea, dehydration is a particular risk. Like adults, they should be encouraged to drink each time they open their bowels; half a glass of fluid is enough for small children. Children can get into trouble with the balance of salts in their blood, especially with profuse diarrhoea. Oral rehydration sachets mixed with boiled and cooled water are the safest remedy. ORS taste awful, though, so it is often more realistic to offer cola with a pinch of salt in it. Otherwise, offer home-made solutions flavoured with fruit cordial or some other tempting cocktail. Getting children to drink is crucial. Babies with severe diarrhoea need checking over by a doctor.

Important note for parents: Infants and very small children have died from too much salt in home-made rehydration drinks, so, if in doubt, give too little salt or none at all. Sugar or glucose and water alone make an acceptable rehydration solution. Babies should continue to be breast-fed. Solid foods should be given as usual.

When to use medicines

Blockers – the 'blocking' medicines such as Imodium, Lomotil and *codeine phosphate* – are not the cure for diarrhoea that they may appear. Blockers work by paralysing the muscles of the bowel, trapping noxious bugs and poisons within the body. Vital fluids may not pour out of your bottom, but they can become pooled in inaccessible pockets. Blockers can be useful if you cannot postpone a bus journey for 24 hours, but they tend to make you feel ill for longer so are best taken in combination with an antibiotic (*see* below). It is dangerous to give blockers to children and anyone with dysentery (diarrhoea with fever and the passing of blood and/or mucus). **Enterovioform** was banned as dangerous years ago, yet it is still available in some places (e.g. Thailand). Avoid this too.

Bismuth appears to reduce the amount of fluids lost during diarrhoea and probably also kills some of the bacteria, yet it does not have the disadvantages of antibiotics. It can be used to prevent or treat diarrhoea and can be taken as *bismuth subsalicylate* tablets twice daily, up to 2.1g in 24 hours. The downsides are that it causes an unpleasant taste, nausea and blackening of the tongue and stools. In the UK it is only available over the counter as a liquid and the volumes required probably make it impractical for British travellers to take abroad.

Antibiotics and treatment of severe/bloody diarrhoea

Diarrhoea is generally short-lived (up to 50 hours), so treatment with drugs is rarely necessary. If, though, diarrhoea is accompanied by fever and/or blood in the faeces, or is very profuse, 'blocking' drugs like *loperamide* must be avoided. Instead, it would be sensible to take an antibiotic as well as plenty of rehydration fluids. This should bring relief quickly and safely. *Ciprofloxacin* 500mg twice daily for three days, *norfloxacin* 400mg twice daily for three days or *levofloxacin* 500mg daily are good remedies for severe and/or bloody diarrhoea. *Ciprofloxacin* is not recommended for young children or growing adolescents, in pregnancy, and probably not for athletes, epileptics or people with other neurological problems. *Ciprofloxacin*, *norfloxacin* and related antibiotics can cause tendon inflammation; tendon ruptures have been reported in competitive athletes after *Cipro* treatment, so mountaineers and trekkers may also experience problems. *Nalidixic acid* (for adults, 1g four times daily for seven days) is an alternative and it is reasonably safe for children; this can be bought as GramoNeg 'oral suspension' in India. With all these drugs you must still take plenty (i.e. litres) of clear fluids: at least two glasses every time you open your bowels. For more on the advantages or otherwise of taking antibiotics, *see* pp.36–8.

Even if you have treated yourself with antibiotics, if the symptoms are not beginning to settle after 48 hours it is wise to consult a doctor, or at least arrange a stool test. Persistent abdominal pain, bloody diarrhoea, a fever, confusion setting in, or diarrhoea that goes on for more than three days suggest that you need medical help.

New treatments

Different antibiotics work well or less well in different regions. At the time of writing, *ciprofloxacin* and related fluroquinolone antibiotics are still the drugs of choice for treating tropical gastrointestinal infections in travellers. However, resistance is developing, especially in Asia, and it is likely that new antibiotics will become more useful in the coming years. A **new antibiotic** to treat travellers' diarrhoea has become available in the USA, Spain, Germany, Italy and other countries. This is *rifaximin* (Normix, Flonorm, Redactiv and Zaxine) and appears to cure with few side effects. It is effective in treating gastrointestinal infections that cause fever. Interestingly, the medicine is not absorbed into the body: it stays in the gut in high concentrations killing gram-positive and gram-negative bacteria. It may also have some curative effect on *cryptosporidia*. The antibiotics *bicozamycin* and *aztreonam* have also been shown to be very effective and safe in the treatment of travellers' diarrhoea, but they have never been marketed and are not currently available; they may reappear in future, however.

Stool tests

Medical laboratories in developing countries are often expert at checking stool samples. Make sure that the sample you give is fresh (preferably still warm). If your stools are very liquid, collect a sample into a washed yoghurt pot or, if the consistency allows, poo onto paper and transfer a small amount into the pot provided by the laboratory. Often these pots come with a spoon. The lab only needs a pea-sized amount. The simplest investigation, which almost any laboratory can do, is look at it under a microscope. If the technician sees mucus or red blood cells (RBC) this indicates dysentery, requiring antibiotic treatment (your result may say 'RBC +', which means that some bloodcells have been seen; '++', quite a few; or '+++', lots). The type of antibiotic depends on the symptoms, not the number of + signs. Explosive, profuse diarrhoea and fever means bacillary dysentery, cured by *ciprofloxacin, norfloxacin, nalidixic acid*; milder symptoms suggest amoebae needing *tinidazole* or *metronidazole* (Flagyl). Worms' eggs can be another finding, but these do not do any harm (and don't usually cause diarrhoea) and can wait for treatment until a more convenient time. More sophisticated laboratories can identify bacteria and work out which antibiotic will kill them most effectively, but this takes a few days and you may be better or far away by the time you get the result. A look under the microscope is all you need unless a serious problem, such as typhoid, is suspected. With most intestinal parasites, you need three negative checks several days apart to be sure you are not infected. *See also* table on p.118.

Diarrhoea that goes on and on

Diarrhoea that goes on for more than three to four days should be treated; if no doctor is available try one of the antibiotics suggested above. Diarrhoea can occasionally persist for months (often labelled **tropical sprue**). Sufferers lose a lot of

> **Case history: Torquay?**
>
> Our luxurious beachside hotel in Turkey offered a wonderful buffet each day. I wanted to avoid putting on too much weight, though, and ate lots of salad. At the end of the second week of the holiday, I developed diarrhoea, which got worse and worse until I was passing almost pure blood. I felt ill, nauseated and developed intermittent feverish shakes. I tried to keep up with fluid loss by drinking, but misjudged it. I became worse and was admitted to a local, small and clean, but isolated hospital for a drip and antibiotics, where they said I'd contracted dysentery from the salad. The subsequent four-hour flight home to the UK was disastrous, with lots of nauseated and bloated trips to the over-popular loo, followed immediately by emergency admission and a week of further in-patient treatment on an infectious diseases ward. The bemused doctor in hospital admissions said, 'So, Simon, I hear you've been to Torquay...?'
>
> *the late Dr Simon Boniface*

weight. It is not a well-understood disease, but often responds to *tetracycline* (250mg four times daily) and *folic acid* (5mg daily) for 6–12 weeks. Experiment to see whether avoiding milk and dairy products, fatty, oily and spicy foods and alcohol helps reduce the symptoms. Persistent diarrhoea often gets better when you get home, even without treatment.

Nearly all diarrhoea in travellers is due to bacteria and viruses, but in a tiny minority it is due to some other cause. Protracted diarrhoea could be the start of another, non-tropical problem such as colitis or even bowel cancer so a proper medical assessment is needed.

Filth-to-mouth diseases

Amoebic dysentery (*Entamoeba histolytica*)

Dysentery sounds scary but this form can be mild, and will not usually make you feel particularly unwell. However, the blood in your stools suggests that you need some treatment: take *tinidazole* (Fasigyn) 2g (4x500mg tablets) daily for three days or *metronidazole* (Flagyl) 800mg (2x400mg) every eight hours for five days. Do not drink alcohol with Flagyl or you will feel ill. If you have no symptoms, but amoebic cysts are found in your stools (*see* 'Stool tests', opposite, and table on p.128), you can take

> **'Irritable bowel syndrome' or is it?**
>
> Normal intestines are lined with microscopic finger-like villi, which increase the surface area for ease of absorption of foods and fluids. Severe or long-lasting bouts of diarrhoea or dysentery temporarily destroy the villi and this further increases the rate at which gut contents whizz through the bowel. Worse, there can be a temporary allergy to milk sugars, which further exacerbates the diarrhoea. This though should settle on six weeks of a lactose- (dairy-) free diet.
>
> Irritable bowel symptoms (IBS) – notably bloating, discomfort, urgency and an erratic bowel habit – is common especially in someone who is stressed. It is also common after tropical trips. *Mebeverine* (Colofac) tablets with meals help a great deal and peppermint can soothe, but see also 'giardia', p.117.

A Case of irritable bowel syndrome from the Canaries?

My patient had returned from the Canary Islands. He'd had diarrhoea for two weeks and felt weak and washed out so he'd treated his lethargy by taking a diet of Complan, cheese and whole milk. These rich foods are exactly the worst foods to eat when the bowel is upset. He was cured rapidly by simply avoiding dairy products, and eating lots of starch: pasta, rice, toast and jam. By avoiding milk for six weeks the villi recover and any temporary 'allergy' to milk sugar disappears completely. In this rehabilitation diet, it is all right to eat yoghurt.

Although persistent diarrhoea can be sparked off by travel, it can also be a sign of a new non-travel-related problem. Post-trip diarrhoea that goes on and on is never 'normal'.

diloxanide furoate 500mg every eight hours for 10 days. 'Blocking' drugs like *loperamide* should be avoided if you have dysentery.

Bacillary (bacterial) dysentery

This form of dysentery causes profuse, explosive and bloody diarrhoea with fever, and makes you feel very unwell. *Shigella* is such a powerful microbe that you need only swallow 10 to be struck with severe bacillary dysentery (*see* 'Stool tests', p. 114). It needs antibiotic treatment and lots and lots of clear drinks. 'Blocking' drugs like *loperamide* make dysentery worse.

Campylobacter

This is the commonest cause in food poisoning and gastroenteritis in Britain; as few as 500 bacteria cause infection. Symptoms start two to five days after eating poorly cooked chicken or other meat or unwashed salad. There is abdominal cramping, profuse (sometimes bloody) diarrhoea, fever, aches and pains, plus fatigue. Vomiting is uncommon. The illness is usually over in five days but can go on for 10. It can be treated with *ciprofloxacin* or *erythromycin*.

Cholera (*Vibrio*)

The disease rarely causes symptoms in well-nourished, healthy people. Profuse watery diarrhoea is often due to ETEC bacteria, not cholera. Normal travellers don't usually need to be immunized against cholera, but the new oral vaccine, Dukoral, protects for two years. It also gives a little short-term (three months') protection against travellers' diarrhoea.

Cryptosporidium

This parasite causes a particularly tedious type of diarrhoea lasting between 10 days and two weeks, with a lot of abdominal cramps. You only need to swallow 10 cysts to become infected with *cryptosporidium*, but heating drinking water to only 65°C (145°F) will kill any cysts. There is no specific treatment, although the new *rifaximin* (Normix, Flonorm, Redactiv and Zaxine) may be effective. *Cryptosporidium* can be acquired from swallowing contaminated water in swimming pools and occasionally it gets into the water supply in the developed world; 2–6% of diarrhoea in the industrialized countries is due to *cryptosporidium*.

Cyclospora

These parasites resemble blue-green algae and were first discovered in travellers in Nepal in 1990. *Cyclospora* outbreaks occur there between mid-April and

Case history: India

While travelling in South America I was incapacitated by two acute episodes of vomiting and diarrhoea, and for most of the trip I had diarrhoea of some sort. I was advised to try taking grapefruit seed extract. I then spent eight weeks in India and Nepal during which time I took grapefruit seed extract every morning. In that two months I had the odd day or two of diarrhoea but on the whole had relatively normal bowels. It tastes disgusting, works really well and is available from your local health food shop.

Sue Garrett, New Zealander based in Hanwell

November, with a peak in July. During this season water should be boiled, as chemical sterilization does not kill the cysts. *Cyclospora* diarrhoea lasts 2–12 weeks if untreated. It tends to cause dramatic weight loss – of as much as 10kg (22lb). It has now turned up all over the less developed world and the USA. Treatment is with *co-trimoxazole* (e.g. Bactrim or Septrin); *trimethoprim* alone will not help.

Giardia

Giardia lamblia are elegant heart-shaped parasites that swim around the intestine propelled by two splendid whiskers. They can be picked up anywhere from Mumbai to Michigan; indeed, they are a hazard of summer and autumn trips to the American northwest and the Great Lakes. *Giardia* can be acquired from swallowing contaminated water in swimming pools. Probably only 10 cysts need to get into your stomach for you to suffer.

Infection, called *giardiasis*, upsets the stomach, causes sulphurous, foul-smelling belches and farts, abdominal distension and often protracted diarrhoea. It is sometimes misdiagnosed as i**rritable bowel syndrome**. *Giardia* is probably the most over-diagnosed, inappropriately treated travellers' ailment; if you think you have it, get a stool check before rushing to take antibiotics. First, try 24 hours on clear fluids and a bland, very low-fat diet (*see* 'What to eat when diarrhoea strikes', p.112). Other microbes cause similar symptoms, and untreated *giardiasis* usually does little harm other than make you an unwelcome guest. One fairly specific symptom is passing stools that stink, float and are difficult to flush away (there are other causes of this, so if treatment for *giardia* doesn't work, find a doctor).

The usual treatment is *tinidazole* (Fasigyn), a single 2g dose daily for two days, or *metronidazole* (Flagyl) 2g (e.g. 5x400mg) daily for three days. Do not drink alcohol with Flagyl or you will feel ill. Treatment failures with *metronidazole* are becoming more common, but a second course often eradicates the parasite. Alternative treatments for recalcitrant *giardiasis* is *albendazole* 400mg four times a day for seven days or *quinacrine* 100mg three times daily, although the latter is not yet widely available. *Furazolidone* is also usually effective against *giardia*. If symptoms return it is best to get another stool sample checked before trying more antibiotics.

To name a few rarer bugs

Isospora is a parasite that occurs especially in the Caribbean and tropical Africa; it causes similar symptoms to *cyclospora* and is also treatable with *co-trimoxazole*; those unable to take Bactrim because they are sulphur-drug allergic should get some benefit from *ciprofloxacin*. Other parasites can turn up in stool samples but not all microbes identified by a laboratory are harmful. There is still a debate, for

Microbes that are commonly detected from stool gazing – through a microscope – after a trip to the tropics

microbe	symptoms	treatments
Shigella	Bacilliary dysentery. Explosive severe diarrhoea usually with fever (>38°C) and cramps	Rehydration plus an antibiotic e.g. ciprofloxacin
Campylobacter	Diarrhoea with abdominal cramps and often blood in the stool; also aching joints for a week	Rehydration plus an antibiotic e.g. ciprofloxacin
Cholera	Usually none in previously healthy travellers	Rehydration; antibiotic rarely necessary
Entomoeba histolytica	Often mild but labelled as amoebic dysentery, which sounds scary	Metronidazole for 10 days
Entomoeba coli	None but these are a sign of faeces having got into the mouth	None needed
Giardia	Can be mild; often bloating and smelly sulphurous gas; can cause long-standing irritable bowel type symptoms	Metronidazole for 3 days or tinidazole twice
Blastocystis hominis	Sometimes none; sometimes persistent mild diarrhoea	Metronidazole for 7 days
Cryptosporidium	Diarrhoea with cramps for 10 days	None available; rehydration
Cyclospora	Diarrhoea associated with weight loss of several kilos; comes and goes over several weeks	Co-trimoxazole for 7 days plus rehydration
Schistosoma (bilharzias)	Fever; sometimes diarrhoea	Praziquantel one big dose
Strongyloides worms	Gastrointestinal chaos	albenzazole or tiabendazole for 3 days
Ascaris, trichuris and other worm eggs	Can be few; Ascaris is sometimes seen in the lavatory bowl	Metronidazole for 3 days

example, about whether **blastocystis** is a cause of diarrhoea in travellers or rather only a marker of faecal contamination. Treatment with metronidazole will eradicate both blastocystis and giardia so sometimes it is worth a try. **Dientomoeba fragilis** is another parasite that is occasionally seen in the stools of travellers with recurrent diarrhoea; sufferers who have a blood count often have increased eosinophils. There is some evidence that infection is transmitted along with pinworm. **Dientomoeba** is treated with tetracycline 500mg four times a day for 10 days.

Finally **microsporidia** (Enterocystozoon bieneusi) are reasonably common parasites (8% of Dutch blood donors carry them) that can cause persistent diarrhoea in people with a poor immune status; albendazole clears it up.

On the Ground: Worms, Guts and Nutrition

Worms 120
  Where is worm heaven? 120
Catching a worm 120
Know your worm 121
Problems from bad food 123
  Local alcohol 123
  Food for free 124
  Risky seafood 124
  Other hazards of exotic eating 127
Nutrition 127

10

Summary

→ Diarrhoea and a great variety of parasites can be acquired from contaminated food that has been inadequately cooked but few will do you much harm.

→ In regions where sanitation is poor, eating rare or raw steak or pork puts you at risk of tapeworm.

→ Worms are alarming but rarely dangerous.

→ Eat piping hot, thoroughly cooked food; avoid salads.

→ Pay attention to local cooking methods and eating habits. They have generally been developed to minimize risks to health; the exception is foods that are served raw.

→ Seafood, freshwater crustaceans and fish should be thoroughly cooked before eating.

→ Avoid eating seafood if you are a long way from the sea.

→ Reject fish with a peppery or bitter taste or which causes a tingling or smarting sensation in the mouth (some tinned fish prepared in Southeast Asia has added pepper or chilli).

→ Never eat fruits and berries unless you know they are harmless; things that look like tomatoes are often highly poisonous.

→ Vegetables or fruits with a bitter, stinging or disagreeable taste may be toxic; if in doubt, try them with the tip of your tongue.

→ Don't worry about whether you are getting a healthy diet (vitamin pills are rarely necessary) but aim for variety in the foods you eat.

Worms

Trying new foods is a delight of travel but some travellers imagine that unpleasant parasites may lurk within that squid, guinea pig or armadillo. Is that concern justified?

Where is worm heaven?

Wormy parasites prevail all over the globe. Wherever disposal of faeces is inadequate, they infest people in large enough numbers to impact on their health. Certainly in communities were people don't get enough food, they add to the burden of those struggling for survival. Worms are unaesthetic but, fortunately, a well-fed traveller is unlikely to be greatly affected if they do acquire a wormy hitch-hiker.

Hookworm occurs in all moist, hot parts of the world. Roundworms are especially hardy parasites, which occur in most unhygienic environments, and can survive the harsh freeze-drying of the high, cold deserts of Tibet. *Trichinella* and tapeworms exist wherever cattle or pigs eat fodder contaminated with human excreta. Threadworms are universal wherever there are children, from Croydon to Cambodia. Other worms, including a range of unpleasant flukes, are acquired by eating raw or lightly-cooked fish and shellfish, or water plants such as watercress that have been polluted by excrement.

Catching a worm

Few parasitic worms are transmitted directly from person to person. Roundworms (and sometimes hookworms) are acquired from contaminated food, via some of the same transmission mechanisms as diarrhoeal diseases (*see* p.100). Worm life-cycles, though, are more complex. Most worm eggs need a period of maturation in soil before they can infect people. Tapeworms and *Trichinella* usually need to pass through an intermediate animal host before they can infect man. Threadworms can be transmitted directly from hand to mouth – most commonly among people in close contact with children. These and some tapeworms are the only worms spread directly from one person to another.

There are differences in the ways each type of worm is acquired, but with the exception of hookworm they can be avoided with good food hygiene. Thorough cooking destroys any that lurk in food. Hookworm is mostly avoided by wearing shoes.

Know your worm

There are many to choose from, but those described here illustrate the most common problems, and avoidance strategies are given.

Roundworm (*Ascaris lumbricoides*)

Roundworms are common. In the non-industrialized tropics and sub-tropics they inhabit 80–90% of children. Roundworms look like large pale unsegmented earthworms and are about 30cm (12in) long. They rarely cause problems unless they're present in very large numbers (100 or more) and, since travellers seldom acquire more than one or two, infestations are generally no trouble, even if passing a roundworm is a horrible experience. These worms may be responsible for vague abdominal symptoms, but most people are unaware of their presence until one that has died of old age emerges a year or so after it stowed away.

It is dangerous to take some worm tablets if you are pregnant, and some treatments are unsafe in children under age two, so be careful if you decide to treat yourself. Waiting to take treatment is a safe option if you are pregnant. Roundworms cannot be passed directly from person to person.

Hookworm (*Ancylostoma and Nector*)

Hookworm can be acquired from contaminated food, but is more often picked up by walking barefoot in damp, shady places where people have defecated. The pollution need not be obvious. Worms penetrate the skin, sometimes causing a transient patch of itchy flaky skin (*see* also 'The geography worm or *Larva Migrans*', p.211). Sunshine and dryness kill hookworm; shoes protect you. Hookworms cause few problems, and any stowaways will die out on returning to a temperate climate. Treatment for hookworm is never urgent (I wouldn't bother to get them treated), but for anyone over the age of two, the remedy is *mebendazole* 100mg twice daily for three days.

Expatriate children can suffer significantly from hookworm. Avoid infestation by discouraging barefoot play; any sand pit should be dried in the sun for a week or two before use. Hookworm cannot be passed directly from person to person.

Strongyloides

Strongyloides worms may also penetrate bare feet in unhygienic places. They cause rashes and diarrhoea but, once diagnosed, treatment is easy (*see also* 'Case history: Madagascar rain forest', p.209).

Threadworm (*Enterobius vermicularis*)

These are tiny and cause intense anal itching, especially at night. A hazard of family life (at home and abroad), they are usually acquired from children, and transmit readily within the household so treat each member of the family. Intolerable itching will drive you to seek treatment; take *piperazine* (Antepar, Pripsen in the UK; Antepar, Vermizine in the USA) for seven days. Cure rates are improved if a second course is given after a week; *piperazine* should not be taken by people with epilepsy. *Mebendazole* (Vermox, Ovex in the UK; Vermox, Wormin in the USA) given as a single 100mg dose, repeated two to three weeks later, is better, but must not be given in pregnancy (expatriates must take care when treating female employees), nor to children aged under age two. Personal hygiene must be scrupulous while the infestation is present. Fingernails must be kept short, and hands washed and nails scrubbed with a brush before meals and after each visit to the toilet. Otherwise, those infected will reinfect themselves and others.

Rarer parasites

Tapeworms look like strips of ribbon or pasta in the stools and, alarmingly, may crawl about. They are avoided by ensuring any meat is well cooked. The **pork tapeworm**, *Taenium solium*, can also be acquired by eating foods contaminated with human excreta: a source can be lettuce irrigated with 'night soil' (human sewage), as happens in China, Bolivia, Peru, Nepal and elsewhere. Cysts then settle in the brain, eyes or muscles. This **cystocercosis** is worth avoiding; see a doctor if you think you are infected.

Undercooked pork, wild boar, walrus, polar bear and even occasionally horse-meat can give you *Trichinella*, which are also called 'muscle worms'. Eating inadequately cooked pork or lamb can give you **toxoplasma**, a parasite which is dangerous in pregnancy. It can also be contracted by contact with cat faeces. Finally, eating off plates licked by dogs carries a risk of acquiring another difficult-to-treat worm infestation, **hydatid disease**.

Guinea worm (*dracunculiasis*, Medina worm, aka the 'fiery serpent') is caught by swallowing 1–2mm-long freshwater 'fleas' (*Cyclops*). The mature female worm develops from the larvae within the water flea; they can measure up to 100cm (39in) in length but are just 1–2mm in diameter. This worm is rapidly nearing extinction. It now only occurs in sub-Saharan Africa. Three-quarters of cases are in Sudan and the parasite is still prevalent in Nigeria, Ghana and Burkina Faso. Water that has been boiled or crudely strained through a cloth is safe. Don't worry about it.

Case history: Bolivia

Sara was 20 and teaching English for a year in La Paz. Suddenly, inexplicably, she began to suffer from fainting fits, and developed little lumps under her skin. Weirder still, she saw shadows passing before one eye. Then a friend noticed that during one of Sara's 'faints' she twitched slightly: this was something more serious than a faint. She went to hospital for tests. She had **cystocercosis**, cysts of the pork tapeworm *Taenium solium*, in her brain, eyes and under the skin. Hospital treatment cured her and she is now fine.

Sara was careful to avoid drinking tap water, but she enjoyed eating out and had a particular liking for lettuce in salads. Much of the lettuce sold in La Paz is irrigated with the city's effluent. This is also a risk in other cities and towns in the developing world.

Capillariasis

This, another worm infestation, is a Southeast Asian seafood special. Capillariasis is a weird wasting disease first described in the Philippines (Luzon and Mindanao), where it was traced to the Philippine delicacy called 'jumping salad', made from live shrimps seasoned with vinegar, garlic and chilli. (The shrimps jump on being sprinkled with vinegar.) Capillariasis also occurs in Thailand and Japan and can be caught from raw crabs, snails and fish. The infestation becomes debilitating if not treated, but is treatable once diagnosed.

Problems from bad food

The term 'food poisoning' usually suggests the contamination of food with the bacteria or viruses that cause diarrhoea and vomiting; such problems are covered in **Bowels**, pp.101–9. Other 'germs' can also reach you through bad food: an outbreak of streptococcal tonsillitis, for example, was traced to poorly prepared food.

In addition to bacterial food poisoning, it is also possible to become ill by consuming foods containing **chemical poisons**. There is such a range of possible contaminants that it is impossible to mention them all. However, most naturally occurring food toxins are well recognized wherever they are met, and local culinary habits have evolved to deal with them.

One natural source of poison is the **cassava tuber** (manioc), from which tapioca is made. When raw it contains enough cyanide to kill, but local cooking methods (boiling, soaking, washing in running water and pounding) reduce this to a non-toxic level. Do not prepare cassava yourself; get a local person to cook it for you. It is only a risky food during disasters or famine, when there is insufficient time or fuel for traditional methods of preparation.

Expatriates who live abroad for years increasingly worry about the profligate use of **pesticides** on crops. In some regions farmers spray fruit and vegetables just before they send them to market, to make them look shiny and attractive. Large numbers of people suffer from pesticide poisoning (about 40,000 people die and a million are made ill or permanently disabled annually, worldwide), but these casualties are the result of unsafe spraying techniques or suicide attempts. I have not heard of any significant poisoning of expatriates or travellers through foods contaminated with pesticides. Even so, this is another reason to peel or thoroughly wash any fruit or vegetables, to reduce the amount of harmful chemicals ingested.

Local alcohol

A more predictable poison is alcohol. Even in its purest 'Highland Malt' form it is toxic, but when its origin is a still in a shack, it is likely to contain additional poisons. Be ready to face the consequences if you drink too much. Beware of spirits; distilled drinks may contain extremely toxic methanol, which can cause permanent blindness. If stills are made from pieces of engine, then lead (from solder) and other toxins can contaminate the distillate. Occasionally very odd things are fermented and this is another source of undesirable additions. The foul-smelling Russian samogon, for example, is sugar-based but sometimes beet, corn and even plywood are fermented.

Strength as well as purity of spirits are sometimes demonstrated by setting light to a spoonful: a yellow flame suggests a tainted brew, red suggests lead but a blue flame suggests some level of purity, although it is no guarantee. Fermented distilled maize seems to have the worst hangover potential compared with grain-based brews.

Undistilled drinks of lower alcoholic content (less than 40%) are unsafe if (as is usual) they are prepared with dirty water (e.g. Tibetan *chang*). An exception is Nepali *toongba*, where boiling water is poured over fermented millet, but make sure the water is boiling and the pot pre-heated. *See* p. 199 for the hazards of drinking home-distilled moonshine in the mountains; p.292 for notes on safe alcohol consumption.

Food for free

It can be tempting, especially in a remote place, to go foraging for free foods such as fungi, berries and salad stuffs. Take great care, though, since some highly **poisonous plants** may resemble familiar edible plants at home. There is, for example, a plant with succulent berries in Madagascar that looks like European deadly nightshade (*Atropa belladonna*). Consequently, there have been deaths among Malagasy people who have innocently eaten deadly nightshade berries in France. Seek local advice.

Avoid red or brightly coloured fruits and berries unless you know them to be harmless. Never eat anything that looks like a tomato (unless you know it is one) even if it smells pleasant, nor any roots, fruit or vegetables with a bitter, stinging or other disagreeable taste. If in doubt, try them with the tip of your tongue. Advice on poisonous plants is also found on pp.285–6. In many regions, wild watercress carries a risk of liver fluke infestation. **Seaweeds** are all edible, except in highly polluted areas: the tastiest are pink, purple, reddish or green.

Risky seafood

Shellfish food poisoning

Shellfish are efficient concentrators of faecal bacteria (including cholera) and often harbour parasites. They should be properly cooked although most normal cooking does not make heavily contaminated seafood safe. For sea-crab to be safe when cooked whole, it should be boiled for 10 minutes (eight is not enough) or steamed for 30 minutes (not 25). Crabs and king (i.e. horseshoe) crabs in Southeast Asia and the Pacific can also be a source of **ciguatera** and **scombrotoxic poisoning** (*see* p.126). If you decide to eat sea cucumber (it resembles elastic bands in texture but doesn't taste as good), ensure they are peeled; the skin can be toxic.

From time to time there are dramatic blooms of tiny dinoflagellate animals, *Gambierodiscus toxicus*, that make tropical seawater look red. These are **red tides** and appear to be a case of nature getting her own back after reef-damage by dynamite, a response to pollution or to storm damage. Red tides are signalled by

A fishy story

Generations of mothers have believed that cod liver oil is good for you, but scientific support for fish oils is relatively recent. In the 1970s, scientists noted that Greenland Inuits had a tiny risk of heart attack despite their very high fat diet. Following this observation, evidence started to pile up about the many benefits of a diet rich in fish oil and the omega-3 essential fatty acids. There are now many capsules on the market – some promoted as 'fats of life' – since it has become clear that fish oils, and in particular omega 3:

→ contribute to a healthy retina and brain;

→ probably help to counteract arthritis and disorders of the skin;

→ reduce the chance of developing certain cancers;

→ have beneficial effects on the blood vessels;

→ reduce blood viscosity;

→ keep blood vessels dilated (relaxed);

→ inhibit the clumping together of blood cells in vessels that cause heart attacks and deep vein thrombosis;

→ reduce the risk of stroke and heart attack.

So if your holiday allows, indulge in oily fish (sardines, mackerel, salmon, herring and trout), and know that a meal containing oily fish in the 24 hours before a long haul flight is protective against travellers' blood clots (DVT).

the deaths of many fish and sea birds. Local fishermen usually know not to catch fish during red tides since they are poisonous, though, as their livelihood is compromised, they may be tempted to sell unsafe fish. Shellfish, being filter-feeders, are especially adept at concentrating red tide poisons, so they must also be avoided at these times. Within half an hour of eating contaminated fish or shellfish, symptoms develop which may lead to fatal paralysis in 12 hours. There is no specific treatment. For other effects of red tides, see p.178.

Paralytic shellfish poisoning (PSP) can also occur without a red tide. Symptoms begin (typically within three hours of eating shellfish) with tingling around the mouth and throat, dizziness and a floating sensation. There can also be headache, nausea and vomiting. The numbness progresses and muscles become affected, so that breathing may stop altogether. It even occasionally occurs in Britain, where the PSP season is May to August, and mussels are usually the culprits.

Seafish food poisoning

Eating fish can be risky, although these are not as common a source of disease as filter-feeding shellfish. Skin any reef-fish or tropical fish before eating, and avoid the gonads (sexual organs). Choose fish with clear eyes and a firm, intact bodies that don't smell bad. One speciality of the coastal regions of Peru is *ceviche*, raw fish marinated with lemon and chillies; this can harbour cholera. Japanese sushi, when it is not properly cleaned, can give you herring worms (anisakiasis: fish nematodes), which you can also get from undercooked, salted or pickled fish in California. Fortunately, the worms find man rather an unsuitable host and die fairly promptly after causing a little stomach ache and nausea. Herring worm disease is no longer the problem it used to be in the Netherlands as all mackerel and herrings are now deep frozen; worms are killed in 24 hours at -20°C.

Surgeon fish

Ciguatera fish poisoning occurs between the latitudes of 35°N and 35°S and is commonly reported in Hawaii, Florida, Puerto Rico and the Virgin Islands but in unpredictable outbreaks. Like red tide poisoning, it is due to fish accumulating dinoflagellate toxins as they feed but is harder to recognize than red tides because there is no obvious change in the sea. An early sign a fish is affected is that it causes tingling or numbness of the mouth; reject it at this stage.

Symptoms start 30 minutes to 30 hours after eating, usually with vomiting, watery diarrhoea and cramps, which all get better in 24–48 hours. Some sufferers experience a bizarre hot–cold reversal where cold objects feel burning to touch and hot objects feel cold. Such sensory confusions can persist for months. There is no specific treatment. Fish liver, viscera, sexual organs or roe of large and also scaleless warm-water shore or reef species are most likely to contain the toxin. Unusually shaped reef fish like **surgeon fish, trigger fish and parrot fish,** as well as **moray eels** (*see* illustration on p.174), may cause ciguatera poisoning. To reduce the chances of ciguatera poisoning, avoid eating bizarre-looking fish or very colourful reef fish.

Trigger fish

Scombrotoxic food poisoning occurs after the red flesh of tuna, mackerel and relatives (such as albacore, skipjack and bonito), and tinned fish, e.g. sardines, anchovies and others (mahi-mahi, bluefish, amberjack, herring), is decomposed by bacteria to produce histamine poisons. These cause a tingling or smarting sensation in the mouth, or a peppery or bitter taste in the fish. If you continue eating you will experience hot flushing of the skin, sweating, itching, abdominal pain, vomiting and dizziness, all of which usually go away within 24 hours. Treatment is not necessary. This is avoided by eating only fresh fish, or by gutting and freezing fish as soon as possible after it's caught. Problems are most common in hot climates, as decomposition begins so quickly.

The **puffer fish** (*fugu*) is said to be outstandingly delicious, but is lethal if improperly prepared. There are 250 cases of poisoning per year in Japan, with 60% mortality. Other fish in Southeast Asia and the Indo-Pacific can also be toxic, so get a local cook to prepare fish for you.

Parrot fish

Finally a word about **large, predatory fish** including shark, marlin and swordfish. These, being at the top of the food chain, accumulate pollutants, and recently it has been realized that they can carry quite high levels of toxic mercury. Adults who eat less than one portion of these fish a week will be in no danger, but pregnant women and children under 16 years old should avoid consuming these fish.

Other hazards of exotic eating

Southeast Asia is renowned for its food, and also for the great variety of interesting parasites you can catch from eating it. Freshwater **crabs**, **raw tadpoles**, **frogs** and **snakes** are sources of gnathostome worms; raw freshwater fish harbour *Clonorchis* liver flukes. Consuming raw **freshwater crabs** in central Africa can give you worm cysts and abscesses in the neck, and undercooked giant African land **snails** and freshwater shrimps in Asia, the Pacific and Central and South America, carry a risk of angiostrongyliasis, a nasty little worm that can set up home in the brain or eyes. Infestation causes headaches, facial paralysis and meningitis but can take a month to appear. Always eat your **shrimps**, **beetles**, **snails**, etc. well cooked. And if you get strange symptoms remind your doctor where you've been lately.

Armadillo meat in Mexico and the USA has been implicated in cases of leprosy. If you must eat armadillos, they should also be well done. The only **birds** known to be poisonous are three species of *pitohuis*, thrush-like birds from Papua New Guinea. They produce a very powerful toxin similar to that of South American poison arrow frogs, so that licking the feathers makes your mouth go numb. Locals know where in Papua New Guinea you shouldn't eat small wild birds. **Fruit bats** are tasty, however.

Nutrition

Some people take **vitamin pills** while travelling. It is better (and cheaper) to take a diet that includes fresh fruit and/or vegetables every day. Even if this is not possible, vitamin deficiency is enormously rare in those taking even a minimally varied diet. Many months of a very poor, monotonous diet are needed before deficiencies develop, unless you already have a long-standing disease of the intestine. In the absence of a nutritional deficiency state or anaemia, **zinc** is probably the only nutritional supplement with proven clinical benefits as a **tonic**. It is required by the body in trace quantities and promotes healing and a healthy appetite.

One cause of protracted diarrhoea is **tropical sprue** (*see* p.114). This is one time when nutritional supplements (and sometimes B_{12} injections) are of proven benefit. Another is when planning a pregnancy. Congenital abnormalities are less likely in children born to women who take *folic acid* supplements before and around the time of conception. In addition, women who are pregnant (or planning a pregnancy) and are taking *proguanil* (Paludrine) antimalarial tablets also need to take *folic acid* 5mg daily (*see* **Special Travellers**, p.77).

Salt tablets are unnecessary. If your body needs more salt your taste for it will increase, so shake more on your food. If you are very salt-depleted, salt will not taste salty, so take salty drinks until they do taste salty again.

Fluoride

In Britain we are accustomed to accepting that **fluoride** is added to drinking water in order to promote strong teeth. Such supplementation is still controversial but fluoride drops may be given to children when water fluoride is less than 0.2 parts per million. Fluoride shelf-life in toothpaste is short so there is no point in expatriates shipping out large quantities from home if fluorinated paste is not available locally.

A more likely problem is difficulty finding unfluorinated paste in regions of naturally high fluoride. In some places natural fluoride levels may be so high as to cause children's teeth to turn blotchy yellow-brown and pitted. Urban water supplies will not have such high levels, but expatriates should be aware that fluoride supplements should not be given to children growing up in these regions, and non-fluoride toothpaste should be used. These are districts of hard water that has drained through evaporite rocks; local water engineers will advise on the water quality in their region. Northern Baluchistan, including Quetta, is one such high-fluoride area, and in India a belt stretches from southern Orissa, down the east of the country to Kanniyakumari and including parts of Sri Lanka. There are other areas of high fluoride in east Africa, Yunan (China), Japan, the Gulf and southwest America. Water from deep-tube wells is more likely to contain high fluoride than shallow-tube well water.

On the Ground:
Malaria

What is malaria? 130
  Risks versus side effects 131
Where is malaria a hazard? 132
  Avoidance 133
  Antimalarial tablets 134
Diagnosing malaria 139
  Self-diagnosis 139
  Treatment and cure 140

11

Summary

→ Find out the malaria risk at your destination(s), and establish whether there is a significant chance of catching the serious form: *Plasmodium falciparum*.

→ The risk determines what tablets to take and whether prophylactics and/or standby treatment are necessary. Take any tablets meticulously, including after returning home.

→ Malaria is a killer, but with good information, the right precautions and bite-avoidance, the risk is small. Not all malarious regions are high risk.

→ Malaria-carrying mosquitoes bite from sundown until sunrise. They like sweaty feet, so take a shower and change into long clothes before dusk.

→ Pregnant women, babies and young children are at highest risk of dying from malaria.

→ All antimalarial tablets have the potential for side effects; each traveller must find which of the effective options suits best. Tablets won't protect if you don't take them as directed.

→ If illness strikes within six days of arrival and three months of departure from a malarious region, see a doctor urgently and remind him/her that you could have malaria.

→ Protection against mosquito bites also has the side effect of helping avoid rarer insect-borne diseases.

What is malaria?

Newspaper headlines might have you believing that all foreign countries are seething with diseases. Don't worry about the headlines but read up on malaria. It is the real risk to travellers to much of the tropics and sub-tropics. It is crucial to know about it if you are venturing into the malaria belt.

People acquire malaria when they are bitten (and only one bite is necessary) by an *Anopheles* mosquito that has previously bitten someone with malaria. Symptoms follow at least seven days later. It often starts as a 'flu-like illness (fevers, chills, aches and pains), but can appear in other guises: diarrhoea, abdominal pain or a cough. Malaria is caused by *Plasmodium* protozoa, fastidious parasites that live within the red bloodcells of animals and also inside the body of the mosquito. Bats, rats, deer, monkeys, birds and even reptiles have their own species of malaria – there are over 100 kinds – but only four prefer to inhabit man.

The nastiest, *Plasmodium falciparum*, can cause cerebral malaria, and in the extreme form of the disease so many bloodcells become full of parasites that when they rupture in unison, the body (particularly the kidneys) is overwhelmed with bloodcell debris. Death then often results, however high-tech the medical care is. The death rate from *falciparum* malaria is around 1% in the best hospitals (UK or Africa), although in Japan the mortality rate has been much higher (10%) due to lack of antimalarials (until 2001) and delays in accessing treatment.

The other three kinds of malaria do not kill, but can be difficult to eradicate completely from the body. Unfortunately, it is the dangerous form that is on the increase, and it is this form with which resistance to prophylactic and curative medicines is the biggest problem.

Malaria used to be an issue in temperate regions, including on Long Island and, until only 50 years ago, Italy. There are five species of *Anopheles* mosquito that are native to southern England and East Anglia and that are able to spread malaria. Oliver Cromwell suffered from the '**ague**'; this was, in fact, malaria. The last cases of malaria caught in England were in Romney Marsh just after the First World War –

> **Case history: Africa**
> A British businessman had been visiting sub-Saharan countries for 26 years, and no longer took antimalarial tablets. He assumed that he was immune. He returned from one trip with fever and chills, but wasn't alarmed and it was three days before he saw his doctor. The businessman developed cerebral malaria and kidney failure, and spent three weeks in intensive care. He recovered completely.

probably spread by local mosquitoes from convalescing soldiers who had returned with malaria. These days the only cases contracted in England are at airports, from mosquitoes that have arrived by plane.

Risks versus side effects

Old Africa hands often say that they've had malaria several times. 'It isn't a serious disease, it is a bit like a mild 'flu. You just take the treatment and soon get better. Besides, taking those antimalarial pills and putting nasty chemical repellents on your skin does your long-term health no good, and isn't it even dangerous to your eyesight? It's better – surely – to just treat the disease as and when you get it. Isn't it?'

I disagree. It is true that, of those who contract malaria, most people do not rapidly succumb, but the kinds of malaria that were most common a few decades ago were often mild, even if they did sometimes niggle on, causing health problems that never settled. This was also true for the ague of the English Middle Ages.

Various factors influence what you should do to protect yourself in a malarious region, and a little simple cost-benefit analysis is often required. There are costs, risks and inconveniences to any strategy to avoid getting malaria, but you need to balance these against the risk of dying from the disease. Globally a child dies from malaria every 30 seconds. The cure is known but still it is a killer, and this stark fact should put some of the rather theoretical worries about long-term use of tablets and repellents into proportion. Drug-resistant malaria, in particular, is on the increase, and the proportion of imported malaria that is due to the nasty *falciparum* form that can cause cerebral malaria is on the increase. Consequently, well-meant advice from old Africa hands can be misleading, and even dangerous. It

The stark reality
→ Among the nearly 2,000 people who return to Britain with malaria each year, up to 16 (1%) die of it.
→ In addition, an unknown number of travellers die from malaria abroad.
→ Malaria can kill within 24 hours of the first symptom.
→ There are about 10,000 reported cases of malaria imported into Europe annually.
→ From 1993 to 2004 Germany reported 3,935 cases, with 116 (3%) deaths.
→ 1,500 people bring malaria into the US each year; there were 185 (1%) malaria deaths from 1963 to 2001.
→ The number of malaria cases treated in Britain between 1987 and 2007 ranged between 1,548 and 2,500 in a year, and a significant number of these people ended up in intensive care.

is more important than ever to take precautions against being bitten and – where appropriate – to take antimalarial tablets meticulously.

The challenge to travellers is to assess the malaria risk, determine whether an antimalarial tablet is necessary and then find a suitable one that gives adequate protection for the relevant destination. Understanding the risk should also determine what kind of repellent to use, and what other precautions to adopt. In some regions it would be entirely appropriate to take no tablets, although some travellers would then opt to carry a curative course of medicines. When illness strikes, a local doctor can be sought, who can advise on whether the treatment is necessary, or whether there is some other cause of fever.

A recent American study looking into all the deaths in the US from imported malaria judged that in 80% of those deaths decisions by the traveller had contributed. Travellers had failed to take suggested antimalarials at all or stopped taking them while abroad or failed to report illness to a doctor until it was too late.

Sources of advice on malaria

www.malariahotspots.co.uk provides a host of accessible information and case histories.

Look at *www.fitfortravel.scot.nhs.uk, www.nathnac.org* or *www.HPA.org.uk/infections.*

CDC, Centers for Disease Control and Prevention, 1600 Clifton Rd, Atlanta, GA 30333, US **t** 800 232 4636, *www.cdc.gov/travel.*

Masta Travellers health line, UK **t** 0906 822 4100, gives tailored travel advice. It also has a website: *www.masta-travel-health.com.*

Where is malaria a hazard?

Malaria is a very widespread disease found in much of sub-Saharan Africa, Asia (including parts of Turkey and Azerbaijan) and South and Central America. Melanesia (Papua New Guinea, the Solomons, Vanuatu) is a high-risk area. Although widespread, most (92%) of those cases imported into Europe come from tropical Africa, especially West Africa. It can be acquired (albeit rarely) at altitudes as high as 2,000m (6,500ft), so mountain areas are not necessarily safe: in Quetta people get it from mosquitoes brought up from the Punjab on the train. Get up-to-date

Case history: Indonesia

A British engineer was working for three years in Surabaya and, knowing that eastern Java is free from malaria, took no antimalarial tablets. He spent a weekend on neighbouring Lombok and took no precautions against malaria there either. Three weeks later he died of cerebral malaria.

This man had spent most of his working life in the tropics; he had contracted malaria in Africa, where treatment had soon got the mild symptoms under control. He was not keen to take antimalarials because of side effects, and because he was sure that malaria was not especially serious.

International hotels at Senggigi Beach, Lombok, are not keen to advertise the risk of *falciparum* malaria: it might be bad for business.

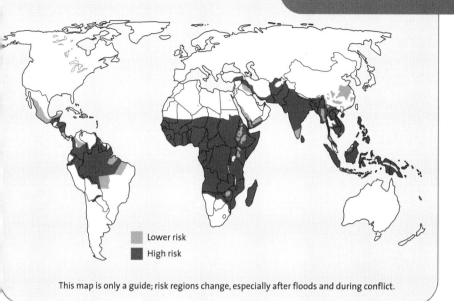

Lower risk

High risk

This map is only a guide; risk regions change, especially after floods and during conflict.

information on risks pre-departure, especially for travel to Africa, where malaria kills at least a million people a year. In Southeast Asia (Cambodia, Vietnam) malaria is often resistant to treatment.

Most capital cities in Southeast and East Asia and South America are malaria-free at present, as are the popular Caribbean resorts, Polynesia and Micronesia. Most of the Republic of South Africa is safe, but in the northeast, including the Kruger National Park, there is still a significant risk.

Pregnant women, babies and young children, people who have no spleen, and anyone who is immunosuppressed (e.g. suffering from cancer, HIV/AIDS, or taking high doses of steroid tablets for more than a week) are all highly susceptible to malaria if they get it. **Pregnant women** are more attractive to mosquitoes and get bitten twice as much as non-pregnant women. Pregnant women who get *falciparum* malaria are at risk of miscarriage and death. Vulnerable travellers should consider whether they need to enter high-risk malarial areas at all. If travel is unavoidable, they must be extra-vigilant about bite protection and meticulous in taking prophylaxis.

Avoidance

Malarial mosquitoes bite from about 5.30pm until dawn. At dusk, put on long clothes and repellents. Sadly, gin and **tonic** does not contain enough quinine to protect you, but you can take other steps to avoid malaria: find out if the disease exists in the region you are going to; investigate the antimalarial tablets available; avoid being bitten; and, on your return, remind your doctor that you have been exposed to the disease.

Antimalarial tablets

Who should take antimalarials?

Taking antimalarial tablets and avoiding bites are your only protection from malaria at present. There is no immediate prospect of a vaccine. *Falciparum* malaria is especially dangerous in children and pregnant women, especially in the last three months. Antimalarials do not pass into breast milk in sufficient quantity to protect infants, so breast-fed babies also need to be given their own antimalarials (*see* pp.136–7).

People born and/or brought up in malarious regions and who suffer from malaria repeatedly build up a partial immunity, so that if they contract the disease they are less likely to become seriously ill. However, this immunity wanes within a year, so that natives of malarious countries become highly susceptible to malaria, just like other travellers (PhD students beware); hence they also need to protect themselves. No antimalarial is infallible, but the few unfortunates who pick up malaria while taking tablets (perhaps doses are forgotten, or poorly absorbed due to diarrhoea) are less likely to get into serious trouble.

Which antimalarial and what side effects

Most malaria tablets are started a week before departure and continued for a month after your return. There is no drug yet known that can prevent the malaria parasite from infecting people. Antimalarials slow parasite multiplication and inhibit their penetration into red blood cells. By taking tablets for long enough, the parasites fade out.

People taking antimalarial tablets often notice side effects. Up to 40% of those taking either *mefloquine* or the *chloroquine + proguanil* combination will report a problem, although many complaints will be trivial and tolerable. Any such symptoms are a price that must be weighed against the major risk of malaria: rapid death. Some side effects can be troublesome enough to make you wish to stop taking the tablets, but in such a case it is important to find an alternative. There is now a good range of prophylactics, so it should be possible to find one that does suit you.

Drug-resistance patterns change: get up-to-date advice on what to take from a travel clinic or information service (*see* 'Sources of advice on malaria', p.132). That said, the efficacy of the 'big three' antimalarials (*doxycycline*, Malarone and *mefloquine*) seems good, with failure rates estimated by the Centers for Disease Control and Prevention at less than 6 per 100,000. The risk of serious side effects seems to be similar with all antimalarials at one in 10,000.

Doxycycline

The antibiotic *doxycycline* is effective against malaria in most destinations, including Africa and the border regions of Thailand and Cambodia. One capsule is taken daily, or there is a soluble formulation for those who are not good at swallowing pills. It can be taken for up to two years continuously. *Doxycycline* is unsuitable for children under the age of 12 and should not be taken by pregnant or lactating women because it binds to growing bones and teeth, and so discolours and weakens them. Doxycycline should not be taken by people with **systemic lupus erythematosis** (it can exacerbate it), nor **myasthenia gravis** (it can make muscle weakness worse), nor anyone known to be allergic to *tetracycline*. Travellers who take *phenytoin*, *carbamazepine* or *phenobarbital* need to double the *doxycycline* dose to one capsule twice daily, but the effectiveness of the anti-epileptic may be reduced. Consider Malarone instead.

Doxycycline can increase sensitivity to sunburn, so it is not ideal for beach holidays; use ample sunscreen whenever you are outside. It can also precipitate vaginal thrush so it is not ideal for honeymoon use. Take the capsules with or after a meal and wash them down with plenty of water. If the capsule gets stuck half way down the gullet, it can cause inflammation. Ideally, you should avoid lying down for 30 minutes after taking it.

Malarone (*proguanil* with *atovaquone*)

Malarone is available on private prescription and is taken daily as a prophylactic in people over 11kg (771/2 pounds) for up to three months. It is called Malanil in South Africa. It is best taken with food or milk. It has the potential to cause side effects, especially mouth ulcers (as *proguanil* alone does), but also weird dreams,

---

Case History: Southern Africa

Bad experiences on high (curative) doses of Lariam made me decide against taking any antimalarial prophylaxis on our fabulous 3,000km, five-week journey through the heart of southern Africa, ending up in the Gonerazhou National Park in Zimbabwe. Knowing the dangers of malaria I took precautions:

→ I applied DEET mosquito repellent on all exposed skin after 4pm.

→ I reapplied mosquito repellent before going to bed (except on my torso, see below).

→ I put on socks, long trousers and long sleeves after 5pm.

→ I burned pyrethrum coils in the hut.

→ I slept under my own mosquito bednet (although it was not treated with insecticide).

It was frightfully hot and I slept naked or near-naked. I was probably bitten when I went out in the night to pee in the bush. I began to feel ill 10 days after we left Gonerazhou; then, the morning after a particularly rich butterfish meal, I vomited. The next evening, I felt as if I had bad 'flu. My body felt stuffed with cotton wool; my limbs ached; I had a fever of 38.4°C; I felt nauseated, had a headache and had the most ghastly, stinky, oily diarrhoea. This was *falciparum* malaria and I started the week-long treatment with *artemesin* (*artemether*). The next 48 hours were bad, with symptoms continuing, but worse, with a temperature of 39.6°C. I felt bad for three to four weeks, suffering energy crashes, intermittent headaches and other pains. The scary thing is how terribly fast the disease progresses. My doctor said that even relatively ineffective prophylaxis with *chloroquine* and Paludrine would have slowed and reduced the severity of my malaria.

Barbara Ikin, Maputo, Mozambique

Commonly used antimalarial prophylactic tablets

Generic drug name	Mefloquine	Proguanil with atovaquone
Trade names	Lariam	Malarone
Frequency	1 weekly	1 daily with food
Dose	250mg tablet	100mg *proguanil* and 250mg *atovaquone*
Start when?	1–3 weeks before travel	1–2 days before travel
Continue until when?	Continue for 4 weeks after return	Continue for 7 days after return
Possible side effects	Mood changes; weird dreams; nausea	Nausea; loss of appetite; mouth ulcers
Notes	Avoid in epilepsy, previous depression, breast-feeding, early pregnancy; avoid pregnancy for 3 months after taking; suitable for children	Not recommended in pregnancy or if trying to conceive or when breast-feeding; not for children under 11kg; paediatric tablets available
Approximate cost for two weeks in a malarious region	£28 for eight tablets	£80 for 24 tablets

insomnia, nausea, poor appetite and gastrointestinal disturbance. It should probably not be taken in pregnancy or if trying to become pregnant.

Malarone should probably be avoided if you have **psoriasis** or **porphyria**. Anyone taking this tablet should be aware that any new problems with vision, muscle weakness, ringing in the ears or hearing problems might be a side effect and a medical opinion should be sought. Some doctors advise three-monthly blood counts in people who take this long term (and outside the licensed indications).

Mefloquine (Lariam)

This is an effective weekly preparation available on private prescription. It should be taken with food, or if it upsets your stomach take half a tablet twice a week. Anyone with a history of fits, depression or psychiatric problems, severe liver disease or who has a close blood relative who is epileptic should avoid it; it is safe for women during the last six months of pregnancy, but those planning a pregnancy should avoid conceiving for three months after stopping *mefloquine*. In Britain, this is currently only licensed for up to a year, although many people take it

Doxycycline	Chloroquine and proguanil	Pyrimethamine and dapsone
Vibramycin	Nivaquine, Aralen or Resochin and Paludrine	Deltaprim (= Maloprim)
1 daily with plenty of water	2 chloroquine weekly and 2 proguanil daily	1 weekly
100mg	2x150mg of chloroquine base and 2x100mg proguanil	pyrimethamine 12.5mg and dapsone 100mg
1–2 days before travel	1 week before travel	1 week before travel
Continue for 4 weeks after return	Continue for 4 weeks after return	Continue for 4 weeks after return
Rash on exposure to sun; loss of appetite; thrush in women	Nausea; mouth ulcers; heartburn	Has caused bone marrow suppression if two tablets taken weekly
Avoid in children, pregnancy and lactation; take after food with plenty of water	Avoid in epilepsy; may make psoriasis worse. Take after food if possible. Proguanil not available in the USA and difficult to find in malarious zones	Sometimes taken with chloroquine. Used in Oceania. Withdrawn in the UK in 2002. Can be taken in the last 6 months of pregnancy but with folic acid
£26 for 50 tablets	Around £18 depending on preparation chosen	£5

for two and, as long as there has been no reaction during the early weeks, it appears safe for such long-term use. It is safe for use in babies (over 5kg/11 pounds) and small children.

The British press has hammered *mefloquine* (Lariam), saying it is a dangerous drug, but it suits many people extremely well. I like it. It should not be dismissed. Like all effective medicines, it causes side effects in some people. A study of 93,668 European travellers to East Africa suggested that *mefloquine* is tolerated best by older people, and seven other studies found that men tolerate it better than women. One in eight women and one in 15 men experience dizziness, feel 'out of it', have disturbed sleep or vivid dreams. Fatigue is another reported side effect. Restlessness and nightmares are less common side effects and the risk of serious problems including paranoia is 1: 6–10,000. New headaches on waking suggest Lariam should be stopped. If you decide to use *mefloquine*, begin taking it two and a half weeks (three doses) before departure and stop it if it seems to cause vivid and unpleasant dreams, mood changes or otherwise alters the way you feel. Avoid alcohol excess (don't binge), LSD and other recreational drugs while taking Lariam.

Homeopathic malaria prophylaxis

It's unusual to see practitioners of conventional and alternative medicine united, but both groups would condemn the use of 'homeopathic malaria prophylaxis' as potentially lethal. Such unanimity comes from the fact that 'homeopathic prophylaxis' is actually a contradiction in terms. The founding principle of homeopathy is to 'treat like with like': so only when a patient has symptoms can the practitioner apply homeopathic principles to choose a remedy. Someone who is completely healthy provides the homeopath with no information on which to base a treatment plan.

I was so worried about this issue that I phoned the Homeopathic Hospital in Glasgow and spoke to Dr Bob Leckridge, who is president of the Faculty of Homeopathy. He told me, 'There is no place for notions of "prophylactic treatment" or "vaccination" in homeopathy. Such ideas do not fit into homeopathic theory at all. In fact, there are now a number of reports of people who have developed malaria after relying on supposed "homeopathy" for protection.'

Conventional antimalarials are admittedly unpleasant to take, but the homeopathic alternative is not an alternative at all.

Dr Grant Hutchison, consultant anaesthetist, Dundee

Chloroquine and *proguanil*

Chloroquine is sold as Aralen and Resochin in the USA. Of the *chloroquine* products available in the UK, Nivaquine tablets are more palatable than Avloclor. Nivaquine is the only paediatric syrup; however, it is terribly bitter and few children tolerate it, even when it is disguised in food.

Adults take two *chloroquine* tablets each week and usually these are taken along with **proguanil** (Paludrine in the UK; not available in the USA) two a day; in mainland Europe, combination tablets containing both drugs are marketed as Savarine. *Chloroquine* and *proguanil* are still a good combination for many travellers unless they are visiting areas with multiple drug resistance. The *chloroquine* + *proguanil* combination is the only antimalarial regime that is available in the UK without prescription, and it is cheap (around £14 for 100 Paludrine and £2.50 for 28 Nivaquine). If *proguanil* is taken by pregnant women, or those wishing to become pregnant, it is necessary to take *folic acid* as well.

Chloroquine can affect the eyes, but only after taking it for at least six years; more frequently, it may cause a slightly queasy stomach shortly after each dose. *Chloroquine* should not be taken by people with epilepsy. *Proguanil* (Paludrine) can cause two troublesome side effects. Taken on an empty stomach it often causes nausea, so take it after a meal or with a glass of milk. Second, it often causes mouth ulcers, so pack something that will ease them (e.g. Teejel or Bonjela). *Chloroquine* and *proguanil* can reduce the appetite and cause heartburn or **indigestion**.

Deltaprim aka Maloprim (*pyrimethamine + dapsone*)

Deltaprim tablets rather went out of favour when several travellers taking two tablets weekly developed bone marrow failure. It is thought to be safe to take if you have taken it before without problems. It is probably also safe in those who haven't taken it before, as long as no more than one tablet weekly is taken. It might be used in regions were there is a lot of *chloroquine* resistance, such as Oceania. It is also suitable for people with epilepsy, although if they take *phenytoin* or *phenobarbital, folic acid* (5mg daily) should also be taken. Children over three months or weighing more than 6kg (13 pounds) can also take it. It was withdrawn in the UK at the end of 2002 because other alternatives are usually considered first by prescribers.

Diagnosing malaria

Even experienced tropical physicians cannot reliably diagnose malaria without a blood test: blood is examined either under a microscope or using an immunological test kit. If possible, you should get a laboratory test done before taking any treatment; this only takes 10 minutes, and in Africa costs about US$1. Dangerous malaria is a possibility if you feel unwell, have a fever over 38°C (100°F) or have 'flu-like symptoms (prostration, aches and pains) seven days or more after arriving in a malarious region, or within three months of returning. Malaria can take up to a year to cause symptoms. If you are far from medical help, be aware that self-treatment is fairly safe, except for anyone pregnant or under 12 years old. Remember that other causes of fever require different treatments; notes to help diagnose them are on pp.256–7.

Self-diagnosis

Several self-diagnostic test kits have been developed. These are highly effective immunological tools, which in skilled hands are reliable in diagnosing malaria. It was hoped that these might be of value to ordinary travellers who, on becoming feverish, could take a spot of their own blood, test it and then decide whether to take drug treatment. Unfortunately, in ill travellers with no laboratory experience, the diagnostic accuracy is very disappointing: in one study 71% were unable to extract blood and a quarter were unable to put the blood on the slide appropriately. In those who managed to complete the test, 10 of the 11 were falsely reassured that they were all right when they were actually incubating serious malaria. So far, then, diagnostic kits are only of proven value when technicians and medics use the kit to perform the test for others.

Symptoms of malaria

There is no sign or pattern of symptoms peculiar to malaria. That is what makes it such a dangerous disease. The most common symptoms include:

→ **Fever** above 38°C (100°F); this is the commonest symptom.
→ **Feeling wiped out** and sore all over (doctors call these 'flu-like symptoms).
→ **Joint pains and aching muscles.**
→ **Shivering.**
→ **Backache.**
→ **Diarrhoea.**
→ **Repeated vomiting.**
→ **Sore throat.**
→ **Headache.**
→ **Convulsions.**

Based on a table in the UK Department of Health's Health Information for Overseas Travel 2001

Case history: Going outside
When relieving yourself outdoors – especially after dark – beware of where you squat and what you squat over. There are many thorny and stinging plants in most regions of the globe, and plenty of places with pods protected by irritating hairs. So check around with a light first. In addition, exposing the *glutei* (bum muscles) allows mosquitoes and other biters an opportunity, or you could disturb fire ants or a snake. In countries where pigs and dogs roam free to scavenge nutrition, there is scope for a different encounter. Squatting children are sometimes cleaned as they poo by dogs, and visitors to China have been alarmed by pigs – squealing with enthusiasm – that charge in to offer this facility.

Treatment and cure

In regions where the risk of malaria is real but low and medical help is more than 24 hours away, some travellers opt to carry a course of malaria treatment. Itineraries must be discussed with a specialist who will determine your particular needs and risks, and you must then travel with a clear understanding and written instructions on when and how to take the cure. Know that standby emergency treatment is a first-aid measure and not a substitute for medical help – which must be sought urgently.

In a malarious region you have to assume that any fever over 38°C (100°F) that continues for more than a few hours is due to malaria, but if you do self-treat, you must still find a doctor as soon as possible.

Quinine is the basis of most cures, but is unpleasant to take, so is usually combined with another medicine. One fast and effective regime is *quinine* (2 x 300mg tablets three times daily for three days) plus *doxycycline* (100mg twice daily for seven days).

Both **Malarone** and to a lesser extent *mefloquine* (**Lariam**) can be used as a cure although not in those already taking these as prophylactics. Malarone can be given to children as long as they weigh over 11kg (24 pounds).

Artemether, a drug first used in China 3,000 years ago, is used to cure malaria. It is now licensed as **Riamet** (*artemether* 20mg and *lumefantrine* 120mg, aka *co-artemeter*) as a standby emergency treatment for travellers who choose not to take prophylaxis; it can only be taken by people over 12 years and weighing more than 35kg (77 pounds). However, it is not as fast-acting as the (albeit less pleasant) *quinine* treatment regime. The course is six doses of four tablets over 60 hours: a total of 24 tablets.

Fansidar is a less popular alternative. *Halofantrine* (**Halfan**) should not be used; it can harm the heart. *Chloroquine* is now rarely used as a cure since its efficacy is waning.

Travellers who acquire the dangerous form of malaria will become ill within three months of leaving a malaria zone. Milder, non-life-threatening forms of malaria may take up to a year to announce themselves. Symptoms of fever, sweats, aches and pains should send you scuttling for medical help at once, as the sooner you start treatment the sooner you'll recover. If you cannot contact your usual doctor, go to a hospital emergency department and say that you could have malaria.

On the Ground:
Bites, Biters and the
Diseases they Spread

Mosquitoes 142
   Do all mosquitoes harm? 142
Avoiding mosquitoes 143
Dealing with mosquito bites 149
Insect-borne diseases 150
Arboviruses 151
   Sand-fly-borne diseases 153
   African and American
   trypanosomiasis 153
Ticks and their diseases 155
   Removing ticks 155
   Tick-borne infections 156

12

Summary

→ Vectors bite for a living and, as a side effect, pass on infection.

→ Mosquitoes are the most important disease vectors, but ticks, sand-flies, black-flies and others are also guilty. The table on p.144 summarizes the main dangerous illnesses; not all are tropical.

→ Most of the exotically named vector-borne diseases are enormously rare.

→ There are tick-borne diseases in the UK, the Mediterranean and the USA, and malaria exists in Turkey.

→ Malaria mosquitoes bite from dusk until dawn; other biters can be active during the day.

→ See a doctor if you have a skin ulcer that will not heal; be especially suspicious if you have visited the American rainforest.

→ Avoid tick and chigger bites by wearing long clothes tucked in, and use a repellent. Consider spraying *permethrin* on your clothes (*see* p.146).

→ Pack plenty of repellent that you know suits your skin.

→ Light-coloured clothes make it easier to spot a tick and also discourage mosquitoes.

→ If you discover a tick on you, get it off (without squeezing or damaging it) as soon as you can, then douse the wound with alcohol or a strong antiseptic.

Mosquitoes

The mosquito is the most deadly animal known to man. It transmits malaria, elephantiasis, dengue, yellow fever and Japanese encephalitis (of which the last two are incurable and can be fatal), as well as a host of rare and never-talked-about diseases, like o'nyongnyong from East Africa, and Finland's inkoo virus.

Do all mosquitoes harm?

Not all mosquitoes are capable of transmitting disease. Males, recognized by their splendid bushy antennae, don't bite at all. Non-malarial mosquitoes tend to be hump-backed, and their bodies rest roughly parallel to the wall, or their bottoms are slightly closer to the wall than their heads. **Culex**, the common house mosquito, rests parallel to the wall. It causes insomnia and occasionally transmits elephantiasis and some viral infections but never malaria. Malaria-carrying **Anopheles** mosquitoes, however, rest with their heads close and bottoms far from the wall. Both *Anopheles* and *Culex* are evening and night-time biters; protect yourself by donning long clothes and repellent at dusk, and sleeping under an insecticide impregnated bednet.

Aedes mosquitoes, which spread dengue and yellow fevers and some geographically restricted viral infections, also rest parallel to the wall. They often have zebra-striped bodies and also have striking black and white striped legs. Hence they are sometimes called tiger mosquitoes. They bite from dawn to dusk (inclusive).

Avoiding mosquitoes

You don't have to be bitten. Defend yourself, especially if bites make you miserable or you are in a region where insect-borne disease is a real risk. Malarious mosquitoes feed on blood and like to bite from dusk until dawn (inclusive), so in the tropics and sub-tropics it is crucial to arm yourself against the dusk assault. The mosquitoes that spread dengue and yellow fevers bite during daylight hours, but they are also active at dusk, so beware the twilight double shift.

Insects that feed on blood home in on a bouquet of smells arising from a human body. They are also attracted to perfumes but repellents confuse mosquito senses. In very buggy regions, take a shower (but avoid perfumed cosmetics) to reduce insect-attracting body odours, then put on long, loose clothes with a good repellent on exposed skin. Alternatively, you could adjourn to the bar where air conditioning and mosquito screens may protect you. When retiring to bed, the best protection is to sleep under a bednet that is impregnated with *permethrin*.

If you **live abroad**, reduce mosquito breeding sites near your house by draining standing water and emptying or covering water tanks and containers. **Travellers** will get bitten less if they select hotels away from accumulations of standing water. Foul black water is where *Culex* nuisance-mosquitoes breed.

Repellents

Choose a repellent to suit your risk. Weigh the inconveniences and potential side effects of any repellent against the possibility of dangerous insect- or tick-borne disease. A cosmetically less-acceptable product might be necessary in malarious Africa, whereas if itching bites and sensitive skin rather than disease are your main issues, then there are a range of attractive products on offer. Citronella-based products (e.g. Mosi-guard) are pleasant, safe and non-irritant,

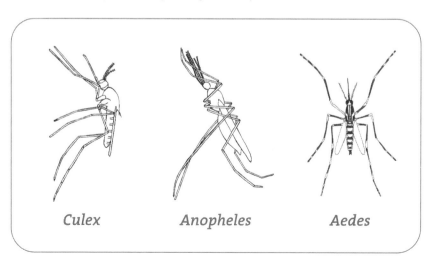

Culex *Anopheles* *Aedes*

Geographical distribution of vector-borne diseases

Chagas' disease (American trypanosomiasis)	Lowland Mexico, Central and South America
Dengue fever	Spreading throughout the tropics and sub-tropics
Dengue haemorrhagic fever	Common in Southeast Asia, the Philippines, the Pacific Islands, India, the Caribbean and tropical South America
Elephantiasis	Humid tropics or coastal regions
Japanese encephalitis	A problem only in Asia, mainly where pigs are kept and rice is grown
Leishmania	Dangerous forms in forests of Central and South America; also Africa, Middle East and South Asia
Malaria	Widespread throughout the tropics and sub-tropics except at altitude
Onchocerciasis (river blindness)	West Africa, South and Central America and a few small areas in East and Central Africa
Oriental schistosomiasis	Patchy distribution in Southeast Asia, China and the Philippines
Plague	A disease of unpredictable outbreaks in very poor living conditions (so unlikely to affect travellers); cases have been reported recently from the USA, Madagascar, China, Myanmar, Vietnam and India
Schistosomiasis (urinary and intestinal; bilharzia)	Savannah and semi-arid regions of Africa, the Middle East and South America (see pp.179–81)
Scrub typhus	East and Southeast Asia including the Philippines, the Pacific Islands including Papua New Guinea, Australia and South Asia (see p.157)
Sleeping sickness (African trypanosomiasis)	Only in Africa in suitable scrubby habitats between the Sahara and the Zambezi
Tick-borne fevers	All continents, temperate and tropical
Yellow fever	Tropical Africa, Central and South America; not in Asia

while DEET will protect you in a high bite-intensity jungle. Note that repellent sticks tend to dry out so are less good for keeping from one trip to the next for infrequent travellers.

Tips for safe use of chemical repellents

→ Test any new repellent on a small area of skin before travel.

→ Apply only to exposed skin and/or clothing.

→ Do not use DEET under clothing or socks.

→ If used with sunscreen, apply repellent 30–60 mins after the sunscreen.

→ Never use repellents on wounds, on irritated or broken skin, or where there is eczema.

→ Do not spray directly onto the face or apply to the hands of young children.

→ Wash any residual repellent off the skin when it is no longer needed.

→ Consider the risk of serious tropical disease when deciding what precautions you need to follow.

→ Natural oils are toxic if swallowed – and so are chemical repellents.

→ Repellents and other skin creams put microscopic holes in condoms.

DEET

Diethyl toluamide or DEET is the gold-standard insect repellent, developed by the US Army in 1946 and registered for general use in 1957. It is used annually by around 200 million people. Its big disadvantage is that it dissolves plastic and ruins many synthetic materials, including watchglasses, pens, sleeping bags, spectacles and some varnishes. Not surprisingly, this makes travellers wonder what such a compound might do to their skin and insides. Yet it is a safe compound. Serious side effects are uncommon (13 cases among the millions of children who have used it), and those likely to have problems are people with very sensitive or broken skin, particularly when lots of repellent is used. Even this ill-advised use will result in little more than a rash or itching. Application under clothes or socks is not recommended, as it will enhance absorption into the body.

Test any product on a small patch of skin before travel, so that if there is a reaction, another product can be tried. DEET must be used with caution in small children (a 6.2% time-release DEET preparation for children is marketed in the USA as Skedaddle) and physicians suggest applying no stronger than a 10% solution of DEET to small children unless the area of exposed skin is minimal, e.g. the ankles. DEET is probably best avoided in pregnancy. It should be applied with care if being put on the face since it tastes nasty, makes eyes sore and irritates the linings of nose and mouth. If used sensibly, though, it is unlikely to harm. Most DEET products protect for up to eight hours, but for only three to four hours in sweaty conditions. When used in addition to long clothes, though, only a small area of skin needs to have repellent applied to it. The right clothes also reduce the problem of needing to reapply repellent frequently when the climate is very humid. There are many DEET formulations on the market, but my favourite is **Ben's 30**, which is water-based and is therefore less likely to irritate, with less absorption than alcohol-based preparations. Other good DEET products are **Jungle Formula Extra Strength, Cutters, Repel** and **Off!**

Those who cannot use DEET might try **Mijex Extra** or **Jungle Formula** (containing Merck 3535), which is about as effective as 30–60% DEET. A chemically similar product to DEET, **Odomos** (*diethylbenzamide*), is sold in India; it is effective, although I haven't been able to confirm manufacturers' claims that it is 'baby safe'. The newish, non-DEET **Autan** is gentler but does not repel African malaria vectors well enough. It does, though, repel many mosquitoes, as well as stable-flies and ticks.

Vitamin B is not repellent

There is no evidence that taking vitamin B_1 tablets protects against mosquito bites, nor does mixing vitamin B complex in cream nor eating Marmite nor (unfortunately) drinking large quantities of beer. Taking vitamin B_1 does seem to reduce the after-bite itch, which might explain why vitamin B is commonly thought to have repellent properties. Don't assume that absence of itch means that you have avoided bites.

Natural oils

There is now a good range of repellents made from pleasant strong-smelling natural oils, including the lemony citronella and eucalyptus. The most effective is **Mosi-guard**, which comes in stick and roll-on preparations, but there are others, including the conveniently packed **Natrapel**. Other types of repellent that are less widely available include **Gurkha** (mild but comes in spray bottles that often leak), Scandinavian **tundra oil**, bog myrtle oil and the Chinese **quwenling**; these and many natural oils work quite well and are kind on the skin, but ultimately are not such effective repellents as chemical preparations. They are fine for most travel purposes (and **bog myrtle** seems especially good against Scottish midges; *www.bogmyrtle.com*), but are not effective enough for use in malarious Africa or other regions of extreme bite-intensity, or where riverine black-flies are a problem.

When selecting a repellent it is important to balance the risk of dying of cerebral malaria, or acquiring some other awful infection on your trip, against the efficacy of the repellent used. I tend to use natural oil products in midgey Scotland, Ulster or the mosquitoey Mediterranean and also during the day in malarious regions, then don long clothes and apply DEET (e.g. **Ben's**) at dusk, and/or retire to an air-conditioned bar.

Repellents on clothes

DEET and *permethrin* can be used to treat clothing, in addition or as an alternative to putting repellents straight onto the skin. The disadvantage of skin applications is that the chemicals sweat off quickly and may irritate. The solution to this challenge is to spray *permethrin* (a contact-insecticide) onto clothes, to make them repellent to biters (especially ticks). This is a particularly effective and useful option in regions where there is a high risk of contracting serious malaria or for those who are really tortured by itching bites. There are also clothes on the market that have permethrin bound into the fabric. They remain repellent through at least 35 washes. However, many garments don't cover enough skin; proofing you own is more adaptable. In regions where insects are less voracious, DEET-soaked repellent anklets offer some protection from mosquitoes that hunt at ankle level (most *Anopheles* and *Culex*), as long as you are upright. However, they don't stop bites completely. Nor do they repel *Aedes* mosquitoes, which roam around more; this is a pity, since *Aedes* bites are a great nuisance in many warm regions.

Bedtime

Research in Africa has shown that sleeping under an insecticide-impregnated bednet protects you from attack by night-biting mosquitoes. In fact, a screen of

Tips for avoiding night-biting mosquitoes

→ Shower just before dusk.

→ At sundown, either retreat to a screened room or put on long, baggy clothes and a good insect repellent.

→ Take special care to protect your ankles with socks or repellents.

→ Sleep under a mosquito net (preferably permethrin treated), use electric mosquito mats or (the least effective) burn mosquito coils.

→ Try to stay only in screened buildings, and spray the room with insecticide regularly; how frequently you spray depends on how frequently the biters return.

→ Fans help baffle the weaker-flying mosquitoes, but some can fly in turbulent air.

→ Wear light-coloured clothes, since dark shades attract mosquitoes.

→ When there are a great number of small flying insects, wear a cotton neckerchief tucked in like a cravat to seal the neck of your shirt.

→ Avoid using scented soaps or perfumes, or wearing shiny jewellery, as mosquitoes like these too.

impregnated cloth dangling around the bed is also effective: mosquitoes choose not to fly over the screen to bite their victims. Bednets (costing from about £20/US$32) are a good investment; they can often be bought for much less overseas, although it might be risky to go shopping in-country unless you know about local availability. Nets treated with *permethrin* will kill any mosquito that lands on the net, so that even if you roll against the net in your sleep (a particular problem with conical nets), mosquitoes won't bite you through it. Impregnation of nets even makes those that have got holes in them protective. It also discourages creepies crawling into bed if you leave the net dangling onto the floor. Nets need to be retreated every six months or after washing. Specialist travel shops and clinics have *permethrin* net treatment kits and also sprays for treating your own net or hotel nets.

Electrical devices

Small, electric hotplates that heat up insecticide-impregnated vaporizing mats are available. The vapour repels or knocks down mosquitoes. They work well except in very large rooms with high ceilings (common in hot climates) and if there is a through-draught. Most types work in a room of $30m^3$ (about $1,000ft^3$); they are less efficient if the device is a long distance from you. If the hotel has provided only one mosquito killer for a big room, ask for another, or use repellent in addition. The best vaporizers contain synthetic insecticides such as *esbiothrin*. Electric **buzzer devices** are useless against mosquitoes, cockroaches, and (as far as I know) all other insects.

Coils

Where there is no electricity you can burn incense coils. Often made in China, they are readily available in most places where mosquitoes are a problem. In West Africa they have been shown to reduce the bite rate by about half: from over 200 per person per night to a mere 100!

Diseases transmitted by small biters

Vector	Vector habits	Disease	Vaccine?
Anopheles mosquitoes	Evening and night biters	Malaria	no
		Elephantiasis	no
		Arboviruses	no
		Skin infections	no
Aedes mosquitoes	Day biters (dawn to dusk inclusive)	Dengue	not yet
		Yellow fever	yes
		Arboviruses	no
		Skin infections	no
Culex mosquitoes	Evening and night biters	Japanese encephalitis	yes
		Elephantiasis	no
		Arboviruses	no
		Skin infections	no
Black-flies	Day biting swarms	Nuisance	no
		River blindness (onchocerciasis)	no
Sand-flies	Evening and night biters	Tropical sores	no
		Kala-azar fever	no
		Sand-fly fevers	no
Tsetse-flies	Painful day biters, attack in swarms	Sleeping sickness (African trypanosomiasis)	no
Cone-nosed bugs	Night biters Hide in crevices in hut roofs and walls	Chagas' disease	no
Rat fleas	Hide in beds etc.	Plague	yes
Bed bugs	Night biters Hide in wall plaster	Pain	no
		Skin infections	no
Mites	Day biters	Scrub typhus	no
		Skin infections	no
Ticks	Attach in daylight	Dozens Scrub and forest	one*

none *means supportive therapy will be given in hospital but that specific treatments that will clear the infection do not exist*

Fans

Ceiling fans may help to baffle mosquitoes a little, but insects are constantly adapting to meet any challenge. Some have become experts at flying in turbulent air and have no difficulty in flying backwards or upside-down in a rainstorm.

Treatment	Continent	Avoiding action
1% die	All	Tablets for malaria; also bite
yes	Tropics	avoidance: long clothes, bednets,
none	Tropics	repellents and insecticides effective
yes	All	against all *Anopheles*-borne diseases
none	Asia, Africa, Americas	Bite avoidance: long clothes,
none	Africa, Americas	repellents and insecticides effective
none	Tropics	against all *Aedes*-borne diseases;
yes	All	discard standing water near home
none	Asia	Bite avoidance: long clothes,
30% die		bednets, repellents and insecticides
yes	Tropics	effective against all *Culex*-borne
none	Tropics	diseases
yes	Hot, humid areas	
no	Africa,	Avoid rivers; also bite avoidance;
can be	tropical America,	long clothes; DEET repellent
dangerous	Tundra, etc.	
difficult	Tropical Americas,	Bite avoidance: repellents;
difficult	Mediterranean,	long clothes; impregnated bednets;
none	Middle East, Asia	fans; sleep above ground
difficult	Tropical lowland	Avoid endemic areas (local advice);
	Africa	repellents; long clothes
90-day	Lowland tropical	Use hammock and net if sleeping
course;	Americas	in wattle-and-daub housing
can be		
dangerous		
antibiotics	Poor housing,	Avoid rats and rodent habitats
	mainly tropical	Vaccine rarely necessary
yes	All	Better hotel; bed away from wall;
antibiotics	All	light on
antibiotics	South and East Asia,	Bite avoidance: repellents;
antibiotics	Australasia	long clothes tucked in
often	All	Bite avoidance: repellents;
difficult		long clothes tucked in

all means all continents except Antarctica
one* means only for 'European' tick-borne encephalitis

Dealing with mosquito bites

Nothing completely takes the itch out of bites, but **tiger balm**, **alcohol**, **calamine**, *crotamiton* (Eurax), **mink oil** and even white, minty **toothpaste** help a little. The convenient marker-pen-sized **After Bite**, containing ammonia, is also quite effective. Anything that cools the bite area is helpful. Antihistamine creams and potions that contain local anaesthetic are not particularly effective, and often cause allergic rashes. Antihistamine tablets can be relieving, however. Sometimes a mild steroid needs to be applied, such as 1% *hydrocortisone* or even the medium-strength steroids like Betnovate or Eumovate.

Try to avoid scratching bites (cut fingernails short), or you risk skin infection. If you scratch a hole in your bite, clean it with antiseptic and cover with a sticking plaster (*see* **Skin**, p.206). Some unfortunate people are hypersensitive to insect bites, which erupt into large, watery blisters; these should not be deliberately punctured. Suffering this in one geographical region will not necessarily mean you will have the problem elsewhere.

Mosquito bites itch a lot during the first six months after you arrive in a new area. Thereafter a kind of immunity develops, so that bites hardly raise a bump. This 'immunity' is geographically localized so that, for example, Peruvians posted from one lowland jungle region to another within their own country complain of the itching and grief the mosquitoes cause at first in a new place. Do not assume you are not being bitten just because you have no itchy bites. In warm climates, if your skin is exposed between dusk and dawn, you may be taking a risk.

A slow-to-heal bump that looks like an infected mosquito bite could be a sign of **scrub typhus**, especially if the person is ill. Treatment is with a course of *doxycycline* (*see also* p.157 and 'Boils' on p.205).

Insect-borne diseases

Elephantiasis

Those who harbour this parasite for years develop elephantine swelling of the legs, hence its name; it's also known as **filariasis** because it is caused by microscopic filarial worms. This is a disease men fear, for it can cause the scrotum to become so distended that a wheelbarrow is needed to transport their sorry member; the largest recorded weighed 102kg (225 pounds). However, this takes decades, and any sane traveller will seek treatment long before things have got that far. The worms can be spread by day- and night-biting mosquitoes. Elephantiasis occurs in much of the tropics, but is treatable. The incubation period is from a few weeks to 15 months. The blood test for filaria is done more than six weeks after leaving a risk area.

Loa-loa

Loa-loa is also caused by filaria, but is spread by **horse-flies** (*Chrysops*) in West and Central African equatorial forests. Visitors (but rarely locals) experience terrific itching, followed by prickling sensations, swelling, aches and pains.

Occasionally a 7cm- (3in-) long worm meanders across the front of the eyeball, an alarming spectacle. Repellents are not very effective against the flies; avoid bites by wearing long clothes and stay in screened buildings where possible. Loa-loa is never life-threatening and it is treatable.

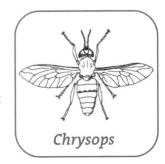

Chrysops

Biting flies

In the USA and parts of Europe, deer-flies, horse-flies and ticks transmit **tularaemia**, a treatable infection causing a range of symptoms from pneumonia to local swellings; often infected people experience no illness at all.

In Asia horse-fly bites are merely painful.

Arboviruses

Viruses spread by insects or ticks, arboviruses, are a hazard in many places: 80 cause disease in humans. There is no specific treatment and few vaccines, so prevention is all-important. Avoid bites, and know how to get ticks off quickly and safely (*see* p.p155–6). Arbovirus diseases may not be regarded as much of a problem locally. Natives who survive an attack in childhood develop good immunity – or die young from them. Travellers, however, may become very ill if infected.

Japanese encephalitis

This is a dangerous, untreatable viral illness spread by mosquitoes that bite from dusk to mid-evening and early morning to daybreak; they can travel many kilometres from their breeding ponds. Fortunately it is very rare in travellers and tourists. There is a vaccine (for further details and a map showing areas of risk, *see* p.46).

Dengue fevers

Dengue is the most common arbovirus infection. It is one of around 200 mosquito-borne viruses affecting man. The first recorded dengue outbreak was in Bangkok in 1953. Now there are about 100 million cases worldwide annually; at least two million are caused by **dengue haemorrhagic fever** (**DHF**), with 140,000 deaths, almost entirely

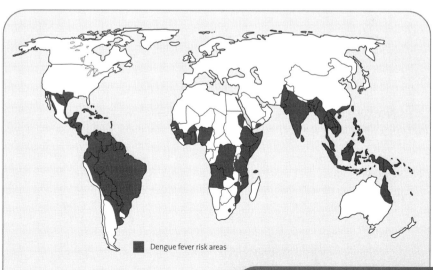

■ Dengue fever risk areas

Dengue fever is a disease of sporadic outbreaks; this map is offered as a guide to likely risk.

Risk areas: dengue fever

among local, urban children. Travellers are unlikely to contract this dangerous form. They do, however, risk classical **dengue fever (DF)** or 'breakbone fever'. The virus is spread by day-biting *Aedes* mosquitoes (*see* pp.142–3). They breed in clean water, including the rainwater that collects in the bracts of big tropical plants, which are common in the gardens of international hotels. DF usually occurs between latitudes 30°N and 40°S: it is endemic in parts of South and Southeast Asia, the Pacific, Africa and the Americas. DF has struck Texas, southeastern US, Greece, Japan and the northeastern tip of Australia but these sporadic outbreaks are rare. Dengue has become a big problem in India recently, as well as in Southeast Asia. New outbreaks are likely in burgeoning tropical cities.

The incubation period is two to eight days. DF comes on suddenly, often with a **behind-the-eyes headache** plus severe muscle and **bone pains** (hence 'breakbone' fever), high fever (40°C/104°F) and a measles-like rash, but the illness lasts no more than 10 days. Complete recovery is the norm, but it can take a month. Symptoms are much milder in children. *Paracetamol* (Tylenol) helps the fever and pain; *aspirin* is not given because this promotes bleeding and will make DHF worse. Dengue is caused by one of four viral subtypes; illness confers immunity to further attacks of the same one, but not the other three.

The dangerous variant, DHF, causes internal bleeding and shock. Left untreated, 50% of all victims die, but with hospital treatment 98% survive. Although experimental research suggests that *ribavirin* and *mycophenolic acid* inhibit the virus, these treatments are yet to be tried and currently doctors offer 'supportive treatment'. DHF is a big problem in Southeast Asia, and since 1996 there have been many cases in Latin America and the Caribbean; it is also present in the Pacific, but so far not in Africa. DHF is not completely understood, but Western travellers are at very low risk. People born in endemic regions who return home are susceptible, however.

Aedes mosquitoes breed in clean water; discourage biters by emptying out vessels like flowerpots and buckets, and disposing of old car tyres. Expatriates should cover or put fish in water tanks to eat the mosquito larvae. In Indonesia there are days when everyone in the community empties their water tanks – in order to eradicate *Aedes* larvae. Several dengue vaccines are under development but none are commercially available as yet.

Chikungunya fever

Chikungunya resembles dengue fever, but there is more lymph-node swelling. It too causes intense **joint pain** and fever. It usually resolves over three to five days but sometimes there is bleeding and some victims have an extensive rash which is longer-lasting. It was first described in Tanzania in 1952 and until the new resurgence of the disease early in 2006 it was thought to be a benign infection. Recently, however, a more dangerous strain struck the Indian Ocean region, with some deaths (in perhaps 4% of cases). There is no specific treatment. Chikungunya is transmitted by both day-flying and night-biting mosquitoes. Spraying has now largely controlled the vectors but it is always worth practising bite avoidance.

West Nile fever is detailed on p.258.

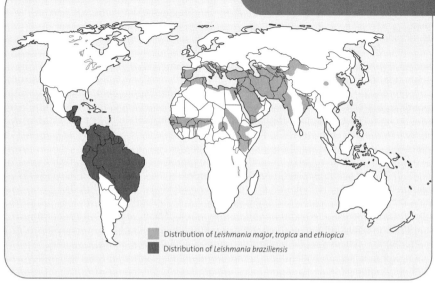

Distribution of *Leishmania major, tropica* and *ethiopica*
Distribution of *Leishmania braziliensis*

Sand-fly-borne diseases

Sand-flies or 'buffalo-gnats' are tiny, brownish, hairy flies. They are most active at twilight, but bite throughout the night. In tropical America, the Mediterranean and Middle East they transmit **leishmania**, a protozoan. This either causes painless tropical sores (*see* **Skin**, p.213) or, in hot, dry regions of the Old World, kala-azar fever.

Sandfly

Sand-flies are so small they can penetrate mosquito nets, though they cannot leave once fed. *Permethrin*-treated nets keep them out, and repellents work well. They are weak fliers, so ceiling fans also help protect you.

In the New World sand-flies are predominantly moist-forest species, and are most likely to bite during the rainy seasons in the forests of Central America, the Amazon basin and Mexico. Lowland, New World leishmania is reasonably common and hard to treat, so precautions against bites must be taken (*see* pp.143–9). The severe form of the lowland disease is *espundia*. In the Andes of Peru and Argentina, sand-flies stay close to villages, where they bite dogs, people and whoever else seems tasty. Ulcers caused by Andean leishmania (*uta*) heal by themselves. Seek medical help if you have an ulcer that will not heal, or any kind of wound that seems to be growing.

African and American trypanosomiasis

Trypanosome parasites cause disease in man and animals. Disease is rare in ordinary travellers, although there have been some cases of sleeping sickness from Tanzania. People are infected by insect vectors that have previously bitten infected domestic or wild animals. Cattle and antelope harbour sleeping sickness parasites in Africa, while in America domestic dogs or forest wildlife are the usual reservoir of Chagas' disease.

Chagas' disease and assassin bugs

Chagas' disease (American trypanosomiasis) may have killed Charles Darwin, but it is a very rare disease in travellers. It is a problem of the rural poor, occurring from the southern USA through into Central and South America. The parasite is most prevalent in Argentina, Venezuela, Chile, Peru and Bolivia; it has been virtually eliminated from Brazil, which formerly accounted for 40% of cases worldwide. It is rare in the Amazon basin, as Indian huts without walls are unsuitable homes for the **cone-nosed** or **assassin bug vectors** (see also pp.143–9). These are substantial (2–2.5cm/1 inch long), shield-shaped, flying nocturnal bugs. They rudely defecate as they take their blood

Cone-nosed bug

meal, and the parasite migrates from the bug's faeces into the victim's broken skin; often, it is aided by the victim scratching in response to the bug-bite. If the parasite gets in, an inflamed bump (a chagoma) may appear at the site of entry, and in half the cases there is a typical swelling of the eyelids, but the first stage of the disease is mild and may go unnoticed. Symptoms generally begin after several years, by which time treatment is difficult. Avoidance of bites, then, is all-important. Avoid sleeping on the floor of a wattle and daub house. A hammock helps protect you, particularly if it has a built-in mosquito net (these are sold in Latin America). There are several other species of cone-nosed bug that bite, usually in self defence; their bite is painful, but they do not feed on blood or transmit disease.

Tsetse-flies and African trypanosomiasis (sleeping sickness)

Tsetse-flies (*Glossina* spp.) transmit sleeping sickness (African trypanosomiasis) in a patchy distribution over parts of sub-Saharan Africa, mostly on forested lake shores and river banks or in forest-savannah mosaics. They like leafy habitats, but one, resplendent in the name *G. longipennis*, survives almost into the Sahara. Local knowledge about the disease is good, so ask before you venture into the bush. Tsetse-flies are active during daylight hours, fly in vast swarms, have a painful bite and are attracted to dark blue. Even sitting between people wearing dark blue can make you a target especially if you flail around. Jungle green is the best colour to wear. Tsetse are about twice the size of a house-fly. Visitors to African game parks have been infected on occasion. A small scab appears at the site of the bite and within a few days there is usually a fever which comes and goes. There is also **headache**, loss of appetite and swelling of lymph glands, especially in the neck. Eventually parasites invade the brain, causing the apathy, sleepiness and then the coma that gives the disease its name. By this time treatment is difficult.

Tsetse-fly

Plague

Bubonic plague has been with us for many thousands of years. There tend to be annual outbreaks of plague in Democratic Republic of Congo, Madagascar, Tanzania, Peru, USA, China, Mongolia and Vietnam. There have been additional outbreaks in India (in 1994), Indonesia (1997) and Algeria (2003).

Outbreaks begin in rats living among people inhabiting unsanitary accommodation. The rats die of the infection, are deserted by their fleas which go in search of a new host. People bitten by these fleas acquire bubonic plague, which is treatable with antibiotics. Travellers are most unlikely to catch the plague. There is a vaccine but it is not very effective. Those exposed to plague may take antibiotics (*tetracycline* 500mg four times daily for 10 days) as a precaution. Symptoms of plague (fever and, usually, painful swellings in the groin or other body 'junction points') require treatment (3g loading dose of *tetracycline* then 3g daily by mouth, or 1g then 500mg four-hourly by intramuscular injection). If you think that you need treatment, see a doctor. The incubation period is two to eight days.

Ticks and their diseases

Ticks are small, slow-moving animals with eight short legs. They attach themselves to larger hosts in order to dine on their blood. They are very widespread, and remarkably well adapted to surviving on an intermittent food supply: the American relapsing fever tick can live without feeding for 10 years. Unfed adult ticks are 3–6mm long, like a sesame seed with legs, but after feeding become the size and colour of a chilli bean. Catching a tick in the act of feeding on you is unattractive in itself, but its bite can be very itchy, particularly if bits of broken mouthparts are left embedded in the skin. Ticks can also carry serious

**An unfed
cattle tick**

infection, although transmission is less likely if the tick has fed for less than 12 hours. Some ticks can cause a transient but life-threatening paralysis.

Ticks are master cat-burglars; they crawl undetected over your skin before settling down to feed in some cosy corner near the genitals, or where the clothing is tight. In tick country wear long clothes, tuck trousers into socks and shirts into trousers. Insect repellent is effective against non-insects including ticks, itch mites and leeches (*see* pp.143–9 for bite-avoidance measures).

Removing ticks

Prompt removal – as soon as you find a tick – will reduce the chance of disease transmission. If the tick is squeezed, crushed or damaged, infection is more likely to be passed on. Some tick-borne pathogens can get in through intact skin, so protect the removing hand in a plastic bag (or surgical gloves if possible).

Ticks are tenacious: a barbed snout and a kind of cement hold them in place, so unless they are still in the process of settling down to feed they are hard to remove. The best method is to grasp the tick with finger and thumb as close to the skin as possible, and pull steadily. This often hurts, since the mouthparts are cemented in. Do not jerk or twist. Once it has been removed, disinfect the skin with alcohol (gin and whisky are fine) and wash your hands with soap and water. It's not necessary to put anything on the tick to make it let go, nor is it wise to apply a flame: this could singe your pubic hair, or make the tick spit, thus increasing the chances of infection.

Very small tick larvae or 'seed ticks' can be scraped off with a knife; ideally, sterilize the skin with alcohol afterwards. In Central American forests seed ticks may crawl on you in enormous numbers. Remove them before they have had a chance to attach by stroking the skin with a finger wrapped in masking tape, sticky side out. This is most easily done by a friend. If the ticks have not been damaged there is less need for skin sterilization, which may not be a practical proposition. Some people, especially when camping or mountaineering, carry tick removers. Reportedly these are useful for detaching very small ticks.

Tick-borne infections

Ticks are efficient disease transmitters because of their longevity, because they feed on blood at each stage of their life cycle and because some diseases (like tularaemia) live in the tick from one generation to the next. There are at least nine tick-borne infections in the USA; Britain's only remaining vector-borne illnesses are spread by ticks: **louping ill**, from sheep ticks in the Scottish borders, and **Lyme disease**. Others occur in Africa, Asia, South America, even Siberia. Some are easily treated with antibiotics. Most are geographically localized, and local doctors know them. They tend to start with fever, aches and pains, and headache.

'European' tick-borne encephalitis (TBE)

'European' tick-borne encephalitis is a viral disease of forests in central and eastern Europe up to an altitude of about 1,200m (4,000ft); it also occurs in parts of Scandinavia and temperate Asia (*see* maps, inside back cover and p.48). This is a nasty disease: 30% of victims suffer neurological complications (residual paralysis in the arms and shoulders) and 1–2% die of it. Deaths occur five to seven days after the start of the neurological signs. TBE ticks live in the undergrowth of deciduous woods, so campers and orienteers are most at risk and might consider immunization. Cases occur between April and November but the peak season for transmission is June to August. *See also* pp.48–9.

Why shun ticks
→ The sight of an engorging tick attached to one's warm and tender parts is unattractive.
→ Most ticks are able to transmit serious infections.
→ The bite site is often itchy and broken skin allows skin infection in.
→ If mouthparts are left in the skin, they can cause long-term itchy discomfort.
→ Some can cause a transient but life-threatening paralysis.

Lyme disease

Lyme disease has almost certainly been around for centuries, wherever *Ixodes* ticks are found. It was first described in Old Lyme, Connecticut, in 1975, when there was an outbreak of what appeared to be **arthritis** in the children. In Britain and Ireland the disease seems to be milder. It occurs mostly where sheep or deer graze among trees and bracken; Lyme disease ticks favour border habitats between woods and meadows and sparsely wooded forest paths. A vaccine against the American strain of the disease was developed and licensed in the USA and proved 76% effective (i.e. not very effective); it was withdrawn in 2002 because it appeared to cause arthritis.

Even in regions where there is a lot of Lyme disease transmission, only 1–2% of people bitten will be infected. Ticks need to be attached for more then 12 hours for Lyme to be transmitted. Then, seven to 10 days after a person is bitten, a slowly enlarging red patch, ring or weal usually appears (in 70% of cases); this does not usually itch. It spreads to a diameter of about 15cms (6in) over a couple of weeks, and may persist for months or disappear after a few weeks. Other common symptoms are aching joints (in 80% of cases), fever, aching muscles and headache. Untreated, the disease slowly progresses, developing into a serious illness that can affect the heart and brain, but antibiotics are effective; usually *tetracycline* in adults and *penicillin* in children are taken for 10–21 days but within four weeks of the bite. If diagnosis is made later intravenous antibiotics are given in hospital.

Rocky Mountain and other spotted fevers

Rocky Mountain spotted fever is a misleading name. In the USA this is now mostly a problem east of the Rockies, although it occurs in every state except Maine, Alaska and Hawaii. The disease also occurs in Mexico, Columbia and Brazil. Pets can bring ticks into homes, so this is occasionally an urban problem; there was even a case acquired in New York City. Victims become unwell after a tick bite with fever, aches and pains, and may become delirious; they usually develop reddish-purple-black spots on the soles of the feet, palms, lower legs and forearms. The rash may spread onto the trunk. It responds to antibiotics.

There are **other tick-borne spotted fevers** that occasionally cause dangerous haemorrhagic (bleeding) disease. These are rare, but occur as close to home as the Mediterranean, as far south as South Africa, and in southern Russia, India and northeast Australia as well as the Americas. They can be treated with antibiotics.

Scrub typhus

Scrub typhus is a treatable rickettsial infection usually spread by ticks (but mites or lice can be the vectors). It is widespread in the scrubby countryside of Oceania, northern parts of Australia, southeast Asia and westwards to southeast Siberia. There are similar tick-borne infections in Columbia and Brazil, and also in the Mediterranean. The site of the tick-bite often leaves a slow-to-heal bump (an eschar) that looks like an infected mosquito bite, but the victim is also ill. Treatment is straightforward and is with a course of *doxycycline*. **African tick typhus** is similar, but usually very mild, with the fever lasting only a few days. It requires no special treatment.

Case history: Australia

Beware of toilet-loving mozzies. On a camping trip in Kakadu, I had a midnight call of nature and returned with a ring of bites circling my buttocks. They were very painful to sit on the next day.

Sam Cowan, Ilford

Tick paralysis

Tick paralysis is a strange condition, most often described in people bitten by *Dermacentor* ticks in the American Pacific Northwest, but known to exist in every continent. It comes on four to six days after a tick attaches. Paralysis begins in the feet and hands; loss of coordination follows, then paralysis of the face, slurred speech and uncontrolled eye movements. By about the eighth day breathing becomes irregular, then stops. Children under age two are most commonly affected. It seems to be due to a toxin secreted by the salivary glands of the tick in a period of rapid egg development.

Fortunately, though, as soon as the feeding tick has been found and removed, symptoms usually disappear in reverse order to that of their appearance. There are no long-term after-effects. There is an antidote in Australia, where paralysis may continue after the tick has been detached.

On the Ground:
Hot Places

Hazards of heat and sun 160
  Skin care in the sun 160
  Heat illnesses 163
Jungle, forests and scrub 164
Deserts 165
Big cities 166

13

Summary

→ Protect yourself from the sun with a hat, suitable clothes and sunscreen.

→ Apply any insect repellent 30–60 minutes after applying sunscreen.

→ When outdoors, wear shoes or some other kind of foot protection.

→ Always carry drinking water.

→ Intense heat and strong sun can cause heat stroke (which can kill or disable) and sunburn (which makes life wretched and can lead to skin cancer); failing to adapt to heat will make you plain miserable.

→ The key to avoiding these problems is to change your behaviour. It's what you do rather than physiological adaptations that protect you – or not.

→ Consider the risks before heading into an unfamiliar environment; prepare properly and take sensible precautions.

→ This chapter also deals with the dangers of desert and forest environments. Sea and freshwater hazards are dealt with in the next chapter.

Hazards of heat and sun

Lots of us travel to enjoy sunshine but sometimes the heat can be too much, especially at first. The hottest place in the Indian subcontinent is northern Sindh, where summer shade temperatures reach 53°C (127°F). For Sindhis, the pace of life slows dramatically as temperatures rise: they know that reducing the amount they expect to achieve is the only way to cope with extreme heat. People sit around and sip tea or bottled drinks, and there is more time to chat. Locals too poor to take shelter and rest, may succumb, as thousands do in the worst hot seasons. Foreigners who slow down protect themselves from physical and mental burnout.

The body adapts to heat by increased sweating and by reducing the amount of salt that is lost in sweat; this change takes one to three weeks. So don't try to do too much at first, and avoid exercise around midday. Wear 100% cotton clothes, as they 'breathe' best: even 30% artificial fibre feels uncomfortable in the heat.

You must increase **water intake** in hot weather, so as to pass a good volume of pale-coloured urine at least three times a day. Passing small amounts of dark, tea-coloured urine usually means you are dehydrated. Make a conscious effort to drink more, as thirst may fail to make you drink enough. Drink at least a large glass of water with every meal. Avoid the temptation to rehydrate with beer: top up with water or soft drinks before alcohol, which is dehydrating. If you let yourself become dry, you will feel awful, and risk kidney stones (*see* p.74) and constipation. Even in extreme heat, it can be difficult to drink enough when all you have is warm plastic-and-chlorine flavoured water. I therefore use a metal (e.g. Sigg) water bottle, iodine if I need a chemical water treatment, and often add a squirt of fresh lime juice. When the heat is so intense that you cannot keep up with water loss from sweating, **oral rehydration sachets** enhance absorption of water into the body.

Skin care in the sun

Tropical sunshine is powerful, so build up exposure sensibly. Sunlight radiation not only ages the skin prematurely, it can also stimulate unpleasant-looking warty growths

Case history: India

I was in India during an unusually hot pre-monsoon when more than 2,500 Indians died of heat stroke. Temperatures were in the forties (110°F), yet I needed to work, walk, think and run a workshop. I found myself struggling up a hill at midday to look at a village water supply. At a point way above the village I cursed bringing no hat, umbrella nor water. Sweat streamed off me; I was parched, scorched, light-headed; my heart was pounding and my head was throbbing. Local colleagues were too polite to tell me to slow down. People most likely to be struck by heat illnesses are those new to heat who exercise hard within the first week of arrival. It takes at least that long for the body to adapt, by producing more sweat and moving fat from beneath the skin to around the central organs. Babies are not good at regulating their body temperature, so they can get into trouble, while older people, especially those taking heart medicines, also need to be extra wary.

After overdoing it the first day I slowed down, and found my main problem was to drink enough. I was rarely able to slake my thirst. American soldiers on desert manoeuvres are required to drink eight litres of fluid a day, and Israeli troops in the Sinai are told to drink 10. British Army doctors recommend 5 litres a day plus half a litre for every hour of physical exercise. My strolls were not on a military scale, but these figures do emphasize the huge volumes that need to be replaced. Yet a litre gulped down all at once tends to sit in the stomach. Adding rehydration salts to drinking water enhances absorption and replaces a little of the salt lost in sweat. Taste for salt increases when you are salt-depleted; in my case, curries and an occasional lime soda (with salt) were enough for my salt requirements.

called **solar keratoses,** and increase the risk of skin cancer. Some say that sunbathing at all in the tropics is daft. If you must do it, build up from 15 or 20 minutes a day, and avoid being out in the midday sun (11am–3pm); short shadows indicate that the sun is at its fiercest. Seek shade when your shadow is shorter than you. Untanned skin can burn in 15 minutes in tropical midday sun. A deep tan only gives as much protection as a factor 3 sunscreen, and sunscreens are by no means an absolute protection: factor 12 delays burning for about three hours. You will burn faster if the sun is reflected off water or other light surfaces, such as a beach, the sea or snow (see p.168), and also on a motorbike or through an open car window.

Skin cancer is not entirely understood, but it seems that while sunscreens protect from burning, they do not eliminate cancer risk. The number of skin cancer cases has risen steadily since pale-skinned people began travelling sunnier places. At special risk are white people living in the tropics (see pp.213–14); it is particularly important for fair children to be protected. The Australian campaign to protect people from skin cancer has a useful ditty – *Slip Slap Slop* – to help remember the precautions to take:

'*Slip on a shirt – Slap on a hat – Slop on some sun cream.*'

Sunscreens

The **ultraviolet** (UV) radiation that reaches us on earth consists of UVA (wavelength 320–400 nanometres) and **UVB** (290–320 nanometres). Shorter wavelengths (UVC at 100–290 nanometres) are – we hope – still intercepted by the ozone layer. UVB causes sunburn, but both UVB and UVA cause skin cancer and skin ageing. Even one episode of severe sunburn appears to greatly increase the risk of skin cancer.

Sunscreens either absorb UV energy or reflect it. Absorbent ones only protect against UVB, although some offer minimal UVA reduction. Reflectant sunscreens (sunblock) contain inert pigments (often zinc oxide or titanium dioxide) that protect against both. Their disadvantage is that they often form a white film on the skin, although many now contain 'microfined' particles of titanium dioxide that are less visible.

The **sun protection factor** (**SPF**) of a sunscreen is a measure of the difference between the dose of UV radiation that produces measurable redness in protected skin and in unprotected skin. Manufacturers' SPFs mainly refer only to UVB protection. Unfortunately, there is no standardization of SPF tests, so direct comparisons between brands aren't easy. In addition, SPFs take no account of a sunscreen's actual performance in real conditions. Nevertheless, SPF does give a rough guide to the degree of protection from UVB. People with sensitive skins should choose an SPF of 15–20, others about 10. It is unnecessary (even undesirable) to use preparations with very high SPFs (25 or more), since even at the Equator the dose of UVB radiation received in a day is not 25 times the amount that will cause sunburn, and very high SPF screens allow extended periods of sunbathing so inviting longer-term damage from large doses of UVA. Be sure to reapply sunscreen frequently (at least every two hours) when in strong sunshine.

There are now clothes and swimsuits that give good protection from UV radiation and, just as sunscreens boast their SPF, **clothes** have an ultraviolet protection factor (**UPF**). Most summer clothing has a UPF of under 15, whereas these special fabrics have UPFs of about 50, higher than the protection offered by the average sun cream. Such sun-protective clothing is available in high street shops.

Sensible clothing and other skin protection

Shirts with collars (rather than T-shirts) protect the back of the neck from burning. Wear trousers, safari shorts or long, full skirts, not short shorts, and keep the sun off your head: umbrellas are cooler than hats when walking or trekking, and more comfortable in tropical rains than a cagoule (black umbrellas get hot, white ones don't screen out enough sun; mine's a grey collapsible). A cotton bush hat can be dunked in water when you're overheating, and a wet neckerchief draped around the neck is very cooling. Cover up when riding on trucks, bus roofs or motorbikes; the cool breeze disguises the fact that you are burning.

Skin cancer and sunburn are not the only reasons for covering skin in the tropics. Being well-dressed helps protect from stinging and biting wildlife (see pp.143–7 and 'Preventing mite bites and tick attachments' box, p.235) and sexual predators. It can also be culturally sensitive and appreciated by locals.

Eyes, as well as skin, suffer from too much sun. Wear sunglasses if there is a lot of glare, or you will suffer from a soreness of the eyes like mild snow-blindness. Use only sunglasses that claim UV protection and carry a national quality mark. A hat with a brim sometimes helps, too, unless glare is being reflected up at you from sea or snow.

Treating sunburn

Calamine lotion, or preparations containing calamine, soothe sunburn but they may not be unavailable abroad. Aspirin helps calm sunburn, and silver sulphadiazine (Flamazine) is also said to help if applied to burned skin. Oily skin treatments, though, trap heat in and make sunburn more uncomfortable. Do not deliberately puncture sunburn blisters. Fluids and heat can be lost through badly burned skin, so drink plenty; you may also develop a degree of hypothermia (reduced body temperature) if you are in a climate with hot days and cold nights.

An emollient cream called tretinoin is claimed to repair years of photo-damage to the skin. Sadly the effect is only temporary, and reversible, so this is no elixir.

Case history: cycling through the Americas

Weight for weight, the cyclist uses less energy to cover a given distance than even superbly designed salmon or dolphins, birds, great cats, the motor car, or any form of jet or rocket engine (*Scientific American*, 1973). Perhaps this explains why the use of bicycles for expeditions has increased so dramatically over the past few years. Certainly, there is no more versatile vehicle known to man. One of its greatest advantages is that once a cyclist has become fit, he or she is far less likely to get ill. On a long expedition, a cyclist's immune system soon gets beefed up, and so long as food-poisoning or serious accidents are avoided, it is possible to cycle for months without having any health disorders. And with good bicycle gearing, climbing hills is no longer a problem, for fitness keeps the cardiac and respiratory changes to a bare minimum and the onset of muscle fatigue is greatly reduced. It is the wind that is the enemy of the cyclist, not mountains! On long expeditions, through such areas as Patagonia or Tibet, it is helpful to cycle during the least windy times of day – and these are often predictable.

I pedalled over 17,000 miles – from California to Tierra del Fuego – for a combined period of three years. Much of this time was spent in the high Andes visiting potters and weavers, sometimes in the remotest villages with no public transport or electricity, and I was never seriously ill. I kept fit by boiling or pilling all my water (and by NEVER getting dehydrated), by cooking most of my own meals (on an Optimus, low-grade petrol cooker) and, when in markets or cafés, only ate meals that I could see boiling before my eyes. I carried a small but comprehensive first-aid kit on the basis that 'a stitch in time...', and for me it worked!

Hallam Murray, Battersea

Medicines and sun sensitivity

If travelling in hot climates, be careful about what you do with any essential medication. If it is put in a bus hold next to the engine it may get cooked – or stolen.

A range of medicines can sensitize the skin to the sun. If you develop a rash that seems sun-sensitive and are taking any non-essential medicine, try stopping the medicine to see if the symptoms settle. Common offenders are high-dose (150 or 200mg daily) *doxycycline* antimalarial tablets (e.g. Vibramycin), *ciprofloxacin* and Bactrim, used to treat diarrhoea. Non-steroidal anti-inflammatories such as *ibuprofen* (e.g. Nurofen) and *diclofenac* (e.g. Voltarol) and many other medicines can also cause this reaction. Unfortunately some tablets prescribed to control diabetes (e.g. *glipizide*, Glibenese, Minodiab; *chlorpropamide*) can also cause this super-sensitivity to the sun, yet clearly these cannot be stopped on suspicion in the middle of your trip. It should, however, be possible to change to a different prescription drug. In this case, seek competent medical advice.

Cold sores

If you suffer from cold sores (due to the *herpes simplex* virus), exposure to strong sunlight may reactivate them. *Aciclovir* cream (*acyclovir*; Zovirax in the UK, USA, Cyclovir in India) is effective in preventing them, if applied early. Apply it when you notice the sensation of an incipient cold sore, even before it appears.

Heat illnesses

Heat exhaustion

Heat exhaustion is a particular risk in hot, high-humidity environments, especially following strenuous exercise in the sun. Overweight people are more prone to it than the very fit, and new arrivals are far more likely to suffer than those who have been in the environment for two weeks or more. There is profuse sweating (which keeps the body relatively cool), and this loss of fluids causes weakness, nausea, dizziness, exhaustion, muscle cramps, restlessness, rapid pulse and vomiting. The skin is very flushed with blood as the body attempts to increase heat loss, but this is at the expense of blood flow to the brain. The body temperature rises but stays below 40°C (104°F).

Take sufferers to a cool, shady place, where they should drink plenty of water. They will probably be very fluid-depleted and may need to drink as much as 2–4 litres in the first hour. If their temperature is 39°C (102°F) or above, they should be actively cooled by removing clothes, fanning and sponging with a cool (not ice-cold) cloth. Cooling should be continued until the victim's temperature is below 39°C.

Sufferers should do no more physical exercise that day; some would say they should be evacuated to hospital. The point at which you decide to evacuate must depend on the competence of the first-aider; if you have no experience of the problem, evacuate – but not if that means a couple of hours in a hot vehicle. If not taken seriously, heat exhaustion can rapidly lead to heat stroke, which is a medical emergency.

Heat stroke or sunstroke

Heat stroke (also misleadingly known as sunstroke) can come on suddenly, or can follow heat exhaustion. It is responsible for some deaths, and sometimes permanent disability. The body temperature is usually above 40°C (104°F), but the most important sign of heat stroke is that the victim becomes confused or behaves irrationally. There may be a lack of coordination, delirium, hallucinations and eventually even convulsions or unconsciousness. Sweating usually decreases, but the skin is not often dry. Pulse and respiratory rates are higher than normal (worrying rates in adults are a pulse-rate of over 100 beats/min, or a respiratory rate over 30/min). The respiratory rate is the number of times the chest rises.

Unconsciousness implies a very grave condition. If the victim has been unconscious for more than two minutes, evacuate him/her to a hospital while continuing cooling. Unconsciousness for longer than two hours is usually followed by permanent disability. Heat stroke is very dangerous. For **prickly heat** and **heat rash**, see pp.206–7.

Jungle, forests and scrub

Tropical and sub-tropical forests are hot, humid places where you can lose a surprising amount of body fluids very quickly. Take it easy at first, and build up the pace of activities over at least a week (even if you're fit). Some people find rainforests oppressively airless and even claustrophobic.

Wear long, loose cotton clothes and insect repellent. They keep off mosquitoes, other insects and ticks (see pp.143–7, 162 and 235) and also protect you from noxious plants (see opposite and p.208). Although most malarial mosquitoes bite at night, some forest-dwelling insects are day-biters, including vectors of dengue and yellow fevers and tropical American sand-fly-borne diseases (see table, pp.148–9). Asian rainforests and deciduous forests in the monsoon are often alive with leeches, which are also kept away by repellents and long clothes (see pp.143–7). Wear proper boots if you expect to stray from paths: you need to be especially cautious about snakes, centipedes and, after

Treating heat stroke

Treatment is as for heat exhaustion:

→ Place victim in the shade.

→ Remove clothing (the victim's, not yours, silly) and fan the victim.

→ Sponge with a cool, wet cloth (but do not apply ice).

→ Gently massage limb muscles to encourage heat dissipation.

→ Encourage drinking, if possible.

→ Monitor the temperature; stop cooling when it is below 39°C (102°F).

→ Beware of the victim's temperature rising again.

→ If the victim is unconscious, raise the legs above the level of the heart.

dark in dry forests, scorpions. Try not to grab at plants to steady yourself; many have thorns, or harbour hordes of aggressive ants. Never put your hands or feet where you cannot see them. Tropical wasps and bees readily get cross with lumbering humans and the more you flail, the more they will sting and call in further reinforcements (*see also* pp.242–3). Always shake out your boots before putting them on.

Noxious plants and wee furry animals

Tropical plants have evolved an impressive array of unpleasant ways to protect themselves. Some are covered in barbed thorns that you may not notice until you come into contact with them; they can be difficult to pull out. Furry-looking seed pods are covered in little hairs that penetrate skin and cause discomfort, only relieved by painstakingly removing each hair with a fine pair of tweezers. Prickly pears, young bamboo and a host of other tropical plants have similar defence mechanisms.

Some plants secrete irritant oils, such as the New World poison ivy and poison oak (*see* illustration, p.208). The giant hogweed, *Heracleum mantegazzianum*, causes a sunlight-sensitive rash (*see* p.208). Avoid any plant that secretes a milky sap; some cause blistering if the sap gets in your eyes. Others are extremely painful stingers. Nepalese nettles (called *sisnu* or *allo*, which look like malignant mutants of the English stinger) are exceedingly unpleasant. Antidotes which, like the European dock, grow with it, include *Artemisia dubia*, a straggly, chrysanthemum-like shrub called *titepati*.

Some small animals, such as Madagascar's cute little tenrecs (*see* illustration, p.252), can deposit masses of very fine spines in the skin, as can furry caterpillars (*see* pp.239–40). Mosquitoes and larger predators love dense undergrowth; do not go into the jungle scantily clad or ignorant of local wildlife hazards (*see* **Animals**, pp.229–52).

Deserts

The risks of heat and sun are more obvious in deserts than many other environments. If driving, consider the possible consequences of vehicle breakdown and carry plenty of water. It might also be wise to invest in a satellite phone or if heading into the desert in Australia or the USA rent a phone locally that will cover the region you plan to explore. Body-fluid losses are huge, especially when you are receiving a cooling breeze through an open window; make an effort to drink more – enough to generate three good volume, light-coloured urinations in 24 hours. Dehydration is also a risk in cold deserts.

Responsible desert relief

Arid environments are deceptively fragile, and for this and aesthetic reasons, leave no trace when you defecate and urinate. Dig a small, deep hole. Drop any toilet paper into the hole too and burn it as much as possible. Then thoroughly fill in the hole with earth and sand. In the desert the wind will sooner or later uncover buried paper, which will then merrily fly around, littering the environment and leaving unhygienic calling cards. Faeces present less of a problem because, especially when covered up, they decompose naturally. After urination, women may either 'drip-dry', burn used paper or, best of all, collect the used paper, place it in a plastic bag and dispose of it when they reach the next garbage disposal facility. Toilet paper does not decompose, so simply dropping it behind a bush or under a stone is irresponsible and will leave it to be whirled around by the wind for weeks, if not months.

Barbara Ikin, Maputo, Mozambique

If stranded without water, do not drink urine but consider other water sources, such as the car radiator (so long as no antifreeze has been added), or condensation, which collects under plastic at night. A major hazard of desert travel in vehicles is encountering unprepared travellers who scrounge water and leave you short. Carry plenty.

Avoid undue heat exposure by wearing a hat and long, loose clothing. Avoid vigorous exercise when it's very hot: the siesta is a sensible adaptation to intense midday heat. Salt tablets are not needed but if your appetite for salt increases, shake more on your food. This replaces the salt lost in sweat. In hot climates ignore the Western anti-salt health dogma.

The major animal hazards of deserts are **snakes** (*see* pp.243–7) and **scorpions** (*see* pp.240–2); some deserts have larger dangerous species, like lions in the Kalahari.

Big cities

It is possible to suffer heat stroke in vehicles. Always carry plenty of water – especially if there is any chance of being stuck in a protracted traffic jam in a big tropical city.

Many major cities, especially those in emerging nations, have a problem with air quality. This is mostly due to car exhausts but industrial air **pollution** also contributes. This is probably not the insidious poison that some people fear but carbon particles in the air reduce visibility, while ozone and sulphur dioxide gases sting the eyes and cause sore throats. This is unpleasant and unaesthetic but people at normal levels of fitness should largely be unaffected by such pollution. However, those who are asthmatic, had childhood asthma or tend to allergic conditions may find they become wheezy again, and both substances will increase the risk of chest infections. Smokers too might expect more respiratory troubles.

People who choose to exercise in polluted city environments often wear **masks** designed for cyclists but not all of these perform to the claims of some manufacturers. Price is not necessarily an indicator of quality and one of the cheapest – Kanco Eezy Breethe – performs well when assessed for leakage and filtering out pollutants, but is difficult to source. This and Respro Techno Gold (£25 from *www.wiggle.co.uk*) and the Techno Gold Upgrade Kit passed the BS EN 149 European Standard test for airborne particles and seem to perform best.

On the Ground: Water

Hazards of the sea 168
  Snorkelling and scuba-diving 169
  Coral 170
  Nasty sea beasts 171
  Dangerous sea fish 175
  Other sea hazards 177

Dangers of rivers and lakes 178
  Schistosomiasis 179
  Black-flies and river blindness 181
  Noxious freshwater creatures 182

14

Summary

→ Use adequate waterproof sunscreen and/or protective clothing, especially when snorkelling or swimming.

→ Apply any insect repellent 30–60 minutes after sunscreen.

→ Wear shoes, 'jellies' or some other kind of foot protection when bathing, strolling along the beach, swimming or paddling.

→ When venturing into an unknown body of open water heed warnings and think twice before bathing where locals say it is dangerous.

→ Avoid sunbathing in the middle of the day: the best sunscreen is shade.

→ Don't attempt a dangerous sport for the first time anywhere if the outfit does not seem geared up for beginners; check that instructors are qualified.

→ Check a reliable travel health source and read about schistosomiasis if travelling to Africa.

→ Accounts of nasty aquatic beasts are often exaggerated.

Hazards of the sea

Few can resist plunging into open water to cool off, or at least indulging in a bit of foot paddling. Water is hazardous stuff though. The salt concentration of sea water is not high enough to act as a disinfectant, and **disease organisms** can thrive in it. Swallowing sea water may give you hepatitis A if you swim in heavily contaminated, land-locked or poorly flushed seas. The Mediterranean and many British beaches are especially unhealthy, despite European laws forbidding the dumping of untreated sewage. Faecal coliform counts (measuring numbers of faecal bacteria) are now published for many UK beach sites; the record is poor. Skin problems are another consequence of bathing in heavily polluted waters (*see also* 'Red tides', p.178).

A depressing number of tourists **drown** each year while bathing in idyllic, inviting tropical seas. Many have been drinking alcohol. People worry about sharks and scorpion fish, but undertows and rip-tides are far more effective killers: in the USA you are 1,000 times more likely to drown than be killed by a shark. Listen to what locals advise about swimming, and if no one else is bathing, pause to think why.

Even in summer, temperate seas are rarely warmer than 15°C (59°F), and at these temperatures swimmers easily tire, get cramp, get into trouble and drown. Beware of swimming too soon (less than two hours) after a heavy meal. **Cramp** can sink even the strongest swimmer. It comes on much more readily if your stomach is very full and if you have any alcohol in your system; the risk is greatest in cooler waters.

Water droplets magnify the **burning** power of the sun. Even waterproof sunscreens wash off or are sweated off quite quickly, so swim wearing a shirt, as well as a good, water-resistant sunscreen. Reapply sunscreen every two hours in strong sunshine. Being out all day in tropical sun – especially reflected off water – can produce soreness of the eyes as well as sunburn. Wear good sunglasses. It is often wise to retire to some shade during the hottest part of the day, but beware that **falling coconuts** kill a surprising number of holidaymakers each year.

Wearing **shoes** or 'jellies' on tropical beaches helps avoid injuries caused by treading on sharp pieces of coral, sea-urchin spines, glass and also used hypodermic

---

Case history: Central America

In three months working at a rehabilitation centre for disabled children on the Pacific coast of Mexico, I was called three times to the beach to resuscitate people who had drowned. All had been drinking alcohol and had been swept out by rip currents. Despite proper mouth-to-mouth resuscitation, none survived.

Don't get drunk and swim.

Jean Sinclair RGN, MSc

---

needles, which are increasingly common on some beaches. Scuba 'fins' offer a little protection, but they do not protect from venomous fish.

Surfers who frolic in the chilly seas around the British Isles have their very own special affliction: **surfers' ear** where there is bony narrowing of the ear canal. It is caused by prolonged cold water immersion. The ears feel blocked but there is no deafness; wearing ear plugs helps. *See also* 'Swimmers' ear', p.178.

Snorkelling and scuba-diving

When planning a trip to explore the submarine world, manta rays, sharks and giant squids might worry you, but the most significant hazard that you must plan for is probably the sun. Tropical and sub-tropical sun burns fair skin in minutes and, if snorkelling, the skin of your back, back of the neck, thighs and calves can burn badly and blister while you are keeping cool just below the surface. Water doesn't protect the skin from radiation, indeed, water droplets can act like magnifying lenses to increase the possibilities of damage. Scuba-divers too risk sunburn, especially when in the boat travelling to a dive site, since the sun is stronger when reflected off water. Wear a waterproof sunscreen and a T-shirt or, even better, an old polo shirt with a collar. When snorkelling, wear long 'shorts'. Ensure that there is high-SPF sunscreen on any exposed parts, including the nape of the neck and the backs of the legs. Consider wearing a **swimsuit** made from special fabrics with their own ultraviolet protection factor, which offer better protection from UV radiation than the average sun cream (*see also* **Hot Places**, pp.160–3).

A large number of diving centres exist all over the tropics. If you have no scuba experience, don't be tempted to 'have a go' unless you are offered training to a recognized standard. The PADI certificate is the most widely recognized international dive-masters' qualification; NAUI or the British Sub-aqua Club Sports Diver certificate are equivalent. Avoid dive centres that do not boast such qualifications. You can burst a lung and die of **air embolism** while ascending from a depth of as little as three metres, and this kind of injury is common in people learning to use compressed air but who are not properly supervised. Check the equipment before use.

It is possible to suffer from **decompression sickness** if you fly soon after scuba-diving. If you have a single dive each day, it should be safe to wait just 12 hours before flying. If you have dived several times a day for several days or you have made dives with decompression stops, an extended time on the surface of 24 hours or more is necessary. If there has been treatment of decompression sickness in a

Sea and shore tips

→ Wear shoes on the beach and when swimming to avoid getting bits of coral and worse in your feet.

→ Avoid sunburn when swimming and snorkelling by wearing a shirt and waterproof sunscreen.

→ Take local advice about where it is safe to snorkel or swim: there may be rip tides, estuarine crocodiles or risk of shark attack.

→ Avoid alcohol or recreational drugs before entering the sea. Drowning is much more likely if you are intoxicated.

→ Be very careful when picking up any tropical sea creatures: lots are armed and venomous.

chamber, it may be necessary to wait as long as seven days before flying, and expert advice should certainly be sought. The British Institute of Naval Medicine runs a 24-hour helpline for divers (see 'Contact information: scuba-diving', below).

Gloves give useful protection if you must collect anything from beneath the waves, although keep in mind that there are some seriously be-weaponed little beasts that demand respect (see pp.171–7). Some of the most attractive cone shells of the tropics possess a venomous harpoon that packs enough poison to kill an adult.

Contact information: scuba-diving

British Institute of Naval Medicine divers' 24-hr emergency helpline: UK **t** (07831) 151 523.

www.bsactravelclub.co.uk: Reports on driving destinations.

www.scuba-doc.com: Full of excellent advice on every aspect of health and diving, but with lovely quirky stuff too.

Coral

After the sun, probably the next most likely hazard when plunging into warm seas is from coral. Its gorgeous colours and the fact it is a haven for all kinds of marine life make it attractive. Live coral looks soft and beautiful, but don't get too close and consider wearing a T-shirt and gloves for protection: a snorkeller wearing gloves can fend themselves off a coral reef in choppy seas. Coral is highly abrasive. The scratches you get by brushing against it will suppurate and be particularly sore and uncomfortable, sometimes for weeks. Wash abrasions thoroughly, remove any coral, sand or debris and apply antiseptic (see p.204). Sea water isn't salty enough to be antiseptic and so continuing to sea-bathe after sustaining abrasions is asking for trouble.

Probably the most common problem from coral is caused by the small fragments that make up many idyllic palm-fringed beaches; these readily penetrate the soles of the feet, and even a small piece is painful and remarkably difficult to extract. You may need to find a doctor to tease it out. Wear shoes when paddling or swimming (see also 'Sea anemones, starfish and sea urchins', p.174). Finally, varieties of **stinging corals**, known as fire corals, can inflict extremely

> **Case history: Central America**
> A strong swimmer and life saver from Ontario, Canada, was standing on rocks on the Pacific coast of Costa Rica, watching the sea for the first time ever. He was well used to large bodies of water – the Great Lakes – but didn't realize that not all waves are the same size. He was washed off his feet by a big 'seventh' wave, and had to swim for nearly half an hour before he struggled back on land, suffering in this time a badly gashed knee that required several stitches. However experienced you are on home ground, local conditions elsewhere may be very different and challenging.
>
> *Jean Sinclair RGN, MSc*

painful and persistent stings, but these are uncommon (hot water immersion may help, *see* 'Treatment of fish stings', p.175).

Nasty sea beasts

Sea creatures need to be able to protect themselves otherwise they end up in something else's stomach. Assume all marine animals to be venomous and treat them with respect. Swimmers and paddlers are stung by venomous fish even in temperate regions, and noxious creatures abound in tropical seas. Fish toxins are inactivated by immersion in very hot water; prevention and treatment are described in detail below. Touch nothing unless you are sure it is harmless, and wear stout gloves if you are collecting anything or rummaging around in crevices. Collecting living creatures is not only bad news for them, it could be for you too.

Cone mollusc

Cone shells

The attractive cone molluscs of the Indo-Pacific measure up to about 23cm (9in) in length, although most are much smaller. They possess a venomous, tongue-like, harpoon tooth, and have stung collectors through the trouser pocket. Stings can cause unpleasant tingling and numbness, and sometimes even paralysis and death from respiratory arrest. Resuscitation can be life-saving, but there is no antivenom. Do not collect live specimens.

The octopus family

Octopus saliva contains a vicious toxin that can be introduced into the skin by a bite from the animal's powerful beak, between the tentacles. Bites are painful and bleed, swell and become inflamed. Blue-ringed octopi, *Hapalochlaena maculosa* and *H. lunulata* of Australia, Indonesia and the Philippines possess such toxic nerve poisons that they can cause fatal paralysis within 15 minutes of a bite. They are only the size of a human hand (10cm/4in long) and can be found in shallow waters.

The flying squid, *Onychoteuthis banksi*, is also dangerous, but since it only comes up near the surface after dark it rarely comes into contact with people. Those bitten are almost always fishermen. Flying squid are sold as food throughout their range; exercise care when preparing them for the table in case they are still alive.

Jellyfish and their kin

Jellyfish, sea wasps, the Portuguese man o' war, fire coral, sea anemones and sea nettles all have venomous stinging capsules called nematocysts. Jellyfish stings are most likely when there are onshore winds. Fortunately, very few species are dangerous and in the region where they commonly cause trouble – the northern coasts of Australia – coastguards warn people if dangerous jellyfish have come inshore.

Worldwide, there are about 30 deaths a year due to jellyfish. Just six species are responsible for these deaths. Three are the **box jellyfish** (*Chironex* spp.), also called 'sea wasps'. These are box-shaped, with tentacles hanging from the four corners of the squarish 'bell'. The largest, most venomous and fast-swimming is ***Chironex fleckeri***, which occurs in Southeast Asia and along the tropical coasts of Australia. They have bodies as big as basketballs (20cm/8in diameter) and tentacles that trail out for 3m (10ft). The tentacles (which carry the sting-cells) are translucent and difficult to see and thus are easy to brush against. Those who are stung experience incredible pain and may collapse and die, sometimes within four minutes. Flooding the stung skin with vinegar inactivates any undischarged stingers. There is a specific antivenom in Australia, which is given by lifeguards. The **Irukandji** (*Carukia barnesi*) is another box jelly that has been causing grief in tropical Australia, yet it is only the size of your thumb. Often, contact with these goes unnoticed, but if people are stung by lots of them they collapse and may not survive (*see* opposite for prevention and treatment).

The **Portuguese man o' war** (*Physalia physalis*), is common in the warm waters of the Atlantic, Pacific and Indian Oceans, and occasionally kills. It possesses a 10–30cm (4–12in) broad, bluish float, with tentacles beneath that trail for 20m (22 yards). The smaller Indo-Pacific species, called the bluebottle in Australia, has just one large tentacle. Vinegar must not be applied after Portuguese man o' war stings because this will make more nematocysts discharge.

Chiropsalmas quadrigatus inhabits the seas of Indo-China, from the Maldives to the Philippines. It also occurs in the Atlantic, from Brazil to North Carolina. There has been one reported death in southeast China

Sea wasp

Irukandji

Portuguese man o' war

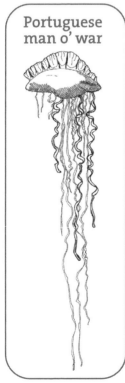

Case History: Australia

I like the big landscapes of tropical North Queensland, but swimming is an amazing palaver. You either put on tights and T-shirt, invest in a 'stinger suit' or use the 'town beach', which is dragged with a net every day. Being a bloke on holiday, and not having packed tights, or a Lycra one-piece, I went for the town beach option.

This was fine except it still seemed like swimming in jellyfish soup with added stingy bits. I watched the 'surf rescue person' do the jellyfish drag. Basically he had a tadpole net and a four-year-old helper. Occasionally he scooped up and picked out a 'deadly' box jellyfish with his fingers. There's a knack obviously. What was interesting was:

→ Sweeping the beach sounds thorough but is in fact stunningly underwhelming.

→ A deadly jelly can be picked up with bare hands if you know how.

→ Jellyfish aren't usually deadly but stings hurt for a long time.

→ The best medicine is vinegar (upmarket tourists may use balsamic).

→ They often sting children because it's mostly children who play along the shoreline where jellies gather.

→ 'Box jellies' aren't the biggest baddies since the Irukandji arrived, but you can't see an Irukandji because they are transparent and smaller than a fingernail.

→ None of the local info on jellyfish seems consistent or gives much confidence in its reliability.

→ After weighing all this up, who wants to go for a swim anyway?

Later, on a snorkelling trip, I rented a 'stinger suit' (not for the fashion conscious) and found that, along with the joy of no jellyfear, you can't get sunburn, so you don't have to grease up with ghastly waterproof suncream. So I thoroughly recommend getting into one (don't worry – they stretch to all sizes).

Edward Howarth, Melbourne

by stings of *Stomolophus nomurai*, which has a 1.5m (5ft) diameter bell. Stay away from big jellyfish wherever you are.

Australians recommend wearing two pairs of tights/panty-hose as **protection** from jellyfish stings. Put one pair on conventionally and then by cutting a hole in the crutch and cutting the feet off the other pair, you can put your arms into the legs, head through the crutch hole and your hands emerge where the feet of the tights were. Then, you tape the two waistbands together to make a whole outfit. I am not sure, however, that I'd feel much like swimming in such garb, so I think I'd wear a proper protective suit, which is available in Australia and is a more chic alternative.

Treatment of jellyfish stings

Try to remove any fragments of clinging tentacles with your fingers or, better still, scrape them off with a credit card. Tentacles still sting after they have broken off the jellyfish. Vinegar (4–6% *acetic acid*) inactivates the stingers of the Indo-Pacific and Australian box jellyfish including the Irukanji, but do not use this on other species. A half-and-half slurry of baking soda and water inactivates the stingers of the unpleasant *Chrysaora* sea-nettle jellyfish and other Atlantic jellyfish. Otherwise immerse in hot (less than 45°C/113°F) water (as for fish stings, *see* p.175) **Never** 'treat' stings by applying alcoholic solutions, such as methylated spirits and suntan lotion, nor by applying kerosene, urine, hot sand or fresh water: these all cause massive discharge of stingers and **exacerbate poisoning**.

Superficial pain usually responds to cold packs or ice applied for 15 minutes. If a victim has stopped breathing, give mouth-to-mouth resuscitation and, if necessary, cardiac massage. The effects of the venom are remarkably short-lived, so that keeping the victim alive for a few minutes with mouth-to-mouth resuscitation means that he or she will probably come around and recover completely, albeit with scars. After a Portuguese man o' war sting, itching can persist for months, and is best treated with a mild steroid ointment or cream like *hydrocortisone* or Betnovate.

Sea anemones, starfish and sea urchins

Anemones sting their prey, so treat them with respect. Even in the tame waters of the Adriatic coast there is one species, *Anemonia sulcata*, that can inflict painful stings, and, like fish stings, this venom is also heat-inactivated (*see* 'Treatment of fish stings', opposite).

Starfish and **sea urchins** have venomous spines and grapples, which can produce dangerous poisoning. Spines embedded in the skin are at best a painful nuisance. Remove them after softening the skin with 2% *salicylic acid* ointment or *acetone* or *magnesium sulphate* paste. This paste is readily available in pharmacies and should be applied under a waterproof dressing; softening may take some days. This technique may also be useful for extracting deeply embedded pieces of coral (*see* p. 170).

Sea snake

Saltwater crocodiles and sea snakes

Saltwater crocodiles (*Crocodilus porosus*) are said to be the most vicious killers in the world; they are bloodthirsty and insufficiently imaginative to fear anything. They are the biggest of the crocodiles, with reliable records of beasts 7m (7½ yards) long and many claims of others in excess of 10m (11 yards). They are found in the sea, mangrove swamps, tidal parts of rivers and estuaries in Southeast Asia, India, Sri Lanka and Australia. Seek local advice before you bathe.

Moray eel

Sea snakes are highly venomous, but fortunately, they rarely bite. Of the few people bitten by sea snakes, some 80% receive no venom and suffer no ill effects. Sea snakes are easy to see because they have striking markings and their vertically flattened, oar-like tail distinguishes them from **eels**. Snakes are sluggish and loll around in warm seas, rocking with the swell. If you happen to be snorkelling above one when it surfaces for a breath, you might get bitten, but the only time that they are commonly provoked into aggression is when they are caught in a fishing net or otherwise harassed. Sea snakes go in for orgies, gathering in numbers to mate; if disturbed at this time they can also be aggressive; I sympathize. If you find a group, stay clear. Afford individuals respect and they will leave you alone.

Dangerous sea fish

About 100 species of fish can administer dangerous stings, and a selection (barracuda, moray and conger eels, garfish, groupers and sharks) can inflict severe bites. Fish stings are common, and there are around 1,500 stingray stings and about 300 scorpionfish stings a year in the USA alone. However, fatalities from fish stings are rare, and so are deaths from shark attacks.

Stonefish

Venomous fish

Stonefish often lurk in shallow water, well camouflaged, half-buried and looking like stones. Impaling a bare foot on their venomous fins or spines is an excruciating experience, but there is a stonefish antivenom. The equally venomous **scorpionfish** and **lionfish** make themselves more conspicuous, and may charge if threatened. Rabbit fish, stargazers, dragonets, catfish and toadfish also carry venom and should be treated with respect.

Lionfish

Weever fish

Venomous fish are not peculiar to tropical waters. European weever fish are common around Britain, especially Cornwall, where they cause many excruciating stings. They also occur in the Mediterranean. It is an undistinguished but tasty little brown fish used to make *bouillabaisse*. Like scorpionfish, they have venomous dorsal fins, and often lie partially buried in sand in shallow water, so that it's easy to tread on them. The sting is so painful that a Welsh trawlerman cut off his toes to get relief.

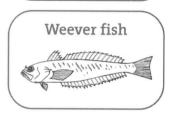

Weever fish

Treatment of fish stings

Fish venom is inactivated by heat, so the treatment (whether the sting is from a tropical or temperate species) is to immerse the affected limb in water that is hot but not scalding (no more than 45°C/113°F). Pain relief is usually immediate, but pain may return. Continued soaking will probably be needed, including a topping up with hot water, for 30–90 minutes; by this time most of the pain will have gone. Repeat the hot soaks if pain returns. Antivenoms exist for some species, and doctors can also inject local anaesthetic, which also gives some relief. *Morphine* and *pethidine* (*meperidine* or Demerol in the USA) do not really help the pain; even where modern medical facilities are available hot water treatment will bring the quickest relief. Subsequently, any pieces of your assailant must be removed, or infection will set in. Foreign bodies, be they fish spines, pieces of coral or rusty nails, will all lead to infection if left in a wound. Debris will also tattoo the skin.

Stingrays

Stingrays are armed with up to 30cm- (12in-) long venomous spines on their tails, which they use to lash out against legs or bodies. They are common in tropical, sub-tropical and most temperate seas. Stingrays occur as far north as Scandinavia and are found in the Mediterranean. They inflict many injuries each year: it is not unusual for victims to receive lacerations 13–17cm (5–6½in) long, as well as the excruciating venom. In Australian coastal waters there is a species that reaches a length of about 5m (5½ yards) and a weight of 350kg (771½lb). There are also nasty freshwater rays in South America. Any ray sting causes awful pain and swelling, which is at its worst 30–60 minutes after being stung. Stings can also sometimes cause collapse and even death. Immersion in hot water neutralizes the venom.

Stingray

Stings are the rays' defence when surprised. Wearing shoes will give you little protection from stingrays (although you will avoid other venomous fish), but adopting a shuffling walk when paddling in shallow water will advertise your presence so that the fish will swim away before you tread on it.

Sharks

Being eaten alive by a shark is an image that nightmares are made of, yet the risk of shark attack is extremely small. There are probably fewer than 100 shark attacks a year worldwide, of which only a small minority – around 10 – are fatal. Compare this with about 400 deaths annually from drowning in Britain's chilly waters alone. You are more likely to be struck by lightning than end up in a shark's belly. And contrast the small number of human deaths due to sharks to the 100 million sharks that are killed annually by people – mainly for shark's-fin dishes. In Australia you are 10 times more likely to be killed by a falling coconut than a shark attack! Attacks in the Mediterranean and Europe are rare: there have been only 78 recorded in the last 100 years.

The nearer you are to the Equator, the less dangerous sharks seem to be. Tropical waters are so well stocked with fish that sharks do not usually trouble to attack something as large and indigestible as a snorkeller or swimmer. The problem with sharks, though, is that they are unpredictable. Most attacks seem to be from 'rogue' individuals, or they occur when someone is unfortunate enough to precipitate or get caught up in a 'feeding frenzy'. Sharks then become so mad that injured

Avoiding shark attacks

Shark attacks are less likely if you:
→ Don't wear shiny jewellery.
→ Avoid murky waters.
→ Don't swim at dusk (when sharks hunt).
→ Avoid splashing or thrashing about – especially if sharks are circling.
→ Don't swim while bleeding.

*See also **www.sharktrust.org***

individuals turn to eat their own entrails. Hungry sharks smell blood and damaged flesh (especially fish oil) from half a kilometre away. Spear-fishermen who carry their catches on their belts may be more at risk of attack; menstruating women may be at increased risk of shark attack, but experts differ on this.

Bull sharks, which can be found in salt and fresh water, seem to be bigger killers than the notorious great white shark of *Jaws* fame. Tiger sharks seem to be the most aggressive and are said to have a go at anything.

A common prelude to an attack is the shark circling its victim. Try to keep calm and swim away steadily, as thrashing will excite the shark. Keep it in view, and if it comes close try banging it on the nose, poking it in the eye and shouting under water: these techniques sometimes work. Shark skin is highly abrasive, and will tear your skin if the shark brushes past you, which could precipitate a feeding frenzy.

Most shark attacks occur around latitudes 30°N and 30°S. There are 30–40 shark attacks annually in Florida, with about three deaths. Take advice before swimming. If there have been shark attacks, or if there are nasty currents or other dangers, locals will know about them.

Other sea hazards

Stinging sea

Swimmers sometimes notice stinging sensations in tropical seas. Unlike 'sea lice' (*see* below) this affects everyone in a similar way, and immediately. Expatriates blame it on stinging seaweed since the problem is most apparent when there is a lot of weed in the water. It is probably due to jellyfish larvae or segments of jellyfish stingers that come in to the beach with the onshore winds and are mixed up in the weed debris. It is an unnerving sensation, but transient.

'Sea lice' or sea-bathers' eruption

This has only recently been recognized; it is also known as **ocean itch**, *caribe* or **sea poisoning**. A few hours after bathing in tropical seas, swimmers notice raised, red weals that last several days. The rash appears most usually on skin that has been covered by bathing suits or in places where the skin is rubbed, such as the armpits, the backs of the knees and, in surfers, where skin has been in contact with the board. In Florida, where it is best-known, 'sea lice' seem to be caused by stings from larvae of the **thimble jellyfish**, *Linuche unguiculata*. These are tiny, near-invisible creatures half a millimetre long that get caught between swimsuits and the skin.

Not everyone is affected in the same way; people who have never met the larvae before will have no rash. The disease seems to be an immune hypersensitivity reaction to jellyfish venom, and those who have encountered larvae several times notice a mild stinging sensation as they swim. They can give an early warning to other swimmers.

The thimble jellyfish is a widespread species, occurring off Central and South America as well as in the Indo-Pacific, including the Philippines. Other jellyfish larvae are probably capable of causing similar problems anywhere in warm seas. On the Florida coast 'sea lice' are only present between April and July (inclusive). They only occur in some years and, as with other jellyfish stings, usually when there are onshore winds.

Treatment of 'sea lice'

'Sea lice' inject venom under the skin, so nothing you put on the skin will go deep enough to counteract it. The only action that is likely to help is to remove bathing suits and take a shower (preferably in salt water initially) after swimming. Showering in fresh water with the swimsuit on will make the venomous cysts of the larvae discharge, aggravating the situation. Anyone who has an attack of 'sea lice' will probably experience another when they wear the same swimsuit again. It is therefore advisable either to throw the swimsuit away or machine-wash it with detergent and tumble-dry it.

Red tides

This phenomenon occurs at unpredictable times in warm seas, turning the ocean red, and can happen anywhere in the tropics. In a red tide, abnormal accumulations of tiny dinoflagellate organisms produce toxins that are released into the sea and sometimes (due to the action of the surf) into the air. These aerosol toxins can cause slight irritation of the airways, a cough, a runny nose, sneezing and sore eyes, and asthmatics tend to wheeze. There is no treatment except to stay away from the red surf; also avoid swimming near a red tide. For problems associated with eating seafood during a tide, see **Worms, Guts and Nutrition**, pp.124–5.

Swimmers' ear

Trips involving lots of time in the water can predispose people to swimmers' ear – an infection of the ear canal. *Aluminium acetate* (as 8% drops) will help prevent recurrences. Alternatively a drop or two of whisky, gin, vodka or rum in the ear several times a day for a few days is as good as eardrops but much cheaper. Very sore swollen ears may need drops containing both an antibiotic and a steroid, obtained from a doctor or pharmacy (*see also* p.268).

Dangers of rivers and lakes

The principal risk of bathing is **drowning**. A surprising number of riverside beauty spots and apparently tranquil pools have claimed the lives of careless revellers. Be wary, especially in limestone areas, where rivers could suck you underground.

In the UK more people drown **inside vehicles** than while swimming. Here is what to do if your car ends up in deep water. When a car plunges into water it settles nose down, as the heaviest bit, the engine, is usually at the front, while the boot (trunk) remains full of air. The submerged car will begin to fill with water, but it is only when it is reasonably full that you will be able to open a door and get out. If you are in the front seats you may be submerged inside the car before enough water has entered to allow you to escape. **Wind down windows** to let the car fill up quickly, so that you can then open the doors or exit through a window.

If you **fall out of a boat** and are swept into a rapid, or are white-water rafting and are taken downstream out of control, ensure that you are travelling feet first; that way, if you hit any boulders or obstacles, your feet will take the impact, not your head. Even if you feel you can make headway by swimming against the current, resist the temptation to swim across the river. You will get swept downstream faster. **Swim heading upstream**, pointing just a few degrees towards the bank you wish to reach. You will slowly progress across in a 'ferry glide'. Ducks and other experienced river users adopt this technique.

Finally, if you get caught up in a **standing wave** at the bottom of a small watershoot or waterfall, you will be held in the water, unable to breathe, just below the surface. The only way to escape is to **swim downwards**. The water at the bottom of the standing wave (canoeists call them 'stoppers') will flush you out and allow you to surface. This is one rare situation where a life jacket may reduce your chances of escape; jettison it if you are caught in a **stopper** and the jacket prevents you from swimming downwards.

Some white-water rivers may be quite polluted, so keep your mouth shut when you fall in and promptly sterilize even the slightest graze with a good drying antiseptic, such as dilute iodine or *potassium permanganate* crystals dissolved in a little water.

Schistosomiasis (bilharzia)

Napoleon called Egypt the land of menstruating men because peeing blood is a symptom of one of the three forms of schistosomiasis. The disease was first described in Egypt in 1851 by German Doctor Theodore Bilharz. His name has lived on as bilharzia, perhaps because it is easier to pronounce than schistosomiasis. The disease used to be so common in Egypt that mothers were said to consult doctors if their sons failed to start 'menstruating' as a normal part of puberty locally. It isn't; it is a cause of debility and failing health.

Bilharzia is caused by a minute worm, which spends part of its life-cycle in freshwater snails and the other part in people. The parasite causes 'swimmers' itch' as it burrows through the skin while you paddle or bathe in infected water. The

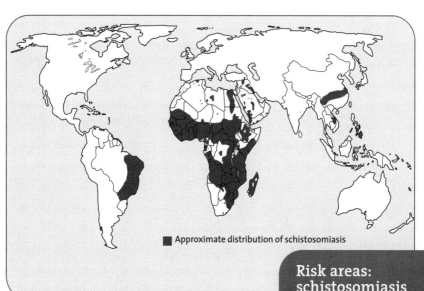

■ Approximate distribution of schistosomiasis

Risk areas: schistosomiasis

Avoiding schistosomiasis

→ If you are swimming, paddling or wading in fresh water that could carry a bilharzia risk, try to get out of the water within 10 minutes.

→ Dry off thoroughly and vigorously with a towel.

→ Avoid bathing or paddling within 200m (219 yards) of villages or places where people use water, especially reedy shores or where there is lots of weed.

→ It is safer to bathe early in the morning than later in the day.

→ If your bathing water comes from a risky source, try to ensure that it is taken from the lake in the early morning and stored snail-free; otherwise it should be filtered (CDC recommends using coffee filter paper!), or add Dettol or Cresol to it.

→ Cover yourself with DEET insect repellent while swimming.

→ If you have been exposed to bilharzia arrange a blood test more than six weeks – but ideally less than 12 weeks – after your last contact with suspect water.

species that occur in Africa and the Middle East (*Schistosoma haematobium* and *S. mansoni*) and in America (*Schistosoma mansoni*) are slow penetrators. Since it takes at least 10 minutes to get through the skin, a quick splash across a suspect stream should do you no harm; vigorous towelling after bathing also kills any parasites caught in the act. Unfortunately, oriental schistosomiasis (*Schistosoma japonicum*) penetrates within a few minutes and is altogether a much nastier parasite.

From the skin, the worm rides the bloodstream, traverses the lungs – where it often causes coughs two to three weeks after the **swimmers' itch** – and finally sets up home to cause an illness with fever. If left untreated, this will settle, but over years, especially if fired by further infections, the disease becomes debilitating, and it can kill after a couple of decades. Travellers are mostly diagnosed and cured in a couple of months; the real sufferers are the poor, who are repeatedly infected and have no access to treatment. Until the 1970s the cure was almost as bad as the disease. Now, though, a single dose of *praziquantel* cures bilharzia. Resistance may be developing although some treatment failures seem to be to do with cures being given too soon. *Oxamniquine* can be used to treat intestinal schistosomiasis and *metrifonate* urinary bilharzia. Avoidance is still better than cure: avoid unnecessary bathing in high-risk areas.

'Swimmers' itch' is even an occasional problem in Britain; schistosomes penetrate the skin, but are unable to complete their life-cycle. An example is *Trichobilharzia* of Loch Lomond, which causes mild, short-lived itching and needs no treatment.

Bilharzia country

Schistosomiasis snails like well-oxygenated, still or slowly moving freshwater with some plant life in it. The snails must first be infected by someone who has the disease urinating or defecating into the water; the risk of infection is therefore greatest in water that is close (less than 100m/300ft) to human settlements. Schistosomiasis is a growing problem in some irrigated areas, mainly in Africa; some criticize irrigation projects for epidemics, but projects that are properly built do not cause problems.

The disease afflicts perhaps 200 million people worldwide (*see* map, p.179), and is prevalent in much of Africa including Madagascar and Mauritius. It also occurs in

Case history: Malawi

Schistosomiasis is a growing concern for travellers to Africa. Many lakes, rivers and irrigation canals carry a risk of infection if people swim, wade or even shower in contaminated water. Blood tests on Malawi expatriates show that two-thirds have been exposed to schistosomiasis, and in 1995 there was an outbreak in a group of people scuba-diving off Cape Clear in Lake Malawi for only a week; three-quarters of them acquired the disease. Diving off a boat into deep offshore water should be a low-risk activity, but showering in lake water or paddling along a reedy shore near a village is high-risk for catching schistosomiasis. This was how the divers became ill.

the Middle East and the tropical Americas (northeast Brazil, the Guianas, Surinam, Venezuela and some Caribbean islands). The Indian subcontinent is clear except for a tiny area in Maharashtra. The oriental form has a patchy distribution: it occurs in parts of China, Taiwan, Vietnam and the Philippines, but Indonesia is free of it except for two remote valleys in central Sulawesi. Schistosomiasis is never acquired from sea bathing.

Black-flies and river blindness (onchocerciasis)

River blindness (onchocerciasis) is a problem in much of tropical sub-Saharan Africa, between 19°N and 17°S, and in central and tropical South America (*see* map, below). The unpleasant worm is transmitted near to fast-flowing rivers where small black-fly vectors breed. These *Simulium damnosum* are a nuisance even in regions (like Asia) where river blindness is absent; their bites cause big lumps in the skin with a bloody speck at the centre, and are itchy for days. Black-flies bite during the day.

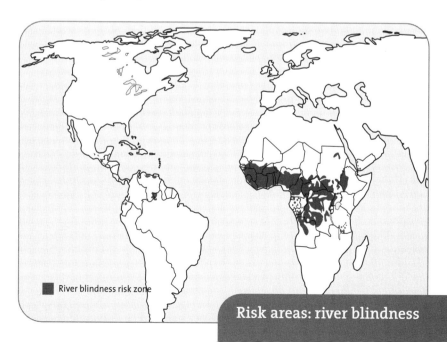

■ River blindness risk zone

Risk areas: river blindness

Onchocerciasis has a variety of manifestations, since it invades many parts of the body, but in travellers it most commonly makes the skin incredibly itchy. Itching is usually confined to a single limb, the arms or just the legs. Generally people need to have had heavy infestations for years before the eyes are threatened. Do not treat yourself; get the problem properly diagnosed. Long trousers, socks and repellents protect the skin from bites in Africa, but in the Americas the arms also need to be well covered.

Black-fly

Noxious freshwater creatures

Aquatic leeches

Aquatic leeches inhabit mountain streams and stagnant water; species that bother people are mostly found in Southeast Asia and Indonesia. They are acquired by swimming in or drinking from infested streams or pools, so drink only boiled or filtered water. Some are slow feeders and stay attached for weeks. If one invades a body orifice (this is enormously rare in travellers) it will probably have to be removed in hospital, but complications are unlikely. If a leech is attached inside the mouth, throat or nose, gargle or sniff a strong salt solution.

Candiru (*Vandellia cirrhosa*)

If you urinate in South American rivers, there is a fish, it is said, that follows the stream to its source, swims inside, sticks out barbed fins and stays put. It can then only be removed surgically, perhaps by penile amputation. The tiny candiru (also called the *carnero* fish) is 40–60mm (1½–2 inches) long and only 4–6mm broad. It embeds itself within the gills of other fish, but the idea of it parasitizing people is exaggerated (*see* 'Case history: willy fish', below).

Crocodiles

Crocodiles are merciless killers, but estimates of the number of human deaths worldwide range between 150 and 1,000 per year. New World crocodilians seem to be less dangerous: most deaths are due to the **Nile crocodile** (*Crocodilus niloticus*) in Africa (including Madagascar) and the **saltwater crocodile** (*see* p.174) in Asia and Australia.

Case history: willy fish

I was working in the village of Aishalton, South Rupununi, in Guyana. It was the usual 4pm social gathering of village worthies – nurse, policeman and so on – at the clinic. A rather distressed small boy was brought in, complete with tiny wiggling candiru fish. The nurse took a look, passed the child to one of the Wapishiana women, and went back to her rum. The fish does not penetrate far into the urethra and the Amerindians are adept at removing them with a thin implement. Penile amputation is a myth popularized by the late William Burroughs in his novel *Naked Lunch*. The nurse told me that she saw one case every couple of years – usually in the dry season when water concentrated in pools attracts both catfish (the main candiru host) and children. Certainly the Amerindians don't regard them as a hazard: compared with stingrays and electric eels, they aren't.

Professor Paul Shaw, University of Sheffield

Case history: Meru Game Park, Kenya

We had driven many miles by the time we came upon a spring that had been converted into a pool for wayward stragglers. After lunch and washing up, we reclined in cool relief until another vehicle arrived, churning up much dust. The parents joined us in the tiny pool while their two young children went to explore a marshy area nearby.

'Daddy! Crocodile!' screamed the girl. We assumed this was a game, until the boy flipped over and disappeared amidst much splashing. Never did four people move so fast. The mother was first to reach the croc. I ensured I arrived last.

As I ran, one of those rare great thoughts came to me. In the Land Rover, we had a massive *panga*, which I diverted to pick up. I observed that mother was pulling the boy, father was trying to wrench the beast's jaws apart and my old friend and expat schoolmaster, Sean, was hitting its head. He was top at boxing at school but it was to no avail. The croc had the boy securely around the waist. I handed the *panga* to Sean, who delivered two blows on the back of its neck. This caused the croc to release the boy, but only for a second while it regained hold on his leg. Another good blow and it let go and slunk off.

There was blood everywhere. Another vehicle arrived with parents of a new baby. The baby's terry-towelling nappies were used to bandage the seven-year-old's midriff for the 200-mile drive to Nairobi Hospital.

Mike West, Steeple Morden

The **mugger crocodile** (*Crocodilus palustris*) of the Indian subcontinent is said not to be aggressive, but in Sri Lanka, in 1988, we saw the remains of a man in one very big mugger living in a freshwater reservoir.

Crocodiles usually hunt victims who are drinking (or washing) at the waterside. The reptile speeds towards the riverbank and, just as it is about to run aground, launches itself at its lunch, exploding out of the water unexpectedly. The only hope for escape is to attack the animal's eyes, its only vulnerable spot. Even if you have a Crocodile Dundee knife to hand you will not be able to sink it through its thick skull. If chased by a crocodile you'll probably get away. They are fast but tire after only 10 metres.

Freshwater stingrays

Freshwater stingrays of South America are very unpleasant and can inflict severe wounds. Avoidance and treatment are as for saltwater rays (*see* p.176).

Piranhas

Piranhas have a nasty reputation stemming originally from a fanciful account written by Theodore Roosevelt. Most species are nearly exclusively vegetarian, while others daintily nibble the ends off fins or scales of other fish. Reliable reports of human deaths are lacking, but the occasional aquarist has been injured by a pet piranha, and their sharp teeth are used by Indians as razor blades. Larger members of the *Serrasalmus* genus may possibly threaten someone who has been injured or otherwise weakened; this is only likely if the piranhas' natural food is scarce, if they have been provoked by waste being dumped in their river, or if they are trapped in a receding pool just before the rains. Most piranhas are about 20cm (8in) long; the largest reach 60cm (2ft). They are not the peril of South American rivers that Roosevelt, Ian Fleming and other tale-tellers make them out to be.

Sharks in fresh water

Perhaps surprisingly, sharks are found in the tidal parts of large river systems. Bull sharks, for example enter Amazonian waters and are aggressive and highly dangerous (see 'Sharks', pp.176–7).

Electric eels and fish

Electric eels and fish are a hazard in tropical South America and a few rivers in West Africa. Cameroonian electric fish can cause unconsciousness and South American eels have been reported to be able to stun a horse. Take local advice, and send the horse in ahead of you when making river crossings.

Water scorpions

Some **true bugs** live in fresh water in temperate and tropical regions. These backswimmers and water scorpions have a surprisingly painful bite for their size, but do not usually bite unless provoked. Thais eat them.

The giant *Belostomatidae* water bugs from the Guianas are the exception. They reach lengths of 10cm (4in). They sometimes attack swimmers, can inflict deep, painful wounds and so are also called 'toe-biters'.

Water scorpion

Infections

Itching can be a problem after bathing in polluted waters, and there are at least two nasty bacterial illnesses – **leptospirosis** (Weil's disease; see p.202) and *Shigella* (bacillary dysentery, see p.116) – that can get you if you swallow water while swimming, rafting, white-water canoeing, etc. These are more likely after flooding. **Hepatitis A** may also be acquired from swallowing the water you are swimming in. If you suspect water is contaminated, try to stay in moving water, and keep your mouth closed.

Case History: Responsible rafting in Nepal

A four day white-water rafting trip down the Kali Gandaki covered about 100km (62 miles) of river, by way of three inflatable Zodiac rafts: two for the 16 rafters and the third for supplies. At night we camped on sand bars. A nylon outhouse was an essential edifice. A paddle dug a half-metre pit and two flat rocks were positioned in each side of the hole for foot grips and to prevent the sides from caving in. Outside the paddle was driven into the ground and crowned with a helmet to act as a vacancy indicator. Helmet on the ground meant the coast was clear; on the paddle meant occupied. A kick of sand over the most recent deposit sufficed as a flush. Paper was put into a plastic bag and later burned; this was the last chore before setting out each morning. The paddle refilled the hole and no-one would ever know we were there.

Jim Soliski, Edmonton

In regions where people are insufficiently wealthy to have bathrooms and lavatories, rivers provide facilities for morning ablutions. Riversides, therefore, may be places to encounter faecal deposits. People camping beside rivers should dispose of their own excreta sensitively and boil drinking water taken from the river.

On the Ground:
High, Cold and Dark

Hazards in the mountains 186
  Who should not ascend? 187
  The right way to walk 187
  'Sahib's knee' and other walkers'
  problems 187
  A harsh environment 188
  Altitude illnesses 190
  Avoiding mountain sickness 193

Other hazards 196
  Exposure (hypothermia) 196
  Frostbite and cold injury 197
  Drinking alcohol at altitude 199
  Altitude effects on women 199
  Avalanches and cross-country
  skiing 199

Caves 201

15

Summary

→ Get the right clothes and footwear for the environments you are exploring. Exposure and frostbite hit poorly prepared travellers. Carry spare socks and change whenever you get wet.

→ Accidents in hostile environments often arise from poor planning and lack of research.

→ Bears are a hazard in some mountain and Arctic regions (*see* pp.248–9).

→ Sunscreens may be necessary even in cold conditions.

→ Check possible threats from unseasonal weather with local sources.

→ Most deaths in the mountains are due to falls and accidents: beware.

→ Above 3,000m (10,000ft) be careful about altitude illness. Know the symptoms (*see* box on p.194). Descend immediately if anyone's health is deteriorating.

→ When venturing high, it is best to be in the company of people you know, so that if someone begins to act strangely you will realize that they are developing high-altitude cerebral oedema.

→ Any limb that has suffered cold injury or chilblains should be rewarmed gently; rubbing damages.

→ Do not venture into caves unless you have reliable lights that last for at least 10 hours and you have told someone your plans.

→ Before entering big tropical caves consider the risks: ask the locals.

→ Trek with a small first-aid kit.

Hazards in the mountains

Mountains attract people. About 50,000 **trekkers** a year visit Nepal alone, and during the season more than 50 people a day cross the Thorong La (a 5,400m/17,700ft pass) near Annapurna. Most have little or no mountaineering experience. This section comprises tips for venturers who are going to altitudes up to 6,000m (20,000ft), but who may not have done much walking at lower altitudes. **High altitude trips** (above 6,000m/20,000ft) need specialist training. Consider attending a course at an approved centre; this will also give you a chance to try out or break in new equipment.

Trekking in the Andes or Himalayas (and even the Alps) combines all the problems of hill walking, plus special altitude risks compounded by the challenge of limited facilities and difficult rescues. Sedentary individuals who decide to go trekking or skiing should start with some pre-trip fitness work. Being fit makes for a more enjoyable and less injury-plagued trip; even doing just 100 step-ups on a chair each day for a week before a trip will strengthen all-important thigh muscles.

Deaths from **altitude illnesses** are now fewer than some years ago; it is **accidents** that take the most lives. Of 148,000 trekkers who visited Nepal over three and a half years, 23 died: nine deaths were accidents, eight from natural causes (mostly heart attacks), four due to altitude illnesses and two to filth-to-mouth diseases. Most accidents were falling off cliff paths. There were also 111 helicopter rescues, many for cases of simple exhaustion. A surprising number of visitors are pushed off cliff paths by pack animals; always stand on the uphill side of the path if you meet a yak or mule, and they will walk around you. It is easy to be misled by conditions in the mountains: bright clear skies and warming sunshine make foul weather seem impossible, so people get caught out.

Allow enough time. **Rushing** makes any trip miserable and exposes you to altitude illnesses, injury and accidents. Nor do you see as much. Only half of the trekkers who set out intending to walk to Everest base camp actually arrive. The others turn back, disappointed, having run out of time and having found themselves unable to cover the distance they expected because of sickness and the strenuous nature of the trek. In Nepal, particularly, you do not need to rush up to great heights to see extraordinary things; lower altitudes are just as interesting, and there are often fewer tourists.

Who should not ascend?

There are two medical conditions that impose an absolute ban on climbing to high altitude: **sickle cell disease** and a propensity to recurrent **pneumothorax** (burst lung). It is probably unwise to climb above 3,500m (12,000ft) when pregnant or if accompanied by babies or toddlers. Those who have had laser surgery for short sight (radial keratotomy) may experience dramatic changes in their vision, sufficient to render them functionally blind, at altitudes over 4,500m (15,000ft); see 'Snow blindness', p.189.

The right way to walk

Walk with a steady rhythm, and pace yourself so you do not need frequent rests; you should be able to keep going all day. If you have to stop for breath or pause because you are tired more often than five minutes each hour you are trying to walk too fast. Go at your own pace, enjoy the scenery and don't try to keep up with macho show-offs. At altitude (e.g. above 4,000m/13,000ft) trekkers need to make a conscious effort to walk slower than their natural rhythm suggests. This is not easy. When forced to walk slowly by shortness of breath, it is important to slow down even further.

Taking proper care of your feet is, naturally, of the utmost importance. The lightest possible footwear is most comfortable in mountains. Unless you are going very high or expect to be walking in snow, almost any robust, comfortable shoes will suffice, but a big range of trekking shoes, boots and socks is available. Take specialist advice on the best shoes for your particular trip and, whatever you wear, ensure that they are comfortable before you go. Remember that many waterproof climbing boots need to be dried out every evening: they do not 'breathe' like leather boots.

Change your socks whenever they get wet, especially in snow, as it's very easy to get frost nip without realizing it. Remove footwear when crossing rivers: wet boots are more likely to rub and cause **blisters**. If a stiff pair of boots is giving you trouble, try the old technique of wearing two pairs of socks (one thick, one thin) to reduce friction and blisters. Any broken skin must be carefully cleaned and incipient patches of infection treated (by soaking feet in hot salty water) before bacteria have a chance to penetrate. Do not puncture blisters: pad them with sticking plaster or moleskin cut into a doughnut shape. Big **toenails** easily 'ingrow' and become infected. To avoid this, cut the nails straight across: leave sharp corners and do not round them off. Keep other nails short. For advice on **athlete's foot** and **cracked heels**, see pp.215–16.

'Sahib's knee' and other walkers' problems

In the days of the Raj, British administrators often pranged their knees when visiting the hills. Sahibs and tourists sustain **knee injuries** because of unfitness and poor walking technique. Going downhill is more strenuous than climbing, and requires more

Case History: Monsoon trekking

Trekking during the monsoon, I walked some of the way with a Nepali. While scrambling down a landslide, I slipped and scraped my knee. When my new acquaintance saw the dribbling blood, he suggested slapping on a handful of a scruffy little weed with blue flowers. He scrunched them up a little and applied the poultice. Not only did the graze stop bleeding immediately, it didn't get infected; yet wounds always go rotten in the monsoon.

I looked the plant up later and discovered that it is called *Stachys* or woundwort. A very similar plant grows on English lawns and heaths.

Simon Howarth

awareness of technique. Fatigue makes people step down onto a straight leg. This jolts the knee joint. To protect the knee and develop a controlled walking rhythm, step down onto a slightly bent knee. The muscles and tendons of the thigh then absorb the impacts. It is hard to do this for long if you are unfit – and you risk injury. Stop when you are no longer able to take your weight on a slightly flexed knee, and rest overnight before long descents. Many trekkers find poles helpful when walking down, and they are especially useful if anyone in your group is in difficulty and needs to be supported.

The **treatment** for knee injuries and other strains and wrenches is rest. If you must continue walking, reduce your daily distance considerably and, if possible, employ someone to carry your pack. Tight strapping with a crêpe or ace bandage will help, although crêpe bandages need to be washed frequently to retain their stretchiness. The treatment of wrenches, sprains and sore joints is dealt with on pp.278–9.

Some **swelling of the feet**, **ankles** and **lower legs** (oedema) is common in mountain walkers even at low altitudes, especially if they are overweight. So long as you continue to feel well this is no cause for concern. If the swelling is uncomfortable, rest with your feet above heart height. If it is accompanied by pain or illness, seek medical help, if possible; do not go any higher, but descend at a gentle pace.

A harsh environment

In the low temperatures that prevail at altitude and in cold deserts it is easy to get seriously cold. Chilling happens most quickly if conditions are windy and/or you are wet. Carry a change of clothes packed in a plastic bag. **Mittens** protect the hands better than gloves (carry spares as mitts often get lost). The skin can become uncomfortably dry and scaly even at modest altitude, but also in cold deserts and the dehydrating atmospheres of the high Andes and Transhimalaya. Drink plenty. Pack moisturizing cream, as well as sun cream and lip-screen. If you have no moisturizer, use butter or cooking grease. **Nosebleeds** are common in high and dry climates. Prevent them by anointing the inside of the nose with a greasy non-perfumed cream such as petroleum jelly, Vaseline, emulsifying ointment or even yak butter or cooking oil.

Mountaineers and trekkers walking in snow will know to protect themselves from the sun with sunscreen and goggles. It is also possible to get sunburned inside the nose from sun reflected up off the snow if sunscreen isn't applied there too.

For the effects and treatment of frostbite and exposure (hypothermia), *see* pp.196–8.

It is dangerous to leave butane stoves burning in your tent all night to keep out the cold. The **carbon monoxide** kills. Others have been burned alive. Beware. Finally be aware that bears are a hazard in any mountain habitats (*see* pp.248–9).

Fluid loss

The body loses more fluid in cold and arid conditions, at altitude and in windy conditions, so you must make a conscious effort to drink more. With any fever, diarrhoea or bad sunburn you need more again. **Thirst** is no guide to whether you are drinking enough. Ensure you are drinking enough to pee three good volumes in 24 hours. Serious dehydration can lead to kidney stones.

Effects of the sun at altitude

Even in places where mountain people live throughout the year (e.g. Ladakh), winter daytime temperatures remain well below -10°C (14°F). It is said to be possible to get sunstroke and frostbite simultaneously, by lying with your feet in the shade and your head in the sun. It is easy to get sunburned despite the cold; even dark-skinned people need to wear sunscreen and a hat. The sun may provoke cold sores if you are prone to them (*see* p.163).

Snow blindness

Nepalis describe snow blindness as like having your eyeballs rubbed in a mixture of chilli and sand. It is painful and disabling. This most frequently occurs at altitude and in snow. It is dangerous because it temporarily blinds in a situation where you may need to see to stay alive. The right treatment is to cover the eyes (tape them closed if it's bad) and descend to recover. Cold compresses may help the pain.

Snow blindness is prevented by filtering out UV radiation with good quality (expensive) glacier goggles; sunglasses aren't good enough. Poor Nepalis protect their eyes by tying on a strip of cloth with slits cut for them to see through.

Another form of temporary blindness, which has been recognized recently, happens in climbers who have undergone a radial keratotomy laser operation for short sight. Altitude temporarily alters the shape of the eyeballs, resulting in extreme long-sightedness that renders the victim unable to perform many tasks. This has led to at least one climber being left for dead and getting badly frostbitten on Everest.

Case history: Chile

I was the leader of the group but I was right at the back on the descent from seeing the lava bubbling in the crater of Volcán Villarrica. I watched the others glissading speedily down on their backsides in the snow, resisting the temptation to join in until the last one – the longest and fastest of all. In waterproof trousers it was great fun, and I then rolled over to make a perfect ice-axe self-arrest. Just as I stopped, though, a crampon spike caught the snow and something snapped! Never glissade down in crampons. Sergio, the group's real technical leader, organized the group to tow me downhill, holding hiking poles. Then, when the snow ran out, Sergio made a rope stretcher, and after wrapping me up and giving me food and water, they carried me down to a four-wheel-drive vehicle. I was in the hospital in Pucón within two hours of the accident and the X-ray showed a broken fibula. Three days later the group flew south while Sergio and I took the overnight bus to Santiago, thence to Heathrow where I used my luggage trolley and hiking pole to support me and my plastered leg as far as the bus. Two months after flying out of Chile I was back with another hiking group.

Tim Burford, guidebook author

Case history: Everest eyeballs

My friend Quin Hollick happened to go for a routine eye test four days after returning from a trip to Everest. His optician saw retinal haemorrhages and, although his sight was and still is fine, she was so concerned that she sent him to hospital. Retinal haemorrhages are small bleeds in the back of the eye and 30–35% of trekkers who ascend to 5,000m (16,500ft) have them. They are more likely in people who haven't been at altitude before and they also happen in people who have a cough. They usually disappear four to six weeks after descent. Anyone noticing a 'hole' in their vision while at altitude must descend urgently, however. Dr Mark Howarth, GP and veteran of several Himalayan medical research expeditions, commented: 'Many opticians in Britain will be very alarmed by the sight of these haemorrhages but unless the bleed is close to the macula (at the centre of the eye) they resolve remarkably well: these high altitude bleeds are surprisingly benign.'

Disturbed sleep: periodic (Cheyne-Stokes) respiration

When people first climb high they often sleep poorly. Some are woken up by a nightmare of being suffocated. During sleep, breathing becomes progressively slower and shallower until it actually stops for a few seconds; then there is a deep sigh and breathing restarts, sometimes waking the sleeper. This is alarming to witness, because as you lie in the darkness you begin to wonder whether your friend is ever going to breath again. Then, when you're just about to struggle across to shake them back to consciousness, a deep sighing inspiration starts them breathing. This is normal in people newly arrived at altitude, and is no cause for concern. *Acetazolamide* (*see* p.195) speeds up acclimatization and reduces sleep disturbance.

Some say that it is unwise to use sleeping pills at altitude; however, a recent study at Everest base camp showed that use of *temazepam* improves sleep and doesn't drop the oxygen content of circulating blood, as had been feared. Even so, *acetazolamide* probably works best to combat high altitude insomnia (*see* p.194).

Altitude illnesses

Mountains kill a lot of people. One-tenth of mountaineers on serious expeditions who climb above 6,000m (20,000ft) die. Yet most of those who are killed in the mountains are not on expeditions: they include many tourists and visitors in the Himalayan region, the Andes, on Mount Kilimanjaro and Mount Kenya. Although falls and other accidents are the major killers, ignorance about mountain sickness makes a significant contribution to the risks and is another important reason why people die in the high ranges.

In South America it is called *soroché*, in Nepal, *aye-lagio*; whatever you call it, mountain sickness is frightening and can kill. Mountain illnesses have been known for a long time; Chinese travellers in 35 BC described the Himalayas as the 'Headache Mountains'. The symptoms, though, are unpredictable and the disease complex. Altitude illnesses are caused by an imbalance of acid and alkali in the blood; this affects breathing controls that normally maintain fluid balances in the body. You need to breathe faster at altitude to take in enough oxygen from the thinner air, but initially the drive to breathe lags behind the body's need for oxygen. When oxygen supplies to the brain are not maintained, headaches and confusion begin. The **headache** is a sign that the brain is swelling (cerebral oedema). The imbalance can also allow fluid to build up in the lungs (pulmonary oedema), which causes **breathlessness** and coughing and sometimes frothy or even bloodstained spit; this can lead to death by drowning.

With sensible rates of ascent, though, and adaptation to altitude over a few days, other longer-term mechanisms switch in: enzyme and hormone changes that allow breathing to settle back to a slower rate. This is acclimatization.

Bad headache, disorientation and excessive breathlessness are signs of severe problems, which can lead rapidly to death. The treatment is to descend at once. Going down as little as 500m (1,500ft) can be sufficient to save someone's life, but descend as far as you can or until the victim is clearly well again. It is rare to be in a situation where you have to ascend before descending, so most deaths are unnecessary.

Altitude illnesses are dangerous because they can come on rapidly, and do not necessarily progress from milder mountain sickness. The early symptoms are non-specific, and the victims are often too disorientated to recognize how ill they are; they may even argue about descending, or can be too apathetic to help themselves. Overruling them can be difficult, but saves lives. Don't wait until morning to see if the victim feels better. If in doubt, descend.

Diagnosing significant altitude illness

Assume any illness at altitude is altitude sickness – especially if it is getting worse. And 'treat' illness with descent. If the problem reveals itself as another disease you will be happier to be closer to home and medical help. Several doctors have produced guidelines for diagnosing mountain illnesses to help decide when descent is necessary, but the symptoms of severe altitude illness so often overlap with other common problems of mountain walkers that none is foolproof. Lists of symptoms are also less useful than deciding whether someone looks ill or not. Headache is worrying, and weird or uncharacteristic behaviour can also be warning symptoms of **cerebral oedema**. There are no signs (except perhaps frothy or bloodstained spit of **pulmonary oedema**) that are especially characteristic of severe altitude illness. It can be difficult to differentiate, say, dehydration and exhaustion from mountain illness: both can cause headache, dizziness, confusion and nausea, but if there is any doubt, the wise action is always to descend. People suffering from mountain illnesses should improve dramatically with descent. Diagnosis in children is even more difficult; pay close attention to any complaints.

Treatment of altitude illnesses

Descent is the only treatment for significant mountain illness. If in doubt, go down while the victim can still walk, as waiting may mean having to evacuate someone who is unconscious or uncooperative after dark. Go down as far as you possibly can but at least 500m (1,640ft). Re-pressurization bags (the **Gamow** weighs 8kg/18lb) are no substitute for descent, and if using them delays going down it may do more harm than good. I have been horrified to hear of people suffering bad enough altitude illness to be repressurized in a bag and then, once 'cured', continuing to ascend. This is dangerous.

The **headache** of mild Acute Mountain Sickness (AMS) can be treated in adults with *acetazolamide*, in a 'loading dose' of 750mg (three tablets) for small adults (under 60kg/130lb) or 1,000mg (four tablets) for large people, then 500mg daily. AMS headache will respond in a few hours; do not climb any higher if you still have a headache. If someone appears to be 'drunk' and disorientated, *dexamethasone* (8mg, then 4mg six-hourly) may help enough for them to walk down; similarly, if someone is having severe trouble breathing, *nifedipine* (20mg slow release six-hourly) should improve their condition enough that they can be evacuated. None of these drugs is an alternative to descent.

If you have to descend, breathe out by puffing against pursed lips. This increases air pressure in the lungs, and acts as a kind of short-term repressurization technique. It also gives someone who is feeling awful something on which to focus their attention.

Who is at risk from altitude illness?

At greatest risk are those who arrive at altitude by plane, helicopter, train or bus, especially if they then climb further without acclimatizing. Lhasa in Tibet (at 3,658m/12,000ft), Cusco in Peru (at 3,415m/11,200ft) and La Paz in Bolivia (at 3,625m/11,893ft) are dangerous, and even people flying into Denver (the 'Mile-High City' at 1,610m/5,280 feet) can feel unwell. In Peru you can experience unhealthily rapid ascent from Lima at sea level to nearly 5,000m (16,400ft) by train in just half a day. Mount Kenya, at just over 5,199m (16,400ft), is not particularly high, but it kills people: the first day's climbing takes you to 3,000m (9,842ft), and on the second day there is a 1,300m (4,265ft) climb to the second refuge. People feeling bad at the second refuge should go back to sleep in Refuge One, and continue when they feel better. Kilimanjaro, at 5,895m (19,340ft), is one of the highest mountains climbed by ordinary tourists without technical mountaineering skills, and is also dangerous.

The fitter you are the faster you can ascend, so the more you can suffer from mountain illness. Clearly, though, there are other risks if you are unfit. If you have escaped mountain sickness on previous ascents, this doesn't mean you'll never suffer. And if you suffered once it does not mean you will suffer every time, although it probably does indicate a propensity. It is impossible to give absolute rules about when a climb or walk must be slowed down or abandoned, but if there is any doubt, descent – or at least taking an extra day to acclimatize – is the wise course. In some regions, immediate rapid descent may not be possible. This might happen (e.g. in the Himalayas) if you have climbed over a ridge and then come down with the intention of camping in a relatively high valley. Thus you would need to ascend before you could lose any significant amount of height. Or, if you are exploring the Andean *altiplano* on local buses or trucks, you may find that a lift is just not available when you need to descend. When over 3,000m (roughly 10,000ft), it is vital that you plan an escape route in case one of your group is struck by mountain sickness. If you or a companion seems to have early symptoms, ascent must be slowed and plans changed. Sleeping at the lowest possible altitude helps protect from altitude illnesses.

Altitude sickness in children

There are several issues to consider when trekking with children. Most parents worry about mountain illness, but as you climb high it also becomes difficult to keep small children warm (*see* p.196) and they get bored, too, if mountain lassitude sets in. I would advise against taking young children above 3,000m (10,000ft). Even at this altitude you must be meticulously cautious; you must know the signs of mountain sickness and be prepared to descend rapidly at short notice. The younger the child, the more careful you must be, as it can be very easy to overlook significant problems in an infant. Experts in mountain medicine caution against going above 2,500m (8,000ft)

Case History: Kanchenjunga base camp

Four of us, walking together over a couple of weeks, had got up to 5,000m (16,500ft). We felt well at this altitude, made two trips to around 5,400m (17,700ft), then decided to climb a 6,200m (20,350ft) peak. As we began this ascent there was an argument about the route; Alan was uncharacteristically short-tempered, but finally we set on up with Alan striding ahead. From a vantage point on a ridge we realized that we had to descend a difficult scree slope to reach our first campsite at the foot of a glacier. I arrived first; the others straggled in over the next hour, Rick carrying Alan's pack and, last of all, Alan supported by Gill. It was 3.30pm; we were at 5,500m (18,000ft). Alan was cold, exhausted and had a headache. Rest, painkillers and hot soup did not revive him but the prospect of descent was horrendous. Alan's headache got worse; then he vomited and became confused. I forced him to get up and was shocked to see him staggering like a drunk. He clearly had cerebral oedema (brain swelling). It was 5pm but I knew that we must descend. I gave him 8mg of *dexamethasone* and 1,000mg of *acetazolamide* but he vomited the tablets.

We headed down a steep gully, with two people at a time taking turns to support Alan, trying to keep him upright. It was soon pitch dark, with a thick mist and no moon. Our progress was excruciatingly slow, managing barely 20m (22 yards) between rests, while Alan's breathing grew weaker. Whenever he sat down, he fell asleep. I gave him more *dexamethasone*, which he kept down, but it didn't seem to help. Luckily, we were able to radio base camp and at 9.30pm we met a rescue party bringing oxygen and injectable *dexamethasone*. By 11.40pm we had all reached the valley, low enough to save Alan. Had we stayed at 5,500m (18,000ft) he would have died.

In retrospect it is easy to see that we should have started down again as soon as we'd reached camp, but we were tired and conditions were difficult. Alan's moodiness was uncharacteristic; alarm bells should ring when a fit man suddenly becomes disproportionately exhausted. And, since we ascended at more than the recommended rate of 300m (984ft) a day, we also might have expected trouble.

Dr Mark Howarth, GP in West Sussex

with children under two; in any case, small children enjoy treks better if you stay well below 3,000m (10,000ft); there is more to entertain them and the climate is kinder. Children can be given *acetazolamide* (at 5mg/kg body weight), but I've never used them on the dozen medium-altitude treks we've done with our children from the age of four months. Even mild symptoms of AMS should be taken seriously; if in doubt, descend. And beware of hypothermia; *see* p.196.

Avoiding mountain sickness

Altitude illnesses are generally only a problem in adults above 3,000m (10,000ft), but some have died of it even at this modest height. The only way to avoid it is to allow plenty of time for acclimatization and, if you notice any symptoms, stop or at least slow your ascent. A recommended safe rate of ascent is to take several days to reach 3,500m (11,000ft), then a further week to reach 5,500m (18,000ft). This gives an average of about 300m (1,000ft) per day, but take rest days and – as always – pace yourself according to the slowest member of the party. Even at this rate, not everyone is able to go high. Many people are also too impatient to ascend at this rate, or it may be that the terrain or the need to reach accommodation makes it difficult to slow down. If you exceed the recommended rate, watch for danger signs. Be especially cautious on a first ascent, or if you have had problems before. Even at recommended

Symptoms of mild Acute Mountain Sickness (AMS)

→ Poor performance.

→ Slight headache.

→ Fatigue.

→ Chest discomfort.

→ Insomnia.

→ Loss of appetite.

→ Nausea.

→ Vomiting.

Action: watch out for increasingly severe symptoms. If you are planning to go higher, consider stopping for a rest day and acclimatization. Descend to sleep lower down if possible, or dramatically slow your ascent. Ascend no further until the headache gets better.

Symptoms of moderate to severe altitude illness

Severe altitude illness may not necessarily lead on from mild AMS, but can cause rapid deterioration over a couple of hours 'out of the blue'. Only some of the listed symptoms will be present.

→ Mood changes.

→ Severe headache.*

→ Disorientation.

→ Confusion* and memory loss.

→ Strange behaviour.*

→ Difficulty with balance, stumbling, acting drunk, etc.*

→ Hallucinations.*

→ Drowsiness (person is difficult to wake up).*

→ Severe nightmares.

→ Unwarranted breathlessness, perhaps even at rest (compared with companions).*

→ Nausea and vomiting.

→ Severe fatigue.

→ Dry cough, frothy spit and even bloodstained spit.*

Note: symptoms marked * are very worrying and should precipitate immediate descent, whatever the time of day or night.

Action: descend at once.

rates, half of trekkers suffer symptoms of mild to moderate AMS (headache, poor appetite, nausea). Some people are inexplicably sensitive to even slow rates of ascent.

Local advice on mountain illness may be misleading; guides and porters who live at altitude may not realize how susceptible foreigners are to these problems. Conversely, with increasing numbers of tourists there are greater opportunities for inexperienced lowlanders, who may know less about the hazards than you do, to work as porters. Some die each year from altitude problems. Take responsibility to ensure that porters you employ directly or indirectly are properly equipped (with shoes, jumpers, blankets, shelter) and watched. **Headaches** should probably be treated with *acetazolamide* (*see* opposite), rather than painkillers. Allow time for rest if porters flag; they will feel they cannot rest however ill they are.

Some trekking agencies proudly announce that they can arrange Gamow bags (*see* p.191) for treating altitude sickness; it is worth asking why they feel this is often necessary: does it indicate poor planning on their part, and/or slowness to descend when symptoms begin? Ask agencies what they know about altitude illness, and what they might do in hypothetical problem situations.

Prevention of altitude illnesses with medicines

Altitude sickness is an acid–alkali imbalance in the blood and body fluids. Peruvians suck limes and other acidic substances in an attempt to correct this. Sherpas say garlic is protective. These might be worth trying, but they won't protect you nearly as well as taking *acetazolamide* capsules.

Acetazolamide (Diamox) tablets hasten acclimatization by increasing oxygen availability to the brain in the critical first few days at altitude. This helps the traveller until longer-term mechanisms take over. It reduces the headache, nausea and insomnia that bother many people above 3,000m (10,000ft), and is excellent if you are ascending rapidly to altitudes of 3,000–4,500m (10,000–15,000ft) by vehicle and cannot slow down your ascent. Some argue that this might encourage people to go higher faster and less safely. It is not an alternative to descent in cases of significant mountain illness. Symptoms more serious than headache or disturbed sleep still warrant immediate descent.

My late friend Dr Tony White ran a test during our expedition to 4,000m (13,000ft) in the Andes. Some of us took *acetazolamide* and others a lookalike placebo. Those of us taking the drug felt better, slept better and had more stamina on caving trips, and our ability to perform psychological tests was much better; unlike those taking placebo, our judgement was as good as at sea level. Clear thinking can be vital in mountains, so I am a fan of *acetazolamide*. The related *benzolamide* is also effective but is yet to become available.

In the West *acetazolamide* is only available on private prescription, and in the UK (like any drug provided for foreign travel, it is not covered by the NHS) it costs about £10 for 10 tablets of 250mg. It is available over the counter in some pharmacies in Nepal, India and South America for about one UK penny a tablet. Take two 250mg tablets or 'sustets' in the morning, beginning three days before ascent and continuing for two more days at altitude. Assuming you try the medicine before ascent (a two-day trial several weeks beforehand is wise, to make sure you are not prone to intolerable side effects), each traveller needs a minimum of 14 tablets. Since the drug speeds your own body's acclimatization mechanisms, it is not necessary to take a second course of five days of Diamox if your route takes you up and down over several ridges or ranges.

Side effects of *acetazolamide*

It is unusual for people to notice any dramatic reactions but, like all drugs, *acetazolamide* has side effects. Those who are allergic to sulfa antibiotics or medicines are likely to be allergic to *acetazolamide* as well, and should not take it. If you take it as a trial (two doses several weeks before ascent) you will be forewarned of any unpleasant reaction. The most common side effect is tingling of the hands and feet, which can be sufficiently annoying to make people want to stop taking the medicine; delaying one or two doses by 24 hours should solve the problem. *Acetazolamide* is a mild diuretic, so be prepared to produce more urine than usual while taking it. Some people also complain of taste disturbance, especially when taking carbonated drinks.

Contact information: mountain medicine
The British Mountaineering Council (BMC), The Old Church, 177–179 Burton Road, West Didsbury, Manchester M20 2BB, UK **t** (0161) 445 6111, **f** (0161) 445 4500, *www.thebmc.co.uk*. Runs mountaineering courses, gives advice and suggests insurers.
Himalayan Rescue Association, *www.himalayanrescue.org*. Provides emergency medical care.
International Mountaineering and Climbing Federation (Union Internationale des Associations d'Alpinisme, UIAA), UIAA Office Monbijoustrasse, 61 Postfach, CH-3000, Bern 23, Switzerland, **t** +41 (0)31 370 1828, **f** +41 (0)31 370 1838, *www.theuiaa.org*. Publishes climbers' information sheets on mountain medicine.

Other hazards

Exposure (hypothermia)

Exposure is most likely when you are cold, wet, hungry and exhausted. As the body temperature falls, you feel inappropriately comfortable. Content, you lose the drive to get to somewhere safe. Sometimes the confusion of exposure makes people act in bizarre ways: they take off their clothes or sit in puddles. This is why it is so dangerous: people die of cold without ever realizing they are in trouble.

Heat is lost more rapidly when the body is wet or chilled by wind. Drinking alcohol also increases heat loss. Make sure you are adequately equipped for your journey. Ask about local conditions before ascent, and be prepared for the worst possible weather: in particular, ensure that everyone has adequate footwear. Wear mittens (*see* p.188). Carry a change of clothes in a plastic bag so that you can get warm and dry once you reach a safe place. The next day, change back into the previous day's sweaty, damp clothes and keep one set dry for night-time. Rest for a day and dry out if you cannot face this.

Watch the people you are walking with and be forceful if you think they are getting into trouble. Stumbling is an early warning sign. People with early exposure shiver, but this ceases as the temperature continues to fall. Exposure and altitude sickness both cloud judgement, so it is up to the unaffected to protect sufferers. They are dangerous enough in themselves, but they also make people prone to accidents, especially in combination with exhaustion. Plan carefully, and be cautious.

Children cool quickly, and are at particular risk of hypothermia if you carry them; exercise keeps you warm while they chill out. Make sure they are warmly dressed, and check often that they feel warm to the touch, especially if it is windy. If their feet and hands are cold but the trunk is warm, they are cold but coping; if their body feels as cold as their extremities the child is seriously cold and you must stop and get them warm. Children carried in backpacks by skiing parents can freeze to death; such deaths occur in the Alps each season.

Treating exposure

The treatment for exposure is slow, gentle rewarming. One technique is to put the victim in a sleeping bag with someone else. Making them too warm too soon can

Hypothermia (exposure)

→ Serious symptoms of profound cold get progressively worse as the core body temperature drops from around 36.5°C (97.5°F) to below 35°C (95°F).

→ Victim feels cold, looks cold, shivering (35°C/95°F).

→ Ability to judge situations impaired; poor decision making (35°C/95°F).

→ Starts to switch off; doesn't care (34°C/93°F).

→ Difficulty with balance, stumbling, confusion (33°C/91.5°F).

→ Not with it; incoherent (33°C/91.5°F).

→ Stops shivering (33°C/91.5°F).

→ Serious risk of heart attack (33°C/91.5°F).

→ Unconscious (31°C/88°F).

→ Pulse and breathing not detectable (30°C/86°F).

→ Death.

adapted from material by Chris Johnson in Expedition Medicine, *ed. D. Warrell and S. Anderson,*
Profile Books/RGS 2002

make things worse, so hot baths are not sensible (even if available), nor is alcohol. The recommended rate of rewarming the body is only by about 1°C per hour, but this can be doubled if shivering starts. Shivering is a good sign; it shows survival processes are returning to normal. Even so, it takes hours to rewarm thoroughly. Space blankets help the body to rewarm slowly and steadily, but do not work well if the wearer is lying uninsulated on the ground. Hot drinks also help in rewarming.

Action: insulate from the ground; shelter from wind; change into dry clothes.

Frostbite and cold injury

Trekkers most often get frostbitten when they try a high pass on a whim. Frostbite means that living tissue has become frozen; in deep frostbite the toes (or other members) look like pieces of chicken from the deep freeze. It is more likely at altitude (where there are high, chilling winds), at extremely low temperatures (below -10°C/14°F), if you are wet, if your boots are constricting, in those with altitude illness and in smokers. Contact with metal makes the skin more susceptible, since it conducts heat away. Beware of metal glasses or earrings in very cold conditions.

Cold injury starts as **frost nip**, usually of the ears, nose, cheeks, fingers, toes or chin. It makes the part numb and blanched (white/very pale), but this is entirely reversible

Case history: Frostbite

Climbing over a high pass in Nepal, the snow was deep and wet for five days, and my boots were not as good as they should have been. I didn't really notice that my feet were always damp until we were warming up in front of a fire after we'd come down. Then the skin of my frost-bitten big toe and the nail slid off like a glove from a finger. It wasn't painful at the time, but it festered in the heat and became very sore as I hobbled the 10 days to the nearest road. I wasn't carrying any dressings and the raw skinless toe was festering and stinking by the time I got back, so my Tibetan landlady treated me with a mixture of bear's bile and extract of musk deer. Even with antibiotics too the infection took weeks to settle.

Simon Howarth

Case history: USA

Camp 4 at 5,000m (16,500ft) on the West Buttress of North America's highest mountain, Denali. Outside the tent, some of the worst recorded weather ever to assail the peak (-40°C/-40°F plus windspeeds of 160kph (100mph) rages around our exposed perch. Inside, I wrestle with bowels that have been hibernating for days. My bowels win. I stagger outside and succeed in releasing multiple crotch zips before my gloved hands freeze. My deposit is frozen before it touches the snow.

Ten months after reaching the summit and the last of my frost-nipped digits finally recovers.

Paul Deegan author of award-winning The Mountain Traveller's Handbook, www.pauldeegan.com

and no damage has been done yet. As the skin rewarms it becomes red and tingly. If the part is not rewarmed the tissues next suffer **superficial frostbite**, with the surface layer actually frozen: the skin looks yellow-grey and is leathery to the touch, but the tissues underneath are still soft. On rewarming the skin is mottled with red-purple patches and some blanched areas. If freezing continues the tissues go on to suffer the most serious end of the spectrum of cold injury, **deep frostbite**.

Climbers will have had times when their feet and hands have been numb for hours. Unfortunately, **deep frostbite** feels no worse; it is not painful until rewarming begins. This painlessness makes it dangerous, as it is easy to injure a frostbitten limb and feel nothing. This is a primary reason why gangrene and infection often set in, with amputation the final result. In deep frostbite the flesh is hard, white or very pale and obviously frozen. The response should be immediate evacuation and the abandonment of a climb or walk. Do not climb again for several months after suffering frostbite.

Treatment of frostbite

The basic treatment is evacuation to a lower, safer place (walk on the still-frozen foot if necessary); do not thaw if there is any chance of it refreezing. Once in a safe haven, rewarm the affected part by immersion in a saucepan of warm – not hot – water (40°C/104°F) for periods of 20 minutes. Deeply frostbitten skin will look mottled blue or grey. Do not knock or even rub the limb. Never immerse in hot water.

After the limb has been defrosted, the skin must be kept clean and used as little as possible. The greatest danger after frostbite is infection, which can enter through any small breaks in the skin. A few hours after thawing the limb swells, and over the next two days huge blisters erupt. These should be left intact; they will be reabsorbed over the next week. The frostbitten limb becomes horribly discoloured, even black and shrivelled if there is gangrene. If frostbite has been superficial, new pink skin will form under the dead shell. If there was deep frostbite the toe or fingertip will eventually, painlessly but revoltingly, fall off.

If surgery is required, there are advantages in waiting at least a few weeks, and it is best done by a surgeon experienced in frostbite damage. Return to a hospital in your home country for this if possible. A frostbitten limb suffers permanent damage that makes it more likely to be frostbitten again so, **once frostbitten, twice frost-shy**.

Trench foot or **immersion foot** was a problem in the First World War, when soldiers were cold, immobile and wet for days. The feet do not freeze, but the condition and its treatment are similar to frostbite. Recovering feet are also prone to infection.

Drinking alcohol at altitude

It is unwise to imbibe large quantities of strong alcohol at altitude. It exacerbates broken sleep and, if the drinker is already suffering mountain sickness, it further reduces the drive to breathe. It will also contribute to poor performance while trekking, as well as increasing the dehydration caused by altitude. It is not necessary to be teetotal when in the mountains, but if you are already feeling 'rough' because of altitude, don't drink spirits as a cure. Be wary too of locally distilled hooch: Peruvian *pisco* is of very variable quality and Nepali *raksi* is fermented and distilled anything. Maize brews have the worst hangover potential, while the connoisseurs say that the best *raksi* is made from millet; even this is fairly toxic. *See also* 'Local alcohol', pp.123–4.

Altitude effects on women

Women taking the combined **contraceptive pill** are at increased risk of pulmonary embolus, deep vein thrombosis and other blood clotting problems at altitude. Women climbing to extreme altitude (above 7,000m/23,000ft) may therefore consider stopping the pill four weeks before ascent, but pack condoms. Alternatively try Depo-Provera or another injectable progestogen contraceptive, but start it several months before your trip (*see* 'Delaying menstruation', p.228).

It is probably best not to climb above 3,500m (12,000ft) when **pregnant**, and you should be extra careful to allow plenty of time for acclimatization. If you are trekking during the first three months of pregnancy, consider the possibility of a miscarriage. This is unpleasant in any circumstances but will be awful if it happens in a remote mountain village. The middle third of pregnancy is the best stage to be intrepid if you want to be, although there may be risks to the unborn child from long stays at extreme altitude. For more on travelling while pregnant, *see* **Special Travellers**, pp.75–8.

Avalanches and cross-country skiing

Avalanches are a cause of injury and death even in Scotland (where wet snow and slab avalanches commonly occur). If you are going out in the hills in snow it is important to know that it is dangerous to climb in gullies or on steep, open slopes, especially convex ones, during or immediately after heavy snowfall. Most avalanche accidents happen within 24 hours of a heavy fall of snow; thereafter, snow usually settles sufficiently to reduce the danger. If out in a heavy fall of snow, keep to safe buttresses or ridges.

Precautions against avalanches

→ Walk/ski in shaded areas before noon.
→ Keep to slopes that have already been exposed to the sun after noon.
→ Avoid deep, snow-filled gullies; they carry a risk of avalanche.
→ Snow-covered convex slopes are prone to avalanche.
→ Sheltered accumulations of snow may avalanche.

Most people who are killed or injured by avalanches are skiers, and true cross-country skiers (not those using prepared pistes) are at the highest risk. Avalanches can occur in many kinds of terrain, even including tree-covered slopes at angles as little as 15°, and skiers have been killed by avalanches less than 20m (66ft) wide and which flowed only 100m (328ft). Knowing about avalanches will protect you.

Loose snow avalanches happen when new loose snow slips off the old snow base; provided the slip is slow, these are not usually dangerous, although if the slope is long and the speed of the avalanche builds up it can develop into the next, highly dangerous kind of avalanche.

Air-borne powder avalanches occur when the flowing snow gains momentum and becomes terrifically powerful. They can travel up to 320kph (200mph), when they uproot trees, shatter buildings and sweep buses off the road.

Wet snow avalanches are most common in the spring when snow is melting. They are heavy, so skiers trapped in them die from being crushed. However, they are rather slow, predictable beasts so can be avoided by those who know the mountains.

Slab avalanches occur when a complete slab of snow breaks away; frequently they are a feature of open, grassy slopes, from snow packed by wind. Slab snow is dangerous because it slips off the underlying snow so easily, yet the smoothed nature of the snow attracts skiers – at their peril.

Avoiding avalanches

Avalanches mostly kill the reckless. Take local advice before setting out. If you choose to venture into avalanche country, travel in a party. Test any slopes by shouting and throwing stones or snowballs ahead of you and then cross one at a time. It is wise to loosen ski bindings and remove the hands from the pole loops since, in an avalanche, it is the moving snow pressing on your equipment which causes fractures. Ideally, leaders should be roped to their mates or should have a length of red cord trailing behind so that if they disappear into the snow, the cord should still be visible and will lead rescuers to them.

If caught in an avalanche, try swimming to stay near the surface. Keep your mouth closed and, as the slide slows, try to clear a space around your mouth and chest to give you room to breathe. Once the avalanche stops moving you will be unable to move and, if rescue doesn't come, you will suffocate in less than an hour.

Ski-slope injuries

→ About one in 100 skiers and twice as many snow-boarders will have their holiday cut short by injury.

→ Many of these are caused by collisions with other skiers; children should wear helmets.

→ Sprains are more common in those who are unfit and who have done insufficient pre-trip fitness training.

→ Those with an old injury are most likely to get injured again.

→ Of those suffering significant trauma, 40% will injure a knee, 25% a wrist and 15% a shoulder.

→ Neoprene joint supports give some protection and should be considered for protecting old injuries.

→ Make sure your insurance covers all your activities, including evacuation off the slopes.

When I asked mountain rescue experts for tips on increasing the chances of survival once buried, they all said: 'avoid the avalanche'.

Equipment should be familiar to you before you head off into the mountain wilderness on your skis and you should realize that tight, ill-fitting boots predispose their owners to frostbite. Take a map and compass and make sure you know how to use them. Carry emergency food and a small survival pack, too.

Caves

Straying more than a few metres into caves takes you into absolute darkness, and it is foolish to enter unless you have reliable specialist lights. If you don't have such equipment or any caving experience, you should only visit 'show caves' with a local guide. 'Exposure' (also known as **hypothermia**, *see* pp.196–7) is a significant risk even in caves situated in reasonably warm climatic zones: wet bodies lose heat fast. Flash floods are also a peril, especially in regions of high rainfall; I've seen whole trees transported a kilometre inside tropical caves by the awesome power of flood-water.

As with many hostile environments, accidents are the big risk but, in addition, there are three special cave diseases: **histoplasmosis**, **leptospirosis** and **rabies**.

Histoplasmosis

This yeast-like fungus is as happy growing on bat or bird dung as in human lungs, so it is contracted by those venturing into enclosed spaces where there is a great deal of bat or bird guano. Disease is only suffered on first exposure to the fungus, and thereafter there is immunity. The illness may be mild or, at worst, there is fever, headache, cough and chest pains, which last between 10 days and three weeks. Usually no treatment is needed except *aspirin* or *paracetamol* (Tylenol). Occasionally there can be serious pneumonia and certain caves in particular regions (including Mexico and South Africa) are known by locals to be dangerous. Cavers in South Africa have worked out which caves to enter first; thus they become 'immunized' against the serious disease that they would otherwise suffer if they entered a 'malignant' cave first. **Smog masks** give some protection, by reducing the number of fungal spores inhaled, although these are uncomfortable to wear in high-humidity, tropical caves, especially if exercising hard.

Where to find *histoplasma*

The *histoplasma* fungus grows in soil contaminated with bird or bat dung or in accumulations of such offerings in barns, chicken houses and beneath bird roosts, as well as in caves.

In the Americas it is principally a tropical microbe, although it has been found in the extreme southeast corner of Canada, in Alaska and in sub-tropical Argentina. It has been isolated in Italy but is not known to have caused disease there. It occurs in Africa, in many parts of Asia and in Australia and should probably be expected in any unsavoury-looking habitat. Fortunately, however, the risk of serious disease is very small unless you enter a small, confined space, disturb a lot of excreta and thus inhale it. Almost everyone who has lived in Tennessee, Kentucky and Ohio will have become naturally immune to the fungus through exposure to spores in soil.

Leptospirosis (Weil's disease)

This infection most often comes from rat (or bat) pee. Infection can arise from drinking infected water, via a skin scratch, or it can get in across the membranes of the nose or eyes in swimmers or sump-divers. Cavers should try to wear sufficient clothes to protect them from abrasions.

The illness begins abruptly with high fever, headache, chills, vomiting, diarrhoea, muscle aches and reddening of the eyes. It responds to *penicillin* and *doxycycline* antibiotics. Those taking *doxycycline* as a malaria prophylactic should also be protected from leptospirosis. The illness can be serious, so if it is suspected, get it properly diagnosed and treated. **Water engineers** and construction workers are at occupational risk from this disease.

Rabies, bats and caves

Rabies is the scariest and nastiest of the cave-related infections, and like the other two cave-related infections is transmitted via the unpleasant media of bat urine and saliva. Large numbers of bats roost in tropical caves and they often carry rabies. In a high-humidity cave atmosphere, it is possible to catch rabies just by inhaling contaminated cave air.

There have been two deaths in the Americas in people who had entered Frio Cave near Uvalde in Texas, which is home to millions of bats. These men had no direct contact with rabid animals and are thought to have inhaled the virus in this unusually high humidity, bat-urine-soaked environment. Anyone entering caves in the Americas should be immunized against rabies (*see* **Immunizations**, pp.49–50; for more on rabies, including the common route of infection, *see* **Animals**, pp.249–52).

Other animal hazards in caves

Caves may be cool refuges for troublesome or dangerous animals, so be particularly careful of what you find inside, especially if you are merely sheltering from the sun or taking a discreet leak. Hornets commonly build nests in cave entrances and you are likely to get stung if they decide you are a threat.

Big animals, including large carnivores, also shelter in caves: I've found fresh puma prints in Peruvian caves. In Madagascar, large, hungry Nile crocodiles take refuge in the subterranean rivers of Ankarana during the dry season. Caves can be home to snakes, too, and even something as small as a European badger would be quite formidable if encountered face to face when you are crawling along a low passage. Cave entrances used by cattle or other mammals to shelter from the heat can also be places to pick up a tick.

On the Ground:
Skin

Skin infection 204
  Dermatology made simple 204
  Skin infection and what to do
  about it 205
  Preventing skin infections 206

Rashes and itches 206
  Plant rashes 208
  Itchy beasts 208
  Fungal infections 211
  Hair loss 212
  Impetigo 212

Other skin problems 213
  Painless tropical ulcers 213
  Skin cancers 213
  Leprosy 215
  Foot problems 215

To bathe or not to bathe... 216

16

Summary

→ Bites go septic fast in hot, moist climates. Use insect repellent and wear long clothes.

→ Skin infections are common in travellers to warm climates. Bathe even the smallest wounds in a good, drying antiseptic.

→ Keep cool by wearing loose, 100% cotton clothes and underwear.

→ Wear shoes, sandals or flip-flops as much as possible: bare feet are prone to injury, and invite parasites and fungal infections.

→ Body-piercing, acupuncture and tattooing can give you hepatitis B or HIV if needles are improperly sterilized.

→ A washcloth or face flannel is an indispensable aid to washing essentials (crutch, armpits, beneath breasts) when it's cold or there is little privacy.

→ A sarong, too, aids modest bathing.

→ Sunburn is one very common but avoidable affliction; 'slip, slap, slop' precautions for avoiding sunburn, and its treatment, are given on pp.160–3.

Skin infection

Hot, moist climates and polluted environments are unkind to the skin. Even the slightest cut or abrasion allows bacteria in and infections can be difficult to cure – especially in the rainy season. Mosquito bites – particularly if scratching breaks the skin surface – are a very common route of infection: apply cream to reduce the itching; tiger balm or calamine preparations help, and so does white toothpaste if you have nothing else. Clean and dress any wounds carefully, and keep them covered; flies love snacking on oozing wounds.

In hot, damp environments tropical ulcers can develop within hours, so look at your legs before retiring for the night. Start treatment as soon as you notice any ulcer. Clean the wound with a good antiseptic, rest with the limb raised above heart height (e.g. raise the leg on two pillows in bed) and consider whether antibiotic treatment is needed (*see* below). Skin infections can spread rapidly, so seek medical help as early as possible.

Dermatology made simple

Antiseptic creams are not the best thing to use in hot, moist climates, because they keep wounds wet, therefore feeding infection. What you need is a powerful antiseptic that also dries the area. I favour old-fashioned *potassium permanganate* crystals dissolved in water (*see* recipe on p.206). Diluted tincture of iodine or *povidone-iodine* preparations are excellent too: Videne powder (Riker Labs) is most convenient, but Betadine products are also good. Aerosol *povidone-iodine* is useful but bulky. You can also use antiseptic wipes (alcohol wipes are good, but they sting open wounds) or *chlorhexadine* (e.g. PHiso-hex or Hibiclens) solutions. A **warning**: both *potassium permanganate* and *iodine* stain disastrously if they spill in your luggage.

Skin infection and what to do about it

An early sign of infection is the skin feeling hot, looking red and perhaps throbbing. Lymph glands often enlarge and become painful at 'junction points' in the body (neck, groin or armpits) and sometimes red tracks appear on the skin. If the redness and heat begin to spread, and especially if you feel feverish (hot and cold), you probably have an infection that needs treatment with antibiotics.

If medical advice is not to hand, take a seven-day course of *flucloxacillin*, 250mg (or *cloxacillin* 500mg) every six hours. If you are allergic to *penicillin* you should take *erythromycin* 500mg (or 250mg if you are of very small build) four times a day for a week. Regular *paracetamol* (Tylenol) or *aspirin* (every four to six hours) will help control the aches and pains that accompany fever. They will make you feel better even before the antibiotics start working (within 48 hours). It is also therapeutic to rest with the affected part raised to heart height to drain away any swelling.

For the treatment of cuts, wounds and abrasions, *see* pp.280–2.

Boils

Boils and abscesses do not need antibiotic treatment unless you have lots of them. They are also hot and red, but the infection is confined to one small area with no 'streaking' or spreading of the redness. Resist squeezing a boil: let it break by itself. Pain killers may be needed and won't interfere with the body's healing processes.

Applying *magnesium sulphate* paste under a waterproof dressing will make the boil or abscess come to a head and expel the poisons faster. Hot compresses (for 15–20 minutes every four hours) are also soothing and helpful. If there are crops of boils in different parts of the body, antibiotics will probably be needed (*see* above); see a doctor if possible, as things that look like boils can be something very different (such as tumbu maggots, *see* pp.230–1) or scrub typhus, *see* p.157. Lines of pustules may be flea bites (*see* pp. 233–4).

Meliodosis

This is a rare and treatable aerobic, gram-negative bacterial infection – due to *Burkholderia* (*Pseudomonas*) *pseudomallei* – that causes skin abscesses and sometimes septicaemia. Most people who are exposed to it get no symptoms at all. It is best known from Southeast Asia and northern Australia, where bacteria get into the body by dust inhalation (helicopter pilots are slightly more susceptible), swallowing uncooked, soil-contaminated foods or directly through the skin. There was a bit of an upsurge following the tsunami-induced chaos early in 2005.

Those with **weak immune systems** (*see* box on p.70) or with **diabetes** (*see* pp.65–7) are the most likely to suffer from meliodosis. It can lie dormant for decades, and then causes problems if people develop diabetes or become debilitated due to other illnesses. If consulting your doctor at home, remind him of previous exotic travels.

If a rash is dry and scaly it should be moistened with greasy creams or ointments. If oozing and wet, it needs to be dried out with an antiseptic, such as potassium permanganate or an iodine-based preparation.

Signs of bacterial skin infection
Some or all of:
→ Spreading redness.
→ Increasing pain.
→ Throbbing.
→ Itching.
→ Pus or fluid discharge.
→ Painful lymph glands.
→ Fever.

Preventing skin infections

If you have minor skin breaks or blisters from walking, soaking the feet in hot, salty water will often prevent infection; it is also very refreshing for tired feet. Bathing in sulphur springs also cures mild skin infections. I can vouch for the efficacy of the springs near Tingo María, Peru, although they turn silver jewellery black.

Treating minor cuts, abrasions and insect bites

Bathe any graze or wound at least twice a day (more if you can) by dabbing it with cotton wool dipped in a solution of half a teacup of boiled water containing a few *potassium permanganate* crystals; it should be about a 0.01% solution. *Potassium permanganate* is cheap and readily available in most developing countries. It also prevents infection far better than Dettol or any cream. Diluted *iodine* or gentian violet are also good drying antiseptics and have similar advantages.

Rashes and itches

A rash can be a sign of many diseases, from harmless heat rash through measles and syphilis to serious typhoid. If you have a widespread rash, it is probably worth consulting a doctor to determine the nature of the problem. In general, if the disease causing the rash is serious, you will feel terribly ill.

Itching without a rash can be due to many causes, and you will probably need to see a doctor to get the correct treatment. Calamine lotion or antihistamine tablets may help (*see* pp.70, 88–9). Itchy rashes become itchier when the skin is hot, so cooling the skin with tepid sponging or fans will help. If you itch, cut your fingernails very short, so that any scratching causes less damage.

Prickly heat

Perhaps a third of people visiting hot destinations are troubled by an itchy, prickly heat rash. It can begin within days of arrival and is worst after two to five months after which time acclimatization tends to occur. Typically there is a fine, pimply rash, often on the chest, and wherever skin rubs on skin or there is friction from clothes or even bedclothes. It is difficult to control.

Case history: Madagascar

Towards the end of seven months in Madagascar, I spent an evening in the company of particularly aggressive mosquitoes. I scratched a bite on the ankle too vigorously and it turned septic. Treatment with antiseptic powder and covering it with plasters seemed to help so that only a small spot remained. In Europe I would have simply left this to dry out and didn't bother to cover it but the infernal flies found it and had a feast. The next day I could hardly walk so took antibiotics and had a good dressing put on it. By evening the whole foot had ballooned frighteningly and I was immobilized in bed with pain, a fever of 40°C (104°F) and I couldn't eat. But with my visa running out and my flight back home booked I had to get to the capital. The two-day bush-taxi journey was out of the question so I flew to Tana where I was impressed with how quickly I was provided with a wheelchair without asking.

I was due to fly back to Paris the following evening but 11 hours in a sitting position was completely out of the question. My insurance had expired after six months and I'd decided to risk not extending it and so, having no insurance and not wanting to pay for extra seats, I decided to stay in Madagascar and have treatment there. By now the infection was creeping up the leg and an enormous sausage-like blood blister spanned the whole foot. A greying doctor at the private and wonderfully clean Clinique St Francois d'Assise Ankadifotsy operated to remove the worst infected tissue. Despite having large doses of intravenous antibiotics, the infection spread up as far as my knee and it was five days before it started to recede. The people looking after me all this time were missionaries who made sure I didn't get into trouble about the out-of-date visa and the parishioners provided me with a '*guarde*' (a lad who was with me all the time, brought food and helped me to the loo – as is normal practice in Malagasy hospitals). The doctor next wanted to operate to remove the large scab which had sealed in the infected tissue underneath. I was scared both about having an open wound covering half my foot as well as the expense the operation might entail and decided to fly home. During the week I spent in hospital, the infection had been successfully confined to the foot and my fever had gone. I paid only about £200.

Back in the 'civilization' of Charles de Gaulle airport I missed my flight because Air France failed to provide a wheelchair. I had to wait eight hours and pay €500 to make the final hop to England. Now, four months later, I still have reduced movement of my ankle, but the scars are healing after skin grafting.

Marko Petrovic

Travelling without health insurance is a false economy: for the young and fit it is cheap. A good travel insurer would have been able to give advice, arrange medical evacuation and even a wheelchair.

Abandon tight or adherent clothes. Wear loose, 100% cotton garments; sleep naked under a gentle ceiling fan; take frequent cold showers (without soap) followed by careful drying (dab, don't rub, the skin with a towel). This usually gives some relief. Calamine lotion can be soothing, and spending time in air-conditioned rooms may also reduce discomfort. If you can't afford an air-conditioned hotel, try chilling in some public building or the lobby of an international hotel. Vitamin C may help. Antihistamines don't.

Allergic rashes

If the skin erupts in a series of raised, red, itchy weals, it may be an allergic reaction to something you have consumed or been exposed to recently. This can be caused by newly started medicines, exposure to certain animals, or unusual foods. Antihistamine tablets help settle the symptoms. The best is *fexofenadine*, but *see* p.70 for others. *Chlorpheniramine* (e.g. Piriton in the UK) and *diphenhydramine* (Benadryl) are also good; they cause drowsiness, so are useful if itches are depriving you of sleep (*see* pp.70,88–9). Consider what could have caused the reaction, and avoid it in future; the next reaction will probably be worse. If a rash appears a few hours after being in the sea, it may be due to 'sea lice' (*see* **Water**, pp.177–8).

Eczema

Eczema is a dry skin condition that is particularly common in children brought up in the over-clean industrialized world. Many children grow out of it. It is commonest in people with family members who have it and many eczema sufferers also have asthma, hay fever and other allergies. Moisturization is the key to controlling eczema and sometimes steroid creams are needed. Ointments are more moisturizing than creams. The mildest steroid – which can be bought over the counter in many places – is 1% *hydrocortisone*. Medium-strength steroids such as Betnovate and Eumovate are sometimes necessary. These stronger steroids should be applied sparingly and thinly and never to the face or genitals. Steroid creams are particularly useful in persistent itching after jellyfish stings and also troublesome insect bites or wasp stings.

Plant rashes

Brushing against **poison ivy**, **poison oak** and **sumac** plants commonly causes rashes in North America. The rash appears several days to a week after contact with the plant and usually starts as red streaks or patches. These develop into blisters, which break down, ooze and crust over; there is often swelling of the underlying skin. The problem usually settles down in four to seven days. There is no special treatment, but cool compresses or calamine lotion can ease it. The **cashew tree** is a relative of poison ivy, and contact with it quite often causes allergic cashew nut dermatitis.

Poison oak

Contact with the stem or the seeds of the **giant hogweed** plant (*Heracleum mantegazzianum*) can, in some people, also cause blistering. This seems to be due to a plant toxin sensitizing the skin so that it becomes highly susceptible to sunburn, and it can leave pigmented patches that persist for seven years. Wearing long clothing whenever you go into jungly areas should protect you from this and other noxious plants and animals. **Primroses** in Europe also cause blistering in some allergic people, causing a reaction not unlike the poison ivy rash. **Nettles** are discussed on p.165.

Itchy beasts

'Nairobi eye' and blister beetles

Some species of small, slim, earwig-shaped **staphylinid beetles** (*Paederus* spp.) secrete toxins if crushed or damaged; these irritate and blister the skin, but after a

Case history: Madagascar rain forest

I woke up feeling as though my body had been through a mangle: muscles I didn't realize I possessed ached. I also had technicolour sores covering my feet, an irritating rash around my middle and dramatic rumblings in my gut. Over the following days, my health deteriorated further: stomach rumbles became severe abdominal pain, intestinal volcanoes erupted with gaseous emissions to match.

Back home, my blood showed a high eosinophil count and I was soon the centre of much interest at the Infectious Disease Unit of the hospital; samples were taken and, finally, they took me up to the lab to look down the microscope – at hundreds of *Strongyloides stercoralis*.

These are ingenious and unique among human worms in having a free-living cycle that can persist in soil for several generations. The larvae burrow through the skin of the feet (especially between the toes). I had been wading around in rainforest streams and flooded rice fields in Masoala and Marojejy. From the skin they enter the bloodstream and lymphatics, causing itchy rashes anywhere. Once in the lungs (where they cause a transient cough and wheeze), the larvae moult to become 2mm-long adult worms. They are coughed up, swallowed and end up in the small bowel, their final retirement home. In this warm, nutritious environment they flourish and live for up to four months. Their eggs are then passed in faeces and hatch into new larvae. The adults can also climb out of the rectum (causing itching) and penetrate the skin to boost the internal infestation again. In this way, the parasite can maintain itself inside someone for 30 years.

After taking some 'horse pills' my visits to the loo became less frequent and eating became a pleasure once more. However, there were still thousands of little corpses floating around my body and my immune system continued to send out the heavy artillery to combat the apparent invasion. I suffered rashes and skin sores for a further couple of months. I recovered fully – but perhaps now I'll think twice before paddling in the tropics.

Nick Garbutt, zoologist and wildlife photographer, Bristol

Rove beetle
(*Paederus* spp.)

one-day delay. If a blister beetle flies into an eye and is damaged, inflammation, irritation and swelling starts after 12 hours or so and continues for several days. The delay in onset makes the problem particularly difficult to recognize and avoid, until it is too late.

These beetles are more abundant if there is plenty of rain. They are found in East Africa and Thailand and southern Spain. Outdoor lighting after dark can attract them in plagues. Even in temperate climates, small staphylinid beetles can fly in great numbers and may enter the eyes of cyclists and bikers, causing a burning sensation. Antihistamine tablets may help. Unless affected skin is close to the eye, apply *silver sulphadiazine* (Flamazine) or calamine to control the burning feeling.

Blister beetles (of the *Meloidae* family) are another widespread family of insects that cause blistering, although without the one-day delay in symptoms. These medium-sized beetles are mostly black or brown, but can be bright metallic blue or green. Again, they only cause blistering if beetle body fluids come in contact with human skin. The **coconut beetles** (family *Oedemeridae*) of the Gilbert Islands also cause severe blistering.

Blister beetle

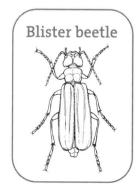

Case history: Pakistan

It was the hot season in southern Pakistan; Jim was very unwell with fever, aches and pains, which he labelled 'flu. Prompted by questions on other aspects of his health, he told me that he had uncomfortable lumps in his groin. These were active lymph glands fighting an infection. He had not noticed that red streaks were tracking up his leg above a tiny cut in the shin. Jim's 'flu was actually a skin infection that had sneaked in through this trivial skin wound. Prompt disinfection would probably have prevented it, but by now he needed a course of *cloxacillin* (500mg four times daily for a week), with which he felt better in 36 hours. Resting with his leg above the level of his heart (lying in bed with his leg propped up on pillows) also aided healing.

Scabies (*Sarcoptes scabiei*)

This is an intensely itchy rash caused by tiny mites burrowing beneath the skin. It tends to be worse at night, and does not affect the head unless the sufferer is under two years old or is very debilitated. Scabies is acquired from prolonged close contact with an infected person (often a child). It is therefore a risk if you sleep in communal accommodation or share a family bed. Symptoms take up to eight weeks to emerge, and in four-fifths of victims are confined to the wrists and hands. The best treatments are preparations containing *malathion* or *permethrin*, applied twice. The solution must be painted all over the body except the face and scalp, including under the nails; it is then left overnight and washed off the next day. Treatment is repeated after seven days. *Benzyl benzoate* is available in many countries, but it is more unpleasant to use and less effective; it usually needs three applications. Expatriates should treat all members of the household, wash all clothes and bedding in very hot water and dry them in the sun. *Malathion* is safe for all. *Benzyl benzoate* and *permethrin* should not be used in pregnancy. *Crotamiton* (Eurax) cream is an anti-itch preparation that also has some anti-scabies effect.

Itching can actually increase for 24 hours after treatment, and persist for as long as two weeks after the treatment has been successful. Hot baths or other things that heat the skin make the itching even worse.

Headlice (*Pediculus humanus*)

Itching of the head and/or body may be caused by lice, however clean you keep yourself. Lice of all kinds are caught by direct contact with someone who has lice, although you can get headlice from a shared brush or comb. Adult lice are translucent and difficult to spot, but the egg cases (nits), firmly cemented to hair, are white and more obvious. They resemble dandruff, but unlike dandruff cannot be picked out of the hair. Fine-toothed combs remove and reveal lice at all stages, so they are a great diagnostic aid. Comb over a sheet of white paper and you will see small things moving in the fallout; they vary in size from minuscule up to a length of about 3mm and breadth of about 1mm. Combing nightly (with a fine comb) is said to prevent lice infestation.

Louse

Natural treatments for headlice

Many villagers in the developing world are skilled at combing out lice and nits and crushing them between the fingernails. A more high-tech treatment is to apply a lot of conditioner to the hair (lice can't cling on to conditioner-covered hair), then comb meticulously for 30 minutes using a fine-toothed comb designed specifically for louse removal, then rinse. Repeat twice a week for two weeks. Four 30-minute sessions of combing are needed for eradication. Wash brushes and combs as well, and dry them in direct sunlight or on a radiator. Shorter hair makes this process easier, and in Asia children are often treated by shaving the head. Natural oils, including neem and tea-tree oils, have insecticidal properties.

Body lice

Body lice are most common in very poor living conditions. There are many louse treatments available, but be particularly careful of what you apply in pregnancy or to small children. Treat bad infestations of head and body lice with *malathion*, *carbaryl* lotion (Quell in the USA; Carylderm in the UK), *permethrin* or *phenothrin*. *Malathion* is the safest and least irritating of the preparations but it is still very strong-smelling and stings if you get it in the eyes; in any case, it can be hard to find. *Benzyl benzoate* is used to treat lice but is less effective than other treatments. Body lice can spread the **nasty louse-borne relapsing fever**. This is very rare in travellers but could be a hazard of spending winters in the Ethiopian highlands or if you sleep in crowded, very poor accommodation in a less developed country. There have been outbreaks in Sudan, West Africa, Vietnam, the Balkans, the Andes and China. For pubic lice (crabs), *see* p.219.

The geography worm or *Larva Migrans*

A worm under the skin causes another very itchy, localized rash. It affects people whose skin has been in contact with soil or sand polluted with dog (or cat) faeces, notably in the Caribbean and Sri Lanka. The dog (or cat) hookworm larva penetrates the skin, then wanders in vain looking for some dog flesh in which to set up home. It searches for weeks, leaving a dry, flaky, red, itchy track. The head advances millimetres each day; the map-like pattern it leaves behind explains why it is called the geography worm.

The worm will do no harm, and eventually dies unfulfilled, but it can be dispatched by freezing the head end with an ethyl chloride spray or carbon dioxide 'snow' (used against warts, and most likely to be found in clinics used by the affluent). An alternative, which is messy but recommended in medical texts, is to crush a few *thiabendazole* tablets, mix them with a bland skin cream and apply it to the area, keeping it in place for 12 hours under a waterproof dressing. Anthelmintics (*thiabendazole* or *albenazole*), taken by mouth for a few days, are also effective, especially if there are several tracks. If a track is on the trunk (between the neck and knees) and progresses faster than a few millimetres a day, this is probably strongyloidiasis and it is best to arrange treatment with tablets within a few weeks.

Fungal infections

Fungal colonization of the skin often causes itching and flaking. The infected area usually has a well-defined edge, redder than the paler centre. Infections in moist areas (under the breasts, within the vagina) may not look the same. Fungal infections are common in sweaty corners, such as the armpits, groin and between the toes. With all these symptoms, wash the affected area, then apply *clotrimazole* (e.g. Canesten in the UK and Asia; Mycelex or Lotrimin in the USA) cream, *miconazole* (e.g. Daktarin in the UK; Monistat Derm in the USA) or *nystatin* two to three times a day. *Terbinifine* (Lamisil) is the most effective antifungal but it is not recommended in children, pregnancy or lactation. The natural approach is to use tea tree oil. Fungal infections beneath toe nails are hard to cure but a clinical trial showed that if tea tree oil was applied daily for six months it cleared fungal infection from beneath toe nails in 80% of victims. More superficial fungal skin infections should respond in perhaps a week. Fungal skin infections encourage bacteria, so if antifungals do not seem to calm an area of inflammation, an antibiotic may be needed; see box on p.206 for warning signs.

If you have an itchy, red area with a well-defined border in the groin or other sweaty corner, smear on an antifungal cream two to three times a day. If this does not work, see a doctor, or consider whether this could be eczema (*see* p.208). Soreness and/or itching around the vaginal opening can be treated the same way, but will often need treatment with antifungal pessaries. Both **crutch rash** and **thrush** are less likely if you wear all-cotton clothing. Underwear is best worn loose: boxer shorts for men and French knickers for women. If you are an expatriate working at a desk, use a cane chair that lets air circulate (but note: bed bugs like cane chairs too).

Hair loss

Hair loss is a distressing symptom that can sometimes happen during travel. It is sometimes blamed on antimalarials, but prolonged flights can also provoke a transient and temporary moult up to three months later (*see* **Flight**, p.88). Poor nutrition and anaemia can cause it and so can fungal infections of the scalp. See a doctor about it if you are worried.

Impetigo

This is a very common superficial infection of the skin, which often begins in a scratched mosquito bite, a graze or a crack at the corner of the mouth. It is an oozing, blistering, golden, crusting, slightly itchy sore that is highly contagious but easily cured. Remove crusts with a mild antiseptic, such as *povidone-iodine* if you have it or salt water if you don't, and treat with an antibiotic cream or powder: *chlortetracycline, fucidin, framycetin, polymyxin* or *neomycin* (e.g. Cicatrin in the UK; Neosporin in the USA). A dilute solution of *potassium permanganate* crystals is also quite effective, and often easy to buy locally, if less convenient to apply while travelling. Spray-on *iodine* (such as Savlon Dry) is a useful preparation. If this doesn't start to control it in 36–48 hours, a week of antibiotics (*flucloxacillin, cloxicillin* or *erythromycin*) can be taken by mouth.

Case history: Peru

I spent four months working in the Peruvian rainforest, at Tambopata. We also explored tributaries by canoe when we slept out in a hammock with no mosquito net. We'd been warned to wear long clothes and apply repellent in the forest but sometimes, especially when labouring, I removed my shirt. Some three months after returning home, I became concerned about a crusty ulcer on my wrist. It was an inch across and just would not heal. I soon had two more lumps further up my arm. Fortunately for me, a friend from the same trip had already been diagnosed with leishmania and I realized that I too might have the disease.

Eventually I ended up at a military hospital, where they took a sample of the ulcer (leaving most of it – to help monitor treatment). The wound was dressed and packed and I received antimony intravenously three times a day for a week. This treatment was frightening: antimony affects the heart and once, when an impatient junior doctor gave the injection too quickly, I felt as if I'd been kicked in the chest! That first round of treatment did not clear the parasites, so I returned to hospital for three more weeks of intravenous therapy. Since I felt very well and had nothing to do, this was intensely boring.

Four of the 30 people on this particular trip contracted *Leishmania braziliensis*, and the friend who sought medical help last needed six months' treatment to eradicate the *espundia* parasites. Soldiers are given a card about ulcers that don't heal; other adventurers beware – keep those little biters away.

Rupert Howes, Brighton

Other skin problems

Painless tropical ulcers

A superficial painless skin ulcer that will not heal over months, particularly after time in Central or South America, needs medical assessment. It may be *espundia* (leishmania), transmitted by sand-fly bites (*see* p.153). Other names for leishmania include Jericho or Delhi boil and dum-dum fever. This usually requires expert treatment in a tropical disease hospital, although a new tablet, *miltefosine* (Impavido), has recently been launched and seems effective, so should simplify treatment. Do not let anyone cut it out, as treatment is difficult and the ulcer is a useful monitor of how well treatment is succeeding. In other regions, especially the Pacific Islands, rapid-growing tropical ulcers are often due to bacteria; again, seek medical help. The usual treatment is antibiotic tablets and rest, keeping the affected limb raised above heart height. Both types of ulcers seem to arise from nothing. A skin sore that will not heal over several months could also be a skin cancer (*see* below). It is important that any non-healing wounds are properly diagnosed.

For **Lyme disease**, initially a non-itchy weal around a tick bite, *see* p.157.

Skin cancers

There are around 40,000 new cases of skin cancer in Britain annually and more than a million in the USA; most are related to excessive sun exposure. Fortunately, the majority of these are either rodent ulcers (also called **basal cell carcinoma, BCCs**) or **squamous cell carcinoma** (SCCs). BCCs don't kill and SCCs are eminently

Case history: miraculous vitamins

When I travelled to India in the 1970s I took vitamin A tablets, called Sylvasun. They claimed to give protection against sunburn and make you tan faster.

Vitamin A tablets and other products containing beta-carotene or canthaxanthin have all been claimed to give protection against the sun. None of these related compounds have been shown to work effectively and they carry the risk of side effects that might harm the eyes and so they are best avoided. The best approach if you are slow to tan is only to expose yourself for short periods initially; people with pale or freckled skin will burn most easily and burning ensures short-term misery, as well as the long-term effect of skin aging and a predisposition to skin cancer.

curable. Both are painless and often start with a red or pearly bump which crusts and scabs over but, even over months, never quite heals. These are easily treated, usually by surgical removal under local anaesthetic. Such tumours are common in older, white expatriates or people who have spent a lot of time outdoors and in sunny places.

Among all those who get skin cancer in the UK, about 5,000 suffer from **malignant melanoma** each year, of whom about 1,500 die. In the US about 60,000 melanoma cases result in over 8,000 deaths. This is an aggressive tumour, which is difficult to treat if caught late. It is becoming more common with increasing tropical travel and its incidence is doubling every 10 years. It is now Britain's second most common cancer in women under 45. Short bursts of intense exposure to strong sun – as in a two-week beach holiday – are a particular risk factor for melanoma in white people.

Those most at risk from skin cancer

→ Fair-skinned people.
→ Those with freckles.
→ Those with red or fair hair.
→ Those who burn easily and tan with difficulty.
→ Those who have been badly/often sunburned, especially as children.
→ People with large numbers of moles (more than 50).
→ Those with existing sun damage (called solar keratoses or 'sun spots'); see p.160–1.
→ People with a close blood relative who has had malignant melanoma (but not just those who have had moles surgically removed).
→ Anyone who has already had a skin cancer diagnosed previously.

Signs that should make you seek treatment

→ A mole that grows larger or becomes thickened.
→ A mole that becomes irregularly shaped or asymmetrical.
→ Development of different colour shades in the same mole.
→ A mole that itches, bleeds, oozes or develops a crust.
→ Dark pigment appears to start streaming out of the mole.
→ Moles over 1cm (half an inch) in diameter, which are more likely to be of concern.

Moles

Moles are slightly raised, pigmented areas of skin. Some skin cancers arise from a mole that changes, or appear in the guise of a new mole. The worst form of skin cancer, malignant melanoma, can kill, but if diagnosed early is curable.

Leprosy

Leprosy is still a common problem in people living in poor, overcrowded conditions in many parts of the world; the disease causes slow destruction of the extremities so that people lose fingers, toes and noses. It first appears as patches of depigmented skin that lack sensation. Lepromatous beggars sometimes touch foreigners deliberately, presumably in the hope that you will be terrified into buying them off, but you cannot contract the disease by touching a leper, or by brushing past people in the bazaar. It is only caught after prolonged and quite intimate contact with an infected person, so the risk of a traveller or expatriate catching it is minuscule. In South America, a similar-looking problem is caused by leishmania (*espundia; see* pp.153 and 213).

Foot problems

Athlete's foot is a dry, scaly rash, often with soreness and itching between the toes; if the skin cracks there may be some oozing too. If you think you have it, get it treated before departure. It is cured by thorough washing and drying, and then applying *terbinafine* (Lamisil) or *clotrimazole* (e.g. Canesten) cream or *miconazole* (e.g. Daktarin) or nystatin two to three times a day. For those favouring a natural approach, **tea tree oil** is also quite effective. To prevent reinfection from sweaty shoes and socks, sprinkle an antifungal powder (e.g. Mycota) into your shoes every night and into your socks each morning. Even the worst athlete's foot may clear up with antifungal powder alone. Thereafter, using lots of antifungal powder protects against reinfection, and is a sensible precaution. Wearing sandals (and going barefoot indoors) when possible also helps. If you have to wear shoes, ensure that your socks are 100% cotton or wool. Severe athlete's foot can become secondarily infected, so if it becomes hot and throbbing, or you feel feverish and unwell, you may need antibiotics (*see* p.205).

One veteran expedition doctor recommended soaking feet in a 4% formalin footbath for 10–15 minutes three times before travelling to hot, moist regions. This hardens the feet for two to three months and may be worth considering if you are going on a tough trip. However, too much formalin treatment will cause the skin to crack, so exercise care.

Sandal-wearers are greatly troubled by **cracked heels**. If this is your problem, keep the offending area of skin thin by abrading it with a skin-grater or pumice after soaking in a bath (do not try this if the skin has already begun to crack). Wearing shoes and socks (the sweat softens the skin) helps too. Otherwise, apply a greasy lubricant: The Body Shop's peppermint foot lotion does the job and smells delicious.

The small parasitic fleas known as **jiggers** can also cause painful swellings between the toes; for these, *see* p.231. For tips on care of the feet when walking, *see* p.187.

To bathe or not to bathe…

In Westerners medical problems are often caused by too much bathing rather than too little. In hot climates you may take several showers a day, and if you use soap each time the skin loses protective oils. Cool water alone is good enough much of the time. If conditions make bathing difficult, just wash armpits, between the legs, between toes and under the breasts with a little soap and a washcloth.

Squat toilets are a challenge: wet the pan before dumping – then they flush easily. In much of the world people do not use toilet paper, but rinse themselves with water after defecation – a basic bidet. This takes practice (and is near-impossible on Western-style WCs). You need to use lots of water. While you are 'a learner' remove all clothes below the waist otherwise water will go all over everything. Squat down low and pour – preferably using a vessel with a spout – directly onto your bottom to flush all the lumpy stuff off. That way you hardly need to use your fingers, except for a bit of gentle waffling and a quick final rub. In a warm climate washing like this is hygienic, will help reduce fungal infections, and the damp area dries quickly even without a towel. It also frees you from carrying toilet paper.

Wash your hands with soap after visiting public toilets. You can acquire others' faecal flora from a door handle. Your own faecal flora will not harm you, but others' will. Air-dry hands by waving them around rather than using a dirty towel.

Showers and legionnaires' disease

The first recognized outbreak of legionnaires' disease attacked 182 American Legion members in a Philadelphia hotel; 29 died. The symptoms were 'flu-like with a pneumonia that did not respond to antibiotics that are usually prescribed for chest infections. Since that first outbreak effective treatment has been identified, so that it generally only causes grave problems in the infirm, immune deficient, frail elderly or heavy smokers. Over 95% of people exposed to the bacteria do not suffer any illness. It is contracted mainly in First World or Western-style hotels, and big institutions like hospitals. Running a shower for a few minutes before bathing will flush out the *Legionella* bacteria and further reduce any chances of infection. Rainforests are an occasional source of human infection. Direct sunshine kills the bacteria; they survive best in above-65% humidity.

On the Ground:
Sex and Genitals

17

Embarrassing bits 218
  Waterworks 218
  Piles 219
  Crabs or pubic lice 219

Sex and libido 220
  HIV/AIDS 220

Men's health 221
  A painful testicle 221
  Discharge or sores 221
  Condoms and the international
  organ standard 221

Women's health 222
  Sexually transmitted infection (STI)
  in women 222
  Discharge 222
  Thrush 222
  Cystitis 223
  Contraception 223
  The pill 224
  Emergency contraception 226
  Unwanted pregnancy 226

Menstruation 227
  Delaying menstruation 228
  Hormone replacement therapy
  (HRT) 228

Summary

→ Not all symptoms below the belt are signs of sexually transmitted disease.

→ Fungal infections around the genitals are common, especially in hot climates – even in nuns (*see* pp.211–12 and 222–3 for treatment).

→ Tight, mixed-fabric clothes around the nether regions predispose to fungal infections. Wear 100% cotton underwear and dress to allow air to circulate.

→ Drink plenty of water to avoid cystitis and kidney stones.

→ Consider the possibly dire consequences of casual sex anywhere. Alcohol and other drugs affect your judgement.

→ If you have an intimate problem, clinics specializing in sexually transmitted diseases will be quickest to sort it out. In many developing countries dermatologists (skin specialists) are also venereologists.

→ Both men and women would be wise to carry a supply of condoms.

→ Condoms are invisibly damaged by contact with sun creams, insect repellents and moisturizing creams, so wash your hands before unwrapping and touching a condom, otherwise an unwanted pregnancy or infection may be the result.

→ Get a check-up in a special clinic promptly if you have any symptoms of sexually transmitted infection: discharge, pain on urinating or genital ulcers.

→ Women needing contraception or planning a pregnancy should discuss their health needs with their doctor several months before travel.

Embarrassing bits

Travel can exert new strains on normal bodily functions. It also often gives the time and opportunity for romance. This chapter will help stop anything turning sour and may help you avoid embarrassing consultations.

Waterworks

Passing blood in the urine usually suggests a bladder infection (cystitis, *see* p.223), requiring antibiotic treatment. Bilharzia can also cause bloody urine (*see* pp.179–81). Some foods and medicines alter **urine colour**: eating beetroot colours urine red, which can look like blood. Very dark urine suggests dehydration (*see* pp.111–2) or hepatitis infection (*see* pp.262–3). In dehydration, drinking a great deal more should lighten the urine colour; try this before seeking medical advice. Everyone should pass good volumes of light-coloured urine at least three times a day; less means you are not drinking enough. People who pass urine hourly are either drinking far too much – or, rarely, may have an endocrine disorder. Men with pain on passing urine may have a sexually transmitted infection (STI) or stone (*see* p.265), and must have a medical check-up at the appropriate clinic. Women who have pain on passing urine probably have cystitis (*see* p.223).

Men over the age of 50 may start to notice difficulties in producing a good stream of urine or they may be troubled by needing to get up to pee in the night. Men with such symptoms should see a doctor to exclude cancer of the prostate. There is evidence that symptoms may be improved by herbal medicines, especially **saw palmetto** and **nettles**.

Travellers who have allowed themselves to become significantly dehydrated – and this is most likely to happen in very hot climates – are storing up problems for the future. Kidney stones may form and cause pain and distress out of the blue years later (*see* 'Pain below the waist', p.265).

Piles

Haemorrhoids or piles may begin during exotic travel. They are precipitated by anything that increases pressure within the abdomen. A common contributory factor in travellers is constipation (*see* pp. 263–4), so drink plenty, eat lots of fruit and avoid constipating food (such as eggs and bananas). Obesity can also bring piles on or make them worse, so keeping slim and fit is advisable. Spending a long time reading on the toilet is also said to encourage them. Mountaineers and hill-walkers sometimes get piles because of the strain of carrying heavy packs combined with exercising and breathing hard at altitude.

Piles are small bulges in the lining of the rectum. Some hang out through the anus like the fleshy end of a little finger. Most itch; some bleed. They are harmless, but can be very painful, or uncomfortable. Treatment while travelling can be difficult. Keep them clean (their shape and position means they are easily soiled, and makes them even more itchy and uncomfortable), keep them lubricated with bland cream (e.g. Anusol, Sudocrem) and try to ease them back inside the rectum. If they are very painful you will need to rest (lying on your side or face down, propping the bottom up on a pillow). Warm baths or cold compresses (crushed ice in a condom) may help.

Occasionally a small blood vessel can leak into a pile so that it becomes intensely painful and looks purple. Lancing big purple piles (of more than 2cm ($^3/_4$in) diameter) or tense painful smaller haemorrhoids with a scalpel surprisingly brings great relief. If there is no one available to do this, it may take as much as a week for the pain to subside, but there will be no long-term damage.

Crabs or pubic lice (*Phthirus pubis*)

These look like minuscule crabs; they feed on blood, and therefore cause a great deal of itching. They are usually acquired from direct (sexual) contact with someone who is infested. Crabs or pubic lice rarely leave the body unless damaged or dying, so transmission via dirty bedding is unlikely though not unknown. If you are hairy, crabs will not necessarily be confined to the pubic region: they can get as far as the eyelashes by way of chest hair and beard. **Treatment** is to apply an aqueous lotion of *malathion, lindane* or *carbaryl* to all hairy parts of the body and leave it on for 12 hours or overnight; it is best to apply a second treatment a week later. Alternatively shaving will get rid of them. If you have crabs, you may have another STI, so you should probably have a check-up at a genito-urinary or skin clinic.

Sex and libido

There are often opportunities for pleasant romantic encounters while travelling, but the risks of acquiring HIV (see below) are considerable. Unprotected sex also exposes you to hepatitis B and a selection of more than 25 other STIs. It is sobering to realize that in the UK, half of all heterosexually acquired HIV is caught abroad. It is foolhardy to have unprotected sex anywhere. A doctor practising in a port in Madagascar told me that 10% of his consultations were for gonorrhoea, a figure not untypical of communities where many people are passing through. So, if you too are passing through, think about the consequences of unsafe sex. Using a **condom** or **femidom** (female condom) reduces the risks, and employing spermicidal pessaries or creams in addition to a 'barrier' diminishes them further, as these sperm-killers are also toxic to viruses. However, beware of contact with other creams, as many oil-based lubricants, and even **sun creams** and **insect repellents**, can invisibly damage condoms, making them porous and allowing sperm to escape.

Sexual appetite may be enhanced or reduced by travel. Many factors that are common in travellers, including fatigue, illness, depression, anger, alcohol consumption and being at altitudes above 3,500m (12,000ft), can temporarily, but reversibly, reduce **libido**.

HIV/AIDS

The human immunodeficiency virus (HIV) that causes AIDS cannot be acquired from mosquito bites. It is commonly spread through sexual contact and less often via contaminated needles or unsterile medical equipment or transfusion. AIDS is a disease of heterosexuals as well as of homosexual men. It is very common in Africa and is increasing in most other parts of the world, especially in major cities. Some countries deny its existence, but it is unlikely any are free from the disease. About 100 British travellers each year pick up HIV overseas, and the rate is rising.

Condoms offer some protection, although oils – and oil-containing sun creams and insect repellents – damage rubber and make microscopic holes that might allow viruses access. Spermicides can be used safely with latex or rubber condoms. Although spermicides destroy the AIDS virus and so should help reduce transmission, very frequent use increases the chances of ulcers forming, and any such broken skin allows easy access for the virus. Ulcers due to STIs or any areas of broken skin therefore make HIV infection much more likely. Any genital infection needs prompt treatment, by a doctor in a special, genito-urinary or skin clinic.

See also **Special Travellers**, pp.70 and 72, for further details on travelling with immunosuppression, and the box on p.37, for information about dealing with emergency exposure to HIV.

Men's health

A painful testicle

A testicle that becomes hot, red and painful needs medical attention. There are two likely diagnoses. If the problem has come on suddenly, it is most likely **torsion** or **twist of a testicle**, when the blood supply is cut off and the testicle dies within a matter of hours. Seek help from a surgeon urgently. More common is **epididymitis**, an infection in which the discomfort tends to come on more gradually; this is cured with a long (usually six-week) course of antibiotics such as *ciprofloxacin*. The pain of both conditions will be helped by wearing supportive underwear (or a jock strap).

Discharge or sores

Discharge from the penis or an ulcer on the genitals may be due to an STI and, even if you do not think you have been exposed to infection, a special clinic is the best place to go for a check-up. Self-treatment is not wise until the problem has been properly diagnosed. Seek help promptly; if the symptoms seem to get better without treatment, it does not necessarily mean the problem has gone away, but it will be more difficult to diagnose if and when it re-emerges later.

Condoms and the international organ standard

It is sensible to pack a supply of condoms for several reasons. First, penile sizes vary: Southeast Asian condoms, for example, may be rather small, while African ones are large. Ensure any condoms bought abroad carry a quality kite mark or equivalent. The shape of penises is also very diverse, so not all condoms fit all comers; specialist shops such as **Condomania** can help if you are non-standard, or you can try a mail order company like **Quick and Direct** (*see* below). Travel with a brand of condoms you know. Carrying them in wallets or jeans' pockets shortens their lifespan, especially in hot climates. Sunscreens, insect repellents and other oily cosmetics put microscopic holes in condoms, so think about what is on the hand that puts the condom on.

Other considerations aside, condoms are also useful items of travellers' equipment. Infantrymen and seasoned jungle travellers use them to carry surprisingly large volumes of water. They are also good waterproof covers for containers. They can be used as temporary fan-belts in cars, washing machines and vacuum cleaners, and can be filled with ice and placed on swollen, painful joints or piles to reduce inflammation and discomfort.

Contact information: stockists of condoms

Econdoms, Quick and Direct, 137a Hersham Road, Walton-on-Thames, Surrey KT12 1RW, UK **t** (01932) 232 443, *info@quickanddirect.com*, *www.econdoms.co.uk*.

Symptoms of sexually transmitted infection (STI)

In women
→ Discharge from the vagina that is thicker, yellower or smellier than normal.
→ Itching around the vagina or pubic region (but often this is simply thrush).
→ Pain on passing urine (but usually this is due to cystitis, see p.223).
→ A painless ulcer or warts in the genital area.
→ Pain during sex (there are other causes).
→ Pain low in the abdomen (there are many other causes).
→ Bleeding between periods or increased pain during periods (though travel often does weird things to women's cycles).

In men
→ Discharge from the penis.
→ Itching around the genital region.
→ Pain on passing urine.
→ A new painless ulcer, spots or warts in the genital area.
→ Pain in the testicles.

Women's health

Sexually transmitted infection (STI) in women

Women should travel with condoms or femidoms so that they can protect themselves from infection (and unwanted pregnancy) in case of unplanned romance. They are also a useful contraceptive back-up if diarrhoea stops absorption of the contraceptive pill. STI in women can cause an unpleasant, greenish vaginal discharge or no symptoms whatsoever. It may compromise future fertility and makes you more vulnerable to acquiring HIV. If you suspect you have an STI, get it treated promptly; most big towns have special clinics.

Discharge

All women experience discharge from the vagina and the consistency varies through the month. Normal discharge is colourless and almost odourless but changes in character in pregnancy and on starting the contraceptive pill. Abnormal vaginal discharge is not always due to an STI; thick, white discharge is common in thrush, and fishy-smelling discharge is probably bacterial vaginosis (treated with metronidozole 2g as a single dose, or with clindamycin cream a 5g applicator full for seven consecutive nights). Tampon-users may notice foul-smelling, dark-coloured or black discharge if they forget to remove the last tampon.

Thrush

Thrush causes itching and sometimes white plaques around the entrance of the vagina. Sometimes there is also cottage-cheesy white discharge. Thrush is common in moist, warm climates, and can follow taking antibiotics. It can also be caused by taking *doxycycline* as an antimalarial. Washing the genital area too much, too often with soap or shower gels aggravates the problem: thrush can therefore be a problem for women who keep themselves too clean. Treatments are as for other fungal infections (*see* pp.211–12), although antifungal pessaries such as *clotrimazole* (e.g. Canesten) are often necessary. *Fluconazole* (Diflucan) capsules, taken by mouth, are available over the counter in the UK. Air circulation helps to clear the infection, so when social circumstances allow it, women should wear skirts or loose-fitting clothes, and not wear underpants. Grapefruit-seed extract has been promoted as a natural cure for thrush, however the antifungal effect of grapefruit comes from chemicals used as preservatives – organic grapefruit has no effect.

Cystitis

Women often suffer from a 'water infection' of the urinary tract and bladder. Such attacks of cystitis can become much more frequent in the tropics, possibly because most people do not drink enough in hot climates, or perhaps because holidays just allow more time for more sex. Cystitis makes women pass urine more frequently, but only small volumes are produced and there is usually great pain at the end of urination. If the only symptom is pain and frequency of urination, try drinking a glass of water containing a teaspoonful of bicarbonate of soda (baking powder), then a further glass every 20 minutes. Excessive quantities of fluids at a different pH from normal unsettle and flush out bacteria. Cranberry juice also works well but may be more difficult to find when you are away. The first couple of times you pass urine it will sting, but the more urine you pass the less it will hurt. The pain should subside after three hours of this routine. If it does not get better with this treatment, if there is blood in the urine or if you have a fever, antibiotics will probably be needed. In this case, take a three-day course of *trimethoprim* 200mg twice a day (not safe in pregnancy) or *co-amoxiclav* (Augmentin) 500mg every eight hours (but not for those allergic to penicillin). Women who are allergic to penicillin and are pregnant should take *cefalexin* 250mg four times a day (unless allergic to *cephalosporins*) or *nitrofurantoin* 100mg every six hours (unless close to the baby's due date). And drink plenty.

Cystitis is not an STI but, like thrush, is common in women who enjoy heterosexual sex. A design fault in the female has positioned the opening of bowel and bladder too close together, so that infection passes from the back passage. Wiping from front to back after using the toilet can help reduce the frequency of attacks, and so does passing urine after intercourse. Also, avoid using antiseptics or perfumed cosmetics in the genital region or cosmetics in bath water. Tight-fitting garments, especially jeans and leotards, can aggravate the problem too. Taking vitamin C (aka *ascorbic acid*) can calm the stinging too.

Cystitis in men or children is not trivial and needs a proper medical assessment.

Contraception

Although the pill is available in most countries, your regular brand may not be. The progestogen-only '**mini-pill**' is certainly hard to find in many Asian countries. In Japan 'normal' steroid hormones, although available, were only licensed as oral contraceptives a few years ago; they are very expensive there and can be hard to find (the International Clinic in Tokyo might be able to help). In general, you should ensure you have enough supplies for your entire time away, although your GP is not able to provide for extended trips except through a private prescription. If you are planning a long trip it may be worth considering using a **progesterone implant** (Implanon), which gives three years' cover, or an **intra-uterine contraceptive device** (IUD or 'coil'), which gives three to five years' cover depending on the device used. Alternatively, an **intra-uterine contraceptive system** (IUS; Mirena) gives five years of contraception and usually causes monthly bleeding to cease. Injectable '**depo**' **contraceptives** have the advantage that they give contraceptive cover for 12 (Depo-Provera) or eight weeks (Noristerat); after some months of use, these usually have the pleasant side effect of reducing or stopping menstrual loss. As with all medicines they have disadvantages, which need to be discussed well in advance – preferably months ahead – of your trip. A family planning clinic or your usual doctor will advise on depo injections, implants and IUDs. Whatever method you decide to use, plan well ahead to ensure that any new contraceptive method suits you several months before departure. Some methods initially cause erratic bleeding.

The pill

Sort out any contraception well before travel. Even in those women who are happy with regular oral contraceptive use, it is still wise to carry condoms, femidoms or possibly a cap to protect themselves from STIs. These are also a useful back-up in case of forgotten pills, a major stomach upset or profuse travellers' diarrhoea. Many women remember their pills by keeping the packet by the toothbrush. Travel disrupts routines and makes it easier to forget. The packet insert gives rules of what to do on missing a pill (*see also* opposite). The new contraceptive ring, which is inserted into the vagina and replaced each month, may be a good solution for some women.

Problems of pill-taking while travelling

Contraceptive pills may not be absorbed properly if you vomit within three hours of taking the pill or if you have very profuse diarrhoea. A slightly upset stomach with a couple of loose bowel motions is not a cause for concern. Taking antibiotics and certain other medicines, including St John's wort, can also reduce the efficiency of the pill. Usually you need to take alternative contraceptive precautions (abstinence, condoms, femidoms or a cap) while taking the antibiotic and for a week afterwards. If taking *doxycycline* as an antimalarial, use additional contraceptive precautions for the first three weeks.

It is also worth carrying condoms as a back-up in case you need to stop taking the pill because you develop jaundice (when the whites of the eyes and then the skin go yellow), *see* p.262–3. You may also like to consider stopping the pill if you experience a great deal of swelling of the ankles. This happens to some people in hot climates and contraceptive pills tend to increase the swelling. Finally, there are some theoretical additional risks to taking the pill when ascending to altitudes over 4,500m (15,000ft). With ascents to very high altitudes (over 7,000m/23,000ft) it may be wise to avoid this type of contraception; *see* **High, Cold and Dark**, p.199.

Rules for taking missed pills

For the mini-pill (progestogen-only pill)

If less than three hours late there is no problem; if more than three hours late:

→ Take the forgotten pill.

→ Take the next pill on time.

→ Use condoms or do not have sex for 48 hours.

→ Keep taking the mini-pill.

→ If you have already had sex before realizing you were late taking your pill, consider taking emergency contraception.

For the combined oral contraceptive pill

If less than 12 hours late, there is no problem; if more than 12 hours late:

→ Take the forgotten pill.

→ Take the next pill on time.

→ Use condoms or do not have sex for seven more pill-days.

→ If fewer than seven pills remain in the current packet, start taking the next packet without a pill-free week.

→ Keep taking the combined contraceptive pill.

→ If you have already had sex before realizing you were late taking your pill, consider taking emergency contraception.

Rules for taking missed pills

If you forget a pill, are late taking one, or vomit within three hours of taking one, following the rules above will ensure contraceptive safety. Women on the pill are most likely to conceive around the pill-free break, so a break of longer than seven days is risky. If you discover you are more than a day late starting the next pack of pills and have had sex in the previous few days, it is advisable to take emergency contraception (*see* overleaf).

Blood clots and the combined pill

Taking the combined oral contraceptive pill increases the risk of a blood clot, and the newer pills carry a slightly higher risk than the older ones (*see* box overleaf). Women who fly frequently may decide to choose a second-generation pill (containing *levonorgestrel* or *norethisterone*, e.g. Microgynon) rather than a third-generation pill (which contains *desogestrel* or *gestodene*, e.g. Femodene, Cilest or Marvelon), or consider other methods of contraception. This might be wise if long-haul travel is planned and the traveller is a smoker, overweight, or there is a family tendency to clots. The risk is highest in women who have recently (within a year) started taking the pill (or HRT tablets). There is no increased risk of clots in women taking the progestogen-only 'mini pill'. Research presented during 2008 suggested that women taking the combined pill but who are immunized against influenza more than half their (albeit small) risk of a clot.

The background risk of deep vein thrombosis (DVT) in the general population is 50 in one million, with an estimated 1–2% death rate. The increased risk of pill-taking is equivalent to the increased risk of death when taking a two-hour drive one Sunday afternoon a year compared to sitting at home. People who have several risk factors for clots and then take a long flight should be aware that risks multiply. They must pay special attention to the precautions and prevention strategies described in the **DVT** feature on pp.15–18.

Female hormones and the risk of a clot

Statistics comparing the background average risk of a thrombosis in the general population – travelling or not – compared with those taking hormones or in pregnancy:

Risk in healthy, non-pill-taker	5 in 100,000 women/year.
Risk in women using HRT patches	5 in 100,000 women/year.
Risk in second-generation pill-taker	15 in 100,000 women/year.
Risk in women taking HRT tablets	20 in 100,000 women/year.
Risk in third-generation pill-taker	25 in 100,000 women/year.
Risk associated with pregnancy	60 in 100,000 pregnancies.

Emergency contraception

So-called 'morning after' emergency contraception is an option after unplanned, unprotected intercourse. There are local restrictions on where it may be obtained but in many destinations it is available from pharmacies, doctors, family planning clinics and hospital emergency departments as *levonorgestrel* (Levonelle). The dose is 1.5mg taken as soon as possible (but within 72 hours of intercourse). Levonelle contains only progesterone and carries no risk of clots. It can be hard to find when you are travelling, so it might be wise to travel with this as a back-up if condoms are used as a contraceptive method. It is 95% effective if taken within 24 hours of unprotected sex, 85% if taken at 25–48 hours and only 58% effective if taken at 49–72 hours. An IUD may also be used for emergency contraception up to five days after unprotected intercourse.

Unwanted pregnancy

Mifepristone is licensed in many regions to terminate an unwanted pregnancy up to nine weeks' gestation. This is an abortifacient (terminates a pregnancy) so it is not available everywhere and is under stricter legal restrictions than emergency contraceptives. In the UK it is only administered in hospital and leads to a miscarriage with some associated discomfort. In some overseas locations, including China for example, doctors will prescribe it to be taken unsupervised at home; however, it would be advisable in this situation to ensure that adequate pain relief is provided. In the UK, referrals for this kind of medical termination, or for surgical removal of a foetus under general anaesthetic, are made by GPs or family planning clinics. Procuring such a termination of an unwanted pregnancy is possible in most European Union countries, excluding Ireland and Malta. It becomes medically and legally more difficult after the 12th week of pregnancy. Although strictly illegal in many other countries, it is often possible to arrange a termination of pregnancy, although this depends on the reasons for the request and the attitudes of individual doctors as well as national laws. Arranging and going through with this unpleasant procedure is difficult in the absence of psychological support and medical back-up. Have a check-up afterwards. Tearfulness is common.

For information about travelling during pregnancy, *see* **Special Travellers**, pp.75–8.

Contact information: contraception

For country information on emergency and other contraception, abortion and helpline numbers, look at the following websites:

www.mariestopes.org.uk.

http://ec.princeton.edu/worldwide/default.asp.

Menstruation

Tampons can be hard to find abroad, so take a supply unless you are prepared to make do with local sanitary towels. It is easy to introduce infection when inserting tampons, yet it is not always easy to find washing facilities when travelling; be as careful as possible about washing your hands, or carry wet wipes. Tampax are available in many big cities worldwide, and to some extent the dispenser solves the hand-washing problem. The two disadvantages of tampons are that it is easy to run out on a long trip and that it may be necessary to carry used tampons (in a ziplock bag) to where you can dispose of them properly.

Proper **disposal** of sanitary towels is difficult. If they are put into the ordinary rubbish system, they may end up being scattered by wind and dogs. The only sensible option is to burn them. Otherwise, washable sanitary towels can be purchased from the sources listed below.

Another alternative would be to travel with a **Mooncup** or a **Divacup**. These collect menstrual blood for up to 12 hours, are removed, the blood jettisoned, the cup washed and can then be reinserted. *See* below for sanitary alternatives.

Menstrual irregularities are sometimes blamed on antimalarials; this may be the case, but it is more likely to be an effect of all the changes that happen during travel. Periods may stop or become erratic, but be aware that the most common reason for a missed period is pregnancy. A doctor should be consulted if there is repeated mid-cycle bleeding or bleeding after love-making. **Period pains** may become more of a problem during travel; pack a remedy assuming the worst. Reducing the quantity you drink for a day or two before the period and for the first day of bleeding often helps reduce pain, although beware of getting dehydrated. *Ibuprofen* (Nurofen in the UK; Motrin in the USA), other non-steroidal anti-inflammatory medicines (*see* **Medicines**, p.36) or *paracetamol* (Tylenol) also help. Otherwise, the contraceptive pill should reduce such symptoms. If periods appear to restart more than a year **after the menopause**, a gynaecological check is needed. The herbal remedy kava does improve menopausal symptoms but the risks of taking it are thought to outweigh the benefits.

Cultural note: menstruating women are considered unclean in many religions, and it would be blasphemy to enter a mosque while bleeding.

Contact information: alternative sanitary protection

Green Baby, 345 Upper St, London N1 3QP, **UK t** 0870 241 7661, *www.greenbabyco.com*. Ecologically friendly, washable sanitary towels.

Plush Pants, 40 Westfield Road, Long Wittenham, Abingdon, Oxfordshire OX14 4RF, UK **t** (01865) 408 040, *www.plushpants.com*. Cloth sanitary towels.

Twinkle Twinkle, Unit 5 Headley Park Nine, Headley Road East, Woodley, Reading RG5 4SQ, UK **t** (0118) 969 5550, *www.twinkleontheweb.co.uk*. Floral sanitary towels.
www.bodykind.com. Makes and supplies the Mooncup.
www.divacup.com. Producers of the Divacup.
www.softcup.com. Sells disposable Softcups, although responsible disposal may be difficult.

Delaying menstruation

Women who are already taking a combined contraceptive pill can miss a period by continuing one 21-pill packet straight after finishing the previous one, without the normal seven pill-free days' break. This is convenient on a short trip or special holiday. Even in established pill-takers, extra or 'break through' bleeds are common if the pill is poorly absorbed due to diarrhoea, so it is wise to pack extra sanitary supplies. Starting the pill simply to control or delay menstruation or miss a period is probably not worth the effort and inconvenience: a study of young women on six-week-long expeditions suggested that many of those who started taking the pill just before the expedition suffered unpredictable bleeding. Packing more tampons, in good, waterproof containers, is a better strategy. Do pack plenty of sanitary protection; it can be hard finding such products overseas, although Tampax seems to be very widely available.

It is also possible to ask your doctor to prescribe *norethisterone* 5mg thrice daily to delay menstruation; it is started three days before the period is expected to start and then the period comes two or three days after stopping these hormone tablets. Injectable contraception (e.g. Depo-Provera) could be especially useful for women planning trips of up to three months. After two or three cycles of this method periods usually cease and, since this is a progestogen-only method, it side-steps the slightly increased risk of thrombosis (a clot) associated with the combined pill. Provided this was initiated four to six months before a trip, Depo-Provera would be an ideal contraceptive for mountaineers (*see* **High, Cold and Dark**, p.199) and other travellers who are at increased risk of clots (*see* 'Flying and DVT', pp.15–18). Implants and IUSs also reduce bleeding; *see* p.224.

Hormone replacement therapy (HRT)

Taking HRT tablets doubles or trebles the risk of thrombosis, with the greatest risk in the first year of use. Research published in the *Lancet* in 2003, however, found that HRT patches don't increase the risk, frequent fliers please note.

Be aware that losing your HRT or having diarrhoea that interferes with absorption of tablets can mean being caught short with a bleed but no protection. Pack with care therefore.

On the Ground:
Animals – Small and Large

Skin invaders 230

Small biters 233
 Six-legged biters 233
 Eight-legged biters 235
 Many-legged biters 237
 Legless biters 237

Small bad beasts 238
 Squirters 239
 Caterpillars 239
 Moths with unusual habits 240
 Dung beetles and flesh-flies 240
 Stingers : scorpions 240
 Stingers: bees, wasps and ants 242

Snakes and nasty reptiles 243
 Venomous land snakes 243
 Other health hazards from snakes 246
 Dangerous lizards? 247

Dangerous large mammals 247
 Man-eaters 247
 African animals 247
 Large Asian species 248
 Monkeys 248
 Bears 248

Dangerous domestic animals 249
 Dog bites and rabies 249
 Cats 250
 Rats and other rodents 250
 First aid for potentially rabid bites 250
 Getting treatment in time 251

Small wild mammals 252

18

Summary

→ Hazards from tropical animals are often over-stated; worry about road accidents, not snakes.

→ This chapter mostly describes animals that are revolting or scary rather than truly harmful. People are often fearful of 'venomous' animals even when the danger they represent is tiny.

→ The USA is home to many dangerous animals, yet most human deaths caused by venomous creatures are from bee stings.

→ Insect repellents deter six-legged assailants, and also leeches, ticks and chiggers. The best repellents are based on DEET (*diethyltoluamide*).

→ Protect yourself against all biters by wearing long baggy cotton clothing – with trousers/pants tucked into socks and shirt tucked into the waistband.

→ When walking outside at night, wear shoes and carry a torch (flashlight) so that you do not stub a toe or stumble on a snake or scorpion.

→ If removing jiggers, maggots, ticks or leeches, make sure they leave both in peace and in one piece.

→ The most common injuries from animals globally are from domestic dog bites.

→ If a dog bites you in an unprovoked attack, assume it is rabid, clean the wound and find a doctor promptly.

→ Never handle wild animals that are inexplicably tame, and do not stroke or pet unknown domestic animals however cute.

Skin invaders

Some travellers like to dine out on accounts of horrific flesh-eaters. And there are insects that lay eggs on human skin so that the young can eat the living tissue. However, only two animals commonly invade man-flesh, and then only in small, discreet areas: you will never be eaten alive. These are tumbu flies and jiggers (not to be confused with chigger-mites). Bot-flies in South and Central America also invade skin. Old and New World screwworms feed on living tissue in wounds, and the Congo floor maggot sucks blood from skin. Other fly maggots can cause benign infestation of dead tissue, and have been used medically for centuries to clean wounds.

Tumbu flies, aka *putsi* (*Cordylobia anthropophaga*)

Tumbu flies are African relatives of blue-bottles or blow-flies. The maggots develop in human skin, causing an inflammation like a boil. The adult fly lays her eggs on clothes that have been left drying in the shade, and maggots usually get to victims by way of clothes or directly from the soil. Eggs or young maggots also contaminate laundry left to dry on the ground. When the clothes are put on, the maggots invade the skin. There they cause 'boils' which usually come in crops, often on the back, arms, waist and scrotum. The 'boils' grow to a maximum size of 15mm in about eight days. The mature grub, which is club-shaped, then falls out through a small hole in the centre of the boil and the inflammation settles down.

The maggot can be encouraged to leave before its eight days are over, but this is not a pleasant spectacle. It first has to be suffocated by placing a drop of mineral oil over its two breathing tubes; these appear as a pair of black dots on

Removing unwanted lodgers

When dispatching unwanted guests, be they jiggers, fly maggots, ticks or leeches, they must always leave intact. If any part of the beast is left behind, it will cause inflammation, which will be difficult to clear and worse than anything the parasite would have done to you if you had left it in peace.

the surface of the boil. If gentle pressure is then applied, the maggot should pop out. Otherwise, as it suffocates it will wriggle violently, and when it emerges it can be grabbed with tweezers and removed. Too much force at this stage will damage the maggot, and if any part of it is left in the skin there will be an unpleasant reaction. Be firm but gentle. You will come to no harm by leaving the maggot alone, although you probably will not want to.

The way to avoid a tumbu infestation is to be careful about where you dry your clothes. Hang them on a line in the sun, or inside where flies cannot reach them. Only take washing in when it is so dry that it is crisp, for the maggot is unlikely to survive a thorough baking in the sun. Iron clothes inside and out. The waistbands of underclothes, bedsheets and babies' nappies (diapers) must also be ironed. Tumbu flies are a problem in hot and high-humidity regions of East, West and southern Africa.

Jiggers

Jiggers, also known as chigoes, *chique* or sand-fleas, are degenerate fleas. They are picked up by walking barefoot in endemic areas, usually where soils are fairly dry and sandy; it is even possible to acquire them indoors. The most troublesome species, *Tunga penetrans*, occurs in tropical Africa, Central and South America. Eight to 10 days after a pregnant jigger has set up home in you, she will have swollen to the size of a small pea, causing a painful swelling at the side of a toenail, between the toes or on the soles of the feet. Left unmolested she will shed several thousand eggs and then die, and her remains will eventually be expelled with a load of pus.

To treat a jigger bite, pick away with a safety pin or needle until you can remove the whole, egg-filled body of the lady jigger. Afterwards, the hole must be doused with antiseptic and a dressing applied to stop infection. If the animal bursts during removal, the eggs will go everywhere and probably re-infest you. Douse with spirit, alcohol or kerosene to kill the remaining eggs (do not smoke while doing this!).

Bot-flies (warble-flies)

Bot-flies (*Dermatobia hominis*) lay their eggs on mosquitoes. When the mosquito takes her blood meal, the hitchhiking fly eggs hatch and the maggots penetrate the victim's skin via the bite hole or a hair follicle. Covering up with long clothes and repellents protects against bot-flies. Once under the skin, they grow until, after two or three months, they measure 2cm ($^3/_4$in). They are unpleasant and unnerving parasites because you can feel (and sometimes hear) them as they fidget. They occur in Central and tropical South America.

Animal hazards and where they occur

Animal hazard	East	Southeast	South	Middle East	Sub-Saharan	North
	Asia				Africa	
Skin-invading maggots				●	●	
Jigger fleas					●	
Ticks	●	●	●	●	●	●
Fleas, lice and bed bugs	●	●	●	●	●	●
Chiggers and scrub itch mites	●	●	●			
Dangerous spiders	●	●	●	●	●	●
Nasty centipedes	●	●	●	●	●	●
Leeches	●	●	●		●	
Venomous caterpillars		●	●			
Itch-inducing (furry) caterpillars	●	●	●	●	●	●
Dangerous scorpions			●	●	●	●
Venomous sea creatures	●	●	●		●	
Stingrays	●	●	●		●	●
Nile crocodiles					●	●
Saltwater crocodiles		●	●			
Potentially lethal snakes	●	●	●	●		
Big game (including bears)	●	●	●	●	●	
Rabid dogs	●	●	●	●	●	●

Asia, East: Japan, China etc.
Asia, Southeast: Indonesia, Thailand, Malaysia
Asia, South: Pakistan, India, Nepal, Bangladesh, Sri Lanka
Pacific, Australasia: Australia, New Zealand
Pacific, Islands: Fiji, Solomons, Papua New Guinea, etc.

One technique for removing remove a bot-fly maggot is to poison the maggot with nicotine from the base of a used, non-filter cigarette. This throws it into quease-making convulsions before it gives in, but subsequently the beast can be squeezed out; get a local who is practised in maggot evictions to do this if you can. In Belize, Barb McLeod has developed a technique that avoids the dying paroxysms. Cover the fly's breathing hole with a generous amount of non-water-based glue: without waiting for this to dry, place a circular patch of adhesive tape on top. The tape should be 1–2cm ($\frac{1}{4}$–$\frac{3}{4}$in) in diameter, depending on the size of the 'boil' and its location. Apply a second seal of glue along the edge of the tape, and allow to dry well. The bot-fly may try to force a new breathing passage by secreting lymph under the edge of the tape. Leave the tape on overnight; by morning the larva should have asphyxiated and can easily be squeezed out or removed with tweezers. Medical texts say that the only way to extract bot-flies is surgically. However, a paper in the prestigious *Journal of the American Medical Association* (1993; **270**: 2087–8) suggests applying strips of bacon over the 'boils'; the maggots love bacon, come out to feast, and can then be caught and removed with tweezers. I go for the McLeod method, because any attempt to grab the live animal risks pulling it apart, which will provoke a nasty inflammatory reaction and infection.

Caribbean	South and Central America	Australasia Pacific	Islands	Habitat
	●		●	rural lowlands
	●			dry, sandy
●	●	●	●	rural
●	●	●	●	poor housing
●	●	●	●	scrub and forest, especially secondary forest
●	●	●	●	warm regions
●	●	●	●	most tropical and sub-tropical rural areas
				moist forest
●	●	●		forest, scrub, plantations
●	●	●	●	rural areas
●	●	●		dry forests, scrub, desert
●	●	●	●	tropical seas
●	●	●	●	shallow sea; tropical South American rivers
				rivers and lakes
		●	●	estuaries, mangrove swamps, coastal regions
●	●			scrub and forest
	●			scrub and forest
●	●		●	villages and towns

Note: This table should only be used as a rough guide, since accurate information on animal hazards is difficult to obtain. Small biting animals which transmit disease are listed in the table on pp.148–9.

Small biters

Mosquitoes, ticks, sand-flies and other little beasts that transmit diseases are covered in **Bites, Biters and the Diseases they Spread**, pp.141–58. For human head and body lice, *see* **Skin**, p.210–11; for crabs (pubic lice), *see* **Sex and Genitals**, p.219. 'Bugs' refer to those insects that entomologists call **true bugs**, the *Hemiptera*.

Six-legged biters

Insects have six jointed legs; many have wings. There are more insect species than all other animals put together. Most make a contribution to the earth's ecological balance; a few make a nuisance of themselves.

Fleas

Fleas are dynamic jumpers. They may be acquired in cheap hotels. They tend to leave a typical breakfast–elevenses–lunch–tea–supper line of bites across the abdomen, then settle down in your sleeping bag. Turning bedding inside-out and

Flea

leaving it out in direct sunlight usually makes them go elsewhere. If this doesn't get rid of them, insecticides may be necessary.

Fleas are difficult to see and even more difficult to catch, for they are small, slippery and fast-moving; they are flat side-to-side, dark nut-brown and look as if they are made from polished leather.

In a very few regions, rat (and rarely human) fleas transmit **plague**, a very rare disease in travellers (*see* p.155).

Stable-flies (*Stomoxys*)

These look like small house-flies, but have a painful bite. They do not transmit disease but occasionally lay eggs in body orifices (*see* 'Dung beetles and flesh flies', p.240).

Horse-flies (*Tabanus*)

These look like streamlined house-flies, but they are much faster and more purposeful than house-flies and indeed most other insects. Their eyes are beautifully coloured and iridescent. Horse-flies can bite through thin cloth; bites are immediately painful and itch for a day or so. They don't often spread disease but can transmit tularaemia (*see* p. 151). They are active during daylight hours, are commonest around cattle and horses and will persist in biting until you kill them, so if they trouble you, find somewhere else to stay. Repellents don't help.

Assassin bugs

Chagas' disease is a debilitating affliction spread by bites of barber or assassin bugs in parts of tropical South America (*see* p.154). Assassin bugs are flat-backed, brown, often shield-shaped, nocturnal insects, which live in wattle-and-daub houses. Their bites are painful; if you plan to use simple accommodation, sleep in a hammock with a mosquito net.

Bed bugs (*Cimex lectularius*)

Bed bugs are what entomologists call true bugs (*Hemiptera*). They are related to assassins, and also have a painful bite. They are a hazard in seedy hotels with cracks and holes in plaster or brickwork; by day they lurk in walls, bed frames and the folds of mosquito nets. The best way to avoid them is to find a smarter hotel, but if you are unfortunate enough to discover bed bugs after settling down for the night, move the bed away from the wall and keep a light on, if possible.

Bed bug

One bed bug takes 10–20 minutes to drink its fill of blood and, if interrupted, will bite repeatedly until it has had enough or you kill it. Bites are painful enough to keep you awake, and are often very inflamed and itchy afterwards. There are seldom long-term problems after bed bug bites, though, and they spread no disease (except insomnia).

Eight-legged biters

Chiggers and mites
Chiggers or red bugs are little red mites known in Britain as harvest mites. They do not enter the skin or suck blood, and should not be confused with the jigger-flea. Only 20 of the 700 species are medically important, as they cause scrub itch. In Asia and the Pacific Islands they transmit scrub typhus (see below). Chiggers are well known to people who walk in long grass, especially in the tropical Americas, for although they are only 1mm long, they make their presence felt. To **keep them off**, apply repellent and tuck trousers into socks, or they will latch on to ankles, the groin, armpits and wherever clothing is tight. They stay on for four days, but welts and severe itching last for 10 days. This is because they leave behind a stylosome (drinking straw), created partly as the body's reaction to their saliva, which continues to irritate and inflame the skin. If you scratch as much as you'd like to, you will get a nasty skin infection.

Scrub typhus mites
The bites of the small Asian mites that transmit scrub typhus (a rickettsial disease that responds to antibiotics) do not itch and so often go unnoticed. True to their name, these mites are common in scrub and secondary forest. Scrub typhus mites occur within a large area of East Asia and the Pacific Islands, down to Queensland, Australia in the south and Sri Lanka and Pakistan in the west.

Other mites
Australian whirligig mites (*Anystis* spp.) are also red and impressively large for mites: up to 1.35mm long. They are beneficial, fast-moving predators, whose bite is painful to humans too. Bites cause a small area of inflammation, which may persist for several days.

The **Mauritian red poison mite** has toxic secretions that, if conveyed to the mouth via the hands, are sufficiently potent to cause unpleasant and occasionally dangerous swelling of the mouth and throat. Wash your hands well if you come into contact with red crawlies in Mauritius.

Spiders
Almost all spiders are venomous, but most are unable to bite into human skin. As a general rule, those that spin elaborate webs need less venom to immobilize their prey, so are less likely to be dangerous. The few spiders that are dangerous either dispense toxins that kill a discreet area of skin (*Loxosceles*, *Lycosa*), or nerve poisons (*Lactrodectus*, *Phoneutria*, *Atrax*). These five genera are described below. Cold compresses or applying ice is sufficient treatment for most spider bites but,

Preventing mite bites and tick attachments
To avoid mites, leeches, chiggers, ticks and the diseases they carry, put on insect repellent; the best are DEET-based (*see* p.145). Wear long sleeves and trousers, and tuck trousers into socks in high grass or scrub. Spraying *permethrin* on your clothes makes you even more repellent.

in Australia, apply a broad, firm compression bandage and immobilize the entire bitten limb in a splint to slow the spread of venom. Most spiders harm by biting. However, some of the very large, hairy spiders flick off body hairs towards the source of their annoyance, and these cause itching; they are particularly unpleasant if they get into the eyes.

Brown recluses or fiddle spiders (*Loxosceles*)

Brown spider

These are long-legged brownish spiders that are widely distributed throughout the Americas, and have also bitten in the Mediterranean, North Africa and Israel. The fiddle describes the violin-like mark on the back of many species. Bites cause localized death of skin tissue and underlying structures. Occasional fatalities occur; there have been about six in the last 100 years in the USA. Men have been bitten on the genitals while on outdoor toilets, so check before you sit. Antivenom is made in Peru, Brazil and Argentina.

South American wolf spiders (*Lycosa rartoria and L. pampeana*)

Wolf-spider bites can cause tissue death resulting in a scar up to 20cm (8in) long. There is an antivenom in Brazil. The European wolf spider, *Lycosa tarentula*, was once blamed for epidemics of bites that, supposedly, could only be cured by dancing the tarantella. However, feared though it is, it rarely kills anyone except the infirm.

Black and brown widows (*Lactrodectus*)

Widows have a very bad reputation but, again, deaths are unusual. They are small black or blackish-brown spiders with a red, hourglass-shaped design on their backs. They are very widespread and occur in much of the Americas, Africa, southern Europe, warm parts of Asia and Australia. Bites are usually on an extremity and, if venom is dispensed, pain spreads from the site up the limb to the lymph nodes in the groin or armpit, and then to the muscles, which suffer cramps and spasms. The victim can become exhausted and dehydrated. Pain is difficult to control even with painkillers, but hot baths may help. Recovery usually takes one or two days, or half an hour if antivenom is given. Deaths are rare but occur occasionally in small children, the elderly or those with long-standing heart or lung disease. Antivenom is made in the USA, Australia, Russia, the Balkans, Italy, South Africa and South America.

Huntsman spiders (*Phoneutria*)

Also called **wandering** or **banana spiders**, huntsman spiders are from South America. They are big – with 4cm (1½in) bodies and 13cm (5in) leg-spans – and aggressive, with rather threatening red colouration around the jaws. Bites cause intense pain, sweating and cramps, but recovery is usually complete in 12 hours. Deaths are unusual, and occur in children and weak adults. Antivenom is made in Brazil.

Funnel-web spiders (*Atrax*)

The nastiest funnel-web spiders fortunately have a very restricted range: they only occur in an area immediately around Sydney, Australia. Because antivenom treatment is available, deaths from funnel-web bites are now rare and, despite its fearsome reputation, the Sydney funnel-web has killed just 13 people in 80 years. They are medium-sized, heavily built 'tarantula'-like spiders that either give a series of superficial bites, or grasp firmly with their legs and drive their chelicerae in with sufficient force to pierce the skull of a chicken.

Many-legged biters

Centipedes

Centipedes are fast-moving predators. Most of their segments have a single pair of legs that protrude to the sides. Bites by

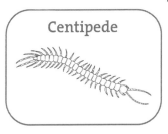

Centipede

big, tropical centipedes are very painful but, worldwide, only one person is recorded as actually having died from a centipede bite; that was in 1923, when a seven-year-old child was bitten in the head by *Scolopendra subspinatus*. The usual treatment is to inject local anaesthetic, but injections of *morphine* or *pethidine* (*meperidine* or Demerol in the USA) may be required for pain.

Centipedes are not good to eat. A 55-year-old Yugoslavian woman accidentally swallowed one. She vomited, cold-perspired, experienced palpitations and then the animal was suddenly discharged from her bowel; later it was identified as *Scolopendra cingulata*.

Millipedes

Millipedes do not bite and are sedate, dignified animals. They are rounded, with legs (two pairs per segment) tucked beneath their bodies to give them an almost snake-like look.

When annoyed, sat on, or rolled on in your sleep, some tropical species secrete an irritant fluid that will inflame the eyes and perhaps the skin. This can be unpleasant, but is not perilous.

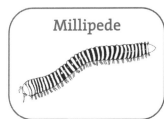

Millipede

Legless biters

Leeches

Leeches do not transmit disease; they harm only if the bite becomes infected. But they are nightmarish creatures – British troops serving in Malaya wore condoms at night because they were so worried about leeches crawling into their urethras,

> ### Case History: Madagascar
> The warm rain was pouring down in the forest of eastern Madagascar, we were soaked to the skin and repellent didn't seem to stay on for long. I was wearing stout walking boots and thick socks. I did an experiment and plastered my right boot thickly with DEET, while the left boot received none. At the end of the day my left ankle was ringed with leech bites and my socks were a squelchy, sticky mess of pink rainwater. My right foot was unscathed. Applying repellent to boots protects for longer, reduces direct skin contact with the insecticide and means that your protection isn't sweated off.

though they needn't have worried. Freshwater aquatic leeches occasionally enter body cavities to cause bleeding from unusual places (see **Water**, p.182), but this is rare and happens only in swimmers.

Leeches are common in rainforests, including in Australia, and in scrub or forest during wet seasons, particularly in Asia. They usually climb onto you from the ground or hitch a ride as you brush through wet undergrowth, or drop down from trees. They can squeeze through shoelace holes and between the fibres of socks. Bites are usually painless (they inject local anaesthetic). You may be unaware of them until you notice a squelching or stickiness in the socks that turns out to be blood. Bites bleed for some hours because of the anticoagulant the leech injects, and, often, leeches have left by the time you find blood.

Leech avoidance and first aid

Avoid leeches by applying DEET insect repellent to the outside of boots (but be aware that DEET dissolves plastics), putting DEET on your ankles (but NOT under your socks) and tucking trousers into socks. Leech country is usually hot and steamy, so if you only apply repellent to the skin you will sweat it off in an hour. Get leeches off with a dab of salt or tobacco and then clean and cover (if possible) any broken skin. Leech bites may itch for weeks, especially if the mouthparts remain in you.

Small bad beasts

What is dangerous?

Local information about dangerous animals is not always accurate. I was told in Sulawesi, for example, that I would be dead in 24 hours after handling a very large, rather attractive millipede. While centipedes have extremely nasty stings, the only noxious property this millipede has is that the juice it might have secreted if upset (which it wasn't) can inflame the eyes if rubbed in. So will snail and slug slime. The secretions of a few tropical millipedes and contact with some damaged beetles in many regions (including southern Spain) may blister skin (see pp.208–9).

Squirters

Tail-less **whip-scorpions**, **cicadas** and a range of other creatures squirt or spit irritant juice when annoyed. If any goes close to your eyes, wash it out with plenty of water. In North America there are a couple of hundred insects known as **walking sticks**; some are known as musk phasmids, as they exude a white liquid with a pleasant musky smell. These are insects to be wary of, however. One species, *Anisomorpha buprestoides*, a 7–12cm- (3–5in-) long, yellow-and-brown-striped insect also known as the **Florida stick**, can spray its 'musk' up to 40cm (16in). When inhaled, this substance causes pain, and if it gets into the eyes the severe burning sensation it provokes takes 36 hours to settle.

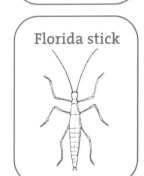

Tail-less whip scorpion

Florida stick

Caterpillars

Furry caterpillars cause great discomfort if you lean on them or they get caught up in your clothes and their hairs are forced into your skin. In rural areas there can be plagues of these attractive-looking insects, and in houses it is easy to lean on one, or pick something up on which one is perched. The fine 'hairs' inject irritant chemicals akin to histamines, which cause irritation for between a few hours and several months. Some caterpillars have large, eye-like markings and spiny-looking appendages to warn you they are unpleasant; these induce blood blisters if you brush against them. Also treat pine processional caterpillars with respect and discourage children from disturbing their web-encrusted colonies; their hairs are highly irritant.

Caterpillar species to watch out for

Hairy moth caterpillars are common all over the world, but only the South American species are really noxious. In Brazil there are very nasty spiny caterpillars. The worst is *Lonomia achelous* (family *Saturniidae*), whose spines deliver a toxin that interferes with blood clotting and can make people very ill. Similarly armed caterpillars are known in Venezuela. Stings by the long-haired caterpillar *Premolis semirufa* (*Arctiidae*) can cause such deep inflammation around the joints that the

Hairy caterpillar

victim may be permanently disabled (a hazard for South American rubber tappers). In Peru there are rufous funnel moth caterpillars (*Megalopyle superba*) that are so large and 'furry' they are known as the **cuy rojizo** or 'reddish guinea pig'. They are notorious for the severity of the skin reactions caused by coming into contact with them. Related caterpillars occur in the southern USA and the Caribbean. Similarly unpleasant species exist in the

Old World tropics and subtropics. Keep away from any furry or spiky caterpillars; striking markings advertise noxiousness.

First aid for removing caterpillar hairs

Sit down in good light and pick each hair out – one by one – with pointed tweezers. Do not use eyebrow tweezers as they will squeeze the remaining venom into the skin. Sticky tape is no help. Be careful what you do with the hairs you pull out; if they enter the eyes they are very dangerous, and if they fall onto your lap they may make that part itch, too. Treat irritation with *paracetamol* (Tylenol) and/or antihistamine (*see* box on pp.88–9), and a cool or tepid bath.

Moths with unusual habits

In Southeast Asia and the southwest Pacific, some moths drink tears from the eyes and also enjoy saliva and other body secretions. This could presumably introduce infection, particularly conjunctivitis. The *Calyptera* genus of moths, from the mountains of Southeast Asia and Papua New Guinea, has a taste for blood and occasionally attacks people at night, usually at or above an altitude of 1,000m (3,000ft) and in the rainy season. Initially the wound is painless, but it hurts when the moth empties saliva into it, and later there is transitory inflammation. The only likely problem arising from this is infection, as these moths also dine on cattle dung.

Dung beetles and flesh-flies

Dung beetles have unpleasant egg-laying habits, and mothers attending my clinics in Sri Lanka commonly complained that insects flew out of their toddlers' faeces as they were deposited on the ground! This bewildering but harmless affliction needs no treatment, and is unlikely to befall even the sleepiest of travellers.

Houseflies, **bot-flies**, **blow-flies**, **flesh-flies** and **hover-flies** occasionally deposit eggs in open wounds and in body orifices so that their maggots can infest the ears, nostrils, eyes and genitals, but this occurs almost invariably in children or very debilitated people.

Stingers: scorpions

Brontoscorpio is my nightmare creature; it was a metre-long scorpion, which fortunately became extinct 300 million years ago. The largest survivors, *Heterometrus* spp. of Southeast Asia and *Pandinus imperator* of West Africa, look terrifying, but their sting is only painful; few scorpions are dangerous to adults. Today there are species capable of lethal stings, mainly to children, in North Africa and the Middle East, South Africa, India and North, Central and South America. Scorpions are most common in dry, arid regions, but do not tolerate extreme heat. They are most in evidence after rain. They are attracted by humidity and so wander into shower rooms. Outside, they hide under stones or rotting logs, so if collecting fire wood, lift or roll logs so that anything lurking underneath flees away from you. Scorpions are nocturnal, so most stings happen at night or when a slumbering

Case history: Sudan

One night, there was great commotion in the women's sleeping quarters where I was staying. Someone was brought in by a group of chanting village women who waved incense over the casualty. An hour saw no improvement in the girl's pain, palpitations and breathing difficulties so she was taken to the healer. He prepared an oily paste containing a mixture of herbs and applied this to the girl's foot – where the scorpion had stung her. Under Islamic tradition, the rest of her body remained completely covered. The paste made the pain ebb away and her heartbeat returned to normal. Two days later the girl was fine again. She'd briefly taken off her shoes after a hard day's work and had been stung when she slipped them back on.

Moral: always check what might be inside your shoes.

Valerie Hovell, Worminghall, Buckinghamshire

Scorpion

specimen is disturbed after it has settled down in your shoe or rucksack. They are occasionally a problem in cities, notably in big towns in lowland Mexico and also in India.

Generally, scorpions with big claws and slim 'tails' rely on claws as their principal weapon, so they are less venomous. Those with small claws and a more substantial 'tail' and stinger are more likely to be dangerous. Exceptions exist: the Middle Eastern *Hemiscorpius lepturus* has a very long, slender stinger, but is very dangerous.

Seek medical help promptly if a child is stung. Mexicans suffer more deaths from scorpions than any other nation, over 1,000 per year, mostly in children under five. Even in Mexico, though, most stings are painful for up to four hours, and only eight of the 25 local species are a serious threat. Antivenom is available for the dangerous ones, like the 5–8cm (2–3in) narrow-bodied, elongated *Centruroides* 'bark scorpions'. These species also occur in Arizona, but rarely kill there as antivenom is readily available. Antivenom is also available for species in Saudi Arabia, although it should not be administered by amateurs. In the absence of antivenom, treatment is with *prazosin* under medical supervision.

Scorpion toxins attack the heart and circulation; some are nerve toxins. The red scorpion of South India unusually causes some **adult deaths**, by poisoning the circulatory system. My own finger is still numb after a sting 23 years ago in Madagascar. A dangerous sting provokes a feeling of being very unwell, profuse sweating, the shakes and a rapid heartbeat. Seek medical help if you can; otherwise rest, let the storm pass and avoid immersing the stung part in cold water, as this increases pain.

Scorpion antivenom and other treatments

Antivenoms are manufactured by institutions in the USA, Germany, Mexico, Brazil, Turkey, Algeria, South Africa, Egypt and Iran. In the UK, the **Lister Institute of Preventive Medicine** stocks some. Scorpion *haemolymph* (their equivalent of blood) neutralizes scorpion venom. An Israeli child was saved by a *haemolymph* injection in lieu of antivenom.

Applying ice packs, immersion in water or cooling by hanging the affected limb out of a car window **increases** the pain. Avoid rubbing or other friction and keep the stung part warm and cushioned. Injecting local anaesthetic in or around a stung finger may give temporary pain relief, but an injection of a powerful, morphine-like drug may be required. However, this treatment will be risky if there are respiratory complications. This may happen after an Indian red scorpion sting, which causes flooding of fluids into the lungs (pulmonary oedema). Seek medical help if you can.

Contact information: stockists of antivenom
Lister Institute of Preventive Medicine, PO Box 1083, Bushey, Herts WD23 9AG, UK **t** (01923) 801 886, *www.lister-institute.org.uk.*

Stingers: bees, wasps and ants (*hymenoptera*)

Normal insect repellent is ineffective against thin-waisted, stinging insects such as bees, ants and hornets, although there are now products to deter wasps. On encountering any air-borne stinging insect, back off calmly; never thrash or flail about. Even a swarm of the feared 'killer bees' should not attack if you stay cool. As they sting, these insects release alarm pheromones which summon others to help in the attack. Wasps and their kin are attracted by sweet things, perfumes and brightly coloured floral patterns.

Honey bees

When a bee stings, its stinger (complete with venom-sack) remains in the skin and continues to pump venom in after the bee has gone. Bees empty 90% of their venom within the first 20 seconds and the remainder within a minute; the longer you take to get the stinger out the more painful the sting will be. Speed of sting removal is more important than technique. Try to scrape or flick it off with your fingernail. Don't fuss about to find an implement with which to scrape or pick it out since this will lose time, and don't grasp a sting with tweezers because that injects the venom remaining in the stinger.

Once the sting is out, apply ice or a cold compress (wet cloth), elevate the part that has been stung, and take antihistamine tablets and/or *aspirin* or *paracetamol* (Tylenol). As a **natural remedy**, applying papaya – or extract of papaya in the form of meat tenderizer (at the ratio of 1:4 tenderizer to water) – probably relieves some of the pain by destroying the venom. It is worth trying.

A severe allergic reaction to stings causes a great deal of swelling and can provoke breathing difficulties; this can be fatal in minutes. Such a severe reaction is unlikely unless there have been previous stings. A hypersensitive individual will usually notice that with each sting they suffer, local swelling becomes increasingly extensive and persistent. Most people in Britain who are allergic to bee stings are bee keepers or their relatives (i.e. people who have been stung lots of times). Allergy is less likely in children than in adults. Those who are allergic should carry an *adrenaline* (*epinephrine*) Epipen or injection (*see* pp.69–70).

Wasps and hornets

Wasps and hornets are not always yellow, black and stripy. The common Asian field wasp is plain orange, and some other species are navy blue. Wasps do not leave their stingers behind, but otherwise their stings require similar treatment to bee stings.

Fire ants (*Solenopsis* spp.)

Fire Ants originated in South America but since the 1920s have spread to the USA, where many people are stung all year round. They have also recently colonized Australia, where they are also becoming a great nuisance. The ants are reddish-brown to black and they are small (less than 5mm long) but when colonies are disturbed, ants will attack in thousands. Some victims experience only temporary discomfort but most suffer pain, itching, swelling and redness around a central weal or welt, which lasts for up to a few hours. Next a small blister forms. Over the next half day or so, the fluid in the blister turns from clear to cloudy, and the area begins to itch. Although the venom is bactericidal, secondary infections due to scratching may happen. As with stings from wasps and bees, fire ant stings can cause dramatic and dangerous allergic reactions, but in only around 0.5% of attacks. Reaction to fire ant stings is similar to reaction to the stings of bees, wasps, hornets and yellow jackets. Most fire ant stings are uncomfortable rather than dangerous. If redness and swelling spreads two or more joints beyond any bite or sting site or over an area greater than 25cm (10in), or if there is difficulty swallowing or breathing or widespread swelling of body parts seek medical help urgently. Antihistamine tablets help (*see* 'Honey bees', p.242 and pp.70, 90–1).

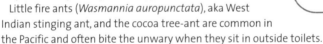

Fire ant

Little fire ants (*Wasmannia auropunctata*), aka West Indian stinging ant, and the cocoa tree-ant are common in the Pacific and often bite the unwary when they sit in outside toilets.

Sweat bees

These 3–4mm long, slow moving, black bees are attracted to sweaty skin, mouths and nostrils. They are easy to kill. Their stings are trivial, but crushing any releases pheromones that summon reinforcements when they can become really annoying. They live in much of the tropics and sub-tropics.

Snakes and nasty reptiles

Venomous land snakes

Few snakes are dangerous. Of nearly 3,000 species worldwide, about 500 are venomous, but fewer than 250 ever cause death or permanent disability. A good proportion of venomous snakes do not have the capability or temperament to be harmful; even those that are venomous and aggressive more often than not give a 'dry' (harmless) bite. However, as the division between harmful and harmless species is far from clear, anyone bitten by a snake should be assessed by an expert. Snake venom is a meat tenderizer produced by modified salivary glands; it partially digests the prey prior to being eaten, so it has very unpleasant effects. There are about 40,000 deaths worldwide per year (mainly in India, from cobra during the rains), but it is exceptional for travellers to be envenomed. Those at high risk are agricultural labourers, who disturb happily basking snakes, or people who are foolish enough to tease snakes – teasing stimulates the snake to increase the dose of venom. Peninsular Malaysia boasts a particularly rich array of venomous species but, even here, only about one in a thousand people bitten by a snake actually dies. It is 'energy-expensive' for a snake to make venom: it takes two to three weeks for a snake to replenish its venom gland, so it won't want to waste it on anything but food-hunting.

Cutting into a snake bite does not flush out venom, but it can sever arteries. **Tourniquets** are also dangerous (*see* below). However, the Nepali chicken's bottom treatment – where the anus of a decapitated chicken is applied to the wound in the belief that it will draw out the venom (*see* 'Case history: Nepal', p.246) – is based in perverse good sense, in that it may help the victim by preventing him from panicking. People bitten by snakes are so scared that they often thrash around in a blind panic, distributing venom more quickly and disastrously. A complicated ritual helps the victim stay calm, an important but difficult part of snake bite treatment. Those managing the situation must appear confident and cool, even if they too are panicking.

Snake bite treatment

Snakes can control whether they dispense venom or not and often bites are 'dry' and harmless – even if the snake is venomous. Travellers are rarely unlucky enough to suffer a dangerous bite, but everyone wants to know what to do if they are on the wrong end of a pair of fangs. Try to get to a clinic or hospital where they know about snake bites. Many 'first aid' measures can make things much worse but, while evacuation is being organized, follow the rules in the box opposite.

A **tourniquet** is a tight band designed to cut off the blood supply to a limb. Using a tourniquet may be appropriate, but only under exceptional circumstances (*see* box, opposite). A great many limbs are lost through incompetently applied tourniquets. Too often they are applied after a bite by a harmless snake or by a venomous one that has dispensed no venom. Home-made tourniquets do little to stop venom spreading through the body, yet can still cut off circulation enough to risk losing the limb. Applying a broad, firm crêpe bandage around the bitten limb and splinting it is a safer, more effective option than a tourniquet. Even the splinted bandage must be released every half-hour, to let blood reach the body's tissues.

Electric shock or stun guns do not inactivate venom, nor do the 'snake stones' of India and Sudan, although they may be useful – like the headless chickens – by helping everyone to stay calm.

Snake habits

It is worth repeating that not all venomous snakes are dangerous. Many of the brightly coloured coral snakes have such small mouths that they are only capable of getting their teeth into an earlobe or finger web. In a review of snake bites in peninsular Malaysia, the only record of coral snake envenoming was one case in 1937 (the victim survived). Some South American species are big enough to bite a finger if offered.

If a snake bites

1. If you are the victim, try to get someone to help you get help. The less you do the better.

2. Keep the victim still. Promote a calm atmosphere. It is likely to have been a 'dry' bite.

3. Clothes should be rolled up or cut, and not removed, because undressing encourages movement, which disperses venom.

4. The bitten part should be washed with clean water and soap, and wiped gently with a clean cloth to remove any venom from the skin surface. In Australia, the venom in the cloth may then be used to identify the snake and then the correct antivenom can be administered.

5. If venom has entered the body there may be swelling, so remove any watches and jewellery.

6. If you have a crêpe bandage, apply this firmly over the bite-site as soon as possible and extend the bandaging to wrap up as much of the bitten limb as you can.

7. Then splint the bitten limb to slow venom absorption and ease pain.

8. Keeping the bitten limb below the level of the heart also helps slow the spread of the venom and is a useful manoeuvre if bandages and splints are not available.

9. Prompt evacuation to a doctor or hospital is the next priority. If the victim begins to show signs of envenomation, antivenom will then be administered in a safe clinical environment. Administering antivenom carries its own risks (*adrenaline/epinephrine* should be available).

10. Finally, if the offending snake can be captured without risk of someone else being bitten, take it to show to the doctor, so that it can be identified to help define proper treatment. Beware, though, that even a severed head is able to envenom in a reflex bite.

11. Never cut into the bite or suck the wound, and avoid using 'Venom-ex' or similar first-aid devices that cut the skin; they are dangerous and do no good.

12. If prompt evacuation is not going to be possible, release the crêpe bandage every half-hour for 15 seconds and remove it completely after two hours.

13. Do not take *aspirin*; *paracetamol* (Tylenol) is safe.

14. Do not apply ice packs or *potassium permanganate*.

15. Don't panic: it is likely no venom has been dispensed.

When to use tourniquets

Tourniquets are only appropriate under the following circumstances:

→ The delay in getting to competent medical help is going to be more than 30 minutes but less than three hours.

→ The biter was an elapid (cobra, krait, mamba or coral snake), a sea snake (*see* p.174) or an Australian snake.

→ You know what you are doing and feel competent and calm enough to take charge of the situation.

→ The tourniquet is released for 15 seconds every 30 minutes.

→ The tourniquet is removed after two hours.

→ You have a watch, and can write down what you are doing.

Other species, like the black-fanged snakes of Madagascar, can only inject venom as their victim is being swallowed, so they can only envenom those who stick a finger down their throats! Others do not have the temperament to attack. **Sea snakes**, for example, have very powerful venom, but attacks by them are rare (*see* p.174). The highly venomous **krait** and feared **bushmaster** are similarly unlikely to bite, even if provoked (don't try it: kraits still claim lives).

Most deaths from snake bites are in the Indian subcontinent, because snakes there are often forced into contact with man. Most feared is the huge **king cobra** or

Case history: Nepal

I arrived at the district hospital in lowland Nepal after the outpatients clinic had finished, but one patient remained. An emaciated little boy squatted in the corridor, quivering in terror, with a string tied tightly around his arm, which was soaking in a bucket. He was scared to death, his fear aggravated by the fact that the local medical staff were scared to touch him. The child had been romping in leaf litter, and the snake he had disturbed had bitten the fleshy part of his hand, near the thumb. Someone had cut into the wound and applied the anus of a beheaded chicken, because the decapitated corpse is supposed to draw out the venom. I asked, 'Is there any antivenom in the hospital?' The Nepali staff laughed. 'No, but you can find it in the bazaar.'

'Can you get some, and we'll take off the tourniquet and observe the child with antivenom ready...'

I took off the tourniquet and the child was fine.

hamadryad (*Ophiophagus hannah*), which can be 4.8m (15ft) long and, in threatening mode, may stand 2m (6ft) off the ground – looking you in the eye. They are usually slow to attack but may do so with enthusiasm, and are efficient dispensers of venom. However, they are a scarce day-active species that live in dense forest, and you are unlikely to meet one. They are fast movers, but cannot outrun a man. The **Indian cobra** (*Naja naja*) claims more victims than any other snake in the world, but is not usually aggressive, and is often timid. It may attack when disturbed. The young can be real delinquents; they appear during the monsoon and are much more dangerous than adults, because they haven't learned to fear people, are more easily excited and are always ready to strike repeatedly and with determination, especially when cornered in a house. Indian cobras are active in the late afternoon, evening and at night.

One of the difficulties of treating snake bites is that the first aid required is different depending on the kind of snake that bites you. **Viper** venom, for example, mainly harms by destroying tissue around the bite-site, so tourniquets make viper bites worse. However, slowing down the circulation of venom is life-saving in snakes whose venom attacks nerves or muscle, including heart tissue, as with bites from **cobra**, **krait**, **mamba** or **coral snake**, **sea snake** and all **Australian snakes**. In these situations, tightly wrap up as much of the bitten limb as possible with a stretchy bandage (you need three crêpe bandages for a leg) and get to a clinic that has antivenom.

Other health hazards from snakes

The most common problem caused by snake bites is **infection**. Even non-venomous British grass snakes will inflict a deep dirty wound that is hard to clean, so there is a risk of sepsis, tetanus and gangrene. Seek medical help after any snake bite.

To avoid snakes

→ Do not sleep on the ground, except inside a tent with a sewn-in groundsheet.

→ Sleep under a mosquito net that is tucked in.

→ When walking around after dark, carry a torch and wear boots or strong shoes and long trousers.

→ When collecting firewood, tip it away from yourself as you lift it to give the snake an easy route of escape.

Pythons and other large, non-venomous constrictors should be treated with respect. They can reach a length of 10m (33ft), and the largest occasionally kill people. A colleague has a gruesome portrait of a python (*Python reticularis*) killed in Sulawesi, which was sliced open to reveal the body of a man consumed on his wedding night. Pythons (*P. sebae*) have swallowed people in Africa and in South America (*Eunectes eunectes*). South American anacondas can weigh up to 230kg (507lb) and have also been known to attack people.

Dangerous lizards?

In Madagascar people say that chameleons are deadly; in Thailand, geckos are also believed to be poisonous, as are cute little skinks in Nepal. All are harmless. There are only two venomous lizards: the **Gila monsters** and the **beaded lizard**. Both are big (45–80cm/18–32in) and live in southwest USA and Mexico. There is no antivenom, but humans are rarely bitten and there are no reliable reports of deaths. The **Komodo dragon** of Indonesia, a flesh-eating monitor lizard that grows to 3m (10ft) long, is not venomous; however, it has killed at least one careless tourist. Beware the **European fire salamander** though. This amphibian not only tastes awful but it can also squirt toxic liquid which burns the eyes and can even cause temporary blindness. Even **toads** in Europe are very poisonous, but they are not harmful unless licked.

Dangerous large mammals

Man-eaters

Buffalo

Wildlife documentaries allow us to watch from our armchairs while animals dispatch their prey, and it's easy to forget that predators can hurt us, too. Few animals will pick a fight, but most will defend themselves if surprised or cornered, and females will be aggressive if they are with their young. Large primates, especially chimpanzees and baboons, are very dangerous. Do not go walking through dense scrub or long grass that could hide a **rhino** or **buffalo**. Big carnivores are probably best faced: running away will do you no good, since they can outrun you, and this is exactly what prey species do. Do something a prey species would not, such as throwing rocks, or running at the animal shouting and waving a big stick. The predator will (you hope) be so confused it will retreat. Don't sleep in a tent containing anything a big animal might relish; bears often rip open tents if they smell food inside, and carnivores or scavengers help themselves to meat. Finally, be aware that a whining child sounds like an animal in distress and might attract predators.

African animals

If venturing into wildlife country on foot, be sure to take a guide who understands animals. Many 'Africa hands' consider buffalo, hippopotamus, chimpanzees and baboons the most dangerous species. Buffaloes are very aggressive, and hippos are likely to trample you by mistake if you frighten them and are between them and a river, their refuge. Hippos come out of the water to graze at dusk, during the night and on overcast days. **Crocodiles** are the other significant predator to respect if you are relaxing by an African river (*see* pp.182–3).

On self-drive safaris it is quite easy to upset an **elephant** inadvertently. Their vision is not particularly good and in dense bush you can unintentionally surprise one or come between cow and calf. Always have an escape strategy ready, look out for ear-flapping and blowing and back off rather than linger for a good photograph. **Kruger lions** got a taste for human refugee flesh during the Mozambican war so listen to advice on where is safe. Lions take about 10 lives a year. **Vervet monkeys**, which hang about picnic sites, often bite people – especially children – and any mammal bite might transmit rabies (*see* pp.250–2). They can also give you Marburg (aka green monkey) virus, which is extremely dangerous too. Ensure that any bite is thoroughly, surgically cleaned.

Large Asian species

In Africa there is generally space for both wildlife and man. In Asia, with more pressure on land, wild animals are in much closer conflict with farmers. **Elephants** can be very disgruntled and ill tempered, and often attack: they kill about 250 people a year in India. Domesticated Asian elephants were also responsible for 65 deaths between 1990 and 2004. Back off if you encounter an elephant that is flapping its ears and blowing. Large cats (leopards and tigers) in the subcontinent seem to become man-eaters more frequently than in Africa, perhaps because they are so often close to villages and their protected areas are too small; talk to local people before camping in big-cat country.

The great Indian **rhinoceros** is dangerous if you meet it at close quarters on foot. Beware of walking through elephant-high grass in reserves where they are common and, if you meet one, climb a tree (adrenaline will rapidly improve your climbing skills), get behind a tree or lie down.

Monkeys

Beware of picnicking near Asian temples. **Rhesus monkeys** may bite to persuade you to part with your lunch. These and other **macaques** can carry herpes B virus, which is often a killer if transmitted to humans. Be sure to get any monkey bite surgically cleaned – although stitching should be avoided if possible.

Bears

Bears are a hazard in places as far distant as the Himalayas, the Rockies and the Arctic. Black bears attack more people than other bears because they are the most numerous bear species – population around 600,000 – and there is more contact. They tend to leave their victims alive – as if to spread the word. Unprovoked, predatory attacks on humans are very rare but they hit the headlines. Black bears

Case history: North America

I was on a solo camping trip to the Adirondack National Park in the USA, where bears have lost their fear of man and like to scrounge from campers. I was dropping off to sleep when I heard a large animal sniffing around outside the tent. Fortunately I had taken good advice. I had used a rope to hang my food (including tinned food, foody rubbish, even toothpaste) up in a tree away from where I was sleeping, so the bear soon lost interest in the tent. He was also perhaps put off a little by my banging of pots and pans. Bears have quite frequently clawed into tents after smelling food inside. In bear country, wash up plates and pots promptly, away from your camp, and burn any rubbish.

Dr Matthew Ellis, paediatrician, Bristol

were responsible for 51 deaths in the whole of the 20th century. For every bear death there were 45 fatalities to dogs, 120 to bee stings, 249 to lightning and 60,000 victims of homicide. Usually bears run when confronted with loud noise.

In contrast, polar bears sometimes prey on humans and they are often unfazed by loud noise. They are exceedingly strong and dangerous. They can break down doors and claw through quarter-inch steel plate if they sense food. The world's largest land predator, they weigh up to 680kg (1,500lb) and, although not the fastest bears, they can move across the snow at 56kmph (35mph) when motivated.

Rural Nepalis are wary of bears, which are short-sighted and attack without provocation if they smell someone. There were eight deaths following **mountain lion** attacks in California in the years 1993–2003.

Dangerous domestic animals

Domestic animals are much more likely to injure us than wild species simply because we are in close and frequent contact. Dogs kill hundreds of people, while healthy wolves have never killed anyone. There have been reports of severe injuries or even deaths after attacks by domesticated camels, cattle, water buffalo, elephants, pigs, cats and even sheep and ferrets. If you need to pass a pack animal on a cliff path, stand uphill, so that it does not push you over.

Be wary of domestic animals and pets you do not know. Tame beasts act as disease reservoirs; parrots with runny noses harbour pneumonia-causing bugs, while pet terrapins, tortoises, snakes and even African pygmy hedgehogs are a common source of exotic salmonella infections. Wash your hands!

Dog bites and rabies

The most common injuries inflicted by any largeish animal, at home or abroad, are dog bites. In England and Wales over 200,000 people attend hospital for dog bites annually, and there are about 10 dog-bite-related deaths a year. There are also about 20 deaths a year in the USA from dog attacks. Worldwide, hundreds of people are killed by domestic dogs. If threatened by dogs, stoop as if to pick up a stone to throw at them; most dogs will retreat if they think you are armed with missiles.

Dog bites frequently become infected, there is a risk of tetanus and, in many countries, rabies. Bites still become infected even if you have both tetanus and rabies cover (*see* pp.43, 49–50); wounds must be carefully cleaned and dressed, and medical help sought (or antibiotics started) if infection sets in (*see* pp.205–6).

Rabies is a huge problem in much of the world. More than 25,000 people die from it each year in India and about 500 in Vietnam. Most are infected by stray dogs. There was a small outbreak of rabies (in dogs) in France late in 2007, which highlights that it is always wise to get proper medical attention after any dog bite and check if rabies jabs are needed. Never handle friendly strays or wild animals that are unusually tame; they may be dying of rabies (*see* 'First aid for potentially rabid bites', below).

Cats

Cats can be quite vicious, and even trivial scratches or bites carry a risk of cat scratch fever, caused by *Rochalimaea henselae* bacteria. This is usually a mild illness causing enlargement of the lymph nodes two to three weeks after a cat bite, scratch or a cat-flea bite. Perhaps one-third of American house cats are infected with the disease, but it will only cause significant problems in the elderly or debilitated. It can be treated with a course of *co-amoxiclav* or *clarithromycin* antibiotics. Recently, some Americans have also caught bubonic plague from their cats.

Rats and other rodents

Rodents can damage your health. They are a reservoir of bubonic **plague**, **leptospirosis** (Weil's disease), **tularaemia** and the dangerous **hantavirus** in the Far East, North America and Europe (*see* pp.155, 202, 151 and 260, respectively). Zoologists intent on handling wild rodents should wear leather gloves and have rabies cover.

First aid for potentially rabid bites

Clean any animal bite by scrubbing with soap under running water for five minutes, then liberally apply *povidone iodine* or alcohol (at least 40% – gin and whisky will do) or 0.01% *aqueous iodine*. Then seek medical help for further wound care (but do not allow anyone to suture the bite). If you are far from a clinic you may need to self-treat with a course of *co-amoxiclav* or *clarithromycin* antibiotics.

If you are in a region where **rabies** is a risk, **even if you have had pre-trip rabies immunization**, you should have two booster injections, or a full course plus rabies immune globulin, RIG, if you are not immune (*see* pp.49–50).

Tetanus cover is also necessary if you have not been immunized in the previous 10 years (if in doubt, get boosted, *see* p.43). If the usual tetanus injection that protects you long term is given at the time of the bite, it may not become effective fast enough to protect you. A special, post-bite immunoglobulin needs to be given if you are not immune, and a course of immunization started for future protection.

The World Health Organization (WHO) used to recommend that dogs that had bitten people should be tied up; if the dog survived for 10 days it was said to be free

Symptoms of rabies

After an incubation period that can be a week, but is usually more, there is:

→ fever; anxiety; sleeplessness;

→ often pain &/or tingling at the bite site.

Then:

→ painful spasms of the throat herald the start of hydrophobia;

→ terror – production of quantities of rope-like saliva;

→ spasms involve other muscles including muscles of respiration;

→ death is inevitable but usually occurs within a week due to respiratory arrest.

from rabies, so posed no risk to the bitten person. These guidelines were developed when the only treatment for suspect bites was the dangerous and painful Semple vaccine (5% suspension of sheep or goat brain) given into the abdomen on 21 consecutive days, followed by booster doses. Serious reactions to it happened as frequently as one in 76 courses and its efficacy was poor (41% of those affected died), but, although it is no longer recommended by WHO, it is still given in some basic clinics where there is no alternative.

If bitten, you need cover with an **inactivated rabies vaccine**. Some embassies can arrange supplies; otherwise you should travel to a clinic in a capital or fly home for treatment. Semple vaccine may be all that is immediately available in some regions, but it is not worth the risk.

Getting treatment in time

A surprising number of people who have been bitten by potentially rabid dogs or other animals have just hoped for the best and had no treatment whatsoever. Yet, once symptoms of rabies appear, it is an incurable, invariably fatal disease, and the mode of death is horrible. The incubation period between the bite and the onset of symptoms depends on the distance of the bite from the brain and the severity of the bite. Generally it is between two and eight weeks, but it can be as little as four days, and as long as several years. The virus travels along the nerves and only causes

Case history: Peru

Matthew was visiting the Ashaninka Indians of the Peruvian Amazon as part of an anthropological research project. They were generous in their hospitality and the party went on late, until he and most of the tribe lost consciousness in the village plaza. Next morning he was disturbed to see two deep tooth-marks in his big toe, from which a puddle of blood was oozing. He could not decide which was more impressive, the power of the local hallucinogen (*ayahuasca*) or the vampire's local anaesthetic, which it administers before it dines. Vampire bats, like any mammal, can transmit rabies and, because of the anticoagulant they secrete, bites bleed a lot and easily become infected – two unexpected consequences of losing your inhibitions through recreational drugs. Luckily the vampire was not rabid.

Despite misleading Transylvanian legends, vampires only occur in the New World, and here they are small mammals. The rabies risk is another reason, when camping in tropical America, to sleep in a zippable tent or hammock with a mosquito net. In a rare plague of vampire bites in a Brazilian village in 1991, 314 people were bitten, three of whom died from rabies.

Case history: East Africa

A 34-year-old woman was brushing her teeth at dusk while camping in Kenya. A bat flew into her face and she sustained two scratches on the side of her nose which bled. No special care or first aid was given to her following the incident. Local advice was that there was no rabies in Kenyan bats; the disease is thought to be a problem spread only by dog bites in the region: there had never been a death from rabies recorded in Kenya blamed on a bat. The woman started to feel unwell 23 days later, with dizziness and nausea. She was admitted to hospital in Amsterdam 26 days after the brush with a bat. Her symptoms – difficulty with speech, walking and odd sensations of the skin of the face – pointed to a disorder of the nervous system and rabies was suspected immediately by the Dutch doctors. All possible treatments – both conventional and experimental – were given to the woman. She died in December 2007: 23 days after becoming ill, and 45 days after sustaining the scratches.

Rabies or rabies-like lyssaviruses (which are just as deadly) occur in all continents except Antarctica. Bat bites come with a rabies risk, even in countries that are said to be free of rabies, including Britain and Australia. In the USA 23 people have died of rabies since 2000, mostly following bat bites.

encephalitis and hydrophobia when it arrives at the brain. At this point there is no treatment that will save the victim. An experimental treatment that saved the life of a 15-year-old girl from Wisconsin in 2004 has sadly failed to save subsequent cases.

Adults tend to be bitten on the leg, so the incubation period for the disease (and thus the interval they have to be vaccinated) may be weeks. It is pure madness, then, not to seek help, even if it is long after the bite. The days of painful injections into the abdomen are long gone, and the post-bite treatment is a series of ordinary injections with fewer side effects than pre-trip immunizations.

Act as soon as possible. Clean the wound thoroughly and do not delay seeking medical treatment. Those with an ostrich-like, head-in-the-sand approach to protecting their health should realize that it is never too late to have post-bite injections. Bites closer to the brain need urgent action. Small children are often bitten on the face by dogs, in which case treatment must be immediate.

Small wild mammals

Any mammal, however small, can carry rabies. Get any bite properly cleaned and dressed and then organize rabies and tetanus cover, and perhaps antibiotics. Some of the most apparently harmless mammals carry secret weapons. Even the neurotic-looking **loris** seems to have a noxious bite; this may be due to microbes in the mouth or even possibly a toxin. Animal bites commonly fester.

Streaked tenrec

The smallest **tenrecs** (Madagascar's equivalent of the hedgehog) will deposit very fine spines in your skin if you handle them. Each spine has to be painstakingly removed with fine tweezers; this takes hours. And handling **hedgehogs** will get you covered in fleas.

On the Ground:
Ailments

Medical evacuation and treatment 254

Risks of medical treatment 255

Exotic diseases 255
  Fever 256
  Other infectious diseases 257
  Some rarities 258

Coughs and chest pains 260
  Hepatitis and jaundice 262

Abdominal symptoms 263
  Muscle cramp 266

Head, nose and throat 266

Eye problems 269

Glasses and contact lenses 271

Dental problems 272

19

Summary
→ The illnesses people catch abroad are seldom serious: sore throats and colds are common everywhere; coughs and chest infections are probably even more frequent than at home.
→ Avoid all unnecessary medical treatment that involves injections, and also do all you can to avoid situations that make medical treatment necessary. Play safe.
→ Injections also carry the risk of HIV and hepatitis B.
→ In many countries, carrying illicit drugs or addictive prescription medicines is a very serious crime; it can even be a capital offence.
→ Intoxication and addiction directly or indirectly kill plenty of travellers each year.
→ Motorcycles are the most hazardous form of transport.
→ Reminder: accidents are the health hazards that most often kill or seriously harm travellers. About half of the deaths that occur while travelling are due to accidents; many are avoidable. Fret less about exotic diseases and consider the risks of accidents at all times when travelling.

Medical evacuation and treatment

Health problems or a serious mishap may interrupt your trip. If possible involve the medical assistance agency arranged by your insurance. They can offer advice on where to seek medical help because when you are taken ill it isn't always possible just to come home. Sometimes it is obvious when you need to involve doctors, but sometimes a consultation with a sympathetic medic may reassure you and you can continue to enjoy your trip. If ever there is any doubt it is best to get a medical opinion.

You need to be reasonably well to be medically evacuated: the last thing a seriously ill person needs is to be confined in an aircraft with relatively little oxygen and no emergency care. Flight constraints can make it difficult or slow to evacuate, so sometimes – and assuming that you are not too unwell – it may be quicker to get to a safe hospital on a scheduled flight rather than by air ambulance. Otherwise you may have to make do with local facilities, at least in the short term. It is perhaps worth noting that, often, the more you have paid for an airline ticket, the easier it will be to reschedule your flight home.

In most destinations you will probably find the best medical care in the capital or a major city, probably at an international clinic (if there is one), but ask embassies, expatriates, or hotel staff where to go for the best facilities. Embassies are generally wonderful in medical emergencies and they are also the people to approach should you need to organize a funeral, cremation or repatriation of a body.

For anyone taken ill in the Indian subcontinent, the best medical care is in private hospitals in Bangkok; treatment is good (as is the food!), acceptably high-tech and relatively cheap. Thai government hospitals are also good, but not quite as good as private facilities. Hong Kong and Singapore are also good but more expensive. In Africa, head for South Africa or Nairobi; in South America, go to any capital city.

Pharmacies are a great source of immediate medical help and advice; in many countries, including in much of southern Europe, appropriate antibiotics or other remedies will be sold for specific problems, and pharmacists have excellent knowledge of medicines. Medical treatment varies widely, even in the West (*see* box, opposite).

Healthcare in Rome

Italians often take advice from pharmacies (*farmacia*); before resorting to the doctor; staff are usually helpful and knowledgeable but may not speak English. Most minor complaints (e.g. a tooth abscess or cystitis) can be sorted at the pharmacy; some will give appropriate antibiotics (although they are not supposed to). They can recommend a dentist and can also give you treatment while you wait for your appointment. Unlike the UK, simple medication cannot be bought in supermarkets, so you need to go to the pharmacy even for *paracetamol*. Some over the counter medicines are expensive by UK standards; expect to pay several pounds for a few *paracetamol*. Condoms are now available at most supermarket check-outs and through vending machines.

The Accident and Emergency departments (*pronto soccorso*) of all major hospitals are usually good for more serious problems like suspected appendicitis, injuries or a child with a fever; most people have good experiences although not many health professionals speak English. People admitted to hospital may have less predictable treatment. You'll need to take everything with you, including toilet roll. The wards are clean but nursing care is not as comprehensive and it is of a different style from the UK; the patient or a relative might, for example, need to remind nurses to give prescribed medication – even nebulizers for an acute asthma attack. Relatives are usually expected to stay and help the patient wash, eat, go to the toilet, etc. Treatment in *pronto soccorso* departments is free in Italy, although if you are sent out with a prescription, you have to find a pharmacy outside which is open. The prescription charge may be higher out of hours. Doctors prescribe lots of medicines for one complaint, so if you are short of cash try to find out which is the most important, e.g. the antibiotic. You can ask the pharmacist just to issue one of the treatments.

Many expatriates in Rome use the **Rome American Hospital** (Via Emilio Longoni 69, **t** (06) 22551) where the staff speak English. Charges are in line with the USA but there is no Accident and Emergency department. You are admitted under the care of a doctor whom you need to find first (although your medical assistance company should give you names and details).

Dr Mary Styles, Rome

Risks of medical treatment

Medical treatment, including blood transfusions, or transfusions of blood products for serious illnesses, are routes of HIV infection that are difficult to avoid. If you need any such treatment, try to select expensive hospitals and clinics where staff say that blood is screened (you can only take their word), and try to ensure that intravenous equipment and syringes are new. Some travellers carry their own hypodermic needles and ask local doctors to use them, although I've never thought this a practical solution. Many paramedics in resource-poor destinations give unnecessary injections, so see a qualified a doctor if possible. The pros and cons of carrying an 'AIDS kit' (containing needles, syringes and intravenous fluid) are covered in '"AIDS kits" and blood transfusions, pp.39–40'. (*See also* 'Therapeutic travel', pp.74–5.)

Exotic diseases

Rare and exotic diseases are such a topic of conversation among travellers that I have included a few notes on the most talked-about pestilences as well as commoner infections. Illnesses detailed elsewhere can be found by referring to the index. I have deliberately avoided mentioning every possible disease by name, but the prevention strategies recommended will protect you from almost all problems. Taking precautions against malaria, for example, will protect you from Japanese encephalitis; eating well-cooked foods rather than salads or raw fish will help you avoid filth-to-mouth diseases as well as all those wonderful unpronounceable parasites.

Fever

Fever is a common symptom of many diseases; it makes most people intermittently feel uncomfortably hot, then chilled to the marrow. Significant increases in body temperature also cause lethargy, aches, pains and headache. Take *paracetamol (acetaminophen/*Tylenol) regularly (every four to six hours) or *ibuprofen* (every eight hours) and drink plenty and you'll feel better. Children and those with ulcers or stomach problems should not take *aspirin*. It's easy to become dehydrated with a fever, especially in a hot climate, which will make you feel even worse.

Trivial infections increase the temperature a touch but fever really makes you feel unwell when it rises above 38°C (100°F), and temperatures above 38.5°C (101.5°F) suggest that you might need treatment with an antibiotic or other prescription-only medicine. If drinking plenty and taking *ibuprofen* or *paracetamol* does not help, think about the cause of the fever and consider further treatment. Do you, for example, have a cough, are you peeing a lot or do you have an area of inflamed skin? Infections that often cause fevers are **colds**, '**flu**, **chest infections** and **skin infections**. In women, **cystitis** is common (*see* p.223), and in children, **middle ear infections** or **tonsillitis**: the sore throat of tonsillitis usually puts children off their food. Usually you will know what is causing the fever, so you can refer to the relevant section of this book. Whatever you have is probably trivial or treatable but, if in doubt, and if simple rehydration and *aspirin* or *paracetamol* do not help, seek a medical opinion. Seek help as soon as possible if a child is ill.

There are two serious but treatable infections that cause high fever and significant illness without many other symptoms to help locate the source of the trouble. **Malaria** and also **leptospirosis** can cause fever and severe illness without

Case history: Cambodia

Ceri consulted me soon after arriving back from Cambodia. Six weeks before, she'd been riding pillion on a motorbike that had crashed; there had been a lot of blood. The Cambodian who was driving felt very guilty and rushed to her help. He too was well bloodied. Ceri was bewildered, shaken and sustained lots of grazes. The driver had dowsed her in petrol to staunch the flow of blood.

Later she became worried that some of the driver's blood could have come in contact with her broken skin and that she was at risk of HIV. A blood test done more than 12 weeks after the accident confirmed that she had not contracted HIV. The experience made her consider her own mortality for the first time, and think about the many dangers of riding on motorbikes.

Case history: Is it malaria?

A five-year-old girl developed a high fever: 39.5°C (103°F). The family had returned from Kenya a month previously and had just stopped taking their malaria tablets. They had decided to take over-the-counter *chloroquine* and Paludrine to protect themselves from malaria, rather than the newer, more effective and palatable antimalarials available in the UK on prescription. The girl's parents were sure she had malaria because they had friends who – a month after leaving Africa – had developed malaria on stopping *chloroquine* and Paludrine. Fortunately the child proved to have common, treatable bacterial tonsillitis. Her huge, inflamed tonsils and swollen, tender lymph glands in her neck faded a couple of days into her 10-day course of *penicillin*.

The parents were right to consult a doctor. East Africa is a high-risk area for malaria.

any obvious focus and with diagnostic tests often staying 'normal' initially. The treatment of leptospirosis is with *doxycycline* or another *tetracycline* antibiotic. Malaria treatment is detailed in **Malaria**, p.140.

Other infectious diseases

Lots of infections – both tropical and mundane – cause rashes and **spots**. Those who notice spots but have no fever and who feel well otherwise are unlikely to have anything nasty.

Chickenpox

Most adults (90%) are immune to chickenpox (*varicella* virus) and there is an effective vaccine. People in the infectious stages of the disease (which is two days before the onset of the rash and until all spots become dry scabs) should not fly. Chickenpox is likely to be more severe in adulthood, and in pregnancy there are implications for the baby. Pregnant women who are exposed to chickenpox and who have not had the disease or been immunized should seek medical advice. Chickenpox is dangerous to those with compromised immune systems, e.g. those who have had cancer or cancer treatment within the previous six months.

'Slapped cheek' disease

This is a common parvovirus infection, which causes fever and characteristic red cheeks, but the infected child remains well and there is not much of a rash elsewhere. Most adults (60%) are already immune, having had a mild form of the disease in early life. However, if a non-immune mother gets it during the first 20 weeks of pregnancy, there can be severe foetal anaemia, which needs careful monitoring and possibly treatment with foetal blood transfusions. A blood test done at the time of exposure to the virus will determine the mother's immune status.

Foot and mouth disease

Foot and mouth is an infection of cattle and is not a risk to humans. The stringent controls that are put in place during a foot and mouth outbreak are to prevent the spread of infection between livestock. There have been one or two cases of agricultural workers becoming infected but these people are in direct and often

> ## Case history: Peru
> About 10 days after arriving in the Andes, my sister fell ill and awoke with spots. We were medical students at the time and had organized a scientific expedition to Peru. We'd nerdishly read up on the nasty tropical diseases we might catch and were worried about *verruga*, aka Oroya fever: a disease that killed locals.
> One of the non-medical members of the team recognized the rash as chickenpox. Later we discovered that Oroya fever is not only very rare, but that it responds to antibiotics and is not especially dangerous.

very close contact with infected animals. Although perhaps aesthetically unattractive, eating cooked meat from an animal infected with foot and mouth is not hazardous to human health. This is a completely different microbe from the virus causing hand, foot and mouth disease, a benign, fever-causing illness that is common in children.

Q-fever
Q-fever is caused by rickettsia, *Coxiella burneti,* harboured in domestic animals and unpasteurized milk. Infection can be mild but it can also cause fever, and fatigue that lasts for months. The right antibiotics clear it.

West Nile fever
West Nile encephalitis is a virus transmitted by mosquitoes that are active from dusk until dawn; it can be mild but when it causes inflammation of the brain, it is extremely serious and there is around an 11% case fatality rate. It occurs in Africa, the Middle East and western and central Asia, and there have been sporadic cases in southern Europe since the 1960s. In 2004 two adults acquired the disease in the Algarve, Portugal, for example. The first recognized case in the USA was in 1999; it is now a problem there each summer. The incubation period is three to 15 days and most fatalities are in the over-50s. The virus affects birds and horses as well as humans.

Some rarities

Anthrax
Anthrax is a disease that can occasionally be caught from animals. The people who may be infected are agricultural, tannery and other workers involved in processing bone, hair and hides. Anthrax can enter the human body by inhalation, when it causes a high fever and severe illness, but more common is the skin form, where, over a period of two to six days, a painless swelling (on the hands, forearms or head) breaks down, weeps and develops a black centre. The illness is treated with one of several readily available antibiotics and is not spread from person to person. Occasionally, travellers are infected from poorly tanned animal skin items. There is a gastrointestinal form, but proper cooking kills anthrax and renders infected foods safe.

Advice for travellers during bird 'flu outbreaks
→ Avoid poultry farms or live bird markets.
→ Avoid close contact with live or dead poultry.
→ Do not eat raw or undercooked poultry products (including blood).
→ Wash hands frequently.

Bird 'flu, aka Avian influenza

Bird 'flu was first identified in Italy over 100 years ago. It is a disease of wild fowl, which affects these birds mildly. When they migrate, they spread it to other birds in new countries. The 1997 avian influenza (type H5N1) that re-emerged in 2003 seems to have started in Southeast Asia and has now become entrenched in domestic chickens and ducks there.

Bird 'flu only rarely spreads to humans. Recent human cases have been reported in Indonesia, Cambodia and Egypt – in people in contact with ill or dead domestic birds. It is a disease of the poor living in intimate proximity with their domestic fowl. The symptoms are vague and usually start two to seven days after exposure to an infected bird. Signs of illness are fever over 38°C (100°F), aches and pains, sore throat, a hoarse voice and then, later in the disease process, crackling sounds on breathing and pneumonia. Some anti-viral drugs are useful in treatment including *oseltamivir* (Tamiflu) and *zanamivir* (Relenza). These are taken for four to seven days and work best if started within hours of the beginning of the illness and definitely within 48 hours. Thermal scanning continues in Beijing and some other Asian airports in order to detect cases.

The risk to ordinary people of bird flu is low, yet over 30 million doses of Tamiflu have been swallowed – mostly in Japan – and there have been a few reports (64 cases in Japan between 2000 and 2004) of nasty psychological side effects, including abnormal behaviour, confusion and hallucinations, so it is important to be aware that this is not a totally benign medicine. In addition, there have been at least two suicides reported in people taking Tamiflu, although there is no proof that the drug was responsible. It can be taken prophylactially but it is probably best kept to cure the disease once someone gets symptoms. For current information on bird flu and other outbreaks see *www.who.int*.

Severe Acute Respiratory Syndrome (SARS)

The outbreak of SARS in February 2003 in Hong Kong spread rapidly into China, Singapore, Vietnam and beyond. There were in all around 9,000 cases worldwide. The last case occurred in China early in 2004 and is no longer a concern anywhere. Although initially it was feared that this infection was highly virulent, more than 90% of people contracting SARS survived.

Ebola virus

Ebola occurs in outbreaks in Congo (formerly Zaïre), Sudan, the Côte d'Ivoire and Gabon. It makes people very ill suddenly with a **high fever**, after an incubation of about seven days; half of its victims die. Since most cases are infected through direct contact with body fluids, this is rarely a disease of ordinary travellers, but may involve hospital staff.

Hantavirus

Hantavirus has caused concern in the Americas (there were cases in California and Brazil in 2004), but also occurs in the Far East and elsewhere. Infection comes from mice, if an infected mouse excretes on or nibbles uncooked food that you eat. Symptoms are **fever**, aches and pains, which can progress to breathing difficulties that may kill up to half those affected. It does not respond to antibiotics. Prevent it by ensuring that all food is peeled, boiled or cooked.

Mad cow, BSE and Creutzfeldt-Jakob disease

In 1996 British scientists identified a new variant of an ugly disease. It was caused by a transmissible agent called a prion, which resulted in abnormal folding of proteins within the brain, leading to brain damage and inevitably death. In cattle it was called mad cow disease or bovine spongiform encephalopathy (BSE). When people who were unfortunate enough to eat BSE-infected meat acquired the disease, they called it Creutzfeldt-Jakob disease (vCJD). The infective agent is not destroyed by cooking. It is related to the awful slow virus infection called kuru, which killed cannibals in Papua New Guinea. Slow viruses have very long incubation periods and receiving a blood transfusion or a blood-product-based injection such as **immune globulin** carries a low but finite risk of acquiring these dreadful infections. Since 1996 huge efforts have been made to eradicate BSE and new cases are no longer appearing. It seems to have been caused by animal remains (probably including sheep carcasses) being fed to cattle: sheep suffer from a related slow virus infection called scrapie.

Coughs and chest pains

Sore throats and colds

Coughs or colds may be the last thing you expect to catch while in hot places, but they are common everywhere. Moist, warm, tropical atmospheres also allow germs to survive for longer between victims. When travel involves mixing with more people (including on planes), you are at increased risk of catching a respiratory infection. The fever these infections cause can largely be controlled by taking *paracetamol* or *aspirin* every four to six hours or *ibuprofen* eight-hourly. Gargling (and then swallowing) soluble tablets helps relieve a sore throat. In adults, sore throats are usually caused by viruses, so antibiotics are no help. If you are feverish increase the amount you drink, as even mild dehydration will make you feel worse. The common cold lasts about a week. If it goes on longer, suspect an allergy and try antihistamine tablets (e.g. Zirtek, Piriton or Benadryl), or see a doctor. If you have a cold and a drippy nose, buy cloth rather than paper handkerchiefs or your nose will get sore. Sipping chicken soup helps mobilize and clear excess mucous, and so do steam inhalations. There is some evidence that the herbal remedy andrographis improves recovery from coughs and colds. Honey helps coughs.

The rate at which someone breathes can be a helpful guide to significant disease in the lungs. Unfortunately it is near-impossible to record your own breathing rate accurately, or the rate of someone who knows you are timing them. The normal respiratory rate of an adult is about 12–20 breaths a minute; a rate of 40 a minute implies something may need treatment, or that the person is hyperventilating through anxiety. If the person is asthmatic, remind them to use their inhaler. Normal respiratory rates in children are below 30, in babies below 40.

If there are breathing difficulties and/or a cough, humidified air helps; in hotels with hot water, fill the bathroom with steam. This is useful in children with croup (which causes a characteristic, rough-sounding cough). Small babies with colds may get cross at being unable to breathe and feed simultaneously. Put a drop of boiled-and-cooled water into each nostril and the baby will sneeze out or sniff in the offending snot.

Cough without fever: some remedies

Honey (by spoonful or in drinks) is a pleasant, soothing, natural remedy for coughs. Cough medicines offer some comfort, but beware of what you buy abroad as some contain bizarre and even addictive concoctions. If available, try *simple linctus* (a soothing syrup), or make your own with equal amounts of fresh lemon/lime juice, honey and rum or whisky in a little hot water. Inhaling infusions of eucalyptus oil, Vicks or tiger balm in hot water also helps. Drinking plenty of water, tea or similar drinks helps to loosen a cough and expectorate phlegm, while gargling with warm water helps settle a tickly cough and can be very soothing.

Coughing up blood

Blood-stained spit, or larger quantities of blood brought up by coughing, is a reason to seek medical help and probably have a chest X-ray. Seeing streaks of blood in the spit is common in acute tonsillitis, however. See a doctor if you have a cough for more than four weeks.

Chest infections and pain

A chest infection may be indicated by a cough and fever (especially if you produce a lot of discoloured, thick spit), or a fever with chest pain (especially if it is worse on breathing in), or by a feeling of tightness in the chest. Treatment with antibiotics is likely to help. Take *penicillin* 500mg four times a day or *amoxicillin* 500mg three times a day for seven days, unless you are allergic to penicillins; in this case, you can take *cefradine* 1g twice daily, or *erythromycin* 250mg four times daily, or *clarithromycin* 250mg twice daily. Otherwise, try *trimethoprim* 200mg twice a day (safe for those allergic to *penicillin*, but not for pregnant women). In addition, take *aspirin* (or *paracetamol*) every four to six hours to control fever and pain. If symptoms do not improve in 48 hours change antibiotics: *penicillin* takers should add *erythromycin* or *clarithromycin*. *Penicillin* is the first choice antibiotic in pneumonia; however, resistance has become common in the Far East, Papua New Guinea, South Africa and Spain and so *clarithromycin* would probably be the best choice in these regions.

Severe central chest pain, especially if crushing or stabbing in nature and without fever, needs urgent, careful medical assessment. Heart problems are most common in

> ## Case history: Nepal
> John had been travelling rough in Nepal for four months and was feeling very unwell. He told me that he'd had bad luck with his health during this trip. He had a splitting headache, a severe stabbing pain in the right side of his chest and aching limbs and back. He had a fever and felt a little disorientated. He had a slight tickly cough, made worse by cigarettes. He looked very unwell, was trembling and was very distressed by pain in his chest whenever he moved, breathed in deeply or coughed. His temperature was 40°C (104°F). He had pneumonia. He was a lot better after 18 hours of *penicillin*, lots to drink and regular *aspirin* (two every four hours).

men over 50, especially if heavy smokers and overweight. Smokers suffer more chest infections in general, and are more at risk from illnesses like **legionnaires' disease** (*see* p.216). A burning pain at the bottom of the ribcage (heartburn; *see* p.265) is likely to be **indigestion**. If the pain is severe or is not relieved by taking antacids, seek medical help urgently.

Tuberculosis (TB)

TB is a potentially serious infection that usually begins in the lungs and is common in those who live in overcrowded housing. Travellers on a short trip to a non-industrialized country are unlikely to risk infection, but there is some risk for expatriates. TB is spread by infected people coughing over others, but since it is not very infectious TB is only caught after a great deal of exposure over a long period. Walking through a market puts you at no risk, but those living in the Indian subcontinent, Africa, Southeast Asia and some countries in Eastern Europe may catch TB from sharing a small, poorly ventilated office with ailing colleagues, or from ill staff at home. Medical personnel looking after the sick in a hospital or refugee camp are at risk. TB can also be contracted from infected cows' milk, but not from bug bites, water, food or crockery, nor from touching an infected person. BCG immunization gives about 80% protection; it is not commonly used in the USA (*see* pp.43–4). People with TB often look quite well, and symptoms tend to come on gradually and insidiously; they include fever, night sweats, lethargy, a cough and, eventually, blood in the spit. Expatriates might ask staff or potential staff if they ever cough up blood, so that treatment can be arranged. Not all persistent coughers have TB, but it is more likely in people who have been coughing for more than three weeks. Even if you have shared a house with local coughers, do not worry about TB unless you notice symptoms. Then, seek a check-up and chest X-ray when convenient. Treatment is easy and effective, but tablets need to be taken carefully for a full six months.

Hepatitis and jaundice

Hepatitis is inflammation of the liver. The common causes in travellers are three viruses: **hepatitis A** (also called infective hepatitis), **hepatitis B** (serum hepatitis) and newly recognized **hepatitis E**. Jaundice (yellowing) due to the hepatitis A or E virus is frequently acquired by travellers, especially in the Indian subcontinent and tropical Central and South America: it is one of many filth-to-mouth diseases (*see* p.115–18). Hepatitis B is acquired in the same ways as HIV: through dirty needles, blood transfusions and unsafe sex. It often needs hospital treatment. For information on hepatitis A and B immunization, see pp.44 and 49.

Hepatitis A usually begins with feelings of profound lethargy, lack of appetite, nausea and generally being unwell. As this begins to go away, the urine becomes dark and the stool pale while the whites of the eyes and the skin turn yellow. At this point, you look worse but feel much better. It is a variable illness, which leaves some people feeling very debilitated for many months, but is not dangerous. Hepatitis E runs a similar course and can be mild but pregnant women can become profoundly ill with it. They must be meticulous about avoiding filth-to-mouth infections.

Western medicine can do little for sufferers of hepatitis A and E, but people experience dramatic improvements by taking ayurvedic medicines (on the recommendation of a Western-trained doctor) and Tibetan *amchi* medicines. There are ayurvedic hospitals in Kathmandu and many Indian cities. During recovery from hepatitis, experiment to see what you can eat and drink. Fatty foods (e.g. fried food, peanut butter, avocado, mayonnaise, coleslaw) and alcohol commonly upset jaundiced people, and it may be necessary to be teetotal for six months or so. Your level of activity should be built up slowly; overdoing it causes profound fatigue. Rest as much as you need, avoid alcohol and, if fatty foods upset you, do not eat them.

Abdominal symptoms

Nausea

Episodes of **nausea**, poor appetite and feeling vaguely unwell are common in travellers. This may be a mild assault by diarrhoea-causing pathogens; 24 hours on a bland, light diet will often settle the problem. It can come from air-borne winter vomiting virus or similar. Antimalarial tablets can cause nausea especially if taken on an empty stomach, so take them after a meal. Whole yoghurt or *lactobacillus* capsules or drinks (see **Bowels**, p.109) should help. Constipation can also be a cause of queasy feelings. It is worth noting that the way English-speakers describe nausea differs on either side of the Atlantic. The British talk of feeling 'sick', which to an American simply means feeling unwell. Brits talking to American doctors need to explain that they are nauseated or that they feel like vomiting.

Constipation

Constipation is a common problem due to dehydration, changes in diet and difficulties taking enough fibre. Wholemeal flour is rarely available in the developing world, but the coarse wheat flour (*atta*) used to make Indian chapattis is wholemeal, and makes very good bread. Cornmeal tortillas in Latin America are also a good source of fibre. Dehydration and immobility make constipation worse (going for a run may help get things going), and painkillers and many other medicines can aggravate it. Uncomfortable constipation can be caused by anti-diarrhoea medicines, especially *paregoric*. Even without 'blockers', travellers often oscillate between diarrhoea and constipation. Eggs and bananas exacerbate constipation, but other fruits help relieve it. Constipation can lead to haemorrhoids (piles); see pp.219.

Natural remedies for constipation

Ispaghula husk, which originated in South America but is available in Britain (as Fybogel, Regulan) and sold in India as flea-seed husk or *saat ispagol*, is a useful regulator. Mix it with a glass of water and swallow it down quickly, before the solution turns the consistency of wallpaper paste. Drink more water or juices while taking this remedy. If you're very constipated it takes a few days and several doses to take effect, but it works very well and counteracts the see-sawing between diarrhoea and constipation that can happen while travelling; it is often suggested to help the symptoms of irritable bowel syndrome. Increasing your **bran** intake will also help, but this is very difficult to find or identify in many destinations. In Indonesia it was sometimes available but since brown = chocolate in Indonesian, the label of brown/chocolate-coloured powder/flour seemed to cover bran, wholemeal flour and also chocolate powder.

If eating more fruit and increasing the amount you drink does not get the bowels moving, and you cannot get bran or ispaghula husk, then take **lactulose syrup** 15ml with breakfast. This is a gentle, natural laxative which takes 36–48 hours to work. With severe constipation you can take twice this dose twice a day (i.e. 60ml a day), but build up the dose gradually. Lactulose syrup is bulky and heavy, so it is not an ideal medicine for backpackers, but if constipation is really getting you down you may wish to stop and rest for a few days. Constipation remedies draw water into the bowel to loosen the stool, so you must also increase yet more the amount you drink. **Senna** is a powerful stimulant laxative and is best used as a last resort.

Once you have started to re-establish a normal pattern try to ensure that you go to the toilet whenever the urge strikes (usually after food or hot drinks). This may be easier said than done, but the constipation is exacerbated by 'hanging on' too long.

Abdominal pain

Pains in the abdomen (tummy) frequently accompany diarrhoea, but are often relieved by passing wind or a motion. In diarrhoea, pain usually comes in waves. If pain is severe, constant, of sudden onset, worsens rapidly, is associated with a high fever, long-lasting (more than four hours) or not accompanied by diarrhoea, it may be a sign of serious disease and a doctor should be consulted. **Appendicitis** often starts as a central, umbilical pain, which moves to the right lower corner of the abdomen and settles there. The severe pain it causes is usually accompanied by vomiting. **Diarrhoea** and **constipation** can both cause painful spasms in the lower left abdomen. A competent medical opinion should sort out the trivial from the serious. New or persistent symptoms are always worth a consultation. Peppermint can be soothing. For burning pains or heartburn (discomfort centrally and below the rib cage but above the navel) and other stomach symptoms, *see* opposite.

Especially in women, a rather diffuse pain can be caused by a urinary infection, when almost always there will be stabbing pain at the end of urination (*see* 'cystitis' p.223). A twisted ovarian cyst can also cause severe low abdominal pain on either side; this requires a gynaecological (hospital) assessment. Pain during love-making, especially if there is also fever, needs a check-up at a genito-urinary clinic.

Pain below the waist

Unremitting pain (it may wake you at night) that originates in the small of the back (beneath the waist-line) to one side of the spine may be a **kidney stone**. This hurts like hell and may move from the back beneath the ribs around to your side and may migrate into the lower abdomen and groin. This is unlikely to harm you but you'll need big doses of prescription pain-killers until the stone has passed into the bladder. Some people need to be admitted to hospital and given pain-relieving injections. If you have managed to access sufficiently strong pills to kill the pain (you'll probably need *diclofenac* and *codeine*) then travel plans don't need to change but it would be wise to arrange a blood test to check kidney function, urate and blood calcium within a couple of weeks. Stones are more likely to form in people who have become significantly dehydrated in hot climates but, once formed, the stone can cause pain unexpectedly and at any time. If you have had kidney stones once, you are more likely to get them again – especially if dehydrated. Fever and loin pain combined need prompt treatment – find a doctor. For pain on peeing *see* pp.218 and 223.

Heartburn and indigestion

A diffuse burning pain at the bottom of the ribcage and/or belching should respond to simple antacids (such as *magnesium trisilicate* or a*luminium hydroxide*, e.g. Amphojel, Aludrox, Maalox, Tums and Magalan) or with *alginates* (such as Gaviscon or Algicon), which put a raft of seaweed extract onto the stomach contents to decrease reflux. Yoghurt and/or peppermint can be settling. Avoiding spicy foods, acidic fruits and juices, and cutting alcohol and cigarette consumption usually helps too.

Gastritis, stomach or duodenal ulcers tend to cause a gnawing pain between the navel and the bottom of the rib cage, in the pit of the stomach. Sometimes it is accompanied by nausea. If simple antacids do not give relief, *omeprazole* (Losec), *lansoprazole* (Zoton), *ranitidine* (Zantac) or *cimetidine* (Tagamet) should help, and heal the inflammation or ulcer. Note that these probably increase the chances of getting gastroenteritis though. *See* also pp.109 and 261. Consult a doctor if the symptoms persist.

Vomiting

The treatment of vomiting is to replace fluids, as for diarrhoea (*see* p.110–12), but clear fluids should be taken in sips. Avoid acidic drinks like orange juice. If there is more vomiting than diarrhoea an airborne virus might be suspected, like Norwalk and norovirus; these can have whole cruise-ships puking but, while distressing, the vomiting, cramps and fevers usually settle in 48 hours. The incubation interval is 15 to 50 hours and unfortunately there is only short-lived immunity after any attack. **Vomited blood** can look like coffee grounds; it is a serious symptom that needs prompt medical assessment. If, however, the blood has been swallowed after a nose bleed, this need cause no concern and no treatment is required. Smears of blood are often apparent in tonsillitis; a doctor can confirm this.

Case history: Philippines

When I lived on Leyte people were always trying to treat me. They were particularly worried because I was foreign and so expected to have no immunity against their bugs and spirits. I quickly learnt never to admit to feeling tired, headachy or sick. Otherwise I would be given bits of fruit to eat or infusions to drink. On one occasion when I was feeling queasy I had large unidentified leaves tied across my stomach. People believe that spirits (especially forest spirits) cause illness so various bits and pieces are hung around the necks of the afflicted. I usually accepted any treatment they gave me, thinking that it might not do much good but it was unlikely to cause any harm.

I didn't carry a medical kit although I did always have a bottle of rubbing alcohol, which smelt nice, and I put it on any bites or scratches. I knew that in the tropics wounds easily become infected and this counter-acted that. My colleagues also wiped their hands in it before eating when out in the rural areas.

The only other thing I used for a bad cut was Propolis, the bee extract that my sister (a bee-keeper) insists cures everything. It seemed to help a colleague who had a very badly infected nic-nic (tiny fly) bite which wasn't responding to antibiotics. Her doctor also recommended bathing it in an infusion of guava leaves and letting the leaves stay on the wound. Her doctor had worked in Cambridge for five years, yet he and many other local doctors use many of the traditional herbal concoctions.

Stephanie Ledger, Cambridge

Muscle cramp

Cramp can be due to poor fitness, overdoing unaccustomed exercise in the heat, or lack of salt. Stretch the cramped muscle gently but firmly and stimulate circulation by massage. **Tonic water** might also be worth trying. If you suspect salt-depletion, drink a couple of glasses of water with a teaspoonful of salt (if it does not taste salty, drink more). In the longer term, shake more salt on your food. Health educators discourage salt consumption in temperate climates, but it is a necessary part of the tropical diet. Salt intake may need to be increased in hot climates but salt tablets are not a useful way of taking in salt.

Quinine, 200–300mg at bedtime, is sometimes prescribed for night cramps. This is worth a try if you are not salt-depleted and cramps are a persistent problem. *Quinine* needs to be taken each night, not intermittently, and it may take up to four weeks for improvement to become apparent.

Head, nose and throat

Headache

A severe headache of an unusual type, or one associated with fever, profuse vomiting or inability to look at light, needs urgent medical help: it could be meningitis or another infection (*see* below). Headache, though, is often a symptom of **dehydration**, and people new to hot climates may be surprised by how much they need to drink. Do not worry about replacing salt lost in sweat, but drink plenty and, if vomiting, take sips of oral rehydration solution.

Carbon monoxide poisoning over weeks, from faulty gas appliances or kerosene fires, can also cause troublesome headaches. If headaches start after a head injury, or you experience recurrent headaches of an unfamiliar type, seek medical help promptly. Headaches caused by altitude are covered in **High, Cold and Dark**, pp.190–5. Expatriates with recurrent headaches should have an eye test (for spectacles) and consider if they are overworking, stressed or drinking too much alcohol. High blood pressure also causes headaches.

Meningitis (*see* p.47) causes fever and a headache so intense that you won't want to roll over in bed or look at light. It is a medical emergency.

Typhoid and **paratyphoid** fevers are filth-to-mouth illnesses common in South Asia and tropical Latin America. The vaccine is only partially effective against typhoid and gives no protection against the similar and now commoner paratyphoid (*see* pp.44–5). The incubation period is about two weeks; then there is headache, aching limbs, tiredness, constipation, cough and fever. Fever increases over the first week to 39–40°C (102–104°F); there may then be a rash of tiny, rose-pink spots on the abdomen or chest. Without treatment, the disease is likely to become very serious by the end of the second week, when diarrhoea starts. By the third week there is a real risk of intestinal perforation and bleeding. Antibiotics cure, so seek medical help if this description fits.

Brucellosis is transmitted by drinking infected unpasteurized cows' or goats' milk. Illness begins after one to three weeks' incubation, with headache, loss of appetite, a feeling of being unwell, constipation, often a cough, fever and profuse sweating. It settles down after about 10 days, but the fever returns repeatedly for months. There may be joint pain. It is treatable with antibiotic injections.

Feeling faint

Feeling you are about to faint is a common symptom if you are unwell. Feeling dizzy on standing up or getting out of bed is known as postural hypotension, which means you have insufficient body fluids circulating to get enough blood to your brain. The most common cause of postural hypotension in travellers is dehydration – from diarrhoea and/or drinking insufficiently in hot weather.

Drink at least 1 litre (1³/₄ pints) of water (or ORS solution, *see* pp.111) and carry on sipping drinks until you need to pass water. Before standing up, sit for a minute with your legs over the side of the bed since this should stop you fainting – until you are topped up with fluids again. A serious but rare cause of hypotension is blood loss. If you think you may have lost blood due to an injury or internal bleeding – if you have vomited 'coffee grounds' (*see* p.265) or passed blood (*see* pp.113–14) – get medical attention urgently.

Occasionally, women with very heavy periods become anaemic and notice dizziness on getting up; a doctor may be able to sort this out, but it is not an urgent matter.

Sinusitis (face pain)

When the normally air-filled sinuses in the skull fill with mucus, there is **pain at the front of the face**, and sometimes even **toothache** affecting several top teeth on one side. Sometimes it can cause intense pain in an eyeball. The best treatment is to liquefy the secretions, by leaning over a large bowl of steaming hot water with a towel draped over you and the bowl and inhaling deeply. Aromatic additions help, e.g. natural oils, tiger balm, friars' balsam, menthol, eucalyptus. Chicken soup also helps dispel mucous. Antihistamines (*see* motion sickness table in **Flight**, pp.88–9) may help, especially if you tend to suffer from hay fever. Decongestants like *pseudo-ephedrine* (Sudafed or Actifed) are sometimes recommended by doctors and pharmacists, but these thicken mucus and – especially if several doses are taken in succession – tend to make things worse. Flying increases sinus pain, so if your sinuses are clogged you might need to delay the trip; alternatively, you could try lots of steam inhalations and then, two hours before take-off, one dose of *pseudoephedrine*. If sinusitis makes you feverish and very unwell, take a seven-day course of *doxycycline* (e.g. Vibramycin), 200mg on the first day, then 100mg daily, with plenty of water during a meal. Do not use *doxycycline* if you are pregnant. *Amoxicillin* 250mg three times a day is a good alternative.

Nose bleeds

Nose bleeds should be treated by rest (sitting upright) and cold compresses on the bridge of the nose. Pinch the nose, releasing the pressure every few minutes. Leaning back will make you swallow blood and provoke a vomit. Recurrent nose bleeds can be a problem in very dry conditions, especially in high, cold deserts (*see* p.188). Bleeding from the nose, gums or elsewhere when you are feverish requires urgent medical assessment.

Earaches and itches

Earache in both ears is more likely due to mucus congestion than infection. Steam inhalations plus *aspirin* can help; one dose of a decongestant like *pseudoephedrine* (Sudafed) might help, and is often useful before a flight, but taking this medicine regularly tends to thicken mucus and aggravate the problem. Menthol chewing gum can help on flights too. If earache is on one side only, with fever, take *penicillin* 500mg every six hours at least half an hour before food, or *trimethoprim* 200mg twice daily for five days.

If an ear becomes inflamed, swollen, distorted or very itchy, there is probably an infection of the ear canal. This is common, especially in hot, moist climates. Treat (two to three times daily) with drops of a combination of an antibiotic (*neomycin*, *gentamicin*, *chloramphenicol* or *framycetin*) with a mild steroid, 0.5% *hydrocortisone* (Otosporin, Audicort, Framycort in the UK; Cortisporin otic drops in the USA). Useful alternatives are drops that acidify the ear canal (*aluminium acetate* 8% or *boric acid* in very dilute form) or even whisky. These all work well, are cheap and are less likely to cause allergy than antibiotic combinations. Introducing any object into the ear can stimulate infection, so never, ever use cotton buds or put anything smaller than your little finger in your ear. On objects in the ear, *see* p.283; for swimmers' ear *see* p.178. People who are prone to recurrent infections of the ear canal would be well advised to pack a remedy in their medical kit.

Sore throats and throat infections

Sore throats can be a problem in very dry environments, especially at altitude when you may find yourself breathing through your mouth rather than the nose. The best treatment is to suck boiled sweets or pastilles, and drink plenty. In adults, throat infections and tonsillitis are usually caused by viruses, so antibiotic treatment is unhelpful. A sore throat is also more likely to be viral (and thus 'untreatable') if accompanied by symptoms of a cold. Drink lots; gargle every two to three hours with one soluble *aspirin* or *paracetamol* (Tylenol), then swallow the gargle (take no more than eight *paracetamol* in 24 hours). Gargling with warm water is also soothing. Treatable, bacterial throat infections cause fever, you often feel very unwell, there are swollen painful neck glands, obviously inflamed tonsils covered in white pus, and no cough. If you take an antibiotic it should be for a full 10 days (even though the symptoms will settle in about two). Take *penicillin* 250mg four times daily for 10 days, or *erythromycin* if allergic to *penicillin*.

Diphtheria has virtually disappeared in the West but is still a problem in many tropical and temperate regions, including the ex-Soviet countries. It starts with a sore throat and can progress rapidly to cause difficulties with breathing; it can also damage the heart and nervous system and, if untreated, can kill. Immunization gives excellent protection (*see* p.43) but, even so, prophylactic *erythromycin* is advised if there has been close contact with someone with diphtheria.

Sore throat and mild feelings of being unwell can also herald **Lassa fever**. This serious infection is acquired in rural West Africa. In many cases the disease is mild and, indeed, children who are exposed to the infection often experience few or no symptoms at all. Infection can come from swallowing the urine of the multimammate rat (usually via contaminated, uncooked food), so it is theoretically a risk for travellers staying in villages and eating uncooked food, but most cases are in health personnel working in unsanitary hospitals. In adults, the first symptoms are an undramatic sore throat, aches and pains; then, after three to six days, there is a sudden deterioration. Those who die succumb seven to 14 days after the first symptoms. Seek medical help promptly if you are, or have been, in West Africa and develop a sore throat within three days of arriving or within 30 days of leaving the region. Lassa fever is one of a clutch of very rare, highly infectious and serious viral haemorrhagic fevers that cause bruising and bleeding. Avoid it by eating properly cooked food.

At home, anyone suffering from a **hoarse voice** for a month or more should see an ear, nose and throat specialist. If there is no obvious cause of prolonged hoarseness (such as a harsh, dry climate), it is wise to do so while travelling too.

Eye problems

Black or yellow eyes

A black eye consists of simple bruising around the eye, so the best treatment is cold compresses, as for bruising anywhere else (*see* p.279). If there seems to be any injury to the eye, or headaches begin after sustaining the black eye, seek medical help immediately. Double vision on looking up after an eye injury is a symptom that needs medical assessment reasonably promptly.

If the whites of your eyes turn **yellow** you have jaundice, probably due to infectious hepatitis (hepatitis A or E); there is no specific treatment (but *see* pp.262–3).

Case history: UK

Alex, aged 11, awoke on a Monday morning with a painful red eye. He'd just returned from a weekend with his cousins and they'd been romping in grass and throwing sticky burdock seeds at each other. He had a slight cold. His family doctor diagnosed viral conjunctivitis and prescribed antibiotic drops. Mild viral conjunctivitis often accompanies colds. Alexander's other symptoms improved but the eye steadily got redder and more swollen. It was uncomfortable to look at light, and the eye watered a great deal. Alexander saw the doctor again on Wednesday, who sent him to the eye specialists at the hospital. The ophthalmologist removed a slender spicule, presumably part of a burr, and the eye immediately started feeling better. The 'foreign body', which was tiny but stuck into the underside of the upper lid, had slightly scratched the intensely sensitive front of the eye. The eye recovered completely within a few more days.

It is very unusual indeed for conjunctivitis to affect only one eye and where one eye is red and painful, expert assessment by a specialist is usually necessary.

Red eyes

Superficial eye infections or pink-eye are very common, especially in the tropics. Infection usually starts in one eye but rapidly spreads to both, making them feel sticky, gritty, red and painful. Recurrent redness and inflammation of the lids can be eyelid eczema, which should respond to 0.5% *hydrocortisone* ointment). Alternatively improved cleaning of the lashes may help; this means rubbing through the lashes with a damp cotton bud. Clearing any dandruff with an antifungal shampoo containing *ketoconazole* also often helps. Hay fever and allergies cause red eyes, which then respond well to *sodium cromoglycate* drops four times a day.

Conjunctivitis

The first thing you may notice is the eyelids stuck together with green gunk in the morning. This is usually caused by **bacterial infection**, and treated with antibiotic drops into both eyes, initially every two or three hours. *Chloramphenicol* works well; newer antibiotics cost more but are probably no better. If symptoms do not start to improve after 36 hours, try *tetracycline* drops or ointment; if this does not work seek medical help. Avoid eye preparations that contain extras, especially *hydrocortisone*, *betamethasone* or other steroids. If you notice a change in your ability to see, or if there is great pain in the eyeball or behind the eye, you should consult a physician or specialist in eyes or internal medicine. If the problem remains confined to one eye only, it is unlikely to be simple conjunctivitis: it could be **iritis** or a **foreign body** in the eye. See an eye specialist.

Conjunctivitis can be caused by **viruses**, when inflammation will be mild, there will be less green discharge and you will probably have a cold and/or sore throat. This will get better without treatment (antibiotic drops usually do no harm, if in doubt). In bacterial and viral conjunctivitis, bathing the eye in warm, slightly salty water will aid removal of any discharge. Getting **noxious chemicals** in the eye, such as slug slime, cicada spit, whip-scorpion squirt or centipede ooze, can also cause conjunctivitis. Again, bathe the eye in warm, slightly salty water. If the inflammation is bad, tape or pad the eye closed and see a doctor.

Sore, gritty or burning eyes

Eye discomfort of this sort can be caused by insufficient tears. This is a common problem in all climates, but is even more frequent in hot and dry regions. Hypromellose or artificial tears are useful and safe, and can be applied as often as necessary – half-hourly if you wish.

Subconjunctival haemorrhage

This is bleeding that turns the white of the eye red; it does not affect the coloured iris. It looks horrendous, but is harmless (unless after a bad head injury, *see* p.276) and needs no treatment. Very rarely, it can be a sign of widespread disease (e.g. louse-borne relapsing fever or a viral haemorrhagic fever) but, if so, other symptoms will be present and it will be obvious that you are very ill.

Redness and swelling around the eye (*periorbital cellulitis*)

A very painful, red, puffy eye accompanied by fever requires medical attention. If you are somewhere remote, take *flucloxacillin* 500mg four times a day (or *erythromycin* if you are allergic to *penicillin*) and find a doctor immediately. If there is no fever the problem may be due to a mosquito bite (*see* p.142) or insects flying into the eye (*see* pp.208–9). Inflammation will be greatest if the insect's body is damaged when you try to remove it from the eye.

Styes

Styes are small boils on the eyelid, which are treated by applying a hot compress (use a face cloth). Pluck out the eyelash at the centre of the stye with tweezers, if possible, since this will aid draining of the pus. Antibiotic creams or drops are unlikely to help with a simple stye. If the infection starts to spread elsewhere on the face, take antibiotic tablets, in the same way as for skin infections (*see* **Skin**, p.205).

If you get a stye that does not discharge and go away, or if one keeps recurring in the same place, this is probably a cyst in the eyelid that is getting repeatedly infected. It can be dealt with as a non-urgent matter with a minor operation under local anaesthetic.

Glasses and contact lenses

If you wear glasses or contact lenses, carry your lens prescription with you. Replacements are usually available and often cheap overseas. Lens wearers should also carry with them as much as possible of their preferred solutions, as they may not be able to find them at their destination.

Remove contact lenses on long flights to reduce soreness. Contact lenses can introduce infection into the eye and this is more likely to happen in a hot, dusty, dry climate, especially if you are travelling rough and hygiene standards are difficult to maintain. There are a selection of microbes that may cause eye problems, of which the most worrying is *Acanthamoeba*. Consider wearing glasses instead of lenses, or at least carry a pair of glasses with you so that as soon as any hint of irritation or infection begins you can change over. At extreme altitude (above 8,000m/26,000ft) contact lenses can deprive the eye of oxygen.

Dental problems

If several top teeth hurt, this is probably sinusitis (*see* p.267–8). Toothache is more likely to be due to a cavity if you can see a hole (although those brought up on fluorinated water will have less obvious holes), and cavities tend to hurt only after eating and drinking and not if you tap it. If the tooth hurts all the time – even when you are trying to sleep – and it is worse on tapping, this is likely to be an abscess. There is often soreness of the gums near the abscess and there can be swelling of the face on the same side as the bad tooth. A course of an antibiotic (usually *penicillin* or *erythromycin*) plus painkillers will be needed. Treatment by a dentist is then usually necessary, but this should take place after the infection has been cleared.

If a **tooth** is **knocked out** and the tooth is a baby tooth, stop the bleeding by getting the child to bite on some cotton wool. There is no need to put a baby tooth back. The permanent tooth that grows in its place may be a little late coming through. If a permanent tooth is knocked out, wash the tooth gently in clean water and ensure that the tooth is clear of bits of dirt. Gently push the tooth back into the socket until the biting edge of the loose tooth is at the same level as the tooth beside it. Hold it in place with the fingers. Next either find a dentist to fashion a guard to hold the tooth in place or see if you can improvise support with two thin rolls of beeswax or some similarly malleable material moulded in front and behind the row of teeth. If a tooth can be put back within an hour of being knocked out there is a good chance that it will survive. After 24 hours there is little hope.

Emergency telephone numbers
In the European Union (EU): t 112.

In the UK: both **t 999** and **t 112** will reach emergency services.

In the USA and Canada: t 911.

Other emergency numbers are found on *http://travel.state.gov/travel* and *www.nhs.uk/countryguidance.*

On the Ground:
Accidents

Collapse 274

Immediate responses and safety 274
  Severe bleeding 275

Unconsciousness and fits 276
  The recovery or unconscious
  position 277

Allergic reactions 278

Strains, sprains, bruises and
  wrenches 278

Cuts, wounds and bites 280
  Burns and scalds 281

Fractures and dislocations 282

Something stuck... 283
...in the ear 283
...in the eye 283
...in the throat 284

Swallowing things accidently 285

Exposure to CS gas 286

20

Summary

→ Anyone planning a trip to somewhere lacking an ambulance service, or travelling with children, should go on a first-aid course to gain knowledge and confidence about what to do in a medical emergency.

→ Accidents away from home are scariest since you may not know how to find help or treatment.

→ Be assured that immediate treatment after an accident is usually straightforward and rarely complicated.

→ This chapter is not a complete first-aid course, but will prompt those with a little knowledge of first aid. Lists and tips will help you cope if disaster strikes.

→ Travel with a small first-aid kit and know how to use it. For suggestions, see pp.32–4.

→ Drink-driving or allowing yourself to be driven by a drunk is bonkers. Check that your bush-taxi driver is sober and has functioning eyes and limbs before entrusting your life to him.

→ Become safety conscious.

→ Be properly insured.

Collapse

After a serious accident, drowning or a major medical crisis (such as a heart attack), people die because either:

→ **air** fails to get into the lungs;

→ or **blood** fails to get to the brain.

This makes resuscitation a simple process. Read on to see what to do.

Immediate responses and safety

→ Take a couple of seconds to assess the situation.

→ Check for danger before trying to help:

- Is the casualty still connected to an electricity supply?
- Is the foul air in the well that overcame him also going to poison you?
- Will he drag you underwater?
- Ensure that you do not make the situation worse in any way.
- See if the victim is in danger of further injury: if there is a chance of a spine or neck injury, movement might be harmful.

→ If anyone else is on hand, get them to help; it is hard to resuscitate someone single-handed – even for an expert.

→ Use your first-aid course techniques and the **ABC mnemonic** (see opposite) to remind you what to do.

→ If you have any broken skin you can acquire hepatitis B or HIV infection by contact with blood; use surgical gloves if possible.

→ Never force an accident victim to move if he has pain. Moving a fractured limb is undesirable as well as agonizing. Someone who has a back injury will generally be in such pain he will realize he must not be moved. If a casualty experiences a great deal of pain when you try to move him, stop and think; you may be making things worse.

Emergency telephone numbers

Emergency numbers vary throughout the world:

In the European Union (EU): t 112.

In the UK: both **t 999** and **t 112** will reach emergency services.

In the USA and Canada: t 911.

Severe bleeding

Establish where the blood is coming from (gently clear away blood with a clean cloth) and press on the bleeding point. Blood loss always looks more dramatic than it is, and gentle mopping often reveals a modest wound. Cuts on the scalp or face bleed copiously and always look horrendous (you may think the victim is close to death), but after cleaning you may find only a tiny nick in the skin. If bright red blood spurts out with each heartbeat, an artery has been severed and you should press hard on the bleeding point until it has stopped (more than 10 minutes). Fortunately, in most accidental injuries crushing and tearing of arteries puts them into spasm, so they often stop bleeding spontaneously. 'Clean' wounds, such as those from glass or stab-wounds, often bleed more because the incision is neat.

Stop the bleeding by applying a clean cloth, if available, and pressing on the bleeding point; pressure with two thumbs (one on top of the other) often works well. Bleeding from a long cut can be reduced by pressing the sides of the wound together with your thumbs, then holding it together with Steri-Strips (*see* overleaf). If lots of blood is coming out of a large, fleshy area (buttock or thigh) you may need to put your hand into the wound to try to get hold of the source of the bleeding.

Press hard for a long time (at least 10 minutes), then put on a dressing and tie or strap it firmly in place; crêpe bandages are useful, or you can use an ambulance

ABC for emergencies

Send for help, then:

A is for Airway: check that the mouth and throat are clear; people often vomit in a crisis, or inhale teeth or debris, or the accident can crush part of the face. Clear the airway with your fingers as far as possible. If there is damage to the face that seems to be interfering with breathing, pull the jaw forward (away from the face), hook the tongue forward with your fingers if necessary and tip the head up and back.

B is for Breathing: check that the victim is breathing by placing your cheek close to their nose and mouth. If they are not breathing give mouth-to-mouth artificial respiration, or another method of assisted ventilation if this is more familiar to you.

C is for Circulation: check that the heart is beating by feeling the chest, or (if you are used to finding them) pulses in the neck or groin; wrist pulses are difficult or impossible to feel if someone has lost a lot of blood or is in shock. If there is no pulse, give cardiac massage. If there is a great deal of bleeding this must also be staunched, or your cardiac massage will soon be to no avail.

Miraculous recoveries have happened after apparent drowning in cold water and after jellyfish stings so continue resuscitation for a long time; do not give up after a few minutes.

> **To stop bleeding**
> Press where the blood is coming from and raise the bleeding part above the height of the victim's heart. Never use a tourniquet.

field-dressing pack. If it gets soaked with blood, put on more cloth and apply firm, direct pressure again. Do not remove the blood-soaked cloth and do not peek to see if bleeding has stopped.

Steri-Strips or **butterfly closures** can be a very useful way of closing a wound, but it is hard to get them to stick if the skin is wet with a lot of blood. Use direct pressure during the initial flow, then pull the wound together with Steri-Strips when the blood is dry. Once bleeding has stopped there is not such an urgent need for qualified medical help, but when you do reach a clinic try to discourage the attendant from stitching the wound (for more on this and on blood transfusions, read the beginning of the **Ailments** chapter, p.254, and **Medicines,** pp.31–40). If there is a deep scalp wound that is bleeding profusely, pull the wound edges together by tying strands of hair together across the wound. Also try to ensure that there isn't any hair in the wound, since this will delay healing. Wait at least five days after the accident before cutting away the blood-caked tangle of hair; doing this too soon will encourage bleeding to restart.

If something is sticking out of the wound, do not remove it unless it is small and superficial like a splinter. Pad the area and apply pressure around the object to staunch the blood flow. Get to competent medical help as soon as you can.

Unconsciousness and fits

Head injury and concussion
It is dangerous to move an unconscious patient who may have a spine or neck injury, or a fracture, and so try to do a quick check first. Any period of unconsciousness after a fall or accident suggests trauma to the brain (concussion), and the longer the period of unconsciousness the more likely the possibility of serious damage: unconsciousness for over a minute or so is worrying. Nausea and vomiting are common after a head injury. Confusion, a change in the victim's normal behaviour, sleepiness or persistent headache after a bash on the head may indicate bleeding within the skull and needs urgent medical assessment.

Unconsciousness or extreme drowsiness with fever is very worrying: it could be **cerebral malaria** (*see* pp.130–1) or **meningitis** (*see* p.47), when looking at light will be intensely painful. Get to a doctor urgently.

Convulsions or fits
People who are fitting may bite their tongue, but this will probably happen in the first moments of the attack, so don't try to force something between the teeth; it is not recommended. The victim will usually be incontinent, and will be sleepy and disorientated after the fit. Gently reassure them, but realize that they may not really be aware of what is going on and will just want somewhere to rest and sleep for a while. It is very rare for people to have a fit for the first time in adulthood; if

Dealing with fits and convulsions

In adults

If an adult is having a fit or convulsion, take the following action:

1. Clear the area of hard objects (chairs, tables, etc.) so that the person does not injure him- or herself by thrashing against them. Drag the victim away from any danger. Do not force anything into his/her mouth.

2. Loosen any tight clothing (if this is easy to do) and wait for the fit to subside.

3. Place the victim in the recovery position (*see* below).

In children

Fits, seizures or convulsions are common under the age of five.

If a child has a fit:

1. Turn the child on his/her side so he/she is less likely to choke.

2. Do not force anything into his/her mouth.

3. Wait for the fit to subside; then, if the child is hot, give a dose of *paracetamol* (Tylenol), strip off clothes and cool the body by sponging with tepid water.

this occurs, it could be a sign of serious disease like **cerebral malaria** or **meningitis**, and the victim must be taken to see a doctor urgently.

The most likely cause of a fit in children is a rapidly rising temperature due to some kind of relatively benign infection. Seek medical help promptly to determine the cause of the fever, as – rarely – it can be meningitis or cerebral malaria, or simple tonsillitis. Do not worry; children grow out of fits induced by fevers, and they do not lead on to epilepsy later.

See box, above, for how to treat adults and children having fits.

Fainting

If someone faints, lie the victim down and elevate the legs above heart height; if you have nothing to prop the legs up on, simply bend them at the knee. Check for the heartbeat by feeling the chest, or find a pulse in the neck or groin if you know how to do this; pulses at the wrist are very difficult to feel in someone who has fainted. If there is no pulse, start resuscitation. If a victim has simply fainted, get them to lie flat for a few minutes after recovery. People are embarrassed by fainting, and often reluctant to lie down to prevent a faint, or to stay down when they are recovering. If they do not, they will faint again.

The recovery or unconscious position

Someone who is breathing but unconscious is at risk of vomiting. Vomit may enter the lungs and choke or drown the victim (drunks are especially vulnerable). It is important not to leave an unconscious person on his/her back, unless injuries make moving difficult.

Kneeling beside the casualty, tilt the head and lift the chin to make breathing easier. Straighten both legs, and place the arm nearest you out at right angles to the body, elbow bent and with the palm of the hand uppermost (like a policeman

Recovery position

Images provided by

St John
Ambulance

stopping traffic). Bring the other arm across the chest and hold the hand against the side of his face nearest to you, palm outwards. With your other hand, grasp the thigh furthest away from you, and pull the knee up to bend the leg so that the foot stays on the ground. Keeping his/her hand against the cheek with one hand and your other hand on the leg, roll him/her towards you until he/she is propped on his side supported by his bent arms and leg. Check the head is tilted so that the chin is up and the neck extended, to help him/her breathe freely (remember **ABC**, *see* p.275). This is easier than it sounds; try it before you need to use it.

Allergic reactions

Severe allergic reactions are scary and can be life threatening. Allergy tends to be announced by dramatic and often widespread swelling, itching and redness of the skin. The tissues around the eyes and mouth become swollen and the airways can become constricted. The best treatment is injection of *adrenaline* (*epinephrine*) and many allergic people carry an Epipen in case of this eventuality. Less dramatic allergic reactions can be treated with an antihistamine tablet (see table in **Flight**, pp.88–9) and *hydrocortisone* is also of some value, although – even when given by injection – this takes a couple of hours to have much of an effect. Skin prick and blood tests are possible to identify allergens.

Strains, sprains, bruises and wrenches

Badly **strained muscles** and **wrenched joints** are best treated with **RICE: R**est, **I**ce, **C**ompression and **E**levation. The best cold compress is ice cubes in a plastic bag or condom, wrapped in cloth. Beware of applying or strapping ice or ice packs directly to a limb: it can burn. If there is no ice, bathing in cool water while gently moving the limb will help. Compression means strapping. Elevation means supporting the damaged part above heart height. Use pillows to chock it up if you are in bed.

Treating sprains and wrenches

Badly strained muscles and wrenched joints are best treated with **RICE:**

> Rest
> Ice (or cold water) compresses
> Compression
> Elevation

Strapping an injured limb firmly with a crêpe bandage provides comfort and allows mobilization – i.e. to start hobbling around again when pain allows. Wash bandages frequently to maintain their stretchiness. Rest and *aspirin* (or another non-steroidal anti-inflammatory medicine; *see* below) relieve pain in the short term, and gentle movements help disperse the bruise and encourage healing. As the part heals, reduce the amount of strapping or the limb will remain weak. It is difficult to balance giving enough support to avoid further injury, while allowing enough mobility to stimulate the return of full power. Twisted ankles improve with gentle exercise.

Non-steroidal anti-inflammatories reduce pain in all wrenches, sprains, strains and even breaks. *Aspirin* is the best known; three more in ascending order of potency are *ibuprofen* (Nurofen in the UK; Motrin in the USA), *naproxen* (Naprosyn) and *diclofenac* (Voltarol). Medicines in this group should not be taken together, but suitable additional painkillers are *paracetamol* (Tylenol) and/or *codeine*. **Pain** is a useful sensation: it says something is wrong and that something needs to be done. Rest, strapping the affected area and taking a non-steroidal anti-inflammatory will help joint pains. But try to avoid taking pills just to carry on, especially if there is no need to carry on. If you do wrench something, try to stop travelling for a while.

With **bruising**, apply cold compresses immediately, and after 12 hours or so use hot compresses or hot baths and elevation, followed by gentle mobilization with a crêpe bandage as support. As a bruise begins to disperse it changes colour, through lurid red, purple, black, brown and green to yellow. If there has been internal bruising or bleeding after an operation, these colours may appear a week or so after the initial injury, and gravity takes them below the wound. They can be quite alarming. Significant bruising or bleeding – for instance, into the knee – can also result in bruising appearing below the site of injury and this new, migrating bruise is tender to touch. This surprises many people but it is all part of the healing process. Bruising, when there has been little to provoke it might be worth getting checked with a medical consultation or blood test. Easy bruising that is associated with a fever is sometimes a sign of some very serious, but rare, tropical infections. See a doctor.

Back pain

Back pain can come on after lifting something awkwardly and in this case it will generally settle with pain-killers and rest. Rest doesn't mean going to bed for days but slowing the pace of travel, and breaking up the day with periods of rest and periods of gently pottering about. Bad backs protest at extended periods of sitting but are improved by lying on your front, including being propped up on the elbows, and lying flat. Sometimes back pain can be bad enough for you to need to take a strong anti-inflammatory such as *diclofenac*, plus *paracetamol* (Tylenol) plus *codeine* and even *diazepam* (2–5mg every four hours) to combat muscle spasm. Hot baths also help. There is some evidence that the herbal remedy **devil's claw** helps long-standing back pain and also osteoarthritis. Pain radiating from the low back down one leg is **sciatica** and needs at least a couple of weeks rest; car travel is especially bad for backache. A physiotherapist then needs to teach you how to strengthen your back to prevent further attacks. Pain in one side of the low back may be a kidney stone (*see* **Ailments**; p.265).

Cuts, wounds and bites

Deep wounds
Deep or very dirty wounds should be washed under a running tap or by pouring on water from a bowl or jug. Don't worry about water sterility – just use lots of it. Make sure there is no mud, gravel or glass in the wound, since these will guarantee infection and delay healing. Pick out any bits with clean fingers.

If there is a lot of bleeding, raise up the bleeding part above the level of the victim's heart if possible and apply firm, direct pressure (*see* pp.275–6). Once the bleeding has stopped, resist the temptation to clear away blood clots, because bleeding will restart. Wash any wound thoroughly, pour in antiseptic if you have it, dab dry, then wrap it all up and seek help if you can. If you are somewhere remote, refer to pp.275–6.

Does it need stitches?
We expect any laceration to be stitched promptly in emergency departments. In hot, steamy, unhygienic environments however this can cause a great deal of trouble, especially if the wound is deep or very dirty, or it is the result of an animal bite. Sometimes stitches are required to stop massive bleeding, but otherwise in tropical environments it is often safer to allow even quite big wounds to heal naturally or delay stitching for a week. Animal bites should not be sutured and need expert attention, since infection is almost inevitable and rabies (*see*

Case history: Sri Lanka

It had been a long, hot morning, and when I found an ice-cream parlour in a fancy shopping mall in Colombo, we were all ready for a break. The place was stylish and newly painted in soft green, with large potted trees on the floor, and the glass-topped wicker tables sparkled with cleanliness. I was cautious about eating dairy products, even those with recognized brand names, while in unknown tropical places, but when I saw a Western family (with the children wearing local school uniforms) inside enjoying treats, I decided that we could eat here safely. Four-year-old Bernard, who had been arguing about what size ice cream he could manage, angrily put his bowl down on the table. The entire top shattered, and splinters flew everywhere. Fortunately, only his middle finger was actually implanted with shards of glass. Bernard had not used any great amount of force, but I will never again trust a glass table without some kind of band or border edging the glass – nor do I travel anywhere now without a plaster.

Iris Gowen, Beijing

Case history: Sumbawa

Ray slipped in remote rainforest on Sumbawa, Indonesia. As he fell he impaled his arm on a cut bamboo shoot that was sticking out of the ground; it went clean through the muscles of his forearm. The paramedic at a local clinic sutured the entry and exit wounds.

A few days later Ray's arm was painful and swollen and he was feverish. The stitches were under tension, so I removed them. This allowed the pus to drain and immediately made the arm more comfortable. I redressed the two little wounds and told Ray to take a course of antibiotics. He cleaned and bathed the wounds three times a day. His tetanus immunization was up to date. The wound settled over the following week. Ray's injury was impossible to clean because it was so deep. Suturing the wound sealed in the dirt. Leaving a wound like this open allows it to expel any foreign or noxious material naturally, so the healing process is faster and infection is less likely to set in.

pp.250–2) is a big risk. Keeping wounds clean is more important than closing them (see below).

Deep or very dirty wounds should be cleaned as described in 'Deep wounds', opposite. If there is a lot of bleeding, do not apply a tourniquet. Stop bleeding by elevation and firm, direct pressure (*see also* 'Severe bleeding', pp.275–6). You will be unable to assess the extent of the injury (or discover the whereabouts of a persistent bleeder) while everything is covered in blood, but do not be too enthusiastic about clearing away blood clots, because bleeding will restart. Wash wounds thoroughly but, during this initial clean-up, don't worry about sterility or about applying antiseptic. Then, once you feel that most of the dirt is gone, bathe the wound in dilute *potassium permanganate* solution or another antiseptic (*see* p.204) and change dressings once a day for the first few days.

All wounds (especially deep, dirty wounds and bites) carry a risk of **tetanus**. You should have been immunized before travel (*see* p.43); if you are not tetanus-immune, you will need both active and passive cover as soon as possible after injury (*see* p.250).

Burns and scalds

Remove the victim from the source of the injury. If it is an electrical burn, beware of being electrocuted yourself: turn off the supply, kick the victim free, or use a broom handle or similar non-conductor to disconnect him from the supply. Electrical burns are often very deep and readily become infected, so seek medical help if you can.

To treat **minor burns**, pour on or immerse in cold water until the burn or scald no longer feels hot to the victim. Do not apply creams, lotions or other potions. If clothes are fused into the burn, as often happens with man-made fabrics, trim away loose pieces; do not pull away adhered cloth. Cover the burn with a clean, dry, non-fluffy dressing. *Paracetamol* (Tylenol) or *ibuprofen* (Nurofen in the UK; Motrin in the USA) help reduce pain and burning, and so does raising the burnt area above heart height.

In **superficial burns**, skin sensation (pain) remains and the skin appears red and mottled. Deep, **severe burns** are generally less painful, because nerve endings have been destroyed. The skin looks white or charred. In cases of extensive burns, the immediate threat to the victim's survival is **loss of fluids** through the burn site. If the victim is able to drink, offer sips of water (or oral rehydration solution). Encourage drinking a cupful an hour (in sips will be easiest); a remarkable amount of water (and heat) can be lost from burnt skin. Keep the victim warm: there is a risk of **hypothermia** (*see* pp.196–7).

The next serious problem in severe and extensive burns is **infection**; evacuation home is probably advisable. Signs of infection include: increasing pain, spreading redness, pus dripping from the wound, itching or a bad smell. It sets in rapidly in warm climates.

Bleeding under a nail

Injuries to fingers or toes can cause bleeding under the nail. Even a tiny amount of blood trapped in such a confined space is intensely painful. Heat the end of an uncurled paperclip in a flame until it is red. Place it firmly on the black nail, at right angles to it, so that it burns through the nail but not to the nail bed. You do not need to apply much pressure; the paperclip should just burn through. Do not use a pin or needle; they are too sharp and you will push through to the sensitive nail bed (ouch!) before making a hole big enough to let the blood out.

The paperclip technique is a very satisfying piece of first aid because as soon as the blood is released, there is immediate relief of pain and you have a very grateful patient. The nail comes off eventually and a new one will grow in its place.

Fractures and dislocations

Often the victim will have heard or felt a bone break; they will feel faint and unwell despite the fact that initially there is not always much pain. There will be swelling, an unnatural shape or position, and a reluctance or inability to move the fractured part. Movement of one end of the fractured bone on the other causes intense pain, so immobilize the limb with whatever you can improvise. You can bandage a broken leg against the good one (with plenty of padding in between), or one finger against another. Cushion the broken limb as much as possible; any movement is excruciatingly painful. Broken limbs swell, so check that any bandaging does not compromise blood supply. Third World paramedics are often very competent bone-setters, but evacuate to hospital if you can. Fingers or toes going numb and/or blue after the bone has been set and plastered is a sign that the limb is in serious trouble and the cast is too tight. Get someone to cut the cast off urgently and replace it with a 'back slab'.

If you **break your nose** it will probably be obviously crooked. It will not be all that painful at first, but take some painkillers and then apply a thumb to either side of the nose and straighten it as best you can. All you need to do is to get it reasonably straight. You will get no better treatment in hospital. Cold compresses will help to reduce bleeding from the nose and will soothe the pain somewhat.

Dislocations are usually hard to treat unless they happen frequently to an individual: some people habitually dislocate shoulders. It may be possible to relocate fingers or toes without anaesthetic. The principle is to pull the digit slowly, steadily and firmly back out straight until it jumps into place. Any rough grinding sensations imply there is also a fracture, which is best splinted and treated by a professional.

Pulled elbow is a very common injury in children between the ages of two and four. It often happens when a parent pulls a reluctant toddler's arm. The child cries immediately and will refuse to move the elbow. The problem is minor; if it happens when you are days from a clinic you may wish to treat it yourself. You need to be firm but not forceful. With one hand, steady the child's upper arm by holding it (between the shoulder and the injured elbow) so that he does not wriggle away. Then, using the other hand, gently move his arm so that the elbow is bent to 90°, and then turn the forearm so that the palm of his hand is facing down towards the floor. Next, holding the forearm near the wrist, gently but firmly rotate the forearm (with the elbow kept at 90°) until the palm is facing upwards. If you get it right the elbow will click home and the child will be comfortable again. No further treatment is required. If the child still refuses to move the elbow, it is either still dislocated or there could be a fracture. Seek medical help and perhaps an X-ray.

Something stuck...

...in the ear

Inexpert attempts to remove objects or insects from the ear canal usually push the offending item further in, which may damage the ear drum. Lie the victim on their side with the problem ear uppermost, and fill the ear with water; the object should float out. Straightening the ear canal by pulling the ear flap towards the crown of the head may help the object float out, and soaking in a bath with ears under water can also help. If this does not work you will need medical help. A medical worker with an ear syringe may be able to flush out the object, but many foreign bodies need to be removed in a hospital Ear, Nose and Throat department.

...in the eye

If something is protruding from the eye, you need to find a doctor; if evacuation is going to take some time, you need to protect the eye. Large objects that have penetrated the eye tend to fall out. Small objects can generally be wiped out gently, using wet cotton wool twisted into a point or the corner of a clean handkerchief.

Getting small objects from up a child's nose

If a small child has pushed a small object or piece of food up their nose, here is a painless way for the parent/carer to get it out. It doesn't always work but it doesn't hurt to try. The parent tells the child that they are going to get a big cuddle and kiss. Close the unaffected nostril with one finger, seal the child's lips with your own and give a short sharp blow into the child's mouth. With a bit of luck the offending object will pop out of the nostril. I found this particularly useful when my youngest daughter developed a temporary fondness for pushing beads up her nose.

Dr Deborah Mills, The Travel Doctor, TMVC, Brisbane Australia

Usually the victim's own instincts will protect the eye sufficiently, but if a difficult evacuation is foreseen it may be sensible to protect the eye from further damage by making a cone-shaped shield from cardboard, stiff paper or plastic. Cut a circle that is larger than the eye socket, and cut a radius (like the first cut when slicing a cake). Then overlap and stick the edges of the cut to form a flattish cone. Many first aid books suggest gently packing around the eye with bandages so that the injured eye is covered, **without** any pressure on it. This can be very difficult in practice and may do more harm than good. Even if the other eye is undamaged, the victim will not want to open the good eye and so will need a great deal of help and support during evacuation.

If there is **something small in the eye**, such as a grain of sand or an eyelash, first ensure that the outside of the eye is clean by wiping with a damp cloth, then, while looking up, grasp the eyelashes of the top lid and pull the upper lid over the lower one. Blink. If this does not work, get someone to pour water into the eye while blinking as much as possible. Use tepid water and pour from close to the eye, or trickle water in from a syringe without a needle. The coloured part of the eye is very sensitive, so pour gently onto the white part. Looking away from the water makes the procedure more comfortable. If this doesn't work, grasp the top eyelashes, roll the upper lid back over a cotton bud and inspect under the top lid where grit often lodges. The surface of the eyeball should be checked too, and any particles gently brushed away with another cotton bud. Even the tiniest of foreign bodies can be very painful; a magnifying glass will help you search.

...in the throat

If someone is choking on an inhaled object or piece of food, stand behind him, put your arms around him, linking hands to form a fist in the middle of the upper abdomen beneath the rib cage, and pull towards you and upwards sharply. The idea is to force air out of the lungs and with it the object. This is the **Heimlich manoeuvre**.

If the victim has collapsed roll them onto their back, get astride them facing their head, put your hands (one on top of the other) just under the rib cage and repeatedly force down and towards their head: this should propel the item out. A small child can be held upside-down and smartly slapped on the back. If you are the victim you can achieve a similar effect by slumping forward onto a chair back; this forces air and the object out.

If you swallow a **fish or meat bone**, it may feel as if the bone has stuck, but this is rare: more often the throat has only been scratched. This requires no treatment. If a foreign body really has stuck in the throat it will be almost impossible even to swallow saliva, and large quantities of additional saliva that are secreted will be spat out. The neck will often also feel very tender on prodding from the outside.

The definitive test of whether it is a scratch or whether there is something stuck is to wait for 12–24 hours while taking a cool, soft diet (but not ice cream unless you are somewhere hygienic). People with a scratch will improve, while those with something stuck will feel worse. The treatment for something stuck in the throat is removal of the object in hospital under general anaesthetic.

Case history: Spain

It is a good idea to get children to sit while eating, but it is hard to enforce. Eighteen-month-old Seb was tottering around the hotel lounge in his socks. He slipped and cracked the back of his head on the polished wood floor. The impact fired the raw carrot that he was munching to the back of his throat and he started to choke. I swept him up and threw him face-down across my knees, positioning his head slightly lower than the rest of his body. I then hit him noisily on the back many times until the chewed carrot all seemed to be back in his mouth and he started to cry.

My oldest son watched in horror. He said, 'He fell over and hurt himself Mummy, and you're hitting him! Why are you hitting him? That's not nice!'

Swallowing things accidentally

Toddlers and small children often swallow noxious or worrying substances and some doctors advise travelling with *ipecacuanha emetic mixture* (which induces vomiting) in case of trouble. The choice is yours but don't expect to be able to buy it overseas. There are plenty of myths about what is and is not dangerous if swallowed. While most **multivitamin** preparations are safe, **vitamin A** and **iron**, if swallowed in overdose, can be very toxic: medical help must be sought and *ipecacuanha* should probably be given to vomit up the tablets. On deciding to visit a doctor, try first to work out how many tablets might have been taken and show the doctor the packet/bottle. If a dangerous quantity has been consumed, a child of 6–18 months takes 10ml of *ipecacuanha*, older children 15ml and adults 30ml; dosing is repeated after 20 minutes, if a vomit has not been achieved. **Essential oils** can cause severe toxicity if swallowed and observation in hospital after such an accident is a wise precaution. 'Mild' **antidepressants** and **sleeping pills** can be very dangerous, even if a child only takes a few tablets accidentally; inducing vomiting with *ipecacuanha* would be wise if possible. **Silica gel,** the desiccant found in electrical and photographic products and shoeboxes, often carries a warning: 'toxic if swallowed'. It is not dangerous if taken in small quantities. Most **antibiotics** and also the **contraceptive** pill are not toxic. An overdose of antibiotics is likely to cause a little diarrhoea at worst. The contraceptive pill may cause nausea and, rarely, even some vaginal bleeding in pre-pubertal girls; this is not dangerous. Even swallowing **mercury** from a thermometer does not cause health problems. Finally, **pencil 'lead'** is not lead at all, but inert graphite; chewing pencils does not cause health problems.

Poisonous plants

Young children may nibble parts of plants, but poisoning is unusual because the bitter taste means most gets spat out. Fruits, berries and seeds are mostly harmless, but representatives of the potato, tomato and aubergine family (*Solanaceæ*) are not only very poisonous but their fruits look like attractive little tomatoes (*see also* p.124). The family also includes **deadly nightshade** and evening-scented **angels' trumpets** (*Datura suaveolens*), common hotel garden shrubs with large, dangling white flowers. The **thorn apple** (*D. stramonium*) is also very toxic, as

Case history: cave rescues

I have spent a lot of time underground in the south-west of England. I enjoyed caving and also researched the ecology of blind, cave-adapted animals in the limestones of Devon and Somerset. I served as a cave rescue warden too.

The call-outs were mostly to inexperienced people who had ventured into a cave or abandoned tin mine with ordinary battery-operated torches / flashlights. They didn't realise that these lights fail after only an hour or so. Hypothermia was a problem we feared. These rescues got me thinking about how truly difficult it would be to navigate through a cave I knew well without a light.

My zoological investigations meant that I visited my underground research site at least twice a week. The cave I was studying had one entrance with a loop of low passage and boulder-strewn corridor comprising just 320 feet (less than 100m) in absolute darkness. I experimented with trying to move, lightless, through my familiar cave and time after time managed to progress only a metre or two before ending up in a blind alley.

Even knowing this small cave well, I realised that if my light failed, I'd be incapable of finding my way out. In absolute darkness, however, the tiniest light can save you. I met one chap who found his way out of a small cave in Somerset - by the light of a cigarette. Even better would be to carry emergency lighting; the glow stick variety are convenient. Accidents seldom happen to the well-prepared venturer.

are **aconites**. The **yellow oleander** (*Thevetia peruviana*) is also commonly grown in tropical gardens and all parts of this shrub are poisonous: one fruit is enough to kill a child, but prompt treatment with an *atropine* injection is life-saving. Native of the Americas, its large, flat seeds are worn as ornaments.

The attractive, bright red berries of evergreen **yew** trees (and hedges) are harmless, but all other parts of the plant are toxic, including the seed inside the berry; however, unless the child crunches the seeds, they will usually be passed without causing trouble. If yew poisoning has occurred, symptoms start within 40 minutes. If there has been no abdominal pain, vomiting or diarrhoea within four hours of swallowing then insufficient poison has been absorbed to do any harm.

If in doubt find a doctor, and take a sample of the plant to show if possible.

Exposure to CS gas

If you are exposed to tear (CS) gas spit out (do not swallow) saliva containing the gas (it will make you nauseous, and you may even vomit). Get into a ventilated area and strip off excess clothes (and wash them in due course). The discomfort will disappear in minutes. The best treatment for discomfort in the eyes is to blow dry air on them; use an electric fan if possible, otherwise get someone to blow on them. Washing or irrigating with water will make the symptoms worse.

On the Ground:
Expatriates

Health and hygiene 288
  A good home environment 288
  Filth-to-mouth pathogens 289
  Other health challenges 289

Special concerns for expatriates 289
  Malaria 290
  Pre-existing problems and pills 290

Psychological welfare 291
  Understanding your stresses 292
  Your motivation 292
  Sex and the single expat 293
  The ideal expatriate 293
  Sad spouses 294

Babies and children 294
  The commonest panic 295

21

Summary

→ Do what you can to make your new home feel homely; try to avoid a 'camping' or 'only here for a short time' mentality.

→ Fit mosquito screens and make an effort to pest-proof your home.

→ In warm climates collections of rainwater (e.g. old tyres and discarded buckets as well as blocked surface drains) provide nursery accommodation for mosquitoes.

→ Psychological problems, alcoholism, workaholism and even nervous breakdown are common in expatriates, especially in unemployed spouses.

→ Form alliances with other outsiders and local colleagues too, if possible. Set up good communications networks with friends at home and elsewhere.

→ It can be challenging to organize regular exercise where the security situation is difficult so consider how this will be achieved.

→ Compared with people who take their alcohol in more dilute form, spirits drinkers are most likely to get into trouble with drinking.

→ Find out about and respect local laws, including those relating to alcohol consumption.

→ Have an exit strategy (including the funds to get out) if the political climate turns nasty or war breaks out.

→ Expatriates are at low risk of illness and accident compared with independent travellers, and longer-term residents can usually improve their home and office environments to make them healthier still.

Health and hygiene

A good home environment

Expatriates should be able to make their immediate environment safer than temporary travellers can ever hope to do, and so their risks should be lesser than casual tourists. Homes can be screened against mosquitoes, and properly fitting screen doors with bicycle inner tube nailed along the bottom also exclude snakes. Tiles and high doorsteps discourage scorpions and venomous centipedes too. Keeping chickens means spilled grain, which encourages rodents, which encourage snakes. Site the chicken house as far as possible from the family home. Compost heaps and rubbish pits encourage snakes, which also like to lurk in piles of rubble, so clear your home environment. The immediate area around the house can be swept and cleared to discourage mosquitoes, flies and snakes. Thick, scrubby vegetation, in particular, should be removed, because it makes a good hiding place for snakes and provides resting sites for mosquitoes. All standing water should be covered or drained, and any small quantities collecting in tyres and pots should be emptied; these and plants that trap water where stems join the trunk (such as bromeliads and travellers' palms) make excellent mosquito breeding grounds.

Rural areas may have no electricity, water supply nor sanitation. You may need to dig a pit latrine or sink a tube well. Separate those two facilities as best you can and think about fly-control. Installing a slab over the pit, which can include a water trap, is probably the best solution, or simply having a cover over the hole is some help. The text to advise on latrine design is *Engineering in Emergencies* (see **Bibliography**, p.306). Ensure runoff from any hand pump drains away properly. Consider whether a generator is going to be useful. Fans and air conditioners help cut down mosquito bites indoors, confuse sand-flies and help avoid prickly heat. Keep an eye on people you employ: you are responsible for their welfare. If they cough up blood, this suggests TB (*see* p.262).

Filth-to-mouth pathogens

While at home expatriates should be at little risk of filth-to-mouth diseases. Ensure a ready supply of boiled and filtered water, teach any employees about basic hygiene and make sure they are healthy. Take care when travelling anywhere else in the country: then you become a traveller, with a traveller's increased health risks.

Other health challenges

Conditions may make it challenging to organize the half-hour exercise sessions that everyone should aspire to twice a week. At home you'll be able to go to a gym or pool, cycle, jog or walk the dog but the security situation, air pollution, climate and facilities may make this a less attractive option overseas. Plan how you might get around this then. Consider whether shipping a cheap exercise bike or rowing machine, or buying a Nintendo Wii system might activate you. Or investigate whether your route to the office can involve stair-climbing.

While in I lived in Kathmandu, I conducted a survey on the health and concerns of my expatriate friends and neighbours. Levels of respiratory disease (which expatriates all talk and worry about because of the air pollution in the city) were no higher than at home, but bouts of diarrhoea were frequent, and more serious illnesses were more common than I expected.

I was surprised by how many of our community had needed to seek medical treatment outside Nepal: there were a few medical evacuations, but most trips were for operations or investigations organized at a few weeks' or months' notice; there were also some unpleasant conditions which would not clear up with local treatment. The high proportion of people requiring treatment in Bangkok or at home suggests that it is essential to ensure that you have good medical insurance, covering medical evacuation. Keeping a summary of any previous complicated medical problems or hospital treatment is also useful on such occasions.

Special concerns for expatriates

Most of the information in this book applies equally to independent travellers and expatriates. Expatriates and tourists all need to be careful about food hygiene and water quality, but it's relatively easy for them to protect themselves from infections. Those living in less well-resourced regions are at increased risk of catching TB (*see* p.262), so should consider BCG immunization (*see* pp.43–4), especially for babies. The risks facing expatriates vary according to where they are based – cities, rural areas, jungle, desert or refugee camps – and on their kind of work. Diplomats, development consultants, businessmen, oil prospectors, missionaries, health workers, zoologists, anthropologists and volunteers all have their own particular risks, requirements, stresses and support mechanisms.

Any sensible expatriate will find out about the local culture and especially local laws. In many Muslim countries, for example, it is illegal to drink alcohol or have alcohol in your bloodstream. The rules on how much alcohol you may have on board when driving are mostly lower overseas than in the UK and even in some European countries it is illegal to have any alcohol in your blood if you are driving (*see also* 'The downsides of drinking', p.12). Be aware that lower limits also mean it is easier to have illegal levels of blood alcohol even the morning after a heavy night.

It is worth planning an exit strategy if the host country has any scope for political instability. One friend was caught up in Kuwait during the first Gulf War and although he had to leave in a hurry and lost everything, he believes he owes his life to being able to buy a ticket out with his American Express card. Get proper training if working in high risk situations, consider buying a satellite phone and be aware that international border regulations might prevent you from being able to evacuate to the nearest competent hospital if you do have an accident or medical emergency.

Malaria

Expatriates are consistently bad at protecting themselves from malaria and insect bites. Try to find out exactly what the local situation is. Many Latin American and Southeast and East Asian cities are free from the disease, so city-bound expats may not need prophylaxis, but it may be necessary for weekend jaunts. Even if malaria is not a local problem, take precautions against being bitten so as to avoid other insect-borne diseases (*see* pp.150–1) and do not be paranoid about the side effects of antimalarials; they are generally safe and tested medicines, even if long-term protection can be challenging. I urge expatriates to follow the advice on pp.134–9. A few expatriates take their tablets carefully and then say, 'Since I am taking my malaria tablets, it's safe to sit outside at dusk [getting bitten] while I sip my gin and tonic.' It is not. Nor does the quinine in tonic protect you. Avoid bites.

Pre-existing problems and pills

Expatriates are often on long-term prescription medicines, even if this is only the contraceptive pill. Know the generic names of any of these medicines (so that you can acquire supplies abroad) and find out whether it is important to take only one manufacturer's version of it. Plan for changes in your plans and realize that even if your medicines seem to be readily available locally, strikes, government coups and other unexpected changes can mean that pharmacies may be closed or supplies interrupted. British GPs tend to prescribe generically (so that any brand may be supplied) but generic substitution is ill-advised with some medications. Certain heart and anti-epileptic medicines come into this category and so does lithium; the reason for this is that different brands can lead to different levels of medicine circulating. Such tablets may be best brought from home.

NHS rules say that GPs may only prescribe three months' supply of medicines and if more is needed for an extended stay overseas then the rest must be given on a private prescription. There may be a fee for the prescription and the pharmacist will also charge for the medicines. This is the case even if you are exempt from prescription charges and also if the medicine itself is usually provided free under the NHS – as in the case of the contraceptive pill.

Psychological welfare

The life of an expatriate appears romantic and attractive. The reality is often long hours, huge pressure to achieve and separation from loved ones. Deadlines rarely leave time to learn a local language, which restricts the social circle. The community is small, introverted and often obsessed by trivia. Life can be isolated. Many expatriates also move rapidly from country to country, so that it is doubly hard for them to adjust to local culture. Even the expatriate community itself is constantly shifting, so friendships often remain at a superficial level. It is important to keep in touch with friends at home, but email mustn't be your only social outlet.

Volunteers are at times even worse off. Geography and lower income may isolate them from other expatriates. Local people may not value their contribution as it seems to come so cheap. Some feel undermined by local conditions: they are often involved in work where success or failure is immediately very obvious to them. Some volunteers may communicate better with locals than most business expats but, however well integrated they are, it can be difficult to relax properly.

Aid work, specifically, can throw people into shocking, stressful situations that are very hard to cope with. **The International Committee of the Red Cross** publishes an excellent booklet, *Coping with Stress* (*see* **Bibliography**, p.306), aimed at those working in conflict situations. It includes a stress self-evaluation scheme. Among the symptoms of severe stress identified are: having difficulty sleeping, feeling tense and irritable, being 'jumpy', feeling distant from others, feeling physically lethargic and reliving traumatic events. Some people have attacks of dizziness, sweating, tightness in the chest and breathlessness.

Pressures at work and distance from familiar supports create tensions, and many expatriates unwind with a drink. Alcoholism is a common problem. Workaholism is too, so that when other members of the family do arrive they may feel excluded. It is healthiest to try to work sensible hours, and then relax properly doing something that allows you to switch off from work completely, though this advice is hard to keep to. If deadlines mean you must work long hours at times, compensate with the occasional long weekend away.

Sensible drinking: a few guidelines

→ Never drink spirits, and preferably no alcohol, before sundown.

→ Avoid alcohol if local laws prohibit it.

→ Do not rehydrate with beer or other alcoholic drinks; quench your thirst with water or fruit juices before moving on to alcohol.

→ Avoid the habit of unwinding with a drink or two at the end of every day.

→ If you consistently drink over 21 units of alcohol a week you are drinking too much. Women should drink fewer than 14 units (one unit is half a pint of beer, one small glass of wine or a small measure of spirits; a bottle of wine is about 10 units).

→ Spirits drinkers seem to be more likely to get into trouble with alcohol than those who take their alcohol in more dilute forms.

→ Abstain from alcohol in the first three months of pregnancy as it increases the chance of miscarriage; current recommendations are to take no more than one unit of alcohol per week throughout pregnancy.

Understanding your stresses

Long-term expats face special challenges. Psychological symptoms rather than tropical disease are common. This is not to say that people go crazy, but that, due to a combination of 'culture shock', stress, isolation, insomnia, depression, feelings of horror at the injustices they are trying to work to correct and maybe alcoholism, they find it difficult to cope. Isolation is often a big issue: you are on show and surrounded by people, yet you may not share a common sense of humour and, because ways of being polite differ in different cultures, people can seem rude or intrusive. Gesticulations, too, may be misinterpreted as insulting. Holding up five fingers to indicate that you'd like to buy five oranges in Pakistan, for example, says that the stall-holder is the fifth son of the fifth wife; as Muslims are only permitted four wives, this means you are calling him a bastard.

Your motivation

Why do people work overseas? Expatriates fit into one of three categories: **mercenary**, **misfit** or **missionary**. Within 'missionaries' are classified non-religious evangelists like myself, preaching good hygiene and preventative medicine. We in the 'missionary' group might seem best suited to thrive under difficult conditions, but in fact we are very likely to have motivation problems. We are fired with a cause we know is right, but because our mission is so important it can throw us into conflicts. Our very passion to do good can make us intolerant or impatient, or aspire to ridiculously unreachable goals. Why don't local staff understand the importance of the work? Why is local bureaucracy slowing me down? Why don't expatriate colleagues support me? Depression and disillusionment easily grow. It is important to realize that it's not possible to change the world much, so we must be satisfied with small contributions. We must not fall into the trap of blaming employers, local bureaucrats or colleagues for difficulties (local staff may also have problems adjusting to you). Try to keep problems in perspective. Even tight deadlines are more likely to be met with a relaxed approach. Keep an eye on your physical health too; you won't be efficient if you are unwell or ill-rested, so take time to go and see a doctor if you have symptoms or if you are worried about your health.

Those most likely to experience problems of motivation, and even clinical depression, are high achievers, people running away from problems at home, or those who have had previous psychological problems. Spouses who have given up a rewarding occupation to follow their partner, or who are worried about their children's health and education, are also under great psychological pressure. Do not mislead yourself with romantic ideals. Be rational and analyse your motivation, temperament and the kind of work you will be involved in before you commit yourself. Only you can judge.

Many companies that send employees abroad now recognize the value of counselling services, although others still provide little or no support. Take up what's on offer if you can. Some employers run debriefings which may help. Courses run by development charities are great places to network and share.

Sex and the single expat

Expatriates are very visible in the communities in which they work, and there will be a lot of interest in your activities. If you have a local lover, even a platonic friend of the opposite sex, everyone will know about it. In some cultures this will cause problems for female expatriates. You may be seen as available to all comers, and receive uninvited nocturnal visitors, or you may simply lose the status at work so important in getting things done. There may be worse problems for a local woman who is known to be liaising with a man to whom she is not married. Asian communities, in particular, are prudish about such things, and a woman in this situation can become an outcast in the community – in which she will continue to live after you have gone home. The more obvious risks of AIDS and sexually transmitted infections are covered on p.220.

The ideal expatriate

Ideally adjusted expatriates, who enjoy their time abroad, keep a balanced approach to work by spending at least a whole day each week thinking about something completely different. They will have a long-term assignment (two years or more), and will take time out to go sightseeing and learn about the culture in which they are living. They will often have an interest they can follow in different countries – a sport, handicrafts, birdwatching, playing a musical instrument – and take some regular exercise. They appreciate a few beers, but never drink alone and seldom touch spirits.

Unemployed spouses will take lessons in the local language. This involves learning about social customs and enriches the experience of a different culture, making it possible to enquire about what things are for, why people do what they do and how novel foods might be prepared. If her/his role is primarily that of home-maker, a spouse should do a lot of their own shopping (rather than just sending out the cook), as this forces them into contact with locals, improves language skills and enables them to find out what is going on locally. Often this will lead to enriching and rewarding social work of some kind.

Sad spouses

Spouses can suffer enormously in adjusting to expatriate life. Often, they have given up excellent employment and/or fulfilling social life to travel, so not only do they lose a key role and friends, they seem to lose all worth, too. It can seem as if they are just trailing along with no job, no status, no interests, and perhaps they are even assumed to be short on grey matter too. Their partner's colleagues may seem stand-offish, being unskilled in making small talk to home-makers. The situation can be worse for accompanying male partners, since locals may be mystified about how any man can stoop to being kept by a woman, and the status of so many is judged by profession.

Even when unemployed spouses have a useful skill, they may not be allowed to work, even as volunteers. Some even feel ousted by domestic servants from the role of cook and housekeeper. Unemployed, childless, professional women have a tough time. Wives of their partner's local colleagues will be educated, but will probably be puzzled by a childless wife who has had a career but has little interest in children, cooking, make-up and clothes, or one who doesn't know how to manage servants. Situations vary, though. Remote rural postings can be hard socially, but rewarding professionally, culturally and linguistically; in big cities with their bureaucracy, it can be more difficult to find work, but there may be social advantages. And expatriate communities are fluid, with people coming and going sometimes at very short notice and with little time for goodbyes. Making and losing friends so frequently can make life a bit sad.

Babies and children

Many expatriates return home in the late stages of pregnancy to have their babies. The deadline for long-haul flights on most airlines is before the 32nd week of pregnancy but this varies according to the airline and the length of flight. Sometimes a pre-flight medical examination is required. After delivery, new mothers understandably want to rush back to their families but there is a lot of sense in staying at home for four to six weeks before returning abroad. It is surprisingly hard to diagnose any diseases in early infancy. Try to breast-feed rather than bottle-feed your baby, and make sure that this is already well established and that there are no feeding problems before leaving. The safest age to travel with small children is while they are exclusively breast-fed.

Travelling with children is a joy as they provide ready introductions to people who would otherwise not approach you. They can cause a great deal of worry when they become ill and you are far from adequate medical facilities, but as long as they are protected from insect bites, eat safe food and have had the right immunizations, they should thrive.

If infants are bottle-fed or drink from training beakers, be meticulous about sterilizing them frequently. Sterilization tablets are often hard to come by, but boiling bottles, teats and cups in water for 15 minutes is effective and can be organized anywhere. You can also use liquid bleach. Getting rid of disposable nappies (diapers) is difficult, and if put into an ordinary rubbish system they will

Precautions for parents

→ Travelling children must have all the usual childhood immunizations, as well as any special travel vaccines.

→ Protect children from the sun (*see* pp.160–2); they should wear a shirt, hat and sun cream even when bathing in the sea or open-air pools.

→ Children should wear long, loose clothes and cover up or come inside at dusk to avoid mosquito bites.

→ The family must become safety-conscious; children have a poor sense of danger, and buildings and equipment may not be made to the standards you are used to.

→ Be aware of the hazards of toddlers swallowing noxious substances; read the advice at the end of chapter 20.

→ Ensure that children drink plenty of fluids if they get diarrhoea (preferably ORS; *see* p.111).

probably be scattered far and wide. Burn them, or use terry-towel nappies with liners and plastic over-pants. Nappy liners are indestructible and block up toilets, but washing them will make a box last ages.

It is wise to contact other expatriate parents for a briefing on **local child-rearing practices**. Attitudes on what is important can be very different, and if this is not understood problems may arise. Some parents assume that, because their children lack a local language, they cannot play with the neighbours, but – if allowed to – younger children usually integrate readily with other children. They have a remarkable aptitude for languages, are skilled in non-verbal communication and many games do not require words to be fun. Most parents will choose, for good reasons, to have their children educated in an English-language school if there is one, but younger children may benefit from attending a local kindergarten or similar early childhood centre, where they will learn the local language.

Adolescents arriving in a new country may not be so adaptable, as they are often going through difficult processes of self-identification. This period of turmoil can start as early as the age of 11, and such confused youngsters can have big problems, particularly if their stay in a new country is for less than a year. They may need a great deal of time and patience; like the well-adjusted adult expatriate, they will cope better if they have a transferable hobby or passion. They will also be more unsettled if the rest of the family is unhappy too.

Contact information: educational packs

World-wide Education Service (WES), Waverley House, Penton, Carlisle, Cumbria CA6 5QU, UK **t** (01228) 577 123, **f** (01228) 577 333, *www.weshome.com*. Sells home-school packages.

The commonest panic

In my experience as acting GP to small expatriate communities, it was common for small children to swallow substances that parents thought noxious or worrying. Some doctors would therefore advise keeping some *ipecacuanha emetic mixture* in case of trouble. *See* p.285 for further advice.

Case history: culture shocked in Taiwan

It is odd the things you miss when you are away from home. Asia is famous for their squat toilets, which Westerners stoop to conquer, indeed some wax lyrical about the joys of being able to sit to perform. To be fair, locals find sit-down toilets equally eccentric. Many times I found puzzling footprints on the edges of toilet bowls. The Chinese were hopping up onto the bowl and squatting.

One day in Taipei, I walked into the bathroom of a busy McDonalds. My guts were grumbling and I knew McDonalds had a sit-down toilet. It smelled a bit ripe but that's hardly a revelation in that city; squat toilets are easier to keep clean. I swung open the cubicle and the stink hit like a ton of fermented tofu. I immediately noticed footprints on the porcelain then saw that the owner of the prints also left behind a deposit – except he missed. His crosshairs shot high and to the right, meaning a direct hit onto the rim. I backed out slowly then took the time to walk over to the Hilton.

Jim Soliski, Edmonton

Contact information: expatriates

Control Risks, *www.control-risks.com.*

InterHealth, 111 Westminster Bridge Road, London SE1 7HR, UK **t** (020) 7902 9000, **f** (020) 7902 9091, *www.interhealth.org.uk.* Experienced in support for Christian missionaries and others.

International Committee of the Red Cross, *www.icrc.org.*

Objective Team, UK **t** (01788) 899 029, *www.objectiveteam.com.* Train for survival – from journalists to gap year students.

RedR, *www.redr.org/london.* Offers excellent courses on many aspects of relief and development work.

When You Get Home:
Return

A post-trip check-up? 298
  Malaria 298
  Sexually transmitted infections 298
  What do stool checks reveal? 299
  Stowaways 299
  Some rarities 300
Psychological welfare 300

22

Summary
→ If you fall ill within three months of returning from the tropics remember the risk of serious malaria and seek medical help urgently (within 24 hours) – even if you have taken your antimalarials.
→ Antimalarial tablets must be continued after leaving a malarious region; although no absolute guarantee against malaria, if unlucky enough to get it, you won't die of it.
→ Other diseases imported from the tropics are unlikely to be serious, but see a doctor if you notice a rash, new lumps or bumps, or are unwell. Remind the doctor about your travels.
→ Don't worry about your health; if you feel well, you almost certainly are well.
→ Few diseases lurk unknown without symptoms; the exceptions are HIV and schistosomiasis.

A post-trip check-up?

Many travellers and expatriates wonder whether they need a medical check-up after returning from an extended or tropical trip. Some choose to arrange a formal post-trip check-up by a specialist in tropical diseases. Generally, though, if a returning traveller feels well, there is no need to have a medical examination. The main exception to this guideline is schistosomiasis (*see* opposite); however, if you have an ulcer which will not heal, or if you are worried you may have malaria, HIV, or Chagas' disease, you should also see your doctor.

The most important thing to remember when you get home is to continue taking your antimalarial tablets for the prescribed interval: for most tablets this is four weeks, or a week for Malarone. If you fall ill (especially if this happens within three months of returning), remind your GP that you have been abroad and that you may have been exposed to malaria. If ill on returning to Australia, present yourself at a hospital that specializes in infectious diseases. Open up communications with friends and relations and be aware that low mood is not uncommon after coming home.

Malaria

Falciparum malaria is the only life-threatening disease commonly imported from warm countries. Any fever or 'flu-like illness within a year (but especially within three months) of return from a malarious region should be assumed to be malaria, and medical help should be sought urgently. Most malaria deaths are in those returning from Africa (Kenya is especially notorious) or Melanesia (Papa New Guinea, the Solomons and Vanuatu). There is no screening test that will diagnose it before symptoms manifest themselves, so travellers and doctors must be aware of it as a possible diagnosis. The safety net is not a clever laboratory test, but alert travellers and doctors who act quickly if symptoms of possible malaria begin. For all other aspects of malaria, *see* **Malaria**, pp.129–40. There are much rarer, but serious, causes of fever in returning travellers, but these will cause problems within a month of return (e.g. Lassa fever, *see* p.269).

Sexually transmitted infections

Inhibitions may be on hold while you were travelling and casual sex may have been especially enticing. Unfortunately it comes with a risk of contracting HIV and 25 other sexually transmitted infections. Returning travellers should consider screening if they have put themselves at risk. Counselling about HIV testing can be arranged through your doctor or a special genito-urinary clinic. *See* also **Sex and Genitals**, pp.217–28.

What do stool checks reveal?

Some doctors advocate screening faeces for parasite eggs or cysts. This may reveal an infestation, but generally they only need treating if they are causing symptoms or squeamishness. If you do experience symptoms that someone thinks may be due to worms or *giardia* (*see* p.117), it is important that three stool samples are sent. These are taken on different days but each must be delivered to the lab fresh. Only if three samples are negative is it likely that the traveller is free from parasites. Both *giardia* and worms produce eggs and cysts intermittently, so one clear sample does not necessarily mean that you are free from parasites.

Lingering intestinal problems are common after a trip to the tropics, particularly among travellers returning from South Asia. Often no cause is found, and the symptoms settle down with time. Sometimes treatments for **irritable bowel syndrome** help (*see* box on p.115)

For more on possible results of stool tests, *see* p.114.

Stowaways

Diseases and parasites are often imported from the tropics and subtropics, especially by people who have been abroad for relatively long periods. With the exception of **schistosomiasis** (*see* below), most of them pose little threat either to the infested individuals or to the general public in contact with them. Passing an earthworm-sized *Ascaris* worm is revolting, but she will have done you no harm and will probably have been alone. Most infestations will die out given time or, if they do start causing problems (as may happen on rare occasions), they can be treated easily.

Amoebae frequently infest travellers, and often cause no symptoms at all. However, they can cause a mild form of dysentery and in a minority amoebae can cause a liver abscess. Unfortunately, screening will be most unlikely to detect these problems before they cause symptoms. Travellers should think about this and realize the benefits of avoiding infestations by eating safe, properly cooked food.

Schistosomiasis (bilharzia)

This little worm is acquired most often by travellers who have been wading or swimming in African lakes, although it is also a problem in parts of the tropical Americas and Asia (*see* map on p.179). A blood test is available to test for the parasite and, since there may be no initial symptoms, you should request one if you have put yourself at risk. Your doctor will often be able to organize it. It should be done more that six weeks (but ideally less than 12 weeks) after the last possible exposure to suspect water. The Rift Valley lakes of Africa are common sites for catching schistosomiasis; a study at the Hospital for Tropical Diseases, London, found that about one-third of the 344 cases treated in 1991–4 got the disease from Lake Malawi. *See also* **Water**, pp.179–81.

Some rarities

Chagas' disease

This is a disease of tropical and subtropical Central and South America, transmitted by bug bites (*see* **Bites, Biters and the Diseases they Spread**, p.154). It is very rarely contracted by travellers, but if you have been exposed to bug bites (you should know because they hurt) while sleeping in a wattle-and-daub village hut, a blood test may help to determine if you have been infected. Screening will be justified in only a very few people.

Leishmania (or kala-azar fever)

Leishmania can emerge months or even years after a bite by an infected Old World sand-fly, and bronchopneumonia is the most common way it manifests itself. The Mediterranean coast is a source of infection, but it is generally acquired from much further afield (*see* **Bites, Biters and the Diseases they Spread**, p.153). If you become ill, remind your doctor about your travels. Those returning from tropical South America must seek medical help if they have a skin wound that does not heal within a couple of months.

Worm troubles

A blood test (ELISA) can detect filarial worms. These cause elephantiasis, loa-loa or river blindness in West and Central Africa, Southeast Asia and South America (*see* pp.150 and 181–2). If you have no symptoms, do not request screening unless you have been home for more than six weeks. If you have symptoms, seek medical help promptly. In a minority of those they infest, tapeworms can end up in the brain (*see* **Worms, Guts and Nutrition**, p.122).

Psychological welfare

Travelling is stressful, though exciting, and coming home usually plunges you into reverse culture shock (*see also* **Reverse culture shock**, pp.97–8); this can be hard to handle, especially if you are worried about finding a new job or setting up home again. Many people say that 'reverse culture shock', experienced on coming home, is worse than the difficulty of coping with new cultures; this seems to be especially true on coming home after a long trip to the developing world. Pace yourself and, if everything seems to be going to pieces, find kindred spirits to talk to. One of the worst things about returning is being isolated by your travelling experiences. Even close friends may be unable to understand the life-changing things you have seen, so that you are distanced from them. Try to engineer new friendships through travel clubs; if you can't find a sympathetic fellow traveller, see your doctor – and, personally, I'd recommend staying out of big supermarkets for a few months. For returning travellers who feel fired to give something back, courses run by development charities are great places to network and share.

Useful Addresses

Travel clinics and health information

In the UK

Allergy UK, 3 White Oak Square, London Road, Swanley, Kent BR8 7AG, t (01322) 619 898, t (helpline), f (01322) 663 480, *info@allergyuk.org*, *www.allergyuk.org*.

AMREF (African Medical and Research Foundation), Clifford's Inn, Fetter Lane, London EC4A 1BZ, t (020) 7201 6070, f (020) 7201 6170. The AMREF websites, *www.amref.org* and *http://uk.amref.org*, provide information for travellers to each East African country. Membership: £15 for one month covers one free evacuation within a 500-mile radius from Nairobi; cover for a year (£30) or life (£100) allows one evacuation a year within a 1,000-mile radius. Money spent funds work for community hospitals throughout East Africa.

Asthma UK, Summit House, 70 Wilson Street, London EC2A 2DB, t (020) 7786 4900; t (helpline) 0800 1216 244, f (020) 7256 6075, *www.asthma.org.uk*. Has information on travel insurance for asthmatics.

The Blood Care Foundation, PO Box 588, Horsham, West Sussex RH12 5WJ, t (01403) 262 652, f (01403) 262 657, *www.bloodcare.org.uk*.

Epilepsy Action, New Anstey House, Gate Way Drive, Yeadon, Leeds LS19 7XY, t (0113) 210 8800, t (helpline) 0808 800 5050, *epilepsy@epilepsy.org.uk*, *www.epilepsy.org.uk*. The helpline issues an 'epilepsy passport' (50p) containing first-aid information about epilepsy, in six European languages.

British Heart Foundation, Greater London House, 180 Hampstead Road, London NW1 7AW, t (020) 7554 0000, *www.bhf.org.uk*. Insurance information for those with heart problems like angina and high blood pressure.

British Mountaineering Council (BMC), 177–9 Burton Road, West Didsbury, Manchester M20 2BB, t (0161) 445 6111, *office@the bmc.co.uk*, *www.thebmc.co.uk*. Runs mountaineering courses and advises on other courses and insurance. *See also* Union International des Associations d'Alpinisme.

British Society for Allergy and Clinical Immunology, Suite 2688–66 Queen Anne's Business Centre, St James' Park, 28 Broadway, London SW1H 9JX, t (020) 7340 9614, f (020) 7340 9617, *www.bsaci.org*.

Department of Health (UK), t 0800 555 777, *www.dh.gov.uk*. Publishes *Health Advice for Travellers* (free), explaining how to get overseas medical treatment. Pick up a copy at a UK post office or doctor's surgery.

Diabetes UK, 10 Parkway, London NW1 7AA, t (020) 7424 1000, *www.diabetes.org.uk*. Issues fact sheets about individual countries, including which insulins are available. Also offers travel insurance.

Divers' 24-hr emergency helpline: t (07831) 151 523. Run by the British Institute of Naval Medicine.

Epilepsy Research UK, PO Box 3004, London W4 4XT, t (020) 8995 4781, *www.epilepsyresearch.org.uk*. Publishes a leaflet entitled *Epilepsy and Antimalarial Medication*.

Expedition Advisory Centre, Royal Geographical Society, 1 Kensington Gore, London SW7 2AR, t (020) 7591 3030, f (020) 7591 3031, *www.rgs.org*. The RGS has lots of experience in travel planning.

Foreign and Commonwealth Office, t (020) 7008 1500, *www.fco.gov.uk/travel*.

The Health Line, t 0839 337 733, gives advice (by fax if required) on specific destinations. The clinic provides a comprehensive pre-departure service, and post-trip consultations are also possible.

Holiday Care Service, 2nd Floor, Imperial Buildings, Victoria Road, Horley, Surrey RH6 7PZ, t (01293) 774 535, *holiday.care@virgin.net*. Offers information on holidays for people with existing health problems, and a list of sympathetic travel insurance companies.

Hospital for Tropical Diseases, Mortimer Market, Capper St, London WC1E 6JB, t (020) 7387 4411, *www.thehtd.org*.

InterHealth, 111 Westminster Bridge Road, London SE1 7HR, t (020) 7902 900, *www.interhealth.org.uk*. Travel service providing comprehensive care for aid workers, missionaries and volunteers: clinical consultations, advice, immunizations and health equipment.

MASTA (Medical Advisory Services for Travellers), at London School of Hygiene & Tropical Medicine, Keppel St, London WC1E 7HT, t 0906 822 4100 (premium rate), *www.masta.org*. Call for a personalized travel health brief. Offers immunization information, arranges membership of the Blood Care Foundation and sells AIDS kits and items such as anti-mosquito anklets.

MASTA Travel Clinics, t (01276) 685 040. Call for the nearest; there are currently 30 in Britain, selling malaria prophylaxis memory cards, treatment kits, bednets and net treatment kits. No post-travel service.

MEDEX Assistance Corporation, Victoria House, 5th Floor, 125 Queens Rd, Brighton, E. Sussex BN1 3WB, t (01273) 223 002, *medexasst@aol.com*. Offers medical cover worldwide for individual travellers, families and expats. Provides medical evacuation assistance and help in locating appropriate medical care, and sells medical kits.

Medic Alert Foundation, Freepost, 1 Bridge Warf, 156 Caledonian Road, London N1 9BR, t 0800 581 420, or:

Medic Alert Foundation International, Turlock, CA 95380 1009, US t (209) 668 3333 or t (toll-free) 1 800 344 3226. Supplies bracelets alerting medics to medical conditions.

Nomad Traveller's Clinic, in the STA shop, 43 Queen's St, Bristol, t (0117) 922 6567.

Nomad Travellers' Store, 40 Bernard St, Russell Sq, London WC1N 1LJ, t (020) 7833 4114.

Nomad Travellers' Store and Medical Centre, 3–4 Wellington Terrace, Turnpike Lane, London N8 0PX, t (020) 8889 7014, *www.nomadtravel.co.uk*. Has a complete range of travel equipment and a user-friendly, on-the-spot immunization and advice service. There are several UK branches, or you can call for information (especially on immunizations) on the **Nomad Travel Health Line, t** 0891 633 414 (premium rate).

Online doctors, t (020) 7806 4028, *doctor@e-med.co.uk*, *www.e-med.co.uk*. For a £30 membership you can arrange online consultations with a British GP from anywhere.

Royal Free Travel Health Centre, Pond St, London NW3 2QG, t (020) 7830 2885, *www.travelclinicroyalfree.com*. Immunizations, kits, and returning travellers clinic. Has a specialist nurse on call, regular clinic staff and a team of aviation psychologists offering flight anxiety treatment.

Royal Geographical Society. *See* Expedition Advisory Centre.

The Stroke Association, Stroke House, 240 City Road, London EC1V PR, t (020) 7566 0300, f (020) 7490 2686, t (helpline) 0845 303 3100, *www.stroke.org.uk*.

Thames Medical, 157 Waterloo Rd, London SE1 8US, t (020) 7902 9000. Competitively priced, one-stop travel health service. Profits go to Inter-Health, which provides healthcare for overseas workers on Christian projects.

Trailfinders Travel Clinic, 194 Kensington High St, London W8 7RG, t (020) 7938 3999. Usually has an expert travel doctor on site.

The Travel Clinic, 41 Hills Road, Cambridge, CB1 7UA, t (01223) 367 362, *www.travelcliniccambridge.co.uk*.

Travel Screening Services, 1 Harley St, London W1G 9QD, t (020) 7307 8756, *www.travelscreening.co.uk*. A private service mainly aimed at business travellers. For a £30 membership you can arrange online consultations with a British GP from anywhere, t (020) 7350 2079, *www.e-med.co.uk* or email *doctor@e-med.co.uk*.

Tropical Medicine Bureau, *www.tmb.ie*. Irish body with a useful website specific to tropical destinations.

Union International des Associations d'Alpinisme, Mountain Medicine Centre, British Mountaineering Council, *see* p.301. Publishes information sheets on the medical aspects of mountaineering. Most are aimed at climbers; a few are for doctors.

In North America

The **Centers for Disease Control** in Atlanta, Georgia, are the central source of travel health information in North America. Contact:

CDC, Division of Quarantine, Atlanta, GA 30333, t (404) 332 4559, *www.cdc.gov/travel*. Publishes the invaluable *Health Information for International Travel* and has an excellent – if scary – website. Local (county and state) public health clinics and special travellers' medicine clinics exist in most large cities in North America; most universities have medical centres too.

Travel reports in **Canada** (Ottawa) are available via **Canada t** (613) 944 6788, or **t** 1 800 267 6788; (fax-call system) **f** 1 800 575 2500.

American Diabetes Association, 1701 North Beauregard Street, Alexandria, VA 22311, t 1 800 342 2383, *lcann@diabetes.org*, *www.diabetes.org*.

Canadian Department of Trade and Foreign Affairs, *www.dfait-maeci.gc.ca*. Provides travel information.

Connaught Laboratories, PO Box 187, Swiftwater, PA 18370, t 1 800 822 2463. Sends a free list of specialist tropical physicians in your state.

International Association for Medical Assistance to Travellers (IAMAT), 736 Center St, Lewiston, NY 14092, t (716) 754 4883. Provides lists of English-speaking doctors abroad, and foreign health information.

MEDEX Assistance Corporation (central office), PO Box 19056, Baltimore, MD 21284, t (toll-free) 1 800 537 2029, t (410) 453 6300, *info@medexassist.com*. Offers medical cover worldwide for travelling individuals, families and longer-term expatriates. Also provides medical evacuation assistance and help in locating appropriate medical care, and sells safe medical kits.

The Society for Accessible Travel and Hospitality, 347 Fifth Ave, Suite 610, New York, NY 10016, t (212) 447 7284. Some useful resources.

South American Explorers, 126 Indian Creek Rd, Ithaca, NY 14850, t (607) 277 0488, *www.sath.org*.

US State Department, t (202) 647 4000, *www.state.gov*. Or, for travel emergencies, call Overseas Citizens Services 24-hr hotline **US t** (202) 647 5225.

Australia

The **Travel Doctor-TMVC** has a network of clinics in Australia, New Zealand and Thailand, all of which are members of IAMAT. Call **t** 1 300 658 844 or 1 300 658 844, which forwards the call to the nearest clinic, or check *www.traveldoctor.com.au*. These clinics might be the best first port of call if taken ill in Australia with travel-related symptoms. Otherwise, the following hospitals specialize in treating imported diseases: **Adelaide:** Queen Elizabeth; **Darwin:** Royal Darwin; **Hobart:** Royal Hobart; **Melbourne:** Fairfield (also has a travel health section); **Perth:** Royal Perth; **Sydney:** Westmead.

China

International SOS, Kunsha Building, 16 Xinyuanli, Chaoyang District, Beijing 100027, t 010 6462 9112, *wwwinternationalsos.com*.

MEDEX Assistance Corporation, Regus Office 19, Beijing Lufthansa Center, No. 50 Liangmaqiao Road, Beijing 100016, China, *medexasst@aol.com*. Offers medical cover worldwide.

Nepal

CIWEC Travel Medicine Clinic, near Yak and Yeti Hotel, Durbar Marg, Kathmandu, Nepal, PO Box 1340, t 977 442 4111, f 977 1 441 2590, *www.ciwec-clinic.com*.

South Africa

Johannesburg Clinic Travel Clinic, t (11) 807 3132.

Switzerland

The Blood Care Foundation, t (22) 362 8963.

International Association for Medical Assistance to Travellers (IAMAT), European HQ: Gotthardstrasse 17, 6300 Zug, *www.iamat.org*.

Vietnam

Vietnam has two American-owned, comprehensive 24-hour healthcare facilities:

Columbia Asia Gia Dinh Clinic, 01 No Trang Long, Binh Thanh Dist, t (8) 803 0678, f (8) 803 0677.

Columbia Asia Saigon 24-hour clinic, 08 Alexandre De Rhodes, Dist 01, HCMC, t (8) 823 8888, f (8) 823 8454, *www.columbiaasia.com*.

Useful websites

General

www.cdc.gov/travel: US Government health information.

www.doh.gov.uk: UK Government site offering health advice for travellers.

www.expeditionmedicine.co.uk

www.fco.gov.uk/travel: official Foreign Office website for travellers. For pre-departure preparation tips, see *www.fco.gov.uk/knowbeforeyougo*.

www.fitfortravel.scot.nhs.uk: travel health information.

www.himalayanrescue.org: Himalayan Rescue Association.

www.icrc.org: International Committee of the Red Cross.

www.internationalsos.com

www.MalariaHotspots.co.uk

www.medicalert.org.uk

www.medicineplanet.com: information site.

www.travelhealth.com: offers extensive reports on risks for a fee of $25.

www.tripprep.com: the Travel Health Online website.

www.WhenNatureCalls.com: disposable toilets.

www.who.int: background information on tropical diseases and treatments, and the latest outbreak news.

Disabled access

www.dmoz.org/Society/Disabled/Travel: useful for US travellers.

www.justmobility.co.uk: has links to other helpful sites.

Herbal remedies

www.24DrTravel.com: supplies echinacea and other remedies by mail order.

www.herbmed.org: herbal medicine information.

www.herbs.org: information on herbal remedies, etc.

In-flight issues

www.aviation-health.org: advice on in-flight health issues. Online shop sells masks to protect from in-flight infections and DVT-preventative flight socks.

www.britishairways.com/travel/healthmedcond/public: information on fitness to fly.

www.dh.gov.uk/dvt: specific information about DVT.

Immunosuppression

www.aidsnet.ch: information for travellers with HIV infection, including entry restrictions for countries.

www.thebody.com: information for travellers with immunosuppression.

Courses

British Airways/Aviatours, UK t (01252) 793 250, *www.aviatours.co.uk*. £235 for courses at seven airports.

British Mountaineering Council (BMC), *see* above. Runs mountaineering courses; advises on other courses.

Life Support, UK t (01229) 772 708. First-aid courses.

Outward Bound, Hackthorpe hall, Penrith, Cumbria CA10 2HX, UK t (01931) 740 000, *www.outwardbound-uk.org*. Survival skills courses.

RedR, *www.redr.org/london*. Offers excellent courses on many aspects of relief and development work.

Royal Free Travel Health Clinic, Pond St, London NW3 2QG, UK t (020) 7830 2885, *www.travelclinicroyal-free.com*. Treatment for flying phobia by psychologists.

St John Ambulance, UK t 08700 104 950, *www.sja.org.uk*. First aid.

TALC (Teaching-aids at Low Cost), PO Box 49, St Albans, Herts AL1 5TX, UK, t (01727) 853 869, *www.talcuk.org*. Sells oral rehydration measuring spoons and thermometers, and distributes the classic books *Where There Is No Doctor, Where There Is No Dentist* and other titles.

Virgin Atlantic, UK t (01423) 714 900, *www.flyingwith-outfear.info, www.virgin-atlantic.com*. Regular courses at main British airports cost £199 + VAT.

Wilderness Medical Training, The Coach House, Thorny Bank, Garth Row, Kendal, Cumbria LA8 9AW, UK t (01539) 823 183, *www.wildernessmedicaltraining.co.uk*. First aid.

World-wide Education, Waverley House, Penton, Carlisle, Cumbria CA6 5QU, UK, t (0118) 958 9993, *www.weshome.com*. Sells home-school packages.

Equipment and supplies

Equipment and information to protect travellers are available from InterHealth, MASTA clinics, Nomad (*see* above) and many outdoor suppliers. Some specialist sources are listed below.

General and medical gear

BCB, Freepost, Cardiff CF1 1YS, UK, t (02920) 433 700, *www.bcbint.com*. Marine safety/adventure equipment and the Mini Potti urinal.

www.bogmyrtle.com. Supplies a natural repellent that is especially effective against midges.

BWtechnologies, 5 Canada Close, Banbury, Oxfordshire OX16 2RT, UK t (01252) 727 820, f (01295) 700 301, *www.bwtnet.com*. Water purifiers.

Cotswold, Broadway Lane, South Cerney, Cirencester, Gloucestershire GL7 5UQ, UK, t (01285) 860 612. Shops in London, Reading, Manchester, Southampton and Bewts-y-Coed. Sell filters, bednets, blister relief kits, etc.

Craghoppers Ltd, Risol House, Mercury Way, Urmston, Manchester M41 7RR, UK, or: PO Box 1944, Leigh-on-Sea, Essex SS9 1TR, UK, t (for a brochure) (0161) 749 1364, t (helpline) (0161) 749 1310, *www.craghoppers.com*.

Field & Trek, Langdale House, Sable Way, Laindon, Essex SS15 6SR, UK, t 0844 800 1001, *www.fieldandtrek.com*. Sells bednet impregnation kits and outdoor equipment.

www.flufightersonline.com. Sells flu protection kits including masks and gloves.

FRÍO, PO Box 10, Haverfordwest SA62 5YG, UK, t (01437) 741 700, *www.friouk.com*. Sells a range of wallets that keep contents cool for several days.

Homeway Medical, West Manchester, Salisbury, Wilts SP4 7BH, UK, t (01980) 626 361, *www.travelwithcare.co.uk*. A range of travel accessories, including flight socks.

Lister Institute of Preventive Medicine, PO Box 1083, Bushey, Herts WD23 9, UK, t (01923) 801 886, secretary@lister-institute.org.uk, www.lister-institute.org.uk. Scorpion antivenom.

Mountain Equipment Co-op, (mail orders) 130 W. Broadway, Vancouver, BC, Canada V5Y 1P3, **f** (in N. America) 1 800 722 1960, **f** (local/intl) (604) 876 6590; **t** (in N. America) 1 800 663 2667, **t** (local/intl) (604) 876 6221, www.mec.ca. Life-time membership is $5. Equipment for self-propelled wilderness activities.

Nomad, Unit 34, Redburn Industrial Estate, Woodall Road, Enfield, Middlesex EN3 4LE, UK **t** 0845 260 0044, **f** (020) 889 9529, orders@nomadtravel.co.uk, www.nomadtravel.co.uk. Millbank bags and water filters, among other supplies (see above).

PharmWest, 520 Washington Blvd No. 401, Marina Del Rey, CA 90295, US **t** (310) 301 4015, **f** (310) 577 0296; Ireland **t** 463 7317, **f** 463 7310, UK **t** (free) 800 8923 8923; www.pharmwest.com. Stocks melatonin for jet lag.

SafariQuip, The Stones, Castleton, Hope Valley, Derbyshire S33 8WX, UK, **t** (01433) 620 320, **f** (01433) 620 061, www.safariquip.co.uk. Mail-order travel accessories for water sterilization, bednets, first aid, etc.

Simpson-Lawrence, 218–28 Edmiston Drive, Glasgow G51 2YT, UK, **t** 0870 9000 0527. Adventure/survival supplies.

Travel Paraphernalia, Presents for Men, 8 Fairfax Road, Heathfield, Devon TQ12 6UD, **t** 0844 854 7777, enquiries@presentsformen.com, www.travelparaphernalia.com. Sells a good range of gimmicks and gizmos.

Young Explorers, PO Box 508, Stratford-upon-Avon CV37 1HW, UK, **t** 0870 879 3741, www.youngexplorers.co.uk.

Contraception and feminine hygiene

Green Baby, 345 Upper St, London N1 3QP, UK, **t** 0870 241 7661, customercare@greenbaby.co.uk, www.green-babyco.com. Washable sanitary pads, nappies and liners.

New Angle Products, Box 25641, Chicago, IL 60625, US **t** (773) 478 6779, www.whizzy4you.com. Produces the Whizzy, a device allowing you to pee while standing up.

Plush Pants, 40 Westfield Road, Long Wittenham, Abingdon, Oxfordshire OX14 4RF, UK, **t** (01865) 408 040, www.plushpants.com. Cloth sanitary towels.

Quick and Direct, 137a Hersham Road, Walton-on-Thames, Surrey KT12 1RW, UK, **t** (01932) 232 443, info@quickanddirect.com, www.econdoms.co.uk. Mail-order condoms in various sizes.

Shewee Ltd, 18 Walton Street, Walton on the Hill, Surrey KT20 7RT, UK **t** 0844 800 8270, info@shewee.com, www.shewee.com. Produces portable devices for peeing while standing up.

Twinkle Twinkle, Unit 5 Headley Park Nine, Headley Road East, Woodley, Reading RG5 4SQ, UK, **t** (0118) 969 5550, www.twinkleontheweb.co.uk.

Restop, 2320 Meyers Ave, Escondido, CA 92029, US **t** (760) 741 6600, **f** (760) 741-6622, info@whennaturecalls.com , www.whennaturecalls.com. Sells portable and disposable sanitation equipment.

In-flight travel supplies

For flight-anxiety courses, see 'Courses'.

Activa Healthcare Ltd, Units 26–27 Imex Business Park, Shobnall Rd, Burton on Trent, Staffordshire DE14 2AU, UK, **t** (01283) 540 957, **f** (01283) 845 361, information@activa.uk.com, www.legshealth.com. Produces flight socks.

Airogym, 10 Crystal Business Centre, Ramsgate Rd, Sandwich, Kent CT13 9QX, UK, **t** (01304) 614 650, info@airogym.com, www.airogym.com. Airogyms for £11 including postage and packing.

Aviation Health Institute, 17c Between Towns Road, Oxford OX4 3LX, UK, **t** (01865) 715 999, **t** (order hotline) (01685) 202 708, **f** (01865) 726 583, www.aviation-health.org. Has an online shop selling travel products, e.g. masks to protect from in-flight infections.

Mediven Travel Ltd, Fields Yard, Plough Land, Hereford HR4 0EL, UK, **t** (01432) 373 500, www.mediuk.co.uk/trav-elsocks.html. Sells flight socks.

Pocket Gym Ltd, Corbin Way, Gore Cross Business Park, Bradpole, Bridport, Dorset DT6 3UX, UK, **t** (01308) 421 150 or **t** (order hotline) 0800 072 0898. Produces the pocket gym, priced at £17.95.

Scholl, Freepost, Scholl, UK, **t** 0800 0742 040, www.schollfootcare.co.uk. Flight socks.

Worldwide Health, Freepost, Alderney GY1 5SS, UK, **t** 0870 740 8282, www.worldwidehealth.com. Stocks melatonin.

Travel insurance

Age Concern Insurance Services, 3–10 Melton Street, London NW1 2EB, UK **t** 0845 601 3348, www.ageconcern.org.uk. Covers almost anyone with very few exclusions; they have no age limits.

British Heart Foundation, see above. Has information on insurance for people with heart problems, including high blood pressure.

British Mountaineering Council (BMC), see above. Advises on insurance for mountaineers.

Club Direct, 5 Brighton Road, Croydon, Surrey CR2 6EA, UK, **t** 0800 083 2466, www.clubdirect.com. Up to age 74.

Columbus, Advertiser House, 19 Bartlett St, Croydon CR2 6TB, UK **t** 0870 033 9988, www.columbusdirect.com.

Coventry Building Society, PO Box 9, High Street, Coventry CV1 5QN, UK, **t** 0845 766 5522, www.coventry-buildingsociety.com. Cover up to age 75.

Diabetes UK (see above). Offers travel insurance.

Independent Travellers Insurance Services (ITIS), 363A Kenton Rd, Harrow HA3 0XS, UK, **t** 0870 241 0370, **f** 0870 241 1683, itis@dircon.co.uk, www.itis.dircon.co.uk.

MEDEX Assistance Corporation (see above). Offers medical cover worldwide.

National Asthma Campaign (see above). Has information on insurance for asthmatics.

Perry Gamble, East Devon Business Park, Honiton, Devon EX14 9RC, UK, **t** (01404) 830 100, www.perrygamble.co.uk. Cover up to age 79.

Saga Services, Saga Building, Middleburg Sq, Folkestone, Kent CT20 1AZ, **t** 0800 015 8055, www.saga.co.uk. Offers travel services, insurance and health information.

Tyser UK Ltd, Acorn House, Great Oaks, Basildon, Essex SS14 1AL, UK, **t** (01268) 284 361, www.tyseruk.co.uk. Insurers who are sympathetic to epileptics; they often offer cover with no extra loading.

Worldwide Travel Insurance Services Ltd, The Business Centre, 1–7 Commercial Rd, Paddock Wood, Tonbridge TN12 6YT, UK, **t** (01892) 833 338, www.worldwideinsure.com.

Bibliography

Since most supporting references are now easily located by way of an internet search, I no longer list my sources, but include a further reading list below. Information on my own scientific publications is at *www.wilson-howarth.com*. I also write as J. M. Wilson.

General medical

CDC Health Information for International Travel 2008. The best English-language publication for up-to-date international disease risk information. Single copies available from CDC (*see*, p.303); multiple copies are sold by the Superintendent of Documents, US Government Printing Office, Washington DC 20401; *see also www.cdc.gov/travel*.

Dawood, R. (ed.), *Travellers' Health* (2002; OUP, Oxford). Each section is written by an expert, so a good text for professionals, but many lay readers find it intimidating.

Department of Health (UK), *Health Advice for Travellers: Anywhere in the World* (leaflet T5; Central Office of Information, HMSO). For lay readers. Includes an application EHIC form, which enable holders (if British residents) to obtain emergency treatment in the EU. Available online at *www.dh.gov.uk/en/Publicationsandstatistics*, by calling t 0845 606 2030, or from UK post offices.

Department of Health (UK), *Health Information for Overseas Travel.* Available at *www.dh.gov.uk/en/Publicationsandstatistics*.

Johnson, C., Anderson, S. R., Dalimore, J., Winser, S. and Warrell, D. A. (ed.), *Oxford Handbook of Expedition and Wilderness Medicine* (2008; OUP, Oxford).

WHO, *International Travel and Health* (2002; WHO Publications, Geneva, Switzerland; HMSO, UK). Authoritative, comprehensive; *www.who.int/ith*.

Wilson-Howarth, J. and Ellis, M., *Your Child Abroad: A Manual for Travelling Parents* (2005; Bradt Publications, Bucks, UK; Globe Pequot, USA); still the only comprehensive medical guide for families. *See www.bradt-travelguides.com*.

'Features', 'Getting ready'

Rowlands, E., *Weather to Travel* (2001; Tomorrow's Guides, Hungerford).

'Special travellers'

Royal College of Obstetricians, Travelling in Pregnancy. Available from RCOG, 27 Sussex Place, Regents Park, London NW1 4RG, t (020) t (020) 7772 6200, *www.rcog.org.uk*.

'Medicines'

'Medical kits and supplies', in Johnson, C, Anderson, S. R., Dalimore, J., Winser, S. and Warrell, D. A. (ed.), *Oxford Handbook of Expedition and Wilderness Medicine* (2008; OUP, Oxford).

'Flight'

Bor, R., Josse, J. and Palmer, S., *Stress-free Flying* (2000; Quay Books, Wiltshire).

'Bowels', 'Worms, guts and nutrition'

Wilson, J. M. and Chandler, G. N., 'Sustained improvements in hygiene behaviour amongst village women in Lombok, Indonesia', *Transactions of the Royal Society of Tropical Medicine & Hygiene*, vol. **87**, pp.615–16 (1993).

Wilson-Howarth, J., *How to Shit Around the World: The Art of Staying Clean and Healthy While Traveling* (2000; Travelers' Tales, Palo Alto, Calif)

'Malaria', 'Biters and insect-borne diseases'

Bröker, E., 'TBD: East Asia', *Journal of the British Travel Health Association*, **12** (2008) 44–47

Harrison, G., *Mosquitoes, Malaria and Man: A History of Hostilities Since 1880* (1978; John Murray, London).

'High, cold and dark'

Bezruchka, S., *Altitude Illness: Prevention and Treatment* (1994; The Mountaineers, Seattle, USA; Douglas & McIntyre, Vancouver, Canada; Cordee, Leicester, UK).

Deegan, P., *The Mountain Traveller's Handbook* (2002; The British Mountaineering Council, Manchester). Distributed by Cordee, Leicester LE1 7HD, *www.cordee.co.uk*.

Howarth, J. W., 'Hazards of trekking in Nepal', *Travel Medicine International*, **15** (1997) 82–7.

Pollard, A. J. and Murdoch, D.R., *The High Altitude Medicine Handbook* (1997; Radcliffe Medical Press, Oxford).

Pollard, A.J. and Murdoch, D. R., 'Children in the mountains', *British Medical Journal*, **316** (1998) 874.

White, A. J., 'Cognitive impairment of acute mountain sickness and acetazolamide', *Aviation, Space & Environmental Medicine*, (1984) 598–603.

Wilkerson J. A. (ed.), *Medicine for Mountaineering* (1985; The Mountaineers, Seattle).

'Animals'

Caras, R., *Dangerous to Man* (1975; Penguin).

Warrell, D. A., 'Venoms and toxins of animals and plants' in Weatherall, D. J., Ledingham, J. G. G. and Warrell, D. A. (ed.), *The Oxford Textbook of Medicine* (1987; OUP, Oxford). Best review of venomous bites, but scary clinical descriptions unmitigated by data on actual risks; lists antivenom sources.

Wilson, J. M., 'The scorpion story', *British Medical Journal,* **295** (1987) 1642–4.

Wilson, J. M., 'A sting in the tail', *Lemurs of the Lost World: Exploring the Forests and Crocodile Caves of Madagascar* (1995; Impact Books, London). What a scorpion sting feels like. Available from 33 Hartington Grove, Cambridge CB1 7UA.

'Ailments', 'Accidents'

Dickson, M., *Where There Is No Dentist* (1983; The Hesperian Foundation, California).

Werner, D., *Where There Is No Doctor* (1977; The Hesperian Foundation, California).

'Culture shock', 'Expatriates', 'Return'

Bierens de Haan, B., *Coping with Stress* (2001; ICRC, Geneva).

Davis, J. and Lambert, R., *Engineering in Emergencies: A Practical Guide for Relief Workers* (2002; Register of Engineers for Disaster Relief, ITDG publishing, Warwickshire).

De Botton, A., *The Art of Travel* (2003; Penguin, London).

Ross Institute of Tropical Hygiene, *Preservation of Personal Health in Warm Climates* (1982; London). Written for long-term, remote stays.

Wilson-Howarth, J. and Ellis, M., *Your Child Abroad: A Manual for Travelling Parents* (2005; Bradt Publications, Bucks, UK; Globe Pequot, USA).

Wilson-Howarth J. and Ellis, M., 'Illness in expatriate families in Kathmandu, Nepal', *Travel Medicine International,* **15** (1997) 150–55.

Index

Generic names of drugs and Latin species names are in italics.

ABC for emergencies 274, 275
abdominal pain 112, 121, 126, 222, 264–5
abortion 226
abrasions 206 *see also* grazes
abscesses 205
accidents 10, 25, 40, 79, 186, 254, 256, 273–86
    road accidents 10, 12, 25, 57
acclimatization
    to altitude 192
    to heat 160–6
    to culture 97–8, 104, 300
    see also adjustment process
acetaminophen 33, 34
    see also paracetamol
acetazolamide 190, 194, 195
    side effects 195
aciclovir 34, 163
acne 74
aconites 286
acute mountain sickness (AMS) 191, 193, 194
ACWY meningococcus vaccine 47
adjustment process 95
adrenaline 69, 278
Aedes mosquitoes 142, 143, 148–9, 152
Africa, health risks 56–7
agranulocytosis 36
AIDS 19, 40, 220, 255
aid and development workers 291
air embolism 169
air pollution 68, 166
air travel 85–92
    disabled travellers 30, 73
    and DVT 15–18, 74, 76, 86
    fear of flying 86
    fitness to fly 29–30, 64, 65, 67, 71
    jet lag 91–2
    medical evacuation 25–6, 254
    stop-overs 10, 11
Airogym 16–17
albendazole 117, 118
alcohol 12, 123–4, 290, 292
    as antiseptic 156, 178, 268
    drinking at altitude 199
    mixing with meds 38
allergies 36, 39, 46, 69–70, 207–8, **278**
altitude illnesses 186, 190–5
aluminium acetate 178, 268
aluminium hydroxide 265
amoebae 115–16, 118, 299
amoebic dysentery 115–16
amoxicillin 21, 37, 73, 78, 261, 268
ampicillin 21, 37

AMS (Acute Mountain Sickness) 191, 193, 194
anacondas 247
anaemia 21, 65, 212, 267
anemones 172, 174
Ancylostoma 121
angels' trumpets 285
angry outbursts 96
animals, dangerous 247–50
ankle swelling 87, 188, 224
Anopheles mosquitoes 142, 143, 148–9
antacids 262, 265
anthelmintics 211 *see also* *mebendazole*
anthrax 14, 258
antibiotics 21, 34, 35, 36–7, 38, 155, 213, 221, 224, 261, 285
    and diarrhoea 113–14
    resistance to 38
    skin infections 205
anticoagulants 72
antidepressants 97
antifungals 211–212
antihistamines 33, 38, 70, 79, 206, 260
antimalarial tablets 67–8, 134–9, 140
antiseptic creams 204
ants 243
anxiety 86, 95
apathy 95, 96, 263
    see also lethargy
appendicitis 264
appetite, lack of 263
aquatic leeches 182
arboviruses 151–2
armadillo meat 127
arnica 92
artemether 140
arthritis 74, 157
Ascaris lumbricoides 121, 118
aspirin 16, 33, 35, 36, 39, 68, 71, 72, 162, 205, 242, 245, 260, 261, 269
asplenic people 66, 73
assassin bugs 154, 234
asthma 46, 49, 64, 68
athletes and banned drugs 87
athlete's foot 215
atovaquone 135–6
Autan 145
avalanches 199–200, 201
Avian influenza 14, 19, 259
ayurvedic medicines 263
AZT 37

bacillary (bacterial) dysentery 116
back pain 279–80
bacterial vaginosis 222

behaviour, abnormal 191, 194, 276
banana spiders 236
bandages 32–4
banned drugs for athletes 87
basal cell carcinoma 213
bathing 216
bats 49, 59, 127, 202, 252
BCG immunization 42, 43–4, 51, 289
beaded lizards 247
bears 188, 247, 248–9
beclomethasone 68, 70
bed bugs 148–9, 212, 234
bednets 146
bee stings 242, 243
beetles 208–9
Belostomid water bugs 184
benzyl benzoate 210, 211
berries (poisonous) 123, 286
Bikholderia (Pseudomonas) pseudomallei 205
bilharzia (schistosomiasis) 52, 55, 57, 60, 108, 118, 144, 179–81, 218, 299
bird flu 14, 19, 259
birds 127
bismuth subsalicylate 113
bites 204, 206, 233–8
    dogs 249–50
    mosquitoes 149–50, 204, 207
black eyes 269–70
black flies 148–9, 181–2
black widow spiders 236
bladder infection *see* cystitis
Blastocystis hominis 128
bleeding
    from nose 188, 268
    from wounds 275–6
    stopping with herbs 188
    under a nail 282
    vaginal *see* menstruation
blister beetles 209
blood
    coughing up 261
    in urine 179–80, 218
    severe bleeding 275–6
    vomited 265
blood clots 225, 226
blood transfusions 39–40, 72, 76, 255
boats, falling out of 178–9
body lice 211
boils 205, 230
    see also skin invaders
bombs 61
bone fracture 30, 282–3
boric acid 268
bot flies 231–2
bowel cancer 115
box jellyfish 172

Index

breast-feeding 109
breathing difficulties 16, 69,
    190–1, 260, 261, 269
breathlessness 65, 69
broken bones 30, 282
broken nose 282
brown spiders 236
brucellosis 103, 109, 267
bruising 278–9
BSE (bovine spongiform
    encephalopathy) 260
bubonic plague 18
buffaloes 247
burning
    abdominal pain see heartburn
    eyes 240, 271 see also
        conjunctivitis
    sensation on peeing see STI
burns 25, 281–2
burst lung (pneumothorax) 65,
    69, 169, 187
bushmasters 245

campylobacter 116, 118
cancer 72, 257
    skin cancer 80, 160, 161, 213–15
candiru 8, 182
capillariasis 123
carbamazepine 67, 135
carbaryl 211, 219
carbon monoxide 188, 266–7
cars under water 178
Carukia barnesi 172
cassava tuber 123
cataracts 30
caterpillars 165, 239–40
cat's claw (remedy) 18
cats 250
caves 201–2
cefalexin 223
cefradine 261
centipedes 237, 238
cephalosporins 223
cerebral malaria 276, 277
cerebral oedema 191
cetirizine 33, 70
Chagas' disease 39, 60, 144,
    148–9, 154, 300
chameleons 247
charcoal 109
cheese 103 see also TBE
chemotherapy 72
chest infections 256, 261–2
chest pains 16, 201, 261–2
chickenpox 77, 91, 257
chiggers 235
chikungunya fever 152
children
    accidental swallowings 285
    altitude sickness 192–3
    diarrhoea 78, 79, 80, 100, 112–13
    expatriates 294–5
    fits and convulsions 277
    hypothermia 196
    pulled elbow 283
    rabies 50, 252
    teeth 272
    travelling with 78–80
chill 265
chimpanzees 247
Chironex fleckeri 172
Chiropsalmas quadrigatus 172
chloramphenicol 35, 38, 268
chlorine 106–7
chloroquine 52, 74, 134, 137, 138, 257

choking 284
cholera 14, 19, 50–1, 101, 102, 103,
    104, 108, 116, 118
Chrysops 150
cicadas 239
ciguatera poisoning 124, 126
Cimex lectularius 234
cinnarizine 88
ciprofloxacin 37, 113, 114, 116, 117,
    118, 221
cities, heat in 166
ciwujia injections 36
CJD (Creutzfeldt Jakob disease)
    50, 260
clarithromycin 261
clopidogrel 71
clothes 28–9, 80, 146, 162, 164
clotrimazole 212, 215, 223
clots see DVT
cloxicillin 37, 212
co-amoxiclav 37, 223
co-trimoxazole 117, 118
cobras 246
coconut beetles 209
coconuts 110, 168
codeine 11, 33, 36, 38, 265
codeine phosphate 33, 113
'coffee ground' vomit 265
cold injury 188, 189, 197–8
    see also hypothermia
cold sores 34, 163, 189
colds 90–1, 254, 256, 260–1
colitis 115
collapse 274–5
collapsed lung (pnuemothorax)
    65, 69, 169, 187
colostomies 30
communicable diseases 65
concussion 276
condoms 218, 220, 221–2, 224
cone shells 170, 171
cone-nosed bug 154
confused behaviour 164, 191,
    194, 276
conjunctivitis 30, 270
constipation 160, 219, 261,
    263–4, 267
contact lenses 30, 271–2
contagious diseases 65
contraception 32, 199, 218, 223–6
convulsions 276–7
coral 170–1
Cordylobia anthropophaga 230–1
coughing 260–1
    and bilharzia 180
    bloodstained spit 191, 261
    and histoplasmosis 201
    and tuberculosis (TB) 262
counterfeit medicines 32
Coxiella 258
crabs
    crustaceans 124
    pubic lice 219
cracked heels 215
cramps
    abdominal 112, 126, 264
    menstrual see period pains
    muscle 164, 168, 266
    and swimming 168
cremation 254
Creutzfeldt Jakob disease 50, 260
crocodiles 174, 182–3, 202, 248
cross-country skiing 199–200
crotamiton 149, 210
croup 261

crutch rash 212
cryptosporidium 108, 116, 118
CS gas exposure 286
Culex mosquitos 142, 143, 148–9
culture shock 93–8, 300
cuts 206
cycling 163
cyclizine 88
cyclospora 108, 116, 117, 118
cystic fibrosis 69
cystitis 218, 223, 256
cystocercosis 103, 122

dapsone 137, 138–9
deadly nightshade 285
deaths 186, 241, 245–6
    accidents 10, 254
    risks 18–19, 25
decompression sickness 169–70
decongestants 90, 268
deep vein thrombosis (DVT)
    15–18, 65
DEET 144, 145, 146, 238
dehydration 16, 87, 110, 111–12,
    160, 161, 165–6, 189, 218–19,
    263, 266
Deltaprim 137, 138
dermatitis 208
dengue fevers 14, 55, 59, 144,
    148–9, 151–2
dental health 24, 29, 272
depression 95, 97, 136, 285
    see also apathy, fatigue,
        lethargy, pyschological
        problems
deserts 165–6
desogestrel 225
dexamethasone 193
DHF (dengue haemorrhagic
    fever) 55, 144, 151–2
diabetes 12, 34, 64, 65–7, 82, 205
diarrhoea 19, 57, 59, 60, 81, 118,
    263, 264
    children 78, 79, 80, 100, 112–13
    and diabetes 65
    oral rehydration 21, 65–6, 110–12
    prevention 109
    severe/bloody 113–15
    travellers' 14, 29, 38, 51, 100–15
diclofenac 36, 265, 280
Dientomoeba fragilis 118
diet
    for jaundice 263
    for diarrhoea 112
diethyl toluamide see DEET
digoxin 39
diloxanide furoate 116
dimenhydrinate 88
diphenhydramine 33, 207
diphenhydramine hydrochloride
    88
diphtheria 43, 51, 269
    risks 53–61
dipyrone 35, 36
disabled travellers 30, 73
discharge
    from eye see conjunctivitis
    from nose see sinusitis
    from penis 221
    from vagina 222
    from wound 206
dislocations 282–3
distalgesic 36
diuretics 71–2, 82, 83, 87
dizziness 164, 191, 267

dogs 249–50
double vision 269
doxycycline 38, 52, 67, 78, 134,
    135, 202, 224, 268
dreams 135, 136
dress codes 12–13
dressings 32–4
drink-driving laws 12
drinks, safe 104–5
drips 36
drowning 12, 25, 168, 178
drowsiness 276
    antihistamines 90
    see also fatigue, lethargy
drug trafficking 12
Dukoral 14, 102, 116
dung beetles 240
duodenal ulcers 30, 265
DVT (deep vein thrombosis)
    15–18, 65, 71, 74, 76, 86
dysentery 57, 101, 103, 104, 110,
    114, 115–16

ears 29–30, 169, 178, 268
    middle ear infection 29–30, 256
    objects in 283
ebola virus 259–60
echinacea 39
Economy Class Syndrome 15, 16
eczema 46, 70, 74
edema *see* swelling
elbow, pulled 284
electric eels/fish 184
electrocution 25
elephantiasis 55, 59, 144, 148–9,
    150
elephants 248
emergency contraception 226
encephalitis 48, 151
Entamoeba 108, 115–16, 118
Enterobius vermicularis 122
ephedrine 90
epidemics 19–20
epididymitis 221
epilepsy 46, 49, 64, 65, 67–8
epinephrine 34, 69, 278
erythromycin 37, 78, 116, 205, 212,
    261, 269, 272
espundia 213
essential fatty acids 18
essential oils 149, 285
ETEC (*enterotoxigenic
    Escherichia coli*) 14, 100, 102,
    103, 108, 116
eucalyptus 146
evacuation 254
expatriates 287–96
    babies and children 294–5
    brushes with the law 11
    culture shock 95
    headaches 267
    home environment 288–9
    psychological warfare 291–4
exposure (hypothermia) 187,
    188, 196
eyes 30, 162, 168, 269–71
    objects in 283–4
eyes
    black eyes 269
    red eyes 270
    retinal haemorrhages 190
    snow blindness 189
    yellow eyes 224, 263, 269
face pain (sinusitis) 65, 267–8
fainting 277

faintness 103, 267
falciparum malaria 57, 130, 134
Fansidar 140
feet 168–9, 215–6
fever 256–7
    louse-borne relapsing 211
fexofenadine 70, 207
fibrositis 74
fiddle spiders 236
filariasis 150
filth-to-mouth diseases 104,
    115–18, 263, 289
fire ants 243
first-aid courses 27
first-aid kits 27–8, 32, 33–4, 91
fish 125–6, 175–7
fish bone 284
fish oils 125
fitness 29
fits and convulsions 136, 164,
    276–7 *see also* epilepsy
flaking skin 211
flea bites 205
fleas 231, 233–4
flesh-flies 240
flies 103, 150, 234, 240
Florida sticks 239
flu 14, 16, 49, 82, 256
flucloxacillin 37, 205, 212
fluconazole 223
flukes 108, 120, 127
fluoride 127–8
flushing of the skin 126
folic acid 67
food
    for children 80
    and diarrhoea 112
    illegal foodstuffs 10
    unsafe/contaminated 101,
        102–4, 120
food allergies 69–70
food poisoning 59, 123–6
food-borne diseases 54, 57, 59, 60
foot and mouth disease 257–8
foot problems 215–16
footwear 168–9
forests 164–5
fractures 30, 65, 282
frostbite 188, 189, 197–8
fucidin 212
funeral arrangements 254
fungal infections 211–12, 218
funnel moths 239
funnel-web spiders 237
frusemide 72

Gamow bags 193
gastritis 265
gastro-colic reflex 112
gastrointestinal disease 54, 59, 80
gastroenteritis 54, 67, 75, 90,
    100, 102, 104
genitals 218, 221–3
gentamicin 268
geography worm 211
gestodene 225
giardia 37, 103, 108, 117, 118, 299
Gila monsters 247
ginger 18, 90
gingko 97
glasses 24, 271–2
glibenclamide 39
Glossina 154
grazes 22, 80, 206, 212
Guinea worm 108, 122

haemorrhage 65
haemorrhoids 219
hair loss 88, 212
Hajj pilgrims 57, 75
halofantrine 140
hallucinations 164, 194
hand, foot and mouth disease 257
hantavirus 250, 260
Hapalochlaena 171
hay fever 46, 69, 70
head injury 267, 276
headaches 139, 152, 154, 156, 157,
    190, 191, 201, 202, 266–7
headlice 210–11
heart attacks 10, 12, 65, 71
heart disease 46, 49, 64, 71, 261–2
heartburn 265
heat exhaustion 163–4
heat hazards 160–3
heat rashes 206–7
heat stroke 160, 164, 165, 166
hedgehogs 252
Heimlich manoeuvre 284
heparin 16
hepatitis A 52, 53–4, 54, 57, 108,
    168, 184, 262, 263
    risks 53–61
    vaccine 15, 42, 44
hepatitis B 24, 29, 36, 39, 75,
    262–3
    immunizations 15, 49, 51
hepatitis E 14, 44, 54, 59, 77, 262,
    263
hepatitis infection 218
herbal remedies 39, 218
high blood pressure 71–2
hippoes 247–8
histoplasmosis 201
HIV 24, 29, 36, 37, 70, 220, 255, 256
hoarse voice 269
hogweed 165, 208
homeopathic malaria
    prophylaxis 138
honey 260
honey bees 242
hookworms 21, 108, 120, 121
hornets 242–3
horse flies 150, 234
HRT (hormone replacement
    therapy) 228
hunger 112
huntsman spiders 236
hydatid disease 122
hydrocortisone 34, 208, 268, 278
hyoscine 88, 90, 112
hypertension 71–2
hypodermic syringes 34
hypotension 267
hypothermia 188, 196, 197, 201

ibuprofen 36, 68, 260
IBS *see* irritable bowel syndrome
ice 100, 219, 221, 278
ice cream 100, 102, 104
immersion foot 198
immune disorders 70–1, 205
immunizations 13–15, 41–61, 72,
    75, 102, 250–1, 289
impetigo 22, 212
imprisonment 11–12
incense coils 147
incontinence 83
independent travellers 29
indigestion 262, 265
infectious diseases 80, 257–8

influenza 256
  immunization 14, 16, 49, 82
injections 36
ingrowing toenails 187
inhalers 68
insect bites see bites
insect repellents 220, 222, 235
insect-bite avoidance 59
insect-borne diseases/infection
  54, 60, 150–1
insomnia 136, 190
insulin 66, 67, 82
insurance 24, 25–7, 64, 81
iodine 106, 204, 205, 206, 212
iron tablets 22
irritable bowel syndrome
  115–16, 117, 299
irukandji 172
Isospora 117
ispaghula husk 110, 264
itching 206-12
  and bacterial skin infections
    205–6
  and bathing in polluted
    waters 184
itch-mites 232
ivy, poison 165, 208
Ixodes ticks 157

Japanese encephalitis 14, 42,
  46–7, 59, 60, 144, 151
jaundice 44, 224, 262, 263
jaw wiring 30, 65
jellyfish 172–4, 177, 208
jet lag 91–2
jiggers 216, 231
joint injuries 200
joint pain 139, 152
  see also dengue fevers, fever,
    malaria
jungles 164–5

kala-azar fever 19, 148, 153, 300
kava 97, 227
kidnapping 25
kidney stones 74, 160, 219, 265
knee injuries 187–8
Komodo dragons 247
kraits 245, 246

Lactrodectus 236
lakes 178–84
lamivudine 37
laparoscopy 30
Lariam 135, 136, 137, 140
larva migrans 211
Lassa fever 269
latulose syrup 264
lavatories see toilets
laws in different countries 10–12
lead, pencil, poisoning 285
leeches 59, 182, 230, 231, 232,
  237–8
leg fractures 30, 65
leg swellings
  ankles 87, 188, 224
  from deep vein thrombosis
    (DVT) 15
  in mountain walkers 188
leg ulcers 204
legionnaires' disease 29, 52, 216,
  262
leishmania 51, 53–61, 144, 153,
  213, 215, 300
leprosy 215

leptospirosis 184, 201–2, 250
lethargy 256, 262–3
  see also fatigue
levofloxacin 113
Levonelle 226
levonorgestrel 225, 226
libido 220
lice 210–11, 219
lindane 219
Linuche unguiculata 177
lionfish 175
lions 248
listeria 108
liver failure 66, 136
liver fluke 117
liver inflammation 262
  see also hepatitis
lizards 247
loa-loa 150
Lonomia achelous 239
loperamide 113
loris 252
louping ill 156
louse see lice
louse-bourne relapsing fever 211
loxosceles 236
lungs
  and breathlessness 69
  burst lung 69, 169, 187
  respiratory disease 288
  respiratory rates 164, 261
  see also breathing
Lycosa 236
Lyme disease 52, 156, 157
lymph glands 205

mad cow disease 260
maggots 230–2
magnesium sulphate 205
magnesium trisilicate 265
malaria 59, 60, 66, 73, 77,
  129–40, 144, 148–9
  antimalarial tablets 43, 66, 67,
    70, 77, 132, 134–9
  avoidance 133–4
  children 80, 257
  diagosing 139
  expatriates 290
  post trip check up 298
  risks 52, 53–61, 131–2
  treatment and cure 140
  vaccines 13, 43
malathion 210, 211, 219
Malarone 67, 134, 135–6, 140
malignant melanoma 214
Maloprim 137, 138
marlin 126
mebendazole 121, 122
mebeverine 112
meclozine/meclizine 88
medical check ups 29, 298–300
medical conditions, pre existing
  27, 64–8, 290–1
medical tourism 74–5
medical treatments 254–5
medicines 31–40, 81, 82
meditation 97
mefloquine 52, 134, 136–7, 140
Megalopyle superba 239
melanoma 214, 215
melatonin 11, 92
meliodosis 205
meningitis 47, 267, 276, 277
meningococcus 47, 52, 57, 73, 75
menstruation 227–8

mercury poisoning 285
metoclopramide 90
metronidazole 37, 38, 114, 117, 118
miconazole 212, 215
microsporidia 118
middle ear infection 29–30, 256
mifepristone 226
millipedes 237, 238
miltefosine 213
mines 61–2
mini-pill 223, 225
miscarriage 76, 77, 226
missed period 227
missed pill 225
mites 148–9, 235
MMR immunizations 51
moles 214, 215
monkeys 248
mood 94–8, 136–7
morning sickness, see nausea of
  pregnancy
morphine 237
mosquitoes 59, 140, 142–50, 164,
  165, 204, 207
moths 240
motion sickness 86, 88–90
mountains 186–95
muscle cramp 266
muscle strains 278–9
Muslim countries 11, 28, 290
myasthenia gravis 135

nails, bleeding under 282
Nairobi eye 208–9
nalidixic acid 113, 114
naproxen 36
nausea 97, 136–7, 138, 263
  and altitude illness 191, 194, 195
  and head injuries 276
  and heat exhaustion 164
  see also vomiting, motion
    sickness
nausea of pregnancy 90
nelfinavir 37
neomycin 212, 268
nettles 165
  see also sea nettles
nitrofurantoin 223
Nivaquine 137, 138
norethisterone 225
norfloxacin 113, 114
norovirus 265
noses
  bleeding 188, 268
  broken 282
  objects in 283
NSAIs (non steroidal anti
    inflammatories) 36, 279
nut allergies 69–70
nutrition 127
nystatin 212

oak, poison 165, 208
ocean itch 177–8
octopus 171
oedema 188, 191
oleander poisoning 286
Onchocerciasis 144, 148–9, 181–2
Onychoteuthis banksi 171
operations 30
oral rehydration 65–6, 110–12, 160
Oroya fever 258
oseltamivir 259
otitis media 29–30
ovarian cyst 264

overdose 285
oxygen
  on aircraft 60, 87
  at altitude 190

pacemakers 71
pain 261
  see also relevant body part
painkillers 33, 36, 38, 205
Paludrine 67, 135, 137, 138
panic attacks 97
paracetamol 20, 22, 32, 33, 34,
  36, 205, 240, 242, 245, 260,
  261, 269, 280
paragoric 263
paralysis 155
paralytic shellfish poisoning
  (PSP) 125
paratyphoid 267
Pediculus humanus 210–11
pencil lead 285
penicillin 36–7, 201, 205, 223, 261,
  268, 269, 272
penis 182, 221, 222
peppermint 112, 264
periobital cellutitis 271
period pains 227
periodic respiration 190
permethrin 210, 211, 235
pesticides 123
pethidine 237
pharmacies 254, 255
phenobarbital 67, 135
phenothrin 211
phenytoin 67, 135
Phoneutria 236
Physalia physalis 172
piles 219
pilgrimages 57, 75
pill, contraceptive 222, 224–5,
  227, 228, 290, 291
pink eye 270
piperazine 122
piranhas 183
plague 18, 51, 144, 148–9, 155,
  234, 250
plants 124, 165, 208, 285–6
plasmodium falciparum 130
pneumococcus 47–8
pneumonia 75
pneumothorax 65, 69, 187
poison oak/ivy 165, 208
poisoning 25, 59, 123–6
  carbon monoxide 266–7
poisonous plants 124, 285
polar bears 249
poliomyelitis 43, 52, 55, 57
polymyxin 212
pork tapeworms 122
porphyria 136
Portuguese man o'war 172
potassium permanganate 22,
  204, 205, 206, 212, 245, 281
povidone-iodine 204, 212
pregnancy 75–8, 133, 199, 257, 294
  nausea of 90
  unwanted 226
prescribed medicines 11, 12, 27
prickly heat 206–7
prisons 211–12
probiotics 109
proguanil 67, 135–6, 137, 138
promethazine 88
propranolol 21
pseudoephedrine 268

psoriasis 74, 136
PSP (paralytic shellfish poisoning)
  125
psuedophedrine 90
public lice 219
puffer fish 126
pulled elbow 283
pulled muscle *see* muscle cramp
pulmonary oedema 191
pulse
  finding a pulse 275, 277
  rates 164
pus discharge
  from genitals 221, 222
  from wound 206
putsi 230–1
pyrimethamine 137, 138–9
pythons 247

Q-fever 103, 258
quinine 140

rabies 49–50, 51, 53–61, 201, 202,
  250–2
rashes 206–8, 210, 211
rat fleas 148–9
rats 250
rays 169, 176, 183
recovery position 277–8
red blood cell disorder 73
red bugs 219
red eyes 270
red streaks on the skin 205
red tides 124–5, 178
reflexology 27, 87
regional health risks 51–61
relapsing fever 155
religious travel 75
responsible travelling 20–2
retinal haemorrhages 190
rhinoceros 247, 248
Riamet 140
rifaximin 116
Rift Valley fever 75
risk assessment 18–19
river blindness 144, 148–9, 181–2
rivers 178–84
road accidents 10, 12, 25, 57
Rocky Mountain spotted fever
  157
rodent ulcer 213
Ross River fever 59
rotavirus vaccine 14
roundworms 108, 120, 121
rove beetles 209

safe destinations 24
St John's wort 97, 224
salbutamol 68
Salmonella 102
salt tablets 266
saltwater crocodiles 174
sand-flies 148–9, 153, 213
sanitary protecton 227
Sarcoptes scabiei 210
SARS (Severe Acute Respiratory
  Syndrome) 19, 259
saw palmetto 218
scabies 210
scalds 211
scaly rash 205
schistosomiasis *see* bilharzia
Scolopendra 237
scombrotoxic poisoning 124, 126
scorpionfish 168

scorpions 54, 57, 184, 240–2
scrotum swelling 150
scrub 164–5
scrub typhus 150, 157, 235
scuba-diving 169–70
sea anemones 174
sea creatures 59, 171–7
seafood 120, 123, 124
sea hazards 168–78
sea lice 177–8
sea poisoning 177–8
sea snakes 174, 245, 246
sea urchins 174
sea wasp 172
self-medication 32
senior travellers 81–3
senna 264
septacaemia 52
Severe Acute Respiratory
  Syndrome (SARS) 19, 259
sex 220, 293
sexually transmitted infections
  (STIs) 218, 220, 221, 222,
  298–9
sharks 176–7, 184
shellfish poisoning 59, 124–5
Shigella 101, 103, 108, 118, 184
showers 216
sickle cell disease 187
sickness *see* nausea
side effects of medicines 38
  acetazolamide 190
  antimalarial tablets 127, 130–2,
  134–9
silica gel poisoning 285
silver sulphadiazine 162, 209
Simulium damnosum 181
sinus problems 29–30
sinusitis 65, 267–8
skiing 199–200
  ski-slope injuries 200
skin cancers 80, 160, 161, 213–15
skin infections 22, 148–9, 204–6
skin invaders 230–3
'slapped cheek' disease 77, 257
sleeping sickness 57, 148–9, 154
sleeping pills 123, 127
smog masks 201
smokers 29, 91, 166, 262
snakes 54, 57, 59, 60, 243–7
snails 123, 127
sneezes 90–1
snorkelling 169–70
snow blindness 189
solar keratoses 161, 214
sore throats 260, 268–9
South American wolf spiders
  236
spectacles 24, 271–2
spiders 59, 235–6
spleen removed 73, 133
spotted fever 157
sprains 29, 278–8
squamous cell carcinoma 213
squat toilets 83, 216
squirters 239
stable-flies 234
staphylinid beetles 208–9
starfish 174
statins 16
steroids 35, 38, 45, 68, 208
STI 222
stinging corals 170–1
stinging seas 177
stingrays 175, 176, 183

Index

stings
  bees, wasps and ants 208,
    242–3
  fish 175–6
  jellyfish 172–4, 177, 208
  scorpions 240–2
stitching wounds 280–1
stomach ulcers 30, 256, 265
stomach pain *see* abdominal pain
Stomoxys 234
stones, kidney 74, 160, 219, 265
stonefish 175
stool checks 114, 299
strained muscles 278
strawberries 102
stress 95, 96, 97, 291–2
strokes 65
Strongyloides 121, 118, 209
styes 271
subconjunctival haemorrhage 271
sun spots 160–1
sun super-sensitivity 38–9
sunburn 80, 160, 162
sunglasses 162, 168
sunscreens 161–2, 168, 186, 222
sunstroke 164, 189
surfers' ear 169
surgery 30
sutures (stitches) 280, 281
swallowing things accidentally
  285
sweat bees 243
sweating 267
swelling
  from allergic reactions 278
  of ankles 87, 188, 224
  of brain 190
  from elephantiasis 142
  around the eye 271
  of the feet 188
  from jiggers 231
  of the lymph glands 152, 205,
    206, 210
  severe and widespread 69, 278
  see also leg swellings
swimmers' ear 178
swimmers' itch 179–80
swimming
  and alcohol 168
  and cramps 168
  in polluted waters 168, 184
  sea bathers' eruption 177
  in sulphur springs 206
  see also sea hazards
swordfish 126
syphilis 39
syringes 34, 35, 40
systemic lupus erythematosis 135

Tabanus 234
tampons 222, 227
tap water *see* water supplies
tapeworms 108, 120, 121, 122
tarantula 237
TBE (tick-borne encephalitis)
  48–9, 52, 156
tear gas 286
teeth 24, 29, 272
Tegretol 67
temazepam 11, 190
tenrecs 165, 252
terbinifine 212, 215
testicles 221, 222
tetanus 42, 43, 250, 281
tetracyclines 35, 37, 78, 115, 135, 155

Thailand 11, 12, 14, 38
thalassaemia 73
therapeutic travel 74–5
thermometers 34
thiabendazole 211
thimble jellyfish 177
thirst 189
threadworms 120, 122
throats
  objects stuck in 284
  sore/infected 260, 268–9
thrombosis 81, 82, 87, 228
thorn apple poisoning 285
throbbing 205
thrush 38, 212, 222–3
thyroid 106
tick paralysis 158
tick typhus 157
tick-borne encephalitis (TBE)
  48–9, 52, 156
tick-borne infections 54, 60, 144,
  156–8
ticks 148–9, 155–6, 164, 202
tiger sharks 127
tigers 248
tightness of the chest 97, 261, 291
  see also allergic reaction
tinidazole 114, 117
tiredness *see* lethargy
toe-biter 184
toenails 187
toilets
  children 30, 78–9
  squat toilets 83, 216
tonic (nutritional) 127
tonic water and malaria 133
tonsillitis 256, 257, 265, 269
toothache 267, 272
toothpaste 149
tourniquets 244, 245, 246
toxoplasma 122
travel sickness 86, 88–90
travellers' diarrhoea 14, 29, 38,
  51, 100–15
trekking 186–8
  see also mountains
trench foot 198
tretinoin 162
trichinella 121, 122
trigger fish 126
trimethoprim 78, 117, 223, 261, 268
trimoxazole 78
tropical sprue 114–15, 127
tropical ulcers 204, 213
trypanosomes 144, 148, 153–4
tsete flies 148–9, 154
tuberculosis (TB) 14, 43–4, 51, 91,
  103, 262
tularaemia 151, 250
Tulsi 84
tumbu flies 230–1
tummy ache
  see abdominal pain
Tylenol 32
typhoid 103, 104, 267
  immunization 13–14, 15, 42, 44–5
  risks 53–61
typhus *see* scrub typhus

ulcers 204, 213, 265
unconsciousness 164, 276–8
underweight people 29
United Arab Emirates (UAE)
  10–11, 12

UPF (ultraviolet protection
  factor) 162
urine
  colour of 160, 218
  and cystitis 223
  in deserts 166
  pain on urinating 218, 222, 223
  passing blood 179–80, 218
  to treat jellyfish stings 173–4
  see also Mini Potti, toilets

vaccines 13–15, 43–51, 66, 72, 75,
  103
vaginal discharge 222
valium 21
vampire bats 251
Vandellia cirrhosa 182
varicella 275
venomous caterpillars 165,
  239–40
venomous fish 175
venomous snakes 174, 243–4,
  288
verruga 258
violent crime 57
vipers 246
vitamin B 146
  as a repellant 146
vitamins 127, 146, 207, 214, 285
vomiting
  black stuff 265
  blood 265
  by an unconscious person 277
  with diarrhoea 100
  food poisoning 123, 125, 126
  from head injuries 276
  from leptospirosis 202
  see also nausea

walking sticks (insects) 239
wandering spiders 236
war zones 61–2
warble flies 231–2
warfarin 16
warts, genital 222
wasp stings 208, 242
water
  intake 160, 161
  organisms in 107–8
  safe sources 104–5
  treatment 105–9
water scorpions 184
weals 207
weever fish 175
Weil's disease (leptospirosis)
  184, 200, 202
West Nile fever 14, 258
wheelchair travellers 73
whip-scorpions 239
whirligig mites 235
white-water rafting 178–9
Whizzy 83
widow spiders 236
wired jaw and flying 30
worms 54, 59, 60, 120–2, 209,
  211, 299, 300
wounds 280–1
wrenched joints 278–9

yellow eyes 269
yellow fever 14, 45, 51, 55–7, 70,
  144, 148–9
yew trees 286

zanamivir 259